JCMS Annual Review
of the European Union
in 2008

Edited by

Nathaniel Copsey
and
Tim Haughton

General Editors: Jim Rollo and Daniel Wincott

WILEY-
BLACKWELL

First published 2009 by Blackwell Publishing Ltd

British Library Cataloguing-in-Publication Data applied for
ISBN 978-1-4051-8914-9

Printed and bound in Markono Print Media Pte Ltd

The publisher's policy is to use permanent paper from mills
that operate a sustainable forestry policy, and which has been
manufactured from pulp processed using acid-free and
elementary chlorine-free practices.
Furthermore, the publisher ensures that the text paper and cover board
used have met acceptable environmental accreditation standards.

For further information on Blackwell Publishing, visit our website:
http://www.blackwellpublishing.com

CONTENTS

JCMS 2009 Volume 47 Annual Review pp. 1–5

The Gathering Storm: A Drama in Two Acts

NATHANIEL COPSEY
University of Birmingham

TIM HAUGHTON
University of Birmingham

Europe's auguries for the year 2008 initially appeared strongly favourable. In high politics, the institutional wrangling that had dominated the first decade of the 21st century appeared to be coming to a successful conclusion. It seemed that the Lisbon Treaty, which preserved so much of the ill-fated Constitutional Treaty in all but name, was slowly rolling towards a long-anticipated full ratification. On the economic front – despite a sky-rocketing oil price – continental Europe was building up a head of steam as the German powerhouse of the euro area expanded at its fastest clip in 12 years during the first quarter of the year. A 'credit crunch' had begun to slow the pace of growth of the American and British economies, but this was at first viewed as merely an appropriate correction to the credit-addicted profligacy for which the Anglo-Saxons were so well known. Apart from a few little local difficulties along the Union's southern and eastern fringes, this credit crunch appeared unlikely to affect the heart of the EU. Indeed, rumours abounded that Rhenish capitalists would take advantage of the turbulence to increase their share of world trade. Across the seas, an unpopular American Presidency was entering its final year in office, ending the era of George W. Bush's muscular, neoconservative unilateralism, which many Europeans had so detested. At the turn of the year, it seemed that 2008 marked the return of a stronger Europe – *Europa Redux*.

By the end of the year, few of these auspicious predictions had come to pass. Hopes of the swift entry into force of the Lisbon Treaty had been dashed by a firm Irish 'no' to the Lisbon Treaty, with a wide margin against of 53.4

per cent to 46.6 per cent. The European economy was nosediving into its deepest recession since the end of World War II, led by the unbalanced German economy, which suffered disproportionately from the rapid contraction of world trade. In foreign relations, Russia's military intervention in South Ossetia led to the sudden collapse of the US-equipped and US-trained Georgian army and marked the re-emergence of a stronger Russia prepared to intervene outside the borders of the Russian Federation to protect Russian citizens 'wherever they may be'. A bright spark could be found in America's choice of Barack Obama, a man hugely popular in Europe, as the 44th President of the United States.

Thus although 2008 was a year of disappointments, shocks and setbacks, it was also – to employ a theatrical metaphor – a play in two acts. The first half of the year was full of sunny optimism; the second of bad news and portentous omens.

The *JCMS AR*'s mission is to describe and analyse the work of the Union over the course of the year. Despite the great dramas of these 12 months, the business of the Union continued, for the most part, much as it always does. Significant developments were discernible in fields such as the battle against climate change and Justice and Home Affairs. In the legal sphere, as Michael Dougan summarizes it succinctly in his contribution to this volume, there was a 'cascade of rulings'. Moreover, the first six months of the year saw the first 2004 entrant in the shape of Slovenia take the helm of the Union. Its EU Presidency provided further evidence of the political maturity of central Europe. When the curtain fell on the Slovene Presidency – to return to our theatrical metaphor – eurocrats mused on the country's efficient and competent handling of the EU's business as they left their seats for the summer interval. Nonetheless, the first act had ended on a dramatic note. After a series of largely unproblematic ratifications in national parliaments in many other EU Member States, the Irish voted 'no' to the Lisbon Treaty, provoking much discussion and debate about how to proceed. The very fact that Ireland was the only Member State to ask its citizens to pass judgement on the treaty only fuelled the fires of critics of the EU such as Czech President Václav Klaus, for example, who could not contain his glee when the result was announced, claiming he could write a better treaty from his hospital bed.

The second act of 2008 opened with a fanfare to mark the launch of the French Presidency, but what followed was the sound of distant gunfire as hostilities broke out between Georgia and Russia in August. The conflict brought into sharp relief the debates about further enlargement (of the Union, of course, but also of Nato of which many EU countries are also members) and the kind of policies that are needed for the EU's neighbourhood. It also highlighted the very different attitudes towards Russia that exist in the EU-27. Throughout the crisis French President Nicolas Sarkozy took centre stage.

Nonetheless, although the Russo–Georgian conflict provoked commentators to draw somewhat overblown parallels with the German reoccupation of the Rhineland in 1936 or the Munich conference of 1938, the real crisis of 2008 was the near collapse of the global banking system. Although the depth of the financial crisis had been becoming steadily more apparent throughout the year, the collapse of Lehman Brothers on 15 September brought the world dangerously close to complete financial meltdown.

The long-term ramifications of the economic crisis are hard to gauge in early 2009, but as a result of their deep integration into global and European markets, some of the smaller and newer EU Member States were hit hard. Latvia's economy, which had been racing ahead before the crisis reaching double-digit growth, ground to an abrupt halt and headed swiftly into reverse, which led to the fall of the first (of possibly many) governments as a consequence of the crisis. Support for integration in many of the new Member States had been fuelled in great measure by the belief that membership would deliver continuing improvements in prosperity.

Dealing with the economic crisis became the most pressing challenge for the latter half of the year, pushing many other issues further down or even off the Union agenda. Nonetheless, as Vivien Schmidt and Milada Anna Vachudova's contributions to this volume highlight, when the Union emerges from the crisis the problems that it was already experiencing will require urgent attention. Vachudova's article focuses on the problems of corruption in the two newest Member States, but the lessons that can be drawn are much wider. If conditionality is a largely incentive-based strategy based on rewards and punishments, how can best – or just better – practice be enforced once a state is already a Member State? This suggests that the EU needs to be tougher during accession negotiations.

Vivien Schmidt's article encourages us to reflect on the major challenges facing the EU, including the existential question of the purpose of the project, and offers some ideas for how the EU can progress. Central to her arguments is a belief in the need for the EU to re-envision its identity as a region state, its democracy by changing rules of decision-making and participation, and its economy by employing more 'democratically legitimate' and 'solidaristic' measures. Her prescription may not find favour with all, but her article highlights the importance not just of dealing with the short-term crises that bedevil politicians, but of also searching for an underlying vision of where the EU should be going. The Russo–Georgian conflict and Kosovo's declaration of independence in February exposed one of the underlying themes of 2008 and a perennial question for European politics: borders. Even Slovenia – an understandably strong advocate of enlargement to the Western Balkans – was willing to run the risk of invoking the irritation of fellow Member States by halting Croatia's accession negotiations as a result of a long-standing border dispute. We will undoubtedly return to the themes raised by Vivien Schmidt and the question of borders in subsequent issues of the *JCMS AR*.

–

This is our first issue of the *JCMS AR* as editors and we are proud to have been entrusted with the editorship for the next few years. Following the example of our predecessors, we have continued the process of incremental change to both the content and focus of the journal. After careful consideration, we decided that the article on political developments in the 27 Member States had become somewhat unwieldy and that our readership would perhaps prefer two shorter, punchier commissioned articles.

The first of these new features is the *JCMS AR* State of the Union address. We intend to publish this feature occasionally to mark significant junctures in European politics by inviting a European leader to give his or her vision of where the Union should be heading over the following few years. We are honoured that the first State of the Union address comes from the President of the European Commission, José Manuel Barroso. In his contribution, President Barroso sets out what he believes the main policy challenges are for the Union over the next five years and examines to what extent these ambitions may be blown off course during the present economic difficulties. Inviting a European leader to set out a policy vision in the *JCMS* follows a long tradition. Older readers will recall that Margaret Thatcher's government first announced her plans for the creation of the Single Market in *JCMS* back in 1984 (Her Majesty's Government, 1984). It is our intention that the State of the Union article will be contributed periodically by a serving European leader or elder statesman and thus help foster an essential dialogue between practitioners and academics.

We have also decided to replace the Review Article with the 'Theme of the Year' contribution, which this year comes from a University of Sussex team composed of Lucia Quaglia, Peter Holmes and Robert Eastwood. It looks at the first stages of the Union's response to the financial crisis that first erupted in August 2007, which dominated the political agenda of the latter part of 2008.

Turning to our other commissioned features, Vivien Schmidt of Boston University kindly accepted our invitation to give the *JCMS AR* Annual Lecture at the UACES annual conference in Angers, France, in September 2009. Her lecture entitled 'Re-Envisioning the European Union: Identity,

Democracy and Economy' offers a bold and exciting set of ideas and suggestions for how Europe can escape from its current malaise. This year's keynote article is supplied by Milada Anna Vachudova on the problems of post-accession conditionality.

We are very happy that most of the *JCMS AR*'s established contributors have decided to stay on and are deeply indebted to them for their efforts and efficiency in providing their insightful contributions on time. Sandra Lavenex and Frank Schimmelfennig stood down this year as authors of the article on relations with the Wider Europe, but we are delighted that Richard Whitman – who also takes over as UACES President this year – and Ana Juncos have agreed to take on this role.

We are honoured to succeed Ulrich Sedelmeier and Alisdair Young as editors of the *JCMS AR* and we hope that our editions of the *AR* will match their distinguished record both in commissioning thoughtful and original contributions that extend the boundaries of knowledge in the field of European Studies and in producing a solid, descriptive analysis of political, economic and legal developments in the European Union over the previous year. We would also like to thank the editors of the *JCMS* over the past year – Willie Paterson, Jim Rollo, Dan Wincott and Charlie Lees – as well as UACES, represented by Alex Warleigh-Lack and David Phinnemore, for entrusting us with this endeavour. We hope that our relationship with the incoming *JCMS* and UACES teams will be just as productive.

Reference

Her Majesty's Government (1984) 'Europe – the Future'. *JCMS*, Vol. 23, No. 1, pp. 73–81.

JCMS 2009 Volume 47 Annual Review pp. 7–16

State of the Union: Delivering a 'Europe of Results' in a Harsh Economic Climate

JOSÉ MANUEL BARROSO
President of the European Commission

If any good has come from the past 18 months of turbulence, it must surely be that the European Union and the multilateralism it embodies have proved themselves more necessary than perhaps at any period since the common market was created. The global economic crisis has brought unprecedented pressure to bear on our economy and consequently on businesses, families and communities. Our banking system has been shaken to its foundations and the knock-on effects on the real economy have been severe. Europe's citizens have begun to feel the effects of the crisis for jobs and prosperity. Since the latter part of 2008, the agenda has been dominated by the need to put together our collective response to the crisis, which has tested both our resilience and the speed of our reaction. We have also faced challenges of co-ordination that have highlighted further the need for solidarity between the 27 Member States. We have stepped up to the plate: on all these counts, the Union has responded effectively to the crisis and forged together a co-ordinated set of policies to set Europe back on the road to prosperity in the European Economic Recovery Plan (EERP).

With elections to the European Parliament just held and a new Commission due to take office, I wish to look forward to the policy agenda of the European Commission over the next five years and share with you my thoughts on what our priorities should be during that period. After five years at the helm of the executive, I will also, briefly, look back on what I consider to be our principal achievements over the past five years.

Nonetheless, the focus remains firmly on the future and on what, concretely, the European Union can and should achieve both for its own people
and for the world.

The policy agenda I wish to set out here is structured under four pillars.
First, and most importantly in the current crisis, I will examine our plan to
drive Europe's economic recovery, considering both those necessary short-
term measures that will protect our citizens from the worst effects of the
recession and a package of structural reform measures designed to ensure
the Union's prosperity through increased competitiveness and productivity
in the longer term. Whilst the economic crisis is the most pressing of all the
challenges we presently face, it will not distract us from the necessity of
continuing our programme to tackle climate change and build a sustainable
Europe. Thus the second part of my article deals with our efforts in this
field. Thirdly, I turn to those policy measures that deal with specific action
to aid Europe's citizens, including a package of measures designed to help
consumers and new proposals to combat terrorism and organized crime. My
fourth area of consideration looks at Europe in the world as well as the
challenges of enlargement and the neighbourhood.

I. Jobs and Growth: Driving European Recovery

A major mobilization of efforts is required for the European economy because
recovery from the present crisis will take time – indeed it is likely to dominate
the policy agenda over the next five years. It is important to set the EU on
track to sustainable prosperity by continuing the programme of structural
reform under the Lisbon Strategy.

The Commission has identified four key areas for Community action
that will restore growth and prosperity. First, it is clear that the European
recovery cannot begin without a significant increase in bank lending to
provide the investment that business needs. We will take steps to break the
cycle of declining confidence and unwillingness to lend, which will in some
cases mean taking direct action on the asset side of bank balance sheets,
putting an end to uncertainty about the valuation and location of future
losses. The banks themselves must reveal the scale of their losses. In
addition the ECB and the other central banks will continue to provide
liquidity.

However, it must be recognized that the banks themselves are at least in
part responsible for the crisis. Unacceptable risks were taken by bankers and
we must ensure there is no repetition. Our financial system must be reformed.
Five key objectives are worthy of highlighting here:

1. The EU will be provided with a supervisory framework to detect potential risks early through a Europe-wide financial supervision system.
2. Where national regulation is insufficient or incomplete, European regulation will be proposed on the principle of 'safety first'. In detail, hedge funds and private equity will be more tightly regulated and steps taken to make derivatives and other complex structured products more transparent.
3. The confidence of European investors, consumers and small businesses in the safety of their savings will be boosted by greater depositor protection.
4. Pay incentive structures in financial firms will be brought in line with performance and recommendations will be made on appropriate remuneration for directors.
5. The Market Abuse Directive will be reviewed with a view to providing tougher sanctions against market wrongdoing.

Second, the real economy of the European Union, which is predicted to decline by an unprecedented rate of 2 per cent in 2009, will be supported by the European Economic Recovery Plan (EERP). At the core of this initiative is an immediate fiscal boost of at least 4 per cent of Union GDP, intelligently targeted at strengthening the European economy for long-term challenges following the Lisbon Strategy's recommendations for growth and jobs. These additional funds will be targeted at building our knowledge base, boosting energy security and adapting to a low-carbon economy. Here again, the co-ordinating role of the Commission is of vital importance to make sure that the Single Market is one of the key drivers for recovery and that the positive spillovers are maximized. Upholding the benefits of the Single Market and promoting its values outside of Europe will provide the EU with a unique launch pad for growth. Although the renewed Stability and Growth Pact allows for government deficits to expand during economic downturns, it is clear that Member States must have plans in place setting out how government budgets will return to positions consistent with sustainable public finances in the longer term.

Third, the European Union will take action to ensure that our people receive the maximum level of support during the painful short-term impact of the crisis. During 2009, it is predicted that Europe will lose some 3.5 million jobs. The role of the Commission in co-ordinating efforts must be centred first and foremost on helping Member States to make the structural improvements to their labour markets that will best allow them to bounce back rapidly after the worst of the crisis subsides. The Globalization Adjustment Fund will be quickly activated to allow workers and communities that are affected by job losses to be supported – and supported swiftly. The European Social Fund will be used to respond to crisis-driven needs, here again in the shortest time possible. The emphasis must be placed on speed and easy access to resources to ensure that we keep our people in employment wherever possible, provide adequate income support, invest in training and skills, ensure that the free movement of workers is preserved and provide sufficient support to tackle youth unemployment. Above all, we cannot allow a generation of young Europeans to suffer the long-lasting and hugely damaging effects of unemployment.

Fourth, it cannot be overlooked that the economic crisis is worldwide and that this demands global action. The experience of 50 years' integration, including in particular the launch of the euro and the expansion of the EU to 27 Member States, means that we are better able to speak with one voice in the world than ever before. We must promote a globalization that is based on those values that have served us so well over the past 50 years. I will return to these issues again in section IV.

II. Energy and Climate

The European Union is leading the way in advancing the agenda on the unprecedented climate change challenges we are facing today. Our efforts reached a turning point in 2007. After the decision of the European Council in March 2007 to set precise, legally binding targets on greenhouse gas and carbon emissions, the EU paved the way towards the momentous deal in Bali of December 2007 to pursue a global agreement on emission reductions by the end of 2009. These proposals have been reviewed and endorsed by the International Energy Agency, and the review shows that the EU, through its Energy Policy for Europe, is now moving closer towards being recognized as a single entity in energy matters. These were major achievements for the present Commission that are already making a significant impact in the fight against climate change.

The EU's climate change policy is a series of specific actions, all of which will be realized by 2020 in line with the headline 20, 20, 20 by 2020 policy goal. To reiterate: we will reduce greenhouse gases by 20 per cent; we will meet the target for an overall share of 20 per cent for renewables in the EU's energy consumption; and we will increase our energy efficiency by 20 per cent. The EU is the first region in the world to commit to such far-reaching and legally binding emission reductions.

However, we cannot simply talk about the importance of these issues, since public opinion demands that we take action. Consumer attitudes are changing – EU citizens value renewable sources and prioritize clean energy.

Many citizens think guaranteeing low energy prices and continuous supply of energy should be a priority for national governments.

Whilst other issues may appear more pertinent in the current financial situation, tackling climate change makes economic sense. Not only do bio-fuels make a good alternative when oil prices rise – as they are likely to do once we emerge from the present crisis – but not tackling climate change could cost Member States up to 20 per cent of GDP. Currently, we are working on plans which will result in an anti-climate change programme that will cost just 0.5 per cent of GDP. Pre-crisis, market revenues for solar, wind, biofuels and fuel cells were forecast to increase by approximately €150 billion by 2016, and record levels of investment in wine, solar and biofuels reflect increased investor confidence as well as a public demand to see greener businesses and more ethical investments.

In the current financial crisis, investment in green energy is crucial, as in the EU alone this sector has a turnover of €30 billion and provides approximately 350,000 jobs. If investment is to continue at the current rate, the green sector will be one of the key industries generating new employment opportunities in the economic downturn. The proposals set out in our climate change policies will need to make use of new technologies and creative ways of dealing with carbon emissions, making businesses across Europe more innovative and resourceful in the ways in which they tackle the problem of climate change. This innovation will boost further growth across the sector. In this sense, the EU's climate and energy package is part of the solution both to the climate crisis and to the current economic and financial crisis. As such it should remain at the heart of the Commission's policy agenda for the next five years.

III. Putting our People First

Over the past five years, we have striven to bring Europeans closer to the heart of the EU project, by focusing much of our attention on implementing policies in areas closest to their hearts, such as their fundamental rights and citizenship, migration, justice, security and safety, consumer protection and health.

We will continue this people-centred approach over the next five years through further concrete measures to strengthen the effective enforcement of consumer protection rules across Europe. Food safety, animal health and animal welfare will be continuously monitored, whilst the Commission will continue the work of the EU Health Strategy to help Member States promote public health to the best effect. We will examine in particular what role the EU can play in helping to reduce health inequalities across Europe. To prepare the future, work on demographic issues will continue in 2009, in close co-operation with the Czech and Swedish Presidencies: an assessment of the EU's preparedness for demographic change will be presented to the Spring European Council. In 2009, the Commission will set out its proposals for the further development of the EU as an area of Freedom, Security and Justice. These will form the basis for discussion with Member States, with a view to adopting the Stockholm Programme, a follow-up to the current Hague Programme. Pursuing the establishment of a common immigration policy will continue to be a priority. In a recent Communication, 'A Common Immigration Policy for Europe: Principles, Actions and Tools', the Commission has committed itself to deliver on a series of objectives and principles, in partnership with the Member States and the other EU institutions. This will guide the Commission's action, where immigration must be fully integrated into the wider EU policies for economic growth, competitiveness and social inclusion. External relations policies must also play a role, through promoting reinforced partnerships with third countries in migration management as well as closer links with development and trade policies.

As citizens move freely within the EU, they must have equal access to justice and the protection of the rule of law. Those who break the law should be prosecuted and judged on an equal basis. To enhance the security of EU citizens, the Commission will also present a series of proposals to deal with specific and new forms of criminality: greater prevention of child abuse and trafficking; reinforced international co-operation to fight and prevent cyber attacks; and combat the risk of terrorist attacks in areas such as chemical, biological, nuclear and radiological threats.

IV. Europe in the World

Europe will face considerable competition in the 21st century, both economically and politically as the emerging powers of Asia, Africa and South America rightly begin to assume more responsibility for global governance. I believe very strongly, however, that Europe still has much to contribute in world politics and global governance and that the enlarged European Union has the power and the capability to shape the global order. During the last 50 years, we have built a peaceful Europe based on freedom and solidarity. In the future, to guarantee and to reinforce such achievements, we need to continue to influence and to shape the world around us.

A united Europe is also a source of power and influence for all its Member States. In all my meetings around the world, I see that other countries look at Europe with different eyes since the last enlargement. Compared to when I was Foreign Minister of Portugal in the early 1990s, the differences are huge. It is a mistake to believe that European states can resolve the main global challenges on their own. In the current world, we need to act together. As is so often the case, our citizens' views are clear on this. Public opinion studies in Europe show on a regular basis that around 70 per cent of Europeans want Europe to be more active and influential in world politics.

This is why we need the right institutions. We cannot face successfully the 21st-century globalization with the institutions of the 20th century. The enlarged Europe cannot act effectively with the institutions that were created in a divided Europe. The Treaty of Lisbon will strengthen the enlarged European Union. The permanent President of the European Council will have an important role in the Union's external relations. A change in the President of the European Council every six months is not the most efficient way to act at the international level. In tandem with the President of the European Commission, the President of the European Council will reinforce the coherence and the cohesion of the Union. The High Representative and, simultaneously, Vice-President of the Commission will also be very beneficial to the Union. The ability to pool intergovernmental and supranational tools will make the Union more effective on the external stage. With the High Representative/Vice-President, the External European Action Service will also be a key part of the framework to improve the effectiveness of the Union's foreign policy.

In answer to the Lisbon Treaty's detractors, let me be quite clear: I find it more than a little contradictory to criticize as undemocratic a text which does a great deal to enhance accountability and transparency. National parliaments get increased scrutiny rights over Commission bills and, if enough of them have misgivings, can force the executive to reconsider them. Minutes of the Council of Ministers go on the record and Europeans get the right to ask the Commission to table legislation in areas over which it has jurisdiction if they can muster a million signatures. Lisbon is not about the EU accruing more power for its own sake: it is about improving and clarifying the bargain between Brussels, national capitals and Europe's people.

On the world stage, without European leadership, the international community will not succeed in meeting the ambitious goals that will set us on the path towards a global politics. There have been very important developments lately. Australia has signed the Kyoto agreement. China has recognized that climate change is a serious problem and wants to join international efforts to address it. Japan is committed to working with us. And, finally, there is a clear change in the United States. The new administration has identified the fight against climate change as a priority. When our main partners start to understand our efforts, we need to have the determination to keep the commitments made for our climate change and energy package. It is crucial for Europe's international standing and authority.

Europe is itself a laboratory of globalization, a successful case of setting transnational rules and standards. This experience makes me believe that we are better prepared than any other great power to propose, not to impose, the organizing principles and values of the global order. To propose our values goes hand in hand with defending our interests. They reinforce each other. The right expression is the 'promotion of the European interest'. It is in our interest to spread our norms and to extend our influence. Let me be clear on this point: if we do not persuade other great powers that our norms are beneficial for world order, it will be very difficult to keep our social, environmental standards, and at the same time our economic growth.

The pressures of global interdependence deeply affect European internal economic and social policies. The growth and the increased competitiveness of the new great powers have a strong impact on our economic, social and environmental policies. To deal with these challenges, we need to act at two levels.

First, we need to promote the power of our example. As other societies improve and become more prosperous and open, their citizens will become more demanding. At first, they want to eat better meals, to drive cars and to live in more comfortable houses. Later they will ask for better environmental standards, for more social and political rights, for more welfare and for a better quality of life. These citizens will find out that European societies are a good example in terms of the balance between economic growth and social justice and between competition and welfare. And their governments will also realize that the adoption of European rules and norms is in many cases the right answer to the demands of their electorate and to the stability and prosperity of their societies. For instance, China already applies European regulations and standards for food safety and in its motor industry. European standards are becoming the global norm – and we must ensure that this remains the case.

Europe must continue to shape the multilateral global agenda. We can help to create a more just globalization if we spread our norms and rules to regulate global discourse. Europe is already one of the leading international norm-setters, in human rights and good governance, in fair trade, in development and aid, in labour and social standards, in environmental protection, and in many other areas. It is not difficult to understand why the European Union is the best prepared to promote a multilateral way of international and transnational governance. Europe has unique historical experience of successful integration and co-operation among sovereign states – an experience that has promoted peace and democracy, freedom and solidarity across a whole continent.

In this respect, the European Union is a true school for global governance. Our main task for the next decades is to make the world understand this. I am fully confident that we will succeed as we did with other difficult and demanding tasks during the last 50 years.

Closer to home, over the next five years we should make considerable progress in integrating our neighbours into European structures through both the Union for the Mediterranean and the Eastern Partnership. The success of these initiatives will testify to the Union's ability to spread the mutual benefits of EU integration and co-operation. We foresee far-reaching integration for our neighbours into the EU economy, easier travel for their citizens to the EU providing that enhanced security arrangements are met, improved energy security arrangements and more financial assistance to allow for the more rapid development of our neighbours' economies. Nonetheless, only with strong political will and commitment on both sides will the Union for the Mediterranean and the Eastern Partnership meet their economic and political objectives. If we get it, it will lead to greatly enhanced security and prosperity for Europe and its neighbours.

Conclusions

It would be naïve to deny that our policy agenda risks being blown off course as a result of the current crisis. The danger is that our sense of urgency may make us forget that there are still long-term challenges that will persist throughout the current shocks. The world will no doubt be different after the current crisis but if we do not face up to these issues of productivity, competitiveness and of responding to demographic changes they will still be waiting for us – perhaps in more intractable forms – when we emerge from the present difficulties.

We have already seen during the present economic downturn that the siren calls for protection of national industries and national jobs at the expense of workers elsewhere are growing ever louder. We cannot allow either the great achievements of the Single Market or our transition towards an ever more globalised economy to be blown off course. When we were building the Single Market in the late 1980s and early 1990s, we created the notion of Social Europe to compensate for the short-term pain of transition to a more efficient economy. We also know that globalization will not automatically create benefits for all at the same time – this is why it was necessary to introduce adjustment mechanisms like the Globalization Adjustment Fund. During the current crisis, the need for collective action, for 'more Europe', is greater than ever before.

Europe has always been at its best when it is at its most ambitious. Along the path of European integration we have faced numerous challenges and setbacks. But Europe's leaders never lost their vision of what a more united Europe could achieve. We should never lose sight of that vision and that idealism, particularly now as we seek to bring our European values, norms and standards to the heart of the new institutions of global economic and political governance.

Above all else, the next Commission must continue to build a 'Europe of results' that will deliver economic reform, modernization of social systems, increased security and a Union that speaks with one voice in world affairs. The *JCMS* is an important and influential publication and I hope that some of the ideas put forward in this article will spark a wider discussion not only between academics and practitioners of European integration, but between students and all European citizens.

José Manuel Durão Barroso

JCMS 2009 Volume 47 Annual Review pp. 17–42

Re-Envisioning the European Union: Identity, Democracy, Economy*

VIVIEN A. SCHMIDT
Boston University

Introduction

Over the past three decades, the EU has brought about massive economic transformation, extensive territorial expansion and major democratic renewal. Most recently, however, the European economy has been in crisis, enlargement in limbo and democracy under pressure. And disagreements have continued about the most basic of questions: what is the European Union? How far should it expand? What should it do in the world? EU identity, in other words, has remained an issue as the European economy has headed into recession and as democracy has stalled at the EU level due to delays with the ratification of the Lisbon Treaty and has become increasingly volatile at the national level due at least in part to the EU itself.

Can the EU cope with these issues? And if so, how? This article suggests that the EU may be able to cope. But this requires (1) re-envisioning EU identity, as a 'region-state' with nation-state members in overlapping policy communities; (2) re-envisioning EU democracy, with new EU rules of the game on decision-making (by giving up on the unanimity rule through opt-outs in place of vetoes), on membership (by abandoning the uniformity ideal) and on participation (through more politics and pluralism); and (3)

* I would like to thank the editors, Nathaniel Copsey and Tim Haughton, as well as Mark Blyth and Fritz Scharpf for their helpful comments.

re-envisioning the EU economy, with new EU initiatives to respond to the economic crisis that are more democratically legitimate and 'solidaristic' as well as more economically effective.

The economy is intimately connected to democracy and identity. The linkages are reasonably clear in any democratic nation-state, as political leaders gain the legitimacy to make decisions about the economy through election by the collectively self-identified 'people', who can sanction them at regular intervals. In the European Union, the relationship between economics, democratic politics and identity is more complex, given its multi-level nature, split between national and EU levels. Tensions between the two levels have grown over the years, as economic decision-making has increasingly moved upwards towards the EU level while politics and identity have largely remained national, along with the mechanisms of electoral sanctions. The most recent illustration of the problems that result from these disconnections between EU-level economics and national-level democracy and identity are the referendums on the Constitutional and Lisbon Treaties, when a question about institutional reform presented citizens for the first time in a long time, if ever, with an opportunity to voice their opinions on the EU directly. Unfortunately for the EU, the negative results in France, the Netherlands and Ireland stem from the fact that the voters focused more on questions of EU economic policies and/or the EU's impact on national democracy and identity than on the institutional question being asked.

Today in particular, as we are on the brink of a period of deep and possibly prolonged economic recession, if not depression, democracy and identity in Europe may be particularly challenged. If the EU does not respond collectively and effectively to the economic crisis, or if it does not bring the public along with it as it responds to the crisis, the European project itself could be jeopardized. It is for this reason that I consider some of the deeper issues related to EU economic integration and their implications for EU democracy and identity.

This article begins by noting the impact of economic Europeanization (and globalization) on democracy, and in particular the way in which, in 'democratizing' the European (and global) economy, Europeanization (together with globalization) has ended up economizing on European democracy. A discussion of EU identity follows, focused on how Member States' four differing discourses about the nature, borders and actions of the EU might co-exist, if not be reconciled, by re-envisioning the EU as a region-state while ending unanimity and uniformity rules. I end with a set of suggestions for how to re-envision the EU in terms of European politics and political economic policies.

I. Democratizing the Economy while Economizing on Democracy

Not long ago, few EU experts would have challenged the view that European economic integration has helped 'democratize' the European economy by contributing to the economic prosperity that has served to raise millions out of poverty while vastly expanding the middle classes, by improving lives through the increasing competitiveness that has brought down prices while increasing productivity and efficiency, and by promoting greater equality of opportunity, environmental protection and quality of life. Today, although none would doubt these achievements, many would now question how democratized the economy really has become, given rising inequalities since the 1980s, as the rich have got richer while the middle classes have not, and current concerns about economic precariousness, social justice and the erosion of national welfare states. But whatever their views on economic democratization, most would have little doubt that in creating the European market, EU institutions have effectively 'economized' on national democracy, as more and more decisions have been moved to the EU level, if not the global.

Thirty years ago, when national capitalism was largely controlled by national governments, the spheres of capitalism and democracy were seemingly coterminous. Today, capitalism has become European (and global) while democracy remains local. Moreover, the national state is no longer the central focus of democracy. It has become denationalized and dispersed, as decision-making has moved upwards to international and (supranational) regional bodies; downwards to (sub-national) regional governments, corporate actors and NGOs; and sideways to regulatory agencies, public/private partnerships and self-regulatory bodies (Bieling, 2007). This is a challenge to traditional views of democracy and legitimacy as situated at the level of the nation-state, in particular when decision-making moves upwards, outside the confines of the nation-state. And for European Union Member States, that democratic challenge is compounded by the presence of the EU as an intermediary layer between the national and the global.

As I have argued elsewhere (Schmidt, 2006), the problem for EU 'democracy' is that it splits between supranational and national levels the four basic democratic legitimizing mechanisms that tend to operate simultaneously in any national democracy. These legitimizing mechanisms are, in Abraham Lincoln's famous dictum, government *by, of* and *for* the people – meaning political participation, citizen representation and governing effectiveness – plus, to add a preposition, *with* the people – meaning interest consultation (Schmidt, 2006, pp. 21–9). Unlike nation-state democracy, the EU has a fragmented or 'split-level' democracy. The EU level is mainly characterized by governance *for* the people through effective rule-making reinforced by transparency and accountability – or 'output' democracy (Scharpf, 1999), in particular through the regulatory state (Majone, 1998) – and by governance *with* the people through the elaborate interest consultation process known as the 'Community Method'. The national level retains government *by* and *of* the people through political participation and citizen representation (or 'input democracy' – Scharpf, 1999).

This split in legitimizing mechanisms does not in and of itself mean that the EU taken as a whole is democratically illegitimate. On the contrary, since the EU benefits from national governments' legitimacy *by* and *of* the people through the indirect representation afforded by national executives in the Council and their implementation of EU rules through national administrations as well as by the (weaker) direct representation afforded by the European Parliament (due to be strengthened by the Lisbon Treaty). There are also good arguments to be made for how the EU's governance *for* the people serves an 'efficiency promoting function' (Menon and Weatherill, 2008) – by doing things for the Member States that they cannot do on their own, such as creating the internal market, speaking for the Member States in international trade negotiations and establishing a European currency with the European Central Bank (ECB) to co-ordinate Member State monetary policies, including responses to the economic meltdown. Moreover, one could also argue that governance *for* the people comes out of what Polanyi (2001) in *The Great Transformation* argued was the constant process of social re-equilibration of economic liberalization in a movement/countermovement of disembedding and re-embedding markets in society. For the EU, this means that alongside EU market-making comes market-correcting, as in European Court of Justice (ECJ) rulings in such areas as gender equality, regional equality, environmental protection and laws promoting family solidarity in the case of labour mobility (Caporaso and Tarrow, 2008). We could also show how the EU's governance *with* the people gives voice to a whole range of actors who may be marginalized in their national polities and whose common interests are better expressed at the EU level. A case in point is the way in which transnational networks of activists have promoted EU and national gender equality and sexual harassment laws through a 'ping-pong effect' of interacting bottom-up and top-down pressures for reform (Zippel, 2006).

But all these positive aspects of EU legitimacy notwithstanding, the split in legitimizing mechanisms causes significant legitimacy problems for democracy in EU Member States by putting pressures on national politics. The central problem is that EU decision-making *for* and *with* the people is largely characterized by '*policy without politics*' – as the politics of national interest in the Council of Ministers, the politics of the public interest in the

European Parliament and the politics of organized interests in the Commission predominate (Schmidt, 2006, pp. 30–3). This makes for depoliticized EU policy debates that do not resonate with European citizens, who are used to the left/right divides of national debates and often worry about EU policies on left/right grounds, especially because they have no direct say over them (Schmidt, 2006, pp. 163–8; Barbier, 2008, pp. 231–5).

EU-level 'policy without politics' generally tends to obscure the real politics that lie behind many policies. This became all too clear with the controversy over the Bolkestein directive on services. Presented as simply a matter of market integration by extending free movement to the services sector, with home-country rules to apply on a range of issues related to pay and social protection, the directive exploded as the focus of public debates in France three months before the referendum on the Constitutional Treaty, with nightmares of 'Polish plumbers' taking French jobs and spurring a race to the bottom in wages and social protection contributing to the negative outcome of the vote (Schmidt, 2007). The services directive quickly came to be perceived more generally by many, in particular on the left in western Europe, as a EU neo-liberal market initiative intended to destroy cherished national labour market and welfare protections. Equally importantly, the kinds of market-correcting decisions seen positively from an EU-level perspective as promoting apolitical governance for all Europeans in a Polanyian movement/counter-movement can be seen negatively from the national-level perspective as a politically neo-liberal post-Polanyian destruction of national labour and welfare systems. Cases seen to epitomize this are not just the Commission's initial proposal for the services directive but also the ECJ decisions in the *Laval* and *Viking* cases curtailing national unions' rights to strike (Höpner and Schäfer, 2007). More indirect, negative effects on national welfare states are also attributed to the pressures on euro area members from EMU (Martin and Ross, 2004). But whether seen as negative or positive in intentions and/or effects, there can be little doubt that the EU has disrupted traditional welfare state boundaries (Ferrera, 2005, 2009). And all of this in turn raises questions about whether the EU really does govern effectively *for* the people.

The effects of EU-level 'policy without politics' on national economic arrangements are not the only problem. EU-level 'policy without politics' has also engendered increasing *'politics without policy'* at the national level (Schmidt, 2006, pp. 33, 163–71). As more and more policies are removed from decision-making, national politics is emptied of substance in policy area after policy area, thereby impoverishing the national political arena (Mair, 2005, 2006). Citizens have responded to this in a variety of ways. These include electoral demobilization – as seen in plummeting citizen participation in elections, despite momentary spikes in game-changing elections; electoral volatility, as voter dissatisfaction leads to rapid cycling of governments, especially in the central and east European countries (CEECs); and electoral radicalization. Some citizens have moved far to the right – blaming EU-sanctioned immigration for unemployment and EU institutions for the loss of national sovereignty and identity. Others have moved far to the left – blaming off-shoring to Asia, 'near-shoring' to eastern Europe and liberalizing EU institutions for challenges to long-standing labour institutions and the welfare state. Yet others have turned to interest group politics, joined social movements and supported INGOs in actively trying to make a difference. But while pluralist politics helps with regard to 'associative democracy' *with* the people, it does little for representative democracy *by* and *of* the people (Schmidt, 2006, pp. 25–8).

Within the EU, pluralist consultation *with* the people has been the result of active efforts by the Commission and increasingly the European Parliament (EP) to bring in interest groups and members of 'civil society' as a way to counterbalance the lack of governance *by* the people and to promote democratic legitimacy (Greenwood, 2007). But regardless of how open to public interest consultation *with* the people the EU may be, the problem for national citizens is that this kind of supranational policy-making is very far from the kind of representative democracy *by* and *of* the people they tend to see as the most legitimate. And it is in any case not open to most of them, given the difficulties of transnational mobilization for most citizens. Even 'civil society' is not what it seems. The problem with all such 'pluralist' policy-making processes *with* the people, whether at the global, EU or even national level in big nation-states like the US, is that 'civil society' is increasingly 'expertocracy' (Skocpol, 2004) and thus removed from actual citizens. As a result, in the pluralist policy-making processes of the EU (much as in the US as well as in supranational institutions), governance with some *of* the people and possibly not *for* all of the people is meant to make up for the lack of governance *by* and *of* the people (Schmidt, 2006, p. 28).

Significantly, the problems of pluralist policy-making *with* only some of the people, together with the EU's *policy without politics*, even affects the sub-national regional level in the case of EU programmes such as the structural funds. In southern Italy, for example, politicians are excluded from a consultation process that has created an 'iron triangle' – between civil servants, consultants and interest groups – which is unaccountable (given the absence of politicians), opaque (since no one knows who is involved or what they are doing) and corrupt (as the EU accountants have recently discovered in Calabria, for example) (Fargion *et al.*, 2006a, 2006b).

How have EU Member State leaders responded to this range of pressures on national politics and rising public concerns about Europeanization? Not in ways that would serve to attenuate public concerns or ameliorate legitimacy problems. Generally speaking, the Commission has consciously sought to depoliticize EU policy by presenting its initiatives in neutral or 'reasonable' language, and by using communications techniques such as its 'Plan D' for democracy (Barbier, 2008, pp. 231–2). National leaders have been perfectly happy with the depoliticized language of EU-level 'policy without politics' because this leaves them free in their national capitals to put any kind of political 'spin' of the left, right or centre on EU policies.

As for what they say about those policies, rather than discourses legitimizing the transfer of decision-making responsibility upwards to the EU as the way to solve national, European and global problems *for* the people, national politicians have tended to engage mainly in blame-shifting and credit-taking. On policy issues, national leaders tend to blame Europeanization for unpopular policies because 'the EU made me do it' and to take credit for the popular ones without ever mentioning the EU – largely because this suited their short-term electoral goals (Schmidt, 2006, pp. 37–43). On 'polity' issues, or the EU's institutional impact on national democracy, national leaders have generally been silent – except at moments of treaty referendums, when it was too late, as we saw in France (Schmidt, 2007), the Netherlands (WRR, 2007) and Ireland. As such, they have not even acknowledged the problems of decreasing national democratic access to decision-making, let alone attempted to remedy them. In all of these cases, national leaders only increase citizens' sense of powerlessness in the face of supranational forces to which they must adapt and over which they have no control. And Commission officials only make it worse when, in pronouncements after referendums, they insist that they will go ahead regardless of voters' views.

It is only very recently that we have begun to see a shift in the discourse, as national leaders have been talking about the need for EU and global action to confront the major challenges of today. The fact that EU leaders have been calling for global financial regulation, global action on climate change, poverty, terrorism and more, are all essential elements of enhanced EU governance *for* the people. This, however, is only one part of the solution. It certainly does nothing for governance *with* the people with regard to increasing access beyond the expertocracy, or 'pluralizing' the EU. It does little for governance *by* and *of* the people, which would require more 'politicizing' of EU-level institutions. And it does little to alleviate citizen concerns about the impact of EU economic policies on national socio-economic arrangements.

This leads us to two questions: politically, how can citizens gain some sense of empowerment in the decisions that affect them at the EU level? Economically, what kinds of new EU-level policies could address citizens' socio-economic concerns, in particular with regard to questions of economic precariousness and social justice? In order to answer these questions about how to reform the EU politically and economically, we first need to answer another set of questions, focused on EU identity and EU institutional rules.

II. Re-Envisioning EU Identity and Institutional Rules

The problem for the EU is that some very basic 'existential' questions remain unanswered related to what it is, how far it should expand and what it should do in the world. And without answers to these questions, it has difficulty reforming its political institutional rules, let alone responding to the need to improve citizens' sense of empowerment and to find innovative EU solutions to their economic problems. Importantly, if citizens are ever to identify more with the EU, let alone be actively engaged with it politically, they need a clearer understanding of EU identity.

A New EU Identity as 'Region-State'?

The Member States have very different answers to questions about the nature, limits and goals of the EU, given that they have at least 27 different visions of the EU. These visions can nevertheless be loosely divided into four basic, non-mutually exclusive discourses about the EU (see Schmidt, 2009; following Sjursen, 2007 for the first three kinds of discourse, Howorth, 2007 for the fourth). They include a pragmatic discourse about the EU as a borderless problem-solving entity ensuring free markets and regional security, which is generally characteristic of the UK, Scandinavian countries and the central and eastern European countries (for which it additionally serves as a cash cow – Haughton and Rybář, 2009); a normative discourse about the EU as a bordered values-based community, most identified with France and Germany, but also Austria, Belgium, the Netherlands, Italy and Luxembourg; a principled discourse about the EU as a border-free, rights-based post-national union, attributed to the Commission and to philosophers like Habermas (2001) and Beck and Grande (2007); and a strategic discourse about the EU as global actor 'doing international relations differently' through multilateralism, humanitarian aid and peace-keeping. This last discourse has increasingly become the preferred one of Member State leaders generally, with the EU depicted as 'project' rather than 'process' (Sarkozy) or as having 'projects' (Brown), in their efforts to govern *for* the people in response to global challenges such as the economic crisis, climate change, poverty and terrorism. But agreement on what to do as an international actor can always be undermined by disagreements on what the EU is and how far it should expand – whether as a widening free market, a deepening values-based community or a democratizing rights-based union – not to mention EU decision rules involving unanimity and uniformity.

This brings us to the question: is it possible to conceptualize the EU in ways that allow these different visions of the EU – borderless problem-solving entity, bordered values-based community, border-free rights-based post-nation union and global actor – to co-exist? Not if the decision-making processes and future boundaries of the EU continue to be thought about as they have up until now. For the moment, the future is conceived of much as for nation-states, with reasonably clear boundaries, membership as a question of 'in' or 'out', uniform rules for all and unanimity for treaties that decide on major institutional reforms, policy initiatives and enlargement to new members. This worked well in the past, when the Member States numbered six, nine or even 12. But at 27 or more, this is a recipe for disaster, as we witnessed with the referendums on the Constitutional and Lisbon Treaties. Today, the unanimity rule, designed for an intergovernmental union of six nation-states, stops the treaty process dead in its tracks while the uniformity ideal imposed by a Commission dreaming of a federal state chokes off differentiated integration. The only real possibility to move forward while reconciling the differing visions of the EU is for Member States to recognize what the EU is and to change the decision rules accordingly. This demands new ways of thinking about the EU.

One such way is to conceive of the EU as a 'regional state' (Schmidt, 2004, 2006), by which I mean an entity with state-like qualities and powers in an ever-growing number of policy domains, with variable boundaries due to its ever-enlarging territorial reach as well as its Member States' increasingly differentiated participation in policy 'communities' beyond the Single Market. Calling the EU a 'regional state' is not of the same order as evoking empires, republics or superstates, which are normative conceptualizations of the EU. Instead, calling the EU a regional state reflects empirical reality.

The 'state' in regional state speaks to the EU's state-like qualities in areas such as international trade, in which the trade representative speaks for the EU as a whole; in monetary policy, which the ECB effectively controls through the EMU and EMS; in competition policy, which the Commission administers with a strong hand on mergers and acquisitions both inside and outside the EU as well as on state aid; and in jurisprudence, as the ECJ has effectively become the authority for the judiciaries of all Member States through the doctrines of supremacy and direct effect as well as the practice of national court referrals of cases to the ECJ for preliminary rulings.

The 'regional' in regional state not only modifies the 'state', suggesting the many ways in which the EU is not a state akin to that of the nation-state, including the fact that its members are themselves nation-states in a regional union. It also refers to the fuzziness of the EU's regional territory – will it stop at the Balkans, Turkey, Georgia and Ukraine, or continue on to Russia or the other side of the Mediterranean? – and to the variability of participation in its policy communities. Although all Member States belong to the Single Market, membership is varied in a wide range of areas, including the single currency (with 16 of 27 Member States), Schengen (minus the UK and Ireland but with Norway, Iceland and most recently Switzerland), ESDP (without Denmark but with the participation of Norway in the Nordic Battle-group and with all members being able to opt in or out), the Charter of Fundamental Rights (with opt-outs for the UK and Poland) and freedom of movement of workers, which excludes Romania and Bulgaria until 2014, and where Germany and Austria have a derogation on free movement of labour from the new Member States until 2011.

Admittedly, international relations theorists may not like the name regional state because 'a state is a state is a state'; comparativists may misunderstand the term because a 'region' for them refers to the sub-national level; and this could be dismissed out of hand if it were seen as concept-stretching. But this is not concept-stretching, it is conceptual innovation. It uses ordinary language to describe a new and as yet un-named political-institutional entity beyond the nation-state. After all, we talk about the city-state of the past as well as the nation-state of the present without difficulty. So why not speak of the region-state for this newest of international political forms? The name itself, however, is not as important as the concept, which encourages us to think beyond the current configuration and to countenance significant changes in the EU's political institutional organization and processes, in particular with regard to ending the unanimity rule and the uniformity ideal.

An End to the Unanimity Rule?

Speaking of the EU as a regional state without the unanimity rule on EU treaties allows one to envision opt-outs rather than vetoes as the *modus operandi* of the EU. This should not be all that hard to imagine, since the EU has already breached the principle of unanimity in a number of cases, includ-ing the UK in the Maastricht Treaty on EMU and the Social Chapter (to which it opted in as of 1997), plus the Charter of Fundamental Rights in the Lisbon Treaty; Denmark with Maastricht on EMU and ESDP; and Ireland, if it passes the Lisbon Treaty, with guarantees on neutrality, abortion, taxation and its own Commissioner (as agreed in the December 2008 Council meeting). Abandoning the unanimity rule would help avoid the hazards of the current process, in which individual Member States have been able to hold the others hostage, delaying the entry into vigour of treaties approved by the others and often watering down measures desired by large majorities in futile attempts to engineer compromise (as in the Social Charter, which was watered down in an effort to get the UK to buy in rather than veto, after which it negotiated an opt-out anyway).

In short, what we need is a '*treaty to end all treaties*', such that opt-outs substitute for vetoes in the 'treaties'. Without the unanimity rule, Member States could reach agreement on the big policy issues to pursue by allowing the occasional negotiated opt-outs for those members with legitimate reservations about participation in a given area. Treaty agreement itself could be decided by a supermajority of members. As former Commissioner Mario Monti (2009) suggests, this could follow the example of constitutional reform by two-thirds majorities in federal states, the proposal from the European Commission to the European Convention that ratification by three-quarters of Member States constitutes adoption of the Constitutional Treaty, or the suggestion by representatives of the European Parliament and some governments (including the French) that a super-qualified majority of four-fifths of Member States suffices for treaty ratification. If any of these rules were agreed, however, the question is what to do about countries that do not ratify, whether because the government refuses, the parliament votes against or the public referendum fails. In cases of referendums, Monti proposes a second referendum, phrased in terms of the country in-or-out of the EU. Although this might be appropriate for treaties that propose major institutional reforms that would affect how the EU functions with all the Member States, it would not be for a whole range of treaties focused on specific policies, in which opt-outs would serve the EU's purposes much better. Moreover, insisting that countries hold a second referendum constitutes a form of blackmail, because it leaves countries no option other than to accept all policies regardless of their position – or to leave the Union. What is more, it might make governments fight even harder at earlier stages to block or water down any potential treaty for which it fears a negative public vote in a referendum.

Exit through opt-out would help avoid both dead-ends on treaties for which only one or two objecting Member States hold the entire EU hostage and the dilution of treaty initiatives in the search for consensus. Opt-outs could also apply to the Single Market in cases that challenge deeply held values, such as abortion in Ireland and Poland, alcohol in Sweden, drugs in the Netherlands (see Kurzer, 2001) or even co-determination in Germany. As Fritz Scharpf (2007) has suggested, opt-outs could be part of a politically controlled procedure in which the Council, upon request, could exempt a Member State from a given EU rule that they see as violating highly salient national interests or values. One caveat is needed. Opt-outs would be agreed only so long as these do not negatively affect the functioning of the proposed policy community (for example, the case of fiscal harmonization, where an opt-out could unfairly advantage the given Member State and/or threaten the viability of the policy community as a whole). At the moment, exceptions to the rules are allowed only in very exceptional circumstances and have a very high bar to cross (as in the case of GMOs – genetically modified organisms – for Austria and Hungary, for which the Member States held out against the Commission proposal to lift the ban in March 2009). By the same token, the requirement of supermajority agreement would not apply to smaller groups of countries interested in deepening their ties beyond where the majority wishes to go, which is covered by the different forms of 'enhanced co-operation' discussed below.

The 'catch-22' is that to end the unanimity rule with a 'treaty to end all treaties', the EU would need Member State unanimity for its ratification. Without the opt-out option, the Member States would not be likely to countenance the supermajority rule for treaties. With that option, some form of treaty to end all treaties is plausible, especially given recent history with regard to the Lisbon Treaty. Ironically, if the Lisbon Treaty were to fail the second Irish test, the EU Member States would be likely to give up on the unanimity rule in favour of supermajorities with opt-outs for treaties much sooner.

An End to the Uniformity Ideal?

An end to the unanimity rule goes hand in hand with accepting more differentiated integration for the Member States and an end to the uniformity ideal. This would again recognize the reality on the ground, that is, that the EU has already given up on uniformity in policy areas other than the Single Market, such as EMU, Schengen, the ESDP and the Charter of Fundamental Rights as well as on uniformity in territory through its range of openings to non-members through 'economic areas', 'neighbourhoods' and 'partnerships'. It would also acknowledge the future prospects of differentiated integration through enhanced co-operation.

The beginning of the end of the uniformity ideal (much as with unanimity) came with the UK opt-out in the Maastricht Treaty on the Social Chapter and EMU. The principle of differentiation was officially recognized, however, when 'enhanced co-operation' was written into the Amsterdam Treaty (albeit in unworkable form), modified marginally in the Nice Treaty and made workable in the Lisbon Treaty through 'permanent structured co-operation' for defence and security policy and 'enhanced co-operation' for all other policy areas by allowing nine participant Member States to move forward as a last resort decision when the Union as a whole cannot attain those same objectives within a reasonable period (Treaty of Lisbon, 2007/C 306/22/2). This could promote significant progress in a range of policy areas. Permanent structured co-operation, for example, would allow European Security and Defence policy to advance through the creation of new integrated structures, better use of resources and more co-ordinated action (Howorth, 2009). Enhanced co-operation could encourage, say, interested euro area countries to go ahead with greater fiscal harmonization; allow for the creation of 'immi-gration zones' that group together countries with similar immigration or asylum policies, for example, the CEECs, the Mediterranean countries and Continental Europe; and might even lead to the creation of 'pools' for health care provision among countries sharing borders. This would be especially useful in countries where cross-border medical shopping upheld by ECJ decisions has increased pressures on welfare states by eroding their borders (Ferrera, 2005). Note that the first instance of enhanced co-operation under the more stringent ECM (enhanced co-operation mechanism) of the Nice Treaty was launched in July 2008 on the issue of divorce law by eight countries, in response to frustration with the obstruction of highly progressive countries like Sweden and conservative countries like Malta (which does not recognize divorce).

Differentiated integration is only increased by the 'outside insiders' like Norway, Iceland and Switzerland which participate in the Single Market as well as in a range of other EU policy communities such as Schengen and ESDP but do not have a vote. It is complicated by initiatives like the Bologna process for higher education harmonization, which was set up outside the EU by EU Member States, includes most Member States (but again not the UK) as well as many non-EU states across Europe, and was aided financially and administratively by the Commission. Such differentiated integration will be further extended by the Eastern Partnerships launched in May 2009, which involve deep and comprehensive free trade agreements, gradual integration into the EU economy, 'mobility and security pacts' to allow for easier legiti-mate travel while fighting corruption, organized crime and illegal immigra-tion, democracy and good governance promotion, and more.[1] The developing Mediterranean Union would, of course, take differentiated integration even further.

The only thing yet to be floated is the concept of graduated membership for countries on the EU's periphery which are candidates for accession (now or in the future). Why should the EU not take the next logical step, by

[1] More information on this is available at: «http://eur-lex.europa.eu/LexUriServ/LexUriServ.do?uri=CELEX:52008DC0823:EN:NOT».

declaring that membership is no longer just a long-term matter of 'in' or 'out' but also a shorter-term question of 'in which areas' or 'out of which areas', once certain basic requirements are fulfilled, including the establishment of democratic practices, respect for human rights and a commitment to free markets. For a country like Turkey in particular, a gradual accession process would help avoid the likelihood that in 15 or 20 years' time it would have been turned off by the non-democratic, hard-bargaining accession negotiations led by the Commission, the ever-present possibility of veto (by Austria or France) and the ever-growing volume of the *acquis communautaire* negotiated without it (Schmidt, 2009). Moreover, graduated membership would be a spur to countries on the EU's borders to continue to liberalize and democratize in hopes of joining, thus enabling the EU to maintain its 'power of attraction' (Leonard, 2005), which could be lost if it fixed its borders at any given point. Graduated membership would also ensure socialization into the consensual policy-making style of the EU – something that was lost on Poland, for example, as a result of the non-consensual hard-bargaining of the accession years – as well as better compliance with EU rules, given the gradual nature of the accession process, by contrast with the precipitous and arguably premature accession of some CEECs, in which politics trumped compliance. And finally, graduated membership need not be seen as a slippery slope, in which one foot inside the EU guarantees full membership in the end – as the French might fear with the case of Turkey. Rather, it is more akin to a long and winding road which gives both EU Member States and prospective members the time to get to know one another by engaging with one another as equals in one policy area after another – rather than as principal and supplicant – leaving both the time to decide whether they want continued accession into more and more areas or not.

But such graduated membership would only be attractive to prospective members, as well as to outside insiders, if it were to come with institutional voice and vote in the sectors in which they participate. This inverts Prodi's promise to the neighbours of 'everything but institutions', since the institutions need to come with policy participation, and both gradually. Otherwise, for countries in the EU's periphery, why try to meet the criteria demanding significant democracy and market opening when neighbourhood policy allows entry into the European market with criteria that are more exhortatory than real with regard to democratization? And for countries like Norway, Iceland or Switzerland that already participate in the Single Market in myriad ways, what is the value-added of graduated membership if they do not have a voice and a vote in the areas in which they participate? Graduated membership with institutional voice and vote is important not only to attract partial members but also to ensure that the policy decisions are not only the best ones because everyone has a say in them but also because they are thereby the most legitimate (Schmidt, 2009).

How an EU with graduated membership would work in any given policy area is open. Some areas may not need much formalization, with the EU Commission operating as a regional 'community organizer' or an administrative support link, as in the Bologna process for higher education. In others requiring significant institutionalization, by contrast, we could take a page from the European Monetary Union, which already has a kind of graduated membership (in which some Member States are in, others out), with highly developed institutional voice and vote for its members through a restricted Council of Ministers (the Ecofin); with a central decision-making body, the ECB; and with the Commission to police euro area members or to warn non-members of any violations. If European Security and Defence Policy (ESDP), for example, were to develop substantially in a similar manner using the 'reinforced structured co-operation' procedure under the Lisbon Treaty, it could ensure institutional voice and vote through a Council of Defence Ministers made up of participating members; central strategic co-ordination through an EU Security Council similar to the US National Security Council; a clear division of Member States into groups based on capacities and potential inputs so as to optimize synergies, resource sharing and generate better outputs; the integration of neighbours such as Georgia and Ukraine into the policy process, much as is already done for Turkey, plus an EU caucus in Nato and more (Howorth, 2009). The Single Market would be notionally easier to manage institutionally, since inside outsiders like Norway already sit on expert committees with regard to standard harmonization and have voice but no vote, thus serving as a model for other soon-to-be graduated members. The question would be how to work out EP representation. But even here, non-members have had delegations to the EP, as in the case of the 2004 and 2007 accession countries, participating in discussions even when they have not had the vote.

Some might ask what such a European region-state would do to identity, and whether it does not actually destroy any possibility of reconciling the four differing visions of the EU. The opposite would be the case, since it would enable countries with opposing visions, in particular those of the EU as market v. the EU as community, to co-exist. Those countries with visions of the EU as a borderless free market and security area could maintain this while participating in the Single Market and, say, ESDP. Those with visions of the EU as a values-based community could sustain this while participating in most policy areas or even deepening their integration through enhanced co-operation. Those with a rights-based vision would be satisfied by the EU's continued democratizing influence in its periphery. And finally, all of this would reinforce the strategic vision of the EU as global actor, since the EU could continue to exert its 'power of attraction' with regard to its neighbourhood, to enhance its reach by deepening inter-regional as well as intra-regional co-operation, and to improve its influence through reinforced structured co-operation in defence and security policy or humanitarian intervention.

III. Re-Envisioning EU Politics and Economic Policy

Re-envisioning the EU as a 'region-state' while reforming its decision rules may help solve problems related to what the EU is, how far it should expand and even what it should do in the world, all of which may help it govern more effectively *for* the people in the international arena. But this does little either for governance *by*, *of* and *with* the people with regard to empowering EU citizens, or for governance *for* the people with regard to socio-economic policy. And for all of this, we need to consider further democratizing reforms, none of which are easy. This is because the ways we normally think about democratizing nation-states are not open to this region-state, at least for the moment. A duly elected president and a fully empowered parliament are not on the agenda, given the lack of a sense of European collective identity and will. Moreover, increasing the power of EU-level institutions could only further increase citizens' sense of powerlessness unless we find ways to increase their input into national as well as EU-level decision-making and respond to their concerns about the EU's impact on national labour and social policy. And this, above all, requires more politicizing and pluralizing of the EU.

Towards New EU Politics?

There have been many proposals for political reform, too many to list let alone to go into detail here (for one, see Hix, 2008). Most such proposals focus on increasing *representative politics*, or governance *by* and *of* the people at the EU level, mainly through more political competition in the European Parliament, Commission and/or the Council. There is little question that politicization could have negative effects on governing effectiveness *for* the people (Majone, 1998; Scharpf, 2003, 2007; Schmidt, 2006, p. 270), by introducing yet another source of division into deliberations already burdened by considerations of national, public and special interests among 27 Member States and more, if graduated membership were to come into effect. The end of '*policy without politics*' could in turn lead to stalemates that would only increase citizens' disaffection from and dissatisfaction with the EU – in particular if the decision rules regarding unanimity and uniformity remain unchanged. This said, *'policy with politics'*, if done right, need not unduly affect governing effectiveness at the same time that it could have positive effects on citizens' sense of identification with the EU and its political legitimacy.

Politicization, in any event, will be increasingly hard to avoid, given the awakening of the 'sleeping giant' of cross-cutting cleavages in Member States, with the rise of splits between pro-Europeans and Euro-sceptics in mainstream parties of the right and the left (Van der Eijk and Franklin, 2004) and the likelihood of much more hotly contested, politicized EP elections than in the past, even if they remain second-order elections. Once the Lisbon (or equivalent) Treaty comes into force, politicization is likely to go further, given the election by the European Parliament of the Commission President. This could engender political campaigns across Europe in EP elections, with primaries organized by the major EU political parties across Europe. All of this could be a good thing for democracy if EU-wide political parties become stronger, if they produce platforms with ideas on policy and polity issues that resonate with citizens, and if this in turn produces substantive political debates across the EU about what it should do. Exactly how the electoral politics would play itself out in practice remains in question, however. Although there are good arguments for increasing the majoritarian politics of the Council and the EP (Hix, 2008), in particular to avoid the stalemates of extremely proportional representation systems, as in Italy prior to the 1990s and arguably also since 2006, the EU lacks the collective identity and legitimacy necessary for the kind of majoritarian, one-party rule of a Britain or a France. It would do better with the kind of proportional representation system of a Germany in which, once the right–left polarization of elections campaigns is over, compromise and consensus-seeking rules, in particular at times of grand coalitions.

The EU's increasing legitimacy cannot be based on electoral politics alone, however. It needs to be linked to institutional reforms providing, for example, for greater EP input at the beginning stages of policy formulation. Reforms here could involve linking relevant EP members and committees to the Commission's expert committees in the comitology process. Even without this, however, the Commission could lay out the political dimensions of its policy initiatives, rather than presenting them as purely technical, while the European Parliament could do more to debate the issues (Magnette, 2003; Schmidt, 2006, pp. 268–9). In addition, the EP could be more fully connected to national parliaments – and needs to be, way beyond the provisions in the Lisbon Treaty. This may be the only way to ensure greater national parliamentary engagement with EU issues, beyond the few that become topics of

Europe-wide controversy, such as the services directive. Greater citizen access to the EP either directly or through the national parliaments is another area crying out for reform, as the Lamassoure report (2008) made clear, since citizens do not know their rights or how to ensure them through EU institutions.

Another remedy to EU legitimacy problems would be through more *pluralist politics*. This is a national task as much as an EU-level one. At the national level, political leaders' discourse should make it clear to national publics that national governments are not the only voices which can speak for national interests and values, but that citizens – as opposed to just experts – can and should have more direct input into supranational decision-making. In addition to informing citizens of the pluralist nature of supranational governance *with* the people, they need to help citizens to organize themselves so as to gain access and influence in European decision-making – providing funding, information and strategic advice – as opposed to trying to avoid citizen involvement. Moreover, they need to put procedures into place to enable citizens to participate in the national formulation processes focused on EU decision-making. All of this would also afford the already activist citizens and social movements better access and input at both EU and national levels.

The EU could also do more to bring citizens in. It already has a range of mechanisms for group citizen access at the EU level, although expertocracy is indeed a problem – but also necessary, especially in highly technical areas. And, of course, stakeholder democracy, even if improved, is not public interest oriented democracy (witness the Calabrian structural funds). Some of the rules of transnational membership for EU funding of eligible groups, moreover, are problematic for public interest groups that tend to be organized nationally. In addition, the EU could do much more to facilitate cross-border citizen initiatives, as a supranational 'community organizer', as it did with the Bologna process.

The EU's open method of co-ordination (OMC) also has great potential with regard to bringing citizens into EU-related adjustment processes. In addition to the economic focus on flexibility and employability of the EES (European Employment Strategy) is the social concern with inclusiveness and poverty alleviation in the Social Inclusion OMC. Until now, however, the OMC's potential has not been realized. It remains mainly government exercises (Zeitlin and Pochet, 2005).

Towards New EU Economic Policies?

Finding ways to politicize and pluralize the EU can work only if the EU does more with regard to policy initiatives that address the socio-economic concerns of the citizens, in particular at this time of economic crisis. But what to do and how to address such concerns is not easy, given not only EU decision rules (on unanimity and uniformity) that make for difficulties in reaching collective agreement on such issues, but also EU economic ground rules that focus responsibility for social solidarity on Member States alone.

While EU engagement in economic market-making has gone way beyond the agreements in the Treaties, EU engagement in socio-economic market-correction has fallen short. The 'negative integration' that follows from the Treaties makes market creation relatively easy for the EU Commission and European Court of Justice. 'Positive integration' is much more difficult, since market correction demands agreement from the Member States – which the decision rules of the EU render near to impossible in the social policy arena in particular (Scharpf, 1999), given the differences among the three basic families of welfare states: liberal Anglo-Saxon, conservative continental and social-democratic Scandinavian (Esping-Andersen, 1990). The problems related to negative integration have been made worse in recent years by the increasingly single-minded – we could even say ideological – focus on market integration to the exclusion of other considerations, in particular with regard to the post-Polanyian impact on areas never intended to be subject to the treaties, such as education, health services and labour (Scharpf, 2007, 2009). Because of actions in these areas, as well as in services liberalization, the EU is perceived in many countries as reducing social protections and rights. The services directive, for example, not only jeopardizes public services generally, it also raises sometimes insurmountable problems for non-profit provision of services. The complicated public tendering requirements can make it very difficult for smaller, non-profit local charities to comply, which risks putting them out of business, thereby reducing social capital in local communities. In the UK, for example, Baroness Barker, spokesperson on health for the Liberal Democrats in the House of Lords,[2] argues that the measure was transposed in such a way as to encourage not only the privatization of public services but also the consolidation and professionalization of voluntary sector providers, which would likely lead to a significant loss of social capital in terms of that extra 30 per cent of benefits normally associated with services provided by small non-profits in local communities – both in terms of lower costs from the use of volunteer help and higher social capital from the solidarity generated by community-based, smaller local charities.

Of equal concern are ECJ judgments on education that undermine national tax-based social solidarity by invoking freedom of movement to allow students from other European Member States to displace country nationals

[2] Mentioned in her presentation at the Harvard Center for European Studies on 3 October 2008.

(for example, the case of German medical students in Austria) and on labour markets that limit labour union rights to strike against what they see as unfair wage competition from cross-border firms (the *Viking* and *Laval* cases in Scandinavia – see Reich, 2008). The problem is that Member States have no real recourse here, given the independence of the ECJ and the impossibility of getting the Council to overturn such judgments. On these issues, as Fritz Scharpf (2009) notes, one wonders why the Member States do not 'just say no', to challenge the court judgment. Instead, Member States appear to have been negotiating compromises with the courts or seeking to create national legislation to get around the problem. If they can do this without undermining the national social fabric, so much the better. But should they have to do this? And what is the impact on national perceptions of EU legitimacy?

In addition to imposing a moratorium on social policy-related areas of negative integration, more positive integration is clearly needed, especially given the economic crisis. Here, I offer just a few ideas, some of which were floated already a number of years ago. For example, in light of the EU's clear need and desire to promote freedom of movement of workers and the unfeasibility of creating a uniform EU minimum wage, why not pick up on Fritz Scharpf's (2003) recommendation to institute an agreement on EU-wide relative standards for wages – related to a percentage of the national median income – and for (subsidized) social assistance. In other areas, we should consider revisiting Philippe Schmitter's (2000) proposal to increase EU-wide social solidarity, such as replacing the Common Agricultural Policy with a negative income tax for the poor. Alternatively, in particular since any serious reform of the CAP is years away, why not set up a social assistance fund by collecting, say, five euros per citizen through nationally based income tax – on a voluntary basis for the moment. Let us call it the European solidarity tax (to build citizens' sense of EU identity) and use it to replenish the Globalization Adjustment Fund in order to deal with the certain rise in unemployment and inequalities resulting from today's global economic crisis. None of this, however, is enough to stop the erosion of national welfare states. For this, we would need to consecrate what Maurizio Ferrera (2009) has called a nested 'social space' in the EU to safeguard or reconstruct domestic as well as inter-regional and supranational sharing arrangements in the social policy arena, whether in education, health, welfare or labour policy.

Finally, the EU needs to do more in the macroeconomic sphere to deal with the economic crisis. Rethinking the EMU criteria in light of the crisis would be one aspect of this, whether in terms of what level of deficits and debt are appropriate for a currency that is now established and credible or in terms of the admissions criteria for new euro area members – instead of leaving the economies of Latvia, Estonia and Lithuania to collapse under the burden of euro-denominated loans and currencies fixed against the euro.

Equally importantly, however, the EU needs some means of funding a financial lending institution of last resort that could be an alternative to the IMF, to bail out EU Member States in dire macroeconomic straits. One of the most disappointing aspects of the European response to the economic crisis is that the Member States retained the principle of 'every man for himself' with regard to weathering the storm. It made sense that the Member States refused to create a bail-out for the east European countries alone in response to the *cri de coeur* of the Hungarian Prime Minister against the creation of a new economic iron curtain. But it does not make sense for the EU to leave it to the IMF to bail out its east European members, especially since the IMF conditions of one-size-fits-all, with budgetary austerity and other measures, are the opposite of what these countries need. In a situation in which the failure of east European banks will have boomerang effects on west European ones – we need cite only Austrian and Swedish banks – and that the slowdown in eastern Europe will have spillover effects in western Europe given the interconnectedness of the economies, the answer is to have a European equivalent of the IMF. A European Monetary Fund (EMF) would be able to tailor its responses much more closely to European specificities, and it will be needed not only by east European countries but also by west European ones, given talks of the dangers of insolvency for Italy, Portugal, Greece and Ireland, possibly even Spain, along with EU neighbours like Ukraine. The EMF need not replace the IMF but act in concert with it, as another source of funding with a different set of objectives that would be better tailored to the economic needs and realities of EU Member States. The EMF need not be an entirely new institution, since the European Bank for Reconstruction and Development (EBRD) or even the European Investment Bank (EIB) could be converted into the EMF. The creation of an EMF would also help build greater solidarity and reduce distrust among Member States at a time when this is most needed.

Conclusion

Europe, like the rest of the world, is in for hard times economically. The EU, which is already suffering politically from a legitimacy deficit, needs to do more to win over its citizens. One way is through the EU acting as a global strategic actor on initiatives *for* the people with regard to financial markets, climate change, terrorism and so forth. But the internal economic policies also need rethinking, with new initiatives to promote EU-wide solidarity, such as a European Monetary Fund, a solidarity tax, as well as a moratorium on the pursuit of 'negative integration' when this undermines areas at the very core of national citizenship and social solidarity, and thereby risks further alienating the public and delegitimizing the EU itself. Any such re-envisioning of the EU's socio-economic policy, however, needs to be done in concert *with* the people, through pluralist processes, and *by* the representatives *of* the people at both national and EU level, through more politics, in particular with regard to politically informed debates and deliberation in and among EU institutions. This in turn requires re-envisioning the EU's political decision-making processes in such ways as to increase democratic access to decision-making at the EU and national levels.

In addition to the political and economic reforms, however, the EU needs to re-envision its identity and change its decision rules. Without some reconceptualization of what the EU really is – a region-state consisting of a regional union of nation-states in overlapping policy communities – along with a revision of its rules, by eliminating the unanimity rule and uniformity ideal, it will continue to suffer from institutional stumbling blocks to action both internally and externally. It is not just that the lack of ratification of the Lisbon Treaty has made EU leadership a game of chance. It is that unanimity rules for treaties make it hard to construct common EU global policy initiatives while the uniformity ideal on top of this makes for policy stalemate and/or dilution. Both together make it very difficult to clarify what the EU is, how far it should go and what it should do in the world, given tensions between EU 'widening' as a market, security area or human rights promoter and EU 'deepening' as an identity-enhancing values-based, political union able to agree on and take global action.

Once the principles of unanimity and uniformity are abandoned, membership of the EU 'region-state' need no longer be seen as an all-or-nothing proposition. Beyond certain basic membership requirements – being a democracy which respects human rights and participates in the Single Market – Member States could opt out of the policy 'communities' of which they do not wish to be a part without stopping the other members from going forward. Where supermajorities of all Member States cannot be attained, enhanced co-operation would allow smaller numbers of Member States to move forward on new initiatives in a wide range of areas, from 'structured' defence policy to immigration zones and health pools. For the Single Market, which all members need to buy into at the outset, the supermajority rule plus exceptional opt-outs would be allowed so long as they do not undermine the functioning of the policy community. Accession, moreover, would become a gradual process of differentiated integration with institutional voice and vote, policy area by policy area, once the initial conditions related to democracy, human rights and the market economy are met. This would help avoid the 'big bang' of accession (or rejection) after long years of hard-bargaining, provide ongoing socialization into the EU's consensual policy-making, ensure implementation of EU rules and promote continued democratization.

Instead of detracting from identity or making a political Europe less manageable, the elimination of the unanimity rule and uniformity ideal plus graduated membership with voice and vote would enable the EU to move forward faster with more efficiency as well as legitimacy. In a region-state of 500 million inhabitants in the current hard borders, and many hundreds of millions more in the neighbourhood as potential 'graduated members', unanimity and uniformity plus in-or-out membership are much more likely to undermine progress and alienate citizens.

If we were to imagine what the EU as regional state would look like on a map, we would likely over time find a rather large core of deeply but not uniformly integrated members, mainly in continental and Mediterranean Europe, including some of the CEECs, with a bit less integration for the UK, the Nordic countries and some other CEECs, and even less as we move eastwards beyond the present borders of the Union. Elsewhere, I have suggested that this is neither a *'Europe à la carte'*, as those who envision the EU as a borderless free market might wish, nor does it encourage retreat to a *'core Europe'* with one dish for all, as those who envision the EU as a values-based community might desire. Rather, this is an elaborate *'menu Europe'* with an ever-expanding range of courses, with a shared main dish (the Single Market), everyone sitting around the table and engaging in the conversation, although some individual countries might occasionally opt to sit out a course while other groups of countries might choose to partake of a new course together (Schmidt, 2008). If we add graduated membership to this, we could imagine additional guests joining the diners at the table for particular courses and, slowly over time, partaking of more and more dishes even as they learn the manners of the table and the rules of the conversation. At the same time, moreover, they, just as those diners who occasionally opt out of a course, would be able to see how much their fellow diners relish the other dishes, in order to decide when and if they will opt in later. The result is likely to be an 'ever closer Union' with greater 'unity in diversity'.

References

Barbier, J-C. (2008) *La Longue Marche vers l'Europe Sociale* (Paris: PUF).
Beck, U. and Grande, E. (2007) *Cosmopolitan Europe* (Cambridge: Polity Press).

Bieling, H-J. (2007) 'The Other Side of the Coin: Conceptualizing the Relationship between Business and the State in the Age of Globalization'. *Business and Politics*, Vol. 9, Issue 3, Article 5. Available at: «http://www.bepress.com/bap/vol9/iss3/art5».

Caporaso, J. and Tarrow, S. (2008) 'Polanyi in Brussels: European Institutions and the Embedding of Markets in Society'. RECON Online Working Paper 2008/01, available at: «http://www.reconproject.eu/projectweb/portalproject/RECON WorkingPapers.html».

Esping-Andersen, G. (1990) *Three Worlds of Welfare State Capitalism* (Cambridge: Polity Press).

Fargion, V., Morlino, L. and Profeti, S. (eds) (2006a) *Europeizzazione e rappresentanza territoriale. Il caso Italiano* (Bologna: Il Mulino).

Fargion, V., Morlino, L. and Profeti, S. (2006b) 'Europeanization and Territorial Representation in Italy'. *West European Politics*, Vol. 29, No. 4, pp. 757–83.

Ferrera, M. (2005) *The Boundaries of Welfare: European Integration and the New Spatial Politics of Social Protection* (Oxford: Oxford University Press).

Ferrera, M. (2009) 'The JCMS Annual Lecture: National Welfare States and European Integration: In Search of a "Virtuous Nesting" '. *JCMS*, Vol. 47, No. 2, pp. 219–33.

Greenwood, J. (2007) 'Organized Civil Society and Democratic Legitimacy in the European Union'. *British Journal of Political Science*, Vol. 37, No. 2, pp. 333–57.

Habermas, J. (2001) *The Postnational Constellation* (Cambridge, MA: MIT Press).

Haughton, T. and Rybář, M. (2009), 'A Tool in the Toolbox: Assessing the Impact of EU Membership on Party Politics in Slovakia'. *Journal of Communist Studies and Transition Politics* (forthcoming).

Hix, S. (2008) *What's Wrong with the European Union and How to Fix It* (Cambridge: Polity Press).

Höpner, M. and Schäfer, A. (2007) 'A New Phase of European Integration: Organized Capitalisms in Post-Ricardian Europe'. MOIFG Discussion Paper no. 07/4. Available at: «http://ssrn.com/abstract=976162».

Howorth, J. (2007) *European Security and Defence Policy* (Basingstoke: Palgrave).

Howorth, J. (2009) 'The Case for an EU Grand Strategy'. *Egmont Papers*, No. 27, pp. 15–24.

Kurzer, P., (2001) *Markets and Moral Regulation: Cultural Changes in the European Union* (Cambridge: Cambridge University Press).

Lamassoure, A. (2008) 'Le Citoyen et l'Application du Droit Communautaire'. *Rapport au Président de la République* (8 June). Available at: «http://www.ladocumentationfrancaise.fr/rapports-publics/084000379/index.shtml».

Leonard, M. (2005) *Why Europe Will Run the 21st Century* (London: Fourth Estate).

Magnette, P. (2003) 'European Governance and Civic Participation: Beyond Elitist Citizenship?' *Political Studies*, Vol. 51, pp. 144–60.

Mair, P. (2005) 'Popular Democracy and the European Union Polity'. European Governance Papers (EUROGOV) No. C-05-03, 2005. Available at «http://www.connex-network.org/eurogov/pdf/egp-connex-C-05-03.pdf».

Mair, P. (2006) 'Political Parties and Party Systems'. In Graziano, P. and Vink, M. (eds) *Europeanization: New Research Agendas* (Basingstoke: Palgrave Macmillan), pp. 303–27.

Majone, G. (1998) 'Europe's Democratic Deficit'. *European Law Journal*, Vol. 4, No. 1, pp. 5–28.

Martin, A. and Ross, G. (2004) *Euros and Europeans* (New York: Cambridge University Press).

Menon, A. and Weatherill, S. (2008) 'Transnational Legitimacy in a Globalizing World: How the European Union Rescues its States'. *West European Politics*, Vol. 31, No. 3, pp. 397–416.

Monti, M. (2009) 'Réferendum: quid agendum? Réflexions pour sortir l'UE de la paralysie assurée'. *Notre Europe* (March).

Polanyi, K. (2001) *The Great Transformation* (New York: Beacon Press).

Reich, N. (2008) 'Free Movement *v.* Social Rights in an Enlarged Union: The *Laval* and *Viking* Cases before the ECJ'. *German Law Journal*, Vol. 9, No. 2, pp. 125–61.

Scharpf, F.W. (1999) *Governing in Europe* (Oxford: Oxford University Press).

Scharpf, F.W. (2003) 'Legitimate Diversity: The New Challenge of European Integration'. In Börzel, T.A. and Cichowski, R.A. (eds) *The State of the European Union*, Vol. 6 (Oxford: Oxford University Press).

Scharpf, F.W. (2007) 'Reflections on Multilevel Legitimacy'. MPIfG Working Paper 07/3. Available at «http://www.mpifg.de».

Scharpf, F.W. (2009) 'Legitimacy in the Multilevel European Polity'. MPIfG Working Paper 09/1. Available at: «http://www.mpifg.de».

Schmidt, V.A. (2004) 'The European Union: Democratic Legitimacy in a Regional State?' *JCMS*, Vol. 42, No. 4, pp. 975–99.

Schmidt, V.A. (2006) *Democracy in Europe: The EU and National Polities* (Oxford: Oxford University Press).

Schmidt, V.A. (2007) 'Trapped by their Ideas: French Elites' Discourses of European Integration and Globalization'. *Journal of European Public Policy*, Vol. 14, No. 4, pp. 992–1009.

Schmidt, V.A. (2008) 'A "Menu Europe" Will Prove Far More Palatable'. *Financial Times*, 22 July, p. 13.

Schmidt, V.A. (2009) 'Envisioning a Less Fragile, More Liberal Europe'. *European Political Science* (forthcoming).

Schmitter, P.C. (2000) *How to Democratize the European Union and Why Bother* (London: Rowman & Littlefield).

Sjursen, H. (2007) 'Enlargement in Perspective: The EU's Quest for Identity'. Recon Online Working Paper 2007/15. Available at: «www.reconproject.eu/projectweb/portalproject/RECONWorkingPapers.html».

Skocpol, T. (2004) *Diminished Democracy: From Membership to Management in American Civic Life* (Tulsa, OK: University of Oklahoma Press).

Van der Eijk, C., and Franklin, M. (2004) 'Potential for Contestation on European Matters at National Elections in Europe'. In Marks, G. and Steenbergen, M.R.

(eds) *European Integration and Political Conflict* (Cambridge: Cambridge University Press).

WRR (Scientific Council for Government Policy) (2007) *Rediscovering Europe in the Netherlands* (Amsterdam: Amsterdam University Press).

Zeitlin, J. and Pochet, P. with Magnusson, L. (2005) *The Open Method of Co-ordination in Action: The European Employment and Social Inclusion Strategies* (Brussels: Peter Lang).

Zippel, K. (2006) *The Politics of Sexual Harassment: A Comparative Study of the United States, the European Union and Germany* (Cambridge: Cambridge University Press).

JCMS 2009 Volume 47 Annual Review pp. 43–62

Corruption and Compliance in the EU's Post-Communist Members and Candidates

MILADA ANNA VACHUDOVA
University of North Carolina at Chapel Hill

Introduction

Some 20 years after the end of communism in central and eastern Europe, the European Union (EU) is still working through the opportunities and challenges of enlarging eastwards.[1] For the EU and its new members alike, enlargement has been a success: ten formerly communist states have joined and experienced the economic and geopolitical benefits of membership after the relative rigours of the EU's pre-accession process. The EU's requirements for membership forced candidates to reform the state and the economy, reducing the role of the state in the economy and improving the transparency and efficiency of state institutions. In many areas, however, strict enforcement was limited to the adoption – and not the implementation – of the *acquis* and the reform of the public administration leaves much room for improvement. For the older Member States, enlargement has also brought economic and geopolitical benefits, tempered with challenges ranging from popular concerns about welcoming workers from the new members to concerns about including so many new members in the EU's institutions.

In 2008 the issue of corruption in the EU's newest members – Bulgaria and Romania – took centre stage as it touched on several sensitive issues within the EU. As Europe followed the United States into economic crisis, what hit headlines in 2008 was blatant corruption in the disbursement of EU

[1] I am indebted to Besir Ceka for his insightful comments as well as for research assistance related to this article.

Journal compilation © 2009 Blackwell Publishing Ltd, 9600 Garsington Road, Oxford OX4 2DQ, UK and 350 Main Street, Malden, MA 02148, USA

funds by parts of Bulgaria's state administration. The EU responded strongly, freezing some funds for Bulgaria. At a time of strapped budgets, rising unemployment and so-called 'enlargement fatigue' throughout the EU, the political pressure to be tough on corruption – at least in new members – is likely to remain high. More broadly, the realization that corruption and organized crime in Bulgaria and Romania are extensive and strongly inter-twined with political parties, the civil service and state agencies intensified an ongoing debate on the power of EU leverage. After all, the EU had by 2000 embraced EU enlargement as its most effective foreign policy tool and pre-sented it as the way forward to stabilize and democratize Balkan states, building efficient public administrations and reviving the economy while also helping to bring ethnic reconciliation and reintegration to the post-conflict region. But Bulgaria and Romania force the question: can EU leverage overcome the difficult domestic conditions that we observe in Balkan states? Is it a matter of adjusting the pre-accession process to include, for example, longer preparations, stricter monitoring and more hands-on assistance from Brussels? Or does continuing with enlargement mean accepting states where corruption is pervasive and intractable before – and after – membership? What happens in Bulgaria and Romania over the next months and years will help determine with what tools – and with how much confidence – the EU pursues enlargement in the Western Balkans. The most likely lesson will be that EU leverage is more powerful well before accession than after it, regard-less of the EU's new tools to encourage post-accession compliance.

I. Why So Much Corruption in Post-Communist Europe?

The collapse of communism created spectacular opportunities for corruption throughout the post-communist region (Moroff and Schmidt-Pfister, 2010). Put most simply, the end of the communist system created a vacuum that necessitated rewriting the rules of the economy and the state. Those in power in the early years could write those rules to benefit themselves. Even when adequate rules were written, actors could rely on political connections, dys-functional state institutions and corrupt judiciaries to perpetuate corrupt practices and prevent prosecution (Kornai and Rose-Ackerman, 2004; Spend-zharova, 2008). Briefly, the effects of corruption are significant: corruption impoverishes society by reducing economic growth, undermining entrepre-neurship and stealing from the state. Corruption also undermines liberal democracy as political elites violate the legal limits of their power, citizens lose trust in state institutions and civil society is oppressed or co-opted by powerful networks.

The EU's ten post-communist members do exhibit substantial variation in levels of corruption over the last 15 to 20 years. This variation generally tracks indicators for the quality of democracy and the extent of market liberalization since 1989. It also tracks more structural conditions, such as the level of economic development in 1989 – or indeed the level of industrialization in pre-communist times. Nevertheless, we can see that the nature of political competition during and after regime change has had an impact on levels of corruption and the success of programmes to combat it. Corruption has been highest in states where a narrow group of elites initially governed with little political competition from other political forces, and with little effective scrutiny from the media and civic groups (see Ganev, 2007; Grzymała-Busse, 2007; Hanley, 2008; O'Dwyer, 2006; Vachudova, 2005).

A useful categorization of the different kinds of corruption at play in post-communist Europe distinguishes between low-level administrative corruption, self-serving asset stripping by officials and state capture by corrupt networks (Karklins, 2002). The states that have experienced extensive capture by corrupt networks since 1989 are the ones that continue to have the greatest problems with endemic, high-level corruption today. Much has been written about the potential windfall of a partially reformed economy for well-positioned elites. Research shows that in such an economy elites can extract greater rents for a longer period of time and at a greater cost to society than elites in a rapidly liberalizing economy, where the state is forced to limit and redefine its role in the economy more quickly (Hellman, 1998; Gould, 2004; Spendzharova, 2008).

Thus in Romania a highly corrupt and unreformed former communist party captured the state and governed virtually unopposed until 1996 (Gallagher, 2005; Vachudova, 2005; Pop-Eleches, 2008). In Bulgaria the unreformed communists faced more competition, but nevertheless benefited from extensive control of the state and the economy until 1997 (and beyond). Elites of different stripes installed themselves as powerful economic actors in a partially reformed economy that was defined by corrupt relationships between state officials and economic actors (Ganev, 2001, 2007). On judicial capacity and independence the Czech Republic was ranked for years as the next most problematic country after Bulgaria and Romania among the EU's ten new post-communist members (see Figure 1). This is surprising given its favourable political and economic conditions at the start of the transition – but less surprising given almost seven years of unopposed rule by the same political grouping once the transition had begun (see Grzymała-Busse, 2007; Hanley, 2008).

The pattern of concentrated rule and partial economic reform has been repeated in different ways but usually with even greater intensity in the

Figure 1: Judicial Framework and Independence Ratings

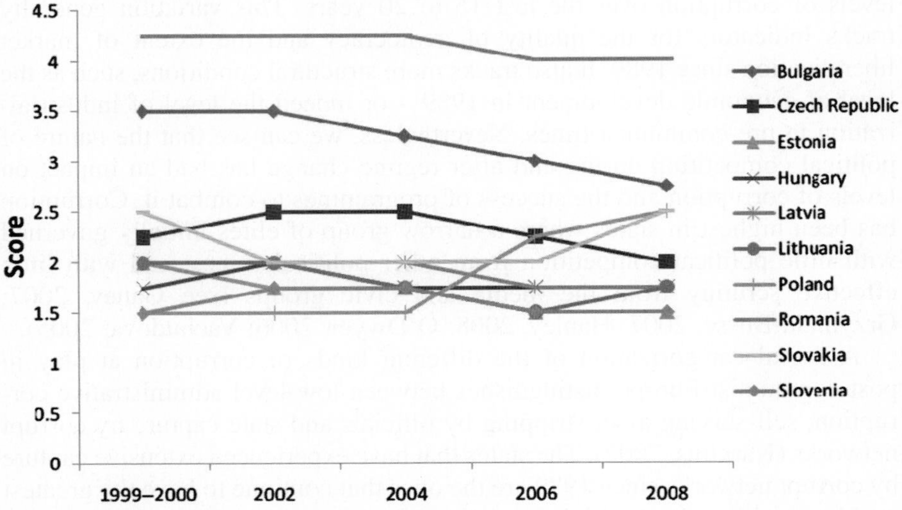

Source: Freedom House's *Nations in Transit* survey, 1995–2008.
Note: *Nations in Transit* is a comparative study of reform in the former communist states of Europe and Eurasia and measures the democratic progress that countries from these regions have made along the following dimensions: electoral process, civil society, independent media, national democratic governance, local democratic governance, judicial framework and independence, and corruption.

Western Balkan states. Authoritarian rule gave ruling elites tremendous power in Croatia and Serbia and Montenegro from 1990 to 2000 even as war and sanctions intensified the grip of organized crime on the economy (Gould, 2004). In the three constituent nations of Bosnia the same nationalist parties have controlled the different parts of the state since 1990, and continue to control much of the country's economic activity for the benefit of the few at the expense of the many. There has been greater political competition in Macedonia and Albania, but in conditions of extremely weak administrative capacity and little or no willingness to combat corruption. Throughout the region, economic and institutional reform has progressed only very slowly as elites protect old clientelistic networks and the rewards of a partially reformed economy; they are benefiting from relationships with organized crime, but are also intimidated and pressured into protecting them from prosecution.[2]

[2] Author interviews with government officials in Belgrade, Sarajevo and Skopje, October and November 2005.

II. Perceptions of Corruption and Variation across States

Corruption is, by definition, difficult to measure. The most widely used quantitative index of corruption is by Transparency International (1995–2008) (see Table 1). This index, however, reports only *perceived* levels of corruption. There may in fact exist a wide gap between perceived and actual

Table 1: The 2000 and 2008 Corruption Perceptions Indices

Rank	Country	2000 CPI score	Rank	Country	2008 CPI score
1	Finland	10	1	Denmark	9.3
2	Denmark	9.8	1	Sweden	9.3
	Sweden	9.4	5	Finland	9.0
9	Netherlands	8.9	7	Netherlands	8.9
10	United Kingdom	8.7	11	Luxembourg	8.3
11	Luxembourg	8.6	12	Austria	8.1
15	Austria	7.7	14	Germany	7.9
17	Germany	7.6	16	Ireland	7.7
19	Ireland	7.2	16	United Kingdom	7.7
20	Spain	7	18	Belgium	7.3
21	France	6.7	23	France	6.9
	Portugal	6.4	26	Slovenia	6.7
25	Belgium	6.1	27	Estonia	6.6
27	Estonia	5.7	28	Spain	6.5
28	Slovenia	5.5	31	Cyprus	6.4
32	Hungary	5.2	32	Portugal	6.1
35	Greece	4.9	36	Malta	5.8
36	Malaysia	4.8	45	Czech Republic	5.2
39	Italy	4.6	47	Hungary	5.1
42	Czech Republic	4.3	52	Latvia	5.0
	Lithuania	4.1	52	Slovakia	5.0
	Poland	4.1	55	Italy	4.8
50	Turkey	3.8	57	Greece	4.7
51	Croatia	3.7	58	Lithuania	4.6
	Bulgaria	3.5	58	Poland	4.6
	Slovak Republic	3.5	58	Turkey	4.6
57	Latvia	3.4	62	Croatia	4.4
68	Romania	2.9	70	Romania	3.8
89	Yugoslavia	1.3	72	Bulgaria	3.6
			72	Macedonia	3.6
			85	Albania	3.4
			85	Montenegro	3.4
			85	Serbia	3.4
			92	Bosnia and Herzegovina	3.2

Source: Transparency International (1995–2008).

levels of corruption, especially if the low-level corruption perceived by citizens in their daily life is of a different magnitude than the high-level corruption linked to state capture that is more likely to be secret (Rose-Ackerman, 1999; Kainberger, 2003; Karklins, 2005). There may also be a wide gap between how much politicians talk about corruption and how little they do about it. Corruption often figures prominently in elections in the region as an argument for electing 'fresh' leaders. This, and the intense press coverage that corruption has received over the last decade or more may inflate perceptions of corruption. Recent studies show that press coverage of corruption in post-communist countries is much greater than in the past, and also greater than in other regions with comparable or higher levels of corruption (Grigorescu, 2006). In 2008, there was much debate about whether Bulgaria or Romania suffered from more high-level corruption (see below). In Sofia, there appeared to be more think tanks publicizing and analysing domestic corruption than in Bucharest, where perhaps corruption stands a greater chance of remaining secret.[3]

Table 1 shows that based on perceptions of corruption in the ten post-communist states accepted to the EU in 2004 and 2007, almost all score in the ballpark of the EU's most corrupt 'old' Member State, Greece, and next in line, Italy. The two consistent exceptions are Slovenia and Estonia. Table 2 presents a different index developed by the World Bank measuring the control of corruption, comparing the scores from 2000 and 2007. The quantitative measures reported annually by Freedom House and qualitative reports produced by the Open Society Institute and other think tanks paint a similarly grim picture of widespread corruption in the post-communist region.[4] Across all three quantitative indexes, the rank orderings of the EU's post-communist members and candidates are generally consistent.

III. The EU and the Fight Against Corruption: Outside of the Acquis

In the run-up to the 2004 enlargement, the EU was fairly effective in requiring candidate states to adopt and implement the *acquis communautaire*. In general, greater attention was paid to those parts of the *acquis* that determine the performance of state institutions and economic actors in the internal market. On the one hand, new members must be competitive in the internal market; on the other, they must enforce EU rules in order to ensure a level

---

[3] The most prominent and active anti-corruption think tank in Sofia is the Center for the Study of Democracy, «http://www.csd.bg», which publishes extensively on Bulgaria's struggle with weak administrative capacity, judicial dependence and organized crime.

[4] Reports and scores by Freedom House can be found at: «http://www.freedomhouse.org». Reports by the Open Society Institute can be found at: «http://www.eumap.org».

Table 2: World Bank's Measure for Control of Corruption

Country	Year	Percentile Rank (0–100)	Country	Year	Percentile Rank (0–100)
Finland	2000	100	Finland	2007	99.5
Sweden	2000	99.5	Denmark	2007	99
Netherlands	2000	98.1	Sweden	2007	98.6
Denmark	2000	97.6	Luxembourg	2007	97.1
Luxembourg	2000	95.1	Netherlands	2007	96.6
Germany	2000	94.2	Austria	2007	94.2
Austria	2000	93.2	Germany	2007	93.2
Ireland	2000	92.2	Ireland	2007	92.8
Belgium	2000	91.7	Belgium	2007	91.8
France	2000	91.3	France	2007	89.4
Spain	2000	90.3	Malta	2007	85
Portugal	2000	86.4	Spain	2007	84.1
Italy	2000	83.5	Portugal	2007	83.6
Malta	2000	79.6	Estonia	2007	80.7
Cyprus	2000	78.2	Slovenia	2007	78.3
Slovenia	2000	76.7	Cyprus	2007	74.9
Greece	2000	75.7	Italy	2007	71
Hungary	2000	75.2	Hungary	2007	70.5
Estonia	2000	72.8	Latvia	2007	66.2
Poland	2000	69.4	Greece	2007	65.7
Lithuania	2000	64.6	Slovakia	2007	65.2
Czech Republic	2000	64.1	Czech Republic	2007	64.7
Slovakia	2000	63.6	Lithuania	2007	61.8
Latvia	2000	58.3	Poland	2007	61.4
Croatia	2000	56.8	Turkey	2007	59.4
Turkey	2000	51	Croatia	2007	58.9
Bulgaria	2000	50	Romania	2007	55.6
Romania	2000	46.6	Bulgaria	2007	53.1
Macedonia	2000	35.9	Macedonia	2007	50.7
Bosnia-Herzegovina	2000	33	Serbia	2007	46.4
Albania	2000	24.3	Bosnia-Herzegovina	2007	44.9
Serbia	2000	8.3	Montenegro	2007	44.4
Kosovo	2000	N/A	Albania	2007	36.7
Montenegro	2000	N/A	Kosovo	2007	25.6

Source: Kaufmann et al. (2008).

playing field. Many observers were concerned about what happens when the leverage of the pre-accession process disappears at accession. After all, the adoption of legislation is generally much easier to track than the quality and durability of the institutions that implement and enforce it (see Dimitrova, 2002). Here, however, the preliminary evidence is more positive than expected: the eight post-communist states that joined the EU in 2004 have outperformed older members in many respects when it comes to enacting EU law and dealing with infringements (Sedelmeier, 2008).

While the fight against corruption as such is not part of the *acquis*, the process of joining the EU can help in indirect ways. Liberalization of the economy, including privatization and the promotion of new small and medium enterprises, reduces the reach of state officials in the economy. Also, the reform of state institutions – including greater transparency and efficiency – may at least constrain the opportunities for corruption across different levels of government. However, the experiences of Bulgaria and Romania, detailed below, show that these indirect measures alone are insufficient when a critical mass of high-level politicians are corrupt, when organized crime has thoroughly penetrated the economy and when the judiciary is weak and corrupt.

Indeed, the blatant problems with corruption in the EU's newest members – Bulgaria and Romania – have pushed the EU into largely uncharted territory. Similar to the protection of ethnic minority rights, EU members are now in agreement that a spirited fight against corruption should be required of candidate states. However, they have never agreed to a set of EU-level anti-corruption policies, just as they have never agreed to EU-level policies to protect ethnic minority rights. Only the most blatant cases of corruption are now being addressed by the EU, just as only the most discriminatory and destabilizing policies against ethnic minorities by candidate state governments have become the subject of EU opprobrium and conditionality. In other words, in protecting ethnic minority rights, the EU could find consensus to 'put out fires', but was not well equipped to do more. The scholarly debate on the success of EU leverage in improving the treatment of ethnic minorities in the candidate states is relevant here. Many scholars have shown that specific changes in minority rights policies were a direct result of the EU's leverage (Kelley, 2004; Vachudova, 2005; Fisher, 2006). And most would argue that changes in legislation, institutions, the agenda of political parties and the tone of the discourse in the country have had an enduring effect. Other scholars, without disputing the initial findings, have argued that the EU's impact was limited in scope and in time. Once the fire had been put out, the EU's leverage waned – and conditions on the ground went into stasis or even regressed (Sasse, 2008).

The absence of a corruption-fighting *acquis* has also meant that it has taken the European Commission more time to develop the tools to compel candidate states to work harder in addressing corruption problems. Here again there is a strong parallel to the provision of ethnic minority rights. The wars in the disintegrating Yugoslavia put encouraging peaceful co-existence among ethnic majorities and minorities in east central Europe squarely on the EU's agenda as early as 1994 with the Balladur Plan. Over the next four years, the Commission became more specific and more insistent in its requirements in this area, culminating in its detailed requirements to the Slovak government in 1998 and later its direct involvement in rewriting the constitution of Macedonia to expand the rights of the Albanian minority.

While the first eight post-communist countries prepared to join the EU between 1997 and 2002, and were subject to the full force of the EU's conditionality, the fight against corruption played a minor role. The problems were not so stark as in Romania and Bulgaria. Moreover, many EU governments that have substantial corruption problems at home were reluctant to see corruption take a prominent place on the EU's agenda *vis-à-vis* the candidate states. As a result, the Commission's admonitions for candidates to tackle even high-level corruption were often watered down for political reasons in the annual Regular Reports.[5]

By 2006, things had changed dramatically as EU governments recognized the extent of the corruption problem in Bulgaria and Romania (Stoyanov, 2008). Figures 1, 2 and 3 show how poorly Bulgaria and Romania score on different corruption measures over time, and how they compare to the average post-communist EU member (Poland) and the best (Slovenia), as well as to the best old EU member (Denmark) and the worst (Greece). These show that in Bulgaria corruption was seen to increase even as Bulgaria was concluding its negotiations and acceding to the EU. The most striking gap between Romania and Bulgaria and the rest of the post-communist EU members is visible in Figure 1, which presents Freedom House scores on the reform and independence of the judiciary.

The Commission reported in 2006 that only feeble attempts had been made by either government to fight corruption, crack down on organized crime and strengthen the judiciary. It asked for immediate action, especially on institutional reform (Engelbrekt, 2007). The Treaty of Accession of Bulgaria and Romania included the same three safeguard clauses as the ones included in the treaties of states that joined in 2004: a general economic safeguard clause; a specific internal market safeguard clause; and a specific justice and home affairs safeguard clause. It also included two new tools. The first is a clause that would have allowed the EU to postpone their membership for one year if they were judged to be 'manifestly unprepared'.[6] This was not

---

[5] Author interviews with officials of the European Commission in 1998 and 2000.
[6] For more information on the safeguard clauses, see: «http://ec.europa.eu/commission_barroso/rehn/pdf/statements/memo_05_396_en.pdf».

Figure 2: Control of Corruption, Comparison across Selected Countries

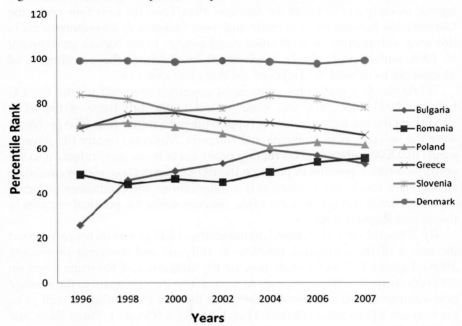

Source: Kaufmann et al. (2008).
Note: The Worldwide Governance Indicators (WGI) project reports aggregate and individual governance indicators for 212 countries and territories over the period 1996–2007, for six dimensions of governance: Voice and Accountability, Political Stability and Absence of Violence, Government Effectiveness, Regulatory Quality, Rule of Law and Control of Corruption.

used. The second is the novel policy, described below, of extending the EU's leverage past the moment of membership by monitoring progress towards a series of benchmarks outlined in the Accession Treaty. Given the gravity of the problem not just in Bulgaria and Romania but also in the Western Balkan states now in the EU's membership queue, the EU's new instruments for fighting corruption are likely to be honed and expanded in the years to come.

IV. Corruption in Bulgaria and Romania Takes Centre Stage in 2008

Bulgaria and Romania were held back from concluding negotiations in 2002 and joining the EU in 2004 with eight other post-communist states due to concerns that their institutions and economies were unprepared to implement the EU's *acquis*. A key component of this concern was widespread

Figure 3: Transparency International Corruption Index

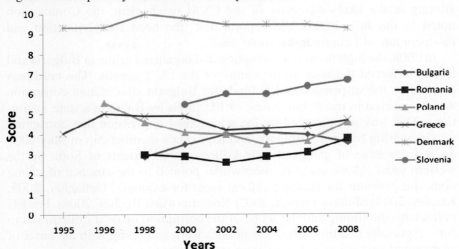

Source: Transparency International's *Corruption Perceptions Index (CPI)*, 1995–2008.
Note: The Corruption Perceptions Index (CPI) is a composite index, which uses yearly surveys of business people and assessments by country analysts from different independent institutions.

corruption, and the lack of transparency and professionalism of state institutions, especially the judiciary. When Bulgaria and Romania did become full members of the EU in 2007, their membership came with an unprecedented condition: an ongoing 'co-operation and verification mechanism' that the Commission would use to monitor whether they lived up to their outstanding commitments in satisfying the requirements of EU membership.

The centrepiece of this extension of the EU's leverage was in the field of judicial reform, corruption and organized crime. The purpose of the co-operation and verification mechanism (CVM) is, according to the Commission, 'to smooth the entry of both countries and at the same time safeguard the workings of its [the EU's] policies and institutions'. The Commission created 'benchmarks' for assessing progress and set up teams to monitor domestic developments in these areas. At the time of writing four progress reports had been published for Romania and Bulgaria in June 2007, February 2008, July 2008 and February 2009.[7] While the EU's previous regular reports on the progress of candidate states were often criticized as too broad and vague, these CVM reports are remarkably detailed, following the activities of

[7] The reports are available at: «http://ec.europa.eu/dgs/secretariat_general/cvm/progress_reports_en.htm».

relevant institutions and tracking the outcome of high-level criminal cases. Hinting at the likely longevity of the CVM mechanism, the Commission noted in the July 2008 CVM reports that 'the need for verification and co-operation will continue for some time'.

In 2008, the high profile of corruption and organized crime in Bulgaria and Romania forced the issue to the centre of the EU's agenda. The headlines focused on the suspension of EU funds for Bulgaria after blatant corruption was discovered in the disbursement of EU funds by Bulgaria's state institutions. This was accompanied by the widespread impression that corruption was increasing following Bulgaria and Romania's membership in May 2007 and by coverage of gangland-style killings on the streets of Sofia by the western press. Many analysts, meanwhile, pointed to the absence of strong domestic pressure for tackling reform (see, for example, Gallagher, 2005; Krastev, 2004; Mungiu-Pippidi, 2002; Noutcheva and Bechev, 2008). For EU politicians, the timing and the scope of the corruption made it difficult not to act – especially at a time when EU publics were struggling with the onset of an economic recession and also voicing strong reservations about the scope of the EU's recent enlargements.

In January 2008 the Commission cut off Bulgaria's funding for road construction after the arrest for bribery of two Bulgarian road agency officials. Some €115 million in money destined for roads were frozen, followed by €121 million in money earmarked for agricultural and rural development. Suspected corruption at two agencies within Bulgaria's ministries of finance and regional development subsequently led the Commission to freeze further funds. The July 2008 publication of the Commission's report on Bulgaria's (poor) progress in meeting the CVM benchmarks was accompanied by confirmation that the European Council had decided to suspend over €500 million of aid to Bulgaria. These funds were intended to help Bulgaria prepare for EU membership by completing reforms and absorbing financial assistance.[8] In the report, the Commission drew a direct link between Bulgaria's poor administrative capacity and its inability to tackle corruption and organized crime (Commission, 2008a).

In late November 2008, the Commission confirmed its decision to revoke the accreditation of the two Bulgarian agencies from disbursing Phare funds, resulting in the irreversible loss for Bulgaria of €220 million of pre-accession funding. A further €340 million remain frozen. These frozen funds may still be recovered by Bulgaria if the Commission approves the government's plan to clean up the two agencies (the Central Financing and Contracting Unit at

[8] Euractiv.com, 24 July 2008; AFP, 23 July 2008.

the Ministry of Finance and the Implementing Agency at the Ministry of Regional Development and Public Work) by the end of 2009.[9]

Using the framework of the CVM, the Commission provided detailed assessments in July 2008 and February 2009 of progress made by Bulgaria during 2008. The July 2008 report was very critical, noting that while important reforms to the judiciary and law enforcement structures had been adopted, the Bulgarian government could show virtually no results in the investigation, prosecution and judgment of high-level level cases of corruption and organized crime: 'While there has been movement on a few cases and widespread publicity given to the "war on corruption", these cases represent a negligible share of such crimes. The statistical information provided is not reliable and sometimes contradictory. Bulgaria has made little progress in freezing or confiscating financial assets resulting from criminal activities' (Commission, 2008b, p. 4).

The February 2009 report had a more positive tone. It noted several concrete achievements in improving Bulgaria's institutional capacity to fight corruption and organized crime, in particular the functioning of the Inspectorate of the Supreme Judicial Council. Its overall assessment, however, continued to point to a lack of results: few cases are prosecuted and virtually none are concluded. The Commission observed that 'in order to demonstrate systemic and irreversible change, Bulgaria needs to show that it has put in place an autonomously functioning, stable judiciary which is able to detect and sanction conflicts of interests, corruption and organized crime and preserve the rule of law. This means in particular adopting the remaining laws needed to complete the legal system and showing through concrete cases of indictments, trials and convictions regarding high-level corruption and organized crime that the legal system is capable of implementing the laws in an independent and efficient way' (Commission, 2009a, p. 3).

Corruption in Romania escaped the headlines in 2008 because the EU did not suspend any of Romania's EU funding. The July 2008 report was relatively positive, noting various efforts by the Romanian government to strengthen the judiciary and prosecute crimes. However, the tone of the February 2009 report was much more negative – indeed, it painted Romania as lagging behind Bulgaria in making progress since the July report. The Commission strongly reproached Romania for strong ties between the judiciary and politicians, noting that the Romanian Parliament continues to block the investigation and prosecution of high-level corruption cases. The report examines the specific situation regarding each of the five benchmarks of the

[9] Euractiv.com, 26 November 2008.

CVM and concludes that momentum has been lost; indeed, work is needed to 'reverse certain backward movements of recent months' (Commission, 2009b, p. 3). The Commission concludes the report by stating that 'Romania must demonstrate the existence of an autonomously functioning, stable judiciary which is able to detect and sanction corruption and preserve the rule of law. This means in particular adopting the remaining laws needed to modernize the legal system and showing through an expeditious treatment of high-level corruption cases that the legal system is capable of implementing the laws in an independent and efficient way' (Commission, 2009b, p. 3).

What we observe today in Bulgaria and Romania are the ongoing consequences of an extended period of state capture. While political power may now be less concentrated, the power of elite networks working in organized crime and siphoning money from the state has proved difficult to shake off, despite the economic liberalization and institutional reform demanded by the EU's pre-accession process. Both economies are widely known to be deeply penetrated with organized crime – and the leaders of these crime rings have direct links to political parties and state institutions. Government officials and civil servants alike consequently show little initiative in prosecuting corruption and the crimes of powerful criminal gangs (see, for example, Center for the Study of Democracy, 2009).

In Bulgaria the 1997 elections brought to power the pro-European 'reformers' in the United Democratic Front (UDF) party. This was Bulgaria's first decisive break with government by its former communist party, the Bulgarian Socialist Party (BSP, often called the Socialists). And while Bulgaria's change of direction was undeniable – toward EU and Nato membership and rapid economic reform – the UDF government was defeated in 2001 amid accusations of rampant corruption among UDF officials. A new centre-right party, the National Movement Simeon II, contested the 2001 elections as a new, untainted and professional political force. It won the elections and was welcomed at home and abroad as an alternative to the corruption-ridden BSP and UDF. However, the fight against corruption under this government was also lacklustre. The elections of 2005 led to a coalition government of the country's three largest parties: the BSP, the National Movement Simeon II and the Movement for Rights and Freedoms (a party supported mostly by ethnic Turks). After far-reaching reform of the economy and the state, Bulgaria was by 2005 a much less corrupt country than it was in the 1990s (Ganev, 2006; Spendzharova, 2008). However, the perception was widespread in Bulgaria as well as abroad that corruption and organized crime penetrated state institutions at the highest level with renewed vigour after this government took power and even more after Bulgaria joined the EU (Center for the Study of Democracy, 2009). Meanwhile, BSP ministers were involved in several dramatic corruption scandals in 2007 and 2008. Notably, in April 2008 interior minister Roumen Petkov was forced to resign after accusations that he was passing information to organized criminals, and evidence that he had met secretly with underworld leaders. Though he was forced to resign, he did not give up his post within the Socialist party, nor did he face any criminal charges.[10]

For their part, Bulgarian citizens view their government officials as steeped in corruption, and overwhelmingly side with the EU. Over 80 per cent of respondents in one poll reported that they did not trust the government, the parliament or the courts. Meanwhile some 75 per cent reported trusting the EU, especially the Commission.[11] Another poll showed that the majority of Bulgarians approved of the EU's decision to freeze subsidies to Bulgaria on account of corruption. Since they believed the money was not reaching them, they 'welcomed funding cuts as a way of hurting the corrupt political class'.[12] In an unprecedented move, Bulgaria's Socialist prime minister, Sergei Stanishev, proposed in February 2009 that the EU send officials to Sofia to help monitor the implementation of laws, manage EU funds and supervise courts, prosecutors and investigators. In view of upcoming elections, some European diplomats interpreted this as a ploy to harness some of the voters' pro-EU sentiments for the BSP-led government. In any case, Commission President José Manuel Barroso rejected the proposal in March 2009, arguing that the direct participation of European experts in the government of Bulgaria would not be appropriate.[13]

Romanian domestic politics has experienced even more high-level political drama surrounding the issue of corruption. The former communist party, led by Ion Iliescu, ruled from 1989 until 1996 under several names, ending its rule as the Party of Social Democracy in Romania (PDSR). In 1996 it was defeated by a broad coalition of parties led by the Democratic Convention of Romania (CDR). Like the UDF in Bulgaria, this government fundamentally changed the trajectory of Romania, orienting it squarely toward fulfilling the requirements of EU membership including tolerance for Romania's Hungarian minority and rapid economic liberalization. The CDR lost the 2000 elections due mainly to the economic hardships of structural economic reform and infighting within the coalition. The former communists, now called the Social Democratic Party (PSD), won these elections and Iliescu

---

[10] *The Sofia Echo*, 13 April 2008.
[11] *The Economist*, 19 March 2009.
[12] Euractiv.com, 26 July 2008.
[13] *The Sofia Echo*, 31 March 2009.

became president once again. This government continued Romania's preparations for EU membership, but was mired in accusations of corruption that
contributed to the PSD's electoral defeat in 2004. Traian Basescu from the
Liberal Democrat Party (PDL) won the presidency in 2004 on a vehement
anti-corruption platform. A coalition government was formed of several
parties under the leadership of Prime Minister Calin Popescu-Tariceanu of the
National Liberal Party (PNL).

It is very difficult to untangle Romanian domestic politics, but what comes
next is generally understood like this: Basescu appointed and supported
government officials that were very energetic in making progress in the fight
against high-level corruption in Romania. But Basescu's opponents charged
that their investigations were politically motivated, targeting politicians from
opposing political parties. The most active was the Minister of Justice,
Monica Macovei, whose work to improve the judiciary and bring cases to trial
was heralded in European capitals as a great breakthrough for Romania.
Many politicians in Romania, however, disagreed and the parliament voted
overwhelmingly in April 2007 to impeach Basescu for infringing on the rights
of the government, the parliament and the judiciary. This impeachment had to
be put to a referendum: 74 per cent of those Romanians who actually voted,
voted against removing Basescu (turnout was 44 per cent).[14] Nevertheless,
Macovei was sacked by the prime minister in 2007.[15]

After a campaign that paid little attention to corruption, the parliamentary
elections of November 2008 resulted in a coalition that brought the PSD back
to power with Basescu's PDL. Observers worry about the ramifications of the
return of the PSD for Romania's fight against corruption, especially since it
is in a strong position *vis-à-vis* its coalition partner, the PDL. Moreover, the
largest number of corruption cases against high-level politicians pursued by
Romania's anti-corruption agency involve politicians from the PSD. So far
the Romanian parliament has habitually used its veto to prevent high-profile
cases against politicians from going to court. And Romania's judges have
routinely doled out only the mildest sentences for those that do. Of the 109
cases that were prosecuted in 2007 by Romania's anti-corruption agency,
headed by Macovei appointee Daniel Moran, only 25 resulted in prison
sentences, mostly for the minimum of three years.[16] Like in Bulgaria, the
Commission will be monitoring closely to see if outcomes improve – or
deteriorate further – under the new government.

---

[14] *Financial Times*, 21 May 2007.
[15] *Financial Times*, 27 March 2007, 12 June 2007.
[16] *Economist*, 31 July 2008. On Daniel Morar and his star reputation in Brussels, see 'Beacon of Hope',
Europeanvoice.com, 11 December 2008.

Conclusion

Since the collapse of communism, the EU has been slow to adapt to its new geopolitical neighbourhood. Over time, however, it has crafted new policies to respond to new problems and new opportunities. This argument can be made for many policy areas including foreign and security policy, justice and home affairs, and immigration. As regards enlargement, after a characteristically slow start, the EU adopted a comprehensive enlargement programme that helped post-communist candidates qualify and prepare for membership. Despite problems with the consistency and the enforcement of the membership requirements, the EU's pre-accession process has had a vastly greater impact on reforming the state and the economy than the efforts of any other external actor. Critically, it has provided long-term incentives for political parties to adopt agendas that are consistent with joining the EU (Vachudova, 2008). And within this process, over time, EU leaders have responded, slowly, to unforeseen problems in candidate states, such as the need to promote ethnic minority rights and ethnic reconciliation and, more recently, to insist on the fight against corruption and organized crime.

Ultimately, in the enlargement process as in other policy areas, the EU's strengths are also its weaknesses. What makes the prospect of co-operating closely with EU representatives – and complying with the EU's extensive requirements – attractive to domestic elites is the promise of eventual membership. The EU can offer this promise because it is an international organization, not a single state. But as an international organization, it is highly integrated – and also highly complex, with a very diverse membership. As a result, as historical institutionalists would predict, rules and policies change only slowly, and novel policies usually develop in response to an external shock (see McNamara and Meunier, 2007; Vachudova, 2007). While the EU's handling of epic levels of corruption in Bulgaria and Romania was certainly timid right through the pre-accession process, it was shocked into more dramatic action beginning in 2006.

Croatia, Serbia, Montenegro, Macedonia, Albania, Bosnia-Herzegovina and Kosovo make up the rest of the EU's membership queue in the Balkans. In these countries, the challenges of tackling corruption and organized crime while building an efficient state administration and an independent judiciary are even greater than in Bulgaria and Romania. Thus the tools that Brussels is developing now to deal with these challenges will be expanded and improved. It is too early to pass a final judgement on the CVM; for that, the next year will be critical. However, the most important lesson that the EU is likely to learn from the accession of Bulgaria and Romania is the same lesson that it learned years ago from Greece: post-accession pressure yields only modest results. In order to be effective, EU leverage must be applied well *before* accession. Indeed, experience suggests that once negotiations for membership have gained momentum, it is already too late to apply strong conditionality and/or turn back (though Turkey will likely end this trend). Earlier junctures, such as opening negotiations or signing association agreements, are more promising (see Grabbe, 2006; Haughton, 2007; Vachudova, 2005).

More difficult, however, than monitoring and evaluating the progress of politicians and state institutions is creating *domestic* pressure for comprehensive reform. EU leverage has always worked much better in concert with domestic pressure towards the same goals. Scholars that have studied corruption in post-communist Europe agree on the importance of domestic pressure – in the form of the media and civic groups – in fighting corruption. They argue that the media, the electorate and civic society have proven to be the most effective promoters of anti-corrupt politics, while the state administration and the judiciary have been the main laggards in this respect (see Holmes, 2006; Karklins, 2005). While the Commission has made a laudable effort in recent years to go against the tide of 'civil society fatigue' amongst Western donors, it needs to find ways to increase domestic pressure on politicians, even as it ratchets up the pressure from Brussels.

References

Center for the Study of Democracy (2009) 'Crime without Punishment: Countering Corruption and Organized Crime in Bulgaria'. Sofia. Available at: «www.csd.bg».

Commission of the European Communities (2005) 'Frequently asked questions about the safeguard clauses included in the Treaty of Accession of Bulgaria and Romania'. MEMO/05/396, 25 October. Available at: «http://ec.europa.eu/commission_barroso/rehn/pdf/statements/memo_05_396_en.pdf».

Commission of the European Communities (2008a) 'Report from the Commission to the European Parliament and the Council on the Management of EU Funds in Bulgaria'. Brussels, 23 July 2008.

Commission of the European Communities (2008b) 'Report from the Commission to the European Parliament and the Council on Progress in Bulgaria under the Co-operation and Verification Mechanism'. Brussels, 23 July 2008.

Commission of the European Communities (2009a) 'Interim Report from the Commission to the European Parliament and the Council on Progress in Bulgaria under the Co-operation and Verification Mechanism'. Brussels, 12 February 2009.

Commission of the European Communities (2009b) 'Interim Report from the Commission to the European Parliament and the Council on Progress in Romania under the Co-operation and Verification Mechanism'. Brussels, 12 February 2009.

Dimitrova, A. (2002) 'Enlargement, Institution-Building and the EU's Administrative Capacity Requirement'. *West European Politics*, Vol. 25, No. 4, pp. 171–90.

Engelbrekt, K. (2007) 'Bulgaria's EU Accession and the Issue of Accountability: An End to Buck-Passing?' *Problems of Post-Communism*, Vol. 54, No. 4, pp. 3–14.

Fisher, S. (2006) *Political Change in Post-Communist Slovakia and Croatia: From Nationalist to Europeanist* (New York: Palgrave Macmillan).

Freedom House (1995–2008) *Nations in Transit* (Washington, DC: Freedom House). Available at: «www.freedomhouse.org».

Gallagher, T. (2005) *Theft of a Nation: Romania since Communism* (London: Hurst).

Ganev, V. (2001) 'The Dorian Gray Effect: Winners as State Breakers in Post-Communism'. *Communist and Post-Communist Studies*, Vol. 34, pp. 1–25.

Ganev, V. (2006) 'Ballots, Bribes and State Building in Bulgaria'. *Journal of Democracy*, Vol. 17, No. 1, pp. 75–89.

Ganev, V. (2007) *Preying on the State: The Transformation of Bulgaria after 1989* (Ithaca, NY: Cornell University Press).

Gould, J. (2004) 'Out of the Blue? Democracy and Privatization in Post-Communist Europe'. *Comparative European Politics*, Vol. 1, No. 3, pp. 277–311.

Grabbe, H. (2006) *The EU's Transformative Power: Europeanization through Conditionality in Central and Eastern Europe* (London: Palgrave).

Grigorescu, A. (2006) 'The Corruption Eruption in East Central Europe: The Increased Salience of Corruption and the Role of Intergovernmental Organizations'. *East European Politics and Societies*, Vol. 20, No. 3, pp. 516–49.

Grzymała-Busse, A. (2007) *Rebuilding Leviathan: Party Competition and State Exploitation in Post-Communist Democracies* (Cambridge: Cambridge University Press).

Hanley, S. (2008) 'Re-stating Party Development in Central and Eastern Europe?' *Czech Sociological Review*, Vol. 44, No. 6, pp. 1155–76.

Haughton, T. (2007) 'When Does the EU Make a Difference? Conditionality and the Accession Process in Central and Eastern Europe'. *Political Studies Review*, Vol. 5, No. 2, pp. 233–46.

Hellman, J. (1998) 'Winners Take All: The Politics of Partial Reform in Postcommunist Transitions'. *World Politics*, Vol. 50, No. 2, pp. 203–34.

Holmes, L.T. (2006) *Rotten States? Corruption, Post-Communism and Neo-liberalism* (Durham, NC: Duke University Press).

Kainberger, H. (2003) 'Corruption in EU Candidate Countries'. Working Paper, Reuters Foundation Programme, University of Oxford.

Karklins, R. (2002) 'Typology of Post-Communist Corruption'. *Problems of Post-Communism*, Vol. 49, No. 2, pp. 22–32.

Karklins, R. (2005) *The System Made Me Do It: Corruption in Post-Communist Societies* (Armonk, NY: M.E. Sharpe).

Kaufmann, D., Kraay, A. and Mastruzzi, M. (2008) 'Governance Matters VII: Governance Indicators for 1996–2007'. *The Worldwide Governance Indicators (WGI) Project* (Washington, DC: The World Bank).

Kelley, J. (2004) *Ethnic Politics in Europe: The Power of Norms and Incentives* (Princeton, NJ: Princeton University Press).

Kornai, J. and Rose-Ackerman, S. (2004) *Building a Trustworthy State in Post-Socialist Societies* (New York: Palgrave).

Krastev, I. (2004) *Shifting Obsessions: Three Essays on the Politics of Anti-Corruption* (Budapest: Central European University Press).

McNamara, K. and Meunier, S. (eds) (2007) *Making History: European Integration and Institutional Change at Fifty* (Oxford: Oxford University Press).

Moroff, H. and Schmidt-Pfister, D. (2010) 'Anti-Corruption for Eastern Europe'. Special issue of *Global Crime*, forthcoming Spring 2010.

Mungiu-Pippidi, A. (ed.) (2002) *Romania after 2000: Threats and Challenges* (Bucharest: UNDP).

Noutcheva, G. and Bechev, D. (2008) 'The Successful Laggards: Bulgaria and Romania's Accession to the EU'. *East European Politics and Societies*, Vol. 22, No. 1, pp. 114–44.

O'Dwyer, C. (2006) *Runaway State-Building: Patronage Politics and Democratic Development* (Baltimore, MD: Johns Hopkins University Press).

Pop-Eleches, G. (2008) 'A Party for All Seasons: Electoral Adaptation of Romanian Communist Successor Parties'. *Communist & Post-Communist Studies*, Vol. 41, No. 4, pp. 465–79.

Rose-Ackerman, S. (1999) *Corruption and Government: Causes, Consequences and Reform* (New York: Cambridge University Press).

Sasse, G. (2008) 'The Politics of Conditionality: The Norm of Minority Protection before and after EU Accession'. *Journal of European Public Policy*, Vol. 15, No. 6, pp. 842–60.

Sedelmeier, U. (2008) 'After Conditionality: Post-Accession Compliance with EU Law in East Central Europe'. *Journal of European Public Policy*, Vol. 15, No. 6, pp. 806–25.

Spendzharova, A. (2008) 'For the Market or For Our Friends? The Politics of Banking Sector Legal Reform in the Post-Communist Region after 1989'. *Comparative European Studies*, Vol. 6, No. 4, pp. 432–62.

Stoyanov, A. (2008) 'Administrative and Political Corruption in Bulgaria: Status and Dynamics (1998–2006)'. *Romanian Journal of Political Science*, Vol. 8, No. 1, pp. 5–23.

Transparency International (1995–2008) *Corruption Perceptions Index (CPI)* (Berlin: Transparency International). Available at: «www.transparency.org».

Vachudova, M.A. (2005) *Europe Undivided: Democracy, Leverage and Integration after Communism* (Oxford: Oxford University Press).

Vachudova, M.A. (2007) 'Historical Institutionalism and the EU's Eastern Enlargement'. In McNamara, K. and Meunier, S. (eds) *Making History: European Integration and Institutional Change at Fifty* (Oxford: Oxford University Press), pp. 105–22.

Vachudova, M.A. (2008) 'Tempered by the EU? Political Parties and Party Systems Before and After Accession'. *Journal of European Public Policy*, Vol. 15, No. 6, pp. 861–79.

JCMS 2009 Volume 47 Annual Review pp. 63–87
DOI: 10.1111/j.1468-5965.2009.02014.x

The Financial Turmoil and EU Policy Co-operation in 2008*

LUCIA QUAGLIA
University of Sussex

ROBERT EASTWOOD
University of Sussex

PETER HOLMES
University of Sussex

Abstract

This article analyses the response of the European Union (EU) to the financial crisis in 2008 under the headings of liquidity, recapitalization and ownership of banks, macroeconomic policies and regulatory policy. It is argued that although at the onset of the crisis governments tended to focus on national-level responses, they quickly realized that international co-ordination would be required. This proved difficult to achieve in many areas, although monetary policy was an exception. Here co-ordination was rapid, not only in the euro area but also between the European Central Bank and other EU national central banks. Even so, within the euro area, the lender of last resort function was carried out by national central banks. Fiscal policy and bank recapitalization were similar across countries, but independently agreed. Competition rules were the one supranational EU regime, but did not act as a significant constraint on Member States.

Introduction

In 2008 the European Union (EU) experienced the worst economic crisis since its creation, one which some claim threatened its very

* Lucia Quaglia wishes to thank the European Research Council (Grant 204398 FINGOVEU) for financial support. We are grateful to Louis Pauly, Jim Rollo, Jim Webber, the participants to the Chevening Fellows in European Political Economy Annual Conference at the University of Sussex and the editors of the *JCMS Annual Review of the European Union* for their perceptive comments. The usual disclaimers apply.

existence.[1] At the time of writing (March 2009), the financial outlays required to support the banking system were unknown but estimates of potential bank losses went as high as £16.3 trillion for the EU as a whole (EU annual GDP in 2008 is officially estimated as €12.5 trillion).[2] Outcomes for unemployment and GDP were not known, but in the fourth quarter of 2008 EU GNP fell at an annual rate of 6 per cent.[3] Even more alarming were the data for world trade. Between October and December 2008 German exports fell by 18 per cent, US exports by 23 per cent and Chinese exports by 32 per cent (Baldwin and Evenett, 2009, p. 1). Even in the three months leading up to November 2008 the IMF estimated that world trade fell at an annual rate of 42 per cent (IMF, 2009b). By contrast, Kindleberger (1986, chapter 8, figure 10) estimated that between 1929 and 1930 the fall in world trade was 19 per cent.

In this chapter we survey the EU response to the financial crisis, focusing essentially on the period from September to December 2008 (for an analysis of the early response to the crisis, see Pauly, 2008). We analyse these responses under the headings of liquidity, recapitalization and ownership of banks, macroeconomic policies and regulatory policy, although at times the lines between these areas may become blurred, for example, between fiscal policy, recapitalization and liquidity provision. Our aim is not so much to explain the crisis or to evaluate the correctness of the policies adopted but rather to assess the degree of co-ordination between the various authorities in the EU as a whole and the euro area. It is too early to make judgements as to the ultimate effectiveness of the institutional arrangements or the policy responses they evoked.

Although at the onset of the crisis national governments tended to focus on national-level responses, they quickly realized that international co-ordination would be required. This proved difficult to achieve in many areas, although monetary policy was an exception. Here co-ordination was rapid, not only in the euro area but also between the ECB and other EU national central banks. Even so, within the euro area, the lender of last resort (LOLR) function was carried out by national central banks (NCBs). Fiscal

---

[1] Münchau, W. 'Eastern crisis that could wreck the eurozone', *Financial Times*, 23 February 2009; *Boston Globe* Editorial 'Europe's Existential Threat', 13 March 2009.

[2] An article reporting this figure from a confidential Commission document appeared in the online *Daily Telegraph* on 12 February, but was quickly removed, but not before it had been recorded elsewhere on the internet. There is no record of any denial. See «http://www.telegraph.co.uk/finance/financetopics/financialcrisis/4590512/European-banks-may-need-16.3-trillion-bail-out-EC-dcoument-warns.html». See also «http://www.creditwritedowns.com/2009/02/are-european-banks-sitting-on-163-trillion-in-toxic-assets.html».

[3] See: «http://europa.eu/rapid/pressReleasesAction.do?reference=STAT/09/28&type=HTML&aged=0&language=EN&guiLanguage=en».

policy and bank recapitalization were similar across countries but independently determined. Supranational competition rules did not act as a significant constraint on Member States.

The article is structured as follows. Section I describes the crisis and gives the arguments for a co-ordinated response. Section II looks at the frameworks for crisis prevention and crisis management. Section III reviews the policies adopted and section IV offers an assessment. Whilst our approach is largely narrative, we try within each section to group together the issues relating to each of our themes: liquidity, recapitalization and ownership of banks, macroeconomic policies and regulatory policy.

I. Anatomy of the Crisis and the Need for a Co-ordinated Response

Anatomy of the Crisis

The crisis that began to have significant effects in Europe from the summer of 2007 was initially a crisis of *liquidity*. Suddenly, on about 9 August, institutions reliant on short-term funding in wholesale money markets discovered that the refinancing of maturing debt could not be taken for granted.[4] The suddenness of this change reflected the link between liquidity and expectations – once fears of *future* illiquidity began to take hold, an immediate liquidity crisis was the inevitable result, especially given the reliance of European banks on footloose wholesale funding: in 2007 deposits funded less than half of the assets of the five largest banks in a number of European countries (De Grauwe, 2008).

An early example illustrating the self-fulfilling nature of the problem was the case of Northern Rock, a UK bank specializing in mortgage lending and reliant on commercial paper for 75 per cent of its funding. Although ostensibly solvent, Northern Rock faced a (re)financing crisis in September 2007, as fears grew among potential lenders over whether Northern Rock would be in a position to repay new short-term loans when they matured and whether the lenders themselves might face liquidity shortages in the interim.[5]

The trigger for the 2007 liquidity crisis may have been the increasing scale of losses on sub-prime mortgage lending in the US – recently estimated at

---

[4] 9 August 2007 saw the sudden widening of spreads between overnight indexed swaps (OIS) and inter-bank lending rates. Since the only difference between an inter-bank loan and the fixed leg of an OIS is that, in the case of the loan, the principal is transferred from the lending bank to the borrowing bank, this spread indicates some combination of liquidity risk and counterparty solvency risk. In the UK, for instance, LIBOR-OIS spreads rose from about 0.10 per cent before the crisis, to fluctuate between 0.50 per cent and 1 per cent between August 2007 and September 2008, before rising about 2 per cent in October 2008 after the failure of Lehman Brothers (Crosby, 2008).

[5] The immediate policy response involved emergency liquidity support and extended deposit insurance. In February 2008, the bank was nationalized.

about \$195 billion (Bank of England, 2008, box 1) and with a relatively limited direct impact on the value of European bank assets – but a vicious circle soon began to take hold, whereby European banks attempted to rebuild liquidity by selling illiquid assets, notably residential mortgage-backed securities. The consequent falls in asset prices eroded bank capital, thus creating a crisis of *solvency* in the European financial system. Although banks reacted to this by raising new private capital, this did not keep pace with spiralling credit losses. It has been estimated that between June 2007 and January 2009, advanced country banks had credit losses and write-downs of \$792 billion, while new capital issuance was only \$446 billion.[6] Public recapitalization amounted to \$380 billion in the period, on paper more than compensating for the net private fall, but it is clear from the behaviour of bank equity prices that the losses so far acknowledged are only a fraction of their likely final value. In January 2009, the IMF estimated the potential deterioration in US-originated credit assets at \$2.2 trillion, up from \$1.4 trillion in October 2008.

Falls in bank capital are not the only factor which has contributed to rises in perceptions of counterparty risk. Uncertainty about the value of bank assets has been increased by the opacity from the point of view of risk of the collateralized debt obligations which constitute a significant fraction of those assets, together with a well-founded loss of confidence in the credit ratings awarded to such assets by the rating agencies, which in modern times have had to rely for their fees on the very institutions whose securities are being rated. Moreover, the decision of the US government to allow Lehman Brothers to fail in September 2008 made it clear that not all risks would be underwritten by governments. The market reaction to this event can be seen in the sharp rise in the so-called 'fear index': the spread between inter-bank lending rates and overnight indexed swap rates that ensued (see footnote 6).

The crises of liquidity and solvency became accordingly self-reinforcing. The individually rational acts of illiquid banks served to erode their collective solvency, while fears of counterparty default intensified the unwillingness of any private agents other than fully insured depositors to lend to the banks. This unwillingness of course extended to banks themselves, so that, as the Governor of the Bank of England remarked in November 2008, the inter-bank offer rate 'is in many ways the rate at which banks do not lend to one another' (King, 2008).

The financial crisis subsequently began to have severe consequences for the real economy as undercapitalized banks with highly uncertain future

---

[6] Bloomberg, reported in IMF (2009a, fig. 2).

sources of finance cut drastically their lending to the non-bank private sector. Quarterly domestic credit growth to the non-bank private sector fell in the euro area from €130 billion in 2007 to €25 billion in the last half of 2009 (IMF, 2009b). Recession spread across the EU: for the euro area, the IMF predicted a fall in Gross Domestic product (GDP) of 2.0 per cent in 2009, a rate of decline unprecedented in the post-war era.[7]

Policy Responses, International Spillovers and the Need for Co-ordination

Facing the financial crisis, national policy-makers had to address three problems simultaneously: *bank illiquidity*, *bank decapitalization* and *recession*. We aim to *describe* the extent to which policies were co-ordinated across the EU and to *assess* the extent to which this co-ordination was appropriate. As far as *assessment* is concerned, identification of the main international spillovers from national policy actions is central, since in the absence of such spillovers co-ordination is unnecessary (see Schoenmaker and Oosterloo, 2005). Also important is whether these international policy spillovers are positive or negative, since this tells us – in cases where governments fail to co-ordinate their actions – whether policy interventions overall are likely to be too big or too small. Fiscal policy provides a good illustration.

Acting alone, a government facing recession will contemplate increasing public expenditure and cutting taxes so as to stimulate demand and stave off rising unemployment. Yet, in deciding how much fiscal expansion to undertake, the government will also take into account its concern about rises in public indebtedness, because of the pressures that extra debt service will exert on the public finances in the future. What the government will *not* take into account are the unambiguous benefits that its fiscal expansion will confer on *other* countries: those countries will enjoy increased demand for their exports, leading to higher output, lower unemployment and *reduced* fiscal deficits. So the fiscal spillover is positive and this implies (as elaborated below) that unco-ordinated fiscal interventions will be too small.

Before *describing* the ways in which policy was co-ordinated in the EU, we provide a thematic classification of policy actions and identify the main international spillovers associated with each policy, against which the EU's response can be assessed. We classify policies under four headings: liquidity, recapitalization and ownership, macroeconomic policy and regulation.

[7] During 1950–2000, the only year that comes close is 1975, when there was a sharp recession in the industrialized countries following the quintupling of world oil prices in 1974. In 1975, average GDP growth in the four largest EU economies was −1.5 per cent (source: Penn World Table Version 6.2, Center for International Comparisons of Production, Income and Prices at the University of Pennsylvania, September 2006. (May 2008 update accessed at «http://dc1.chass.utoronto.ca/pwt/»)).

Liquidity

Measures to enhance bank liquidity may be addressed to either the asset side or the liability side of bank balance sheets. Liquidity is enhanced on the asset side to the extent that central banks either purchase illiquid assets outright or accept them for the purposes of collateralized lending. The scale of such interventions, the range of assets accepted as collateral and the terms under which such assets are accepted all affect bank liquidity. There have been important differences within the EU (i.e. between the European Central Bank, the ECB and other central banks) in how these policies have been applied.

On the liability side, government guarantees of deposit and non-deposit liabilities are the important policy instruments. There is considerable scope for variation and there was considerable variation. For example, guarantees in respect of non-deposit liabilities may be restricted to 'new' borrowing and granted only under certain conditions, such as a defined quantum of recapitalization (UK). There may be a blanket guarantee of such liabilities (Ireland). Some form of guarantee or support may be offered to a particular class of non-deposit liabilities, such as inter-bank claims (Italy). National central banks, both inside and outside the euro area may offer emergency liquidity assistance to individual banks under such terms as they choose, with the credit risk remaining at national level.

Liquidity support creates both positive and negative spillovers. Almost any action that raises system-wide liquidity under present circumstances will confer systemic benefits. But negative spillovers are also present. More favourable guarantees given to bank liabilities in one country than another may expose a bank in the unfavoured country to a run. More generous collateral conditions at one central bank than at another may induce international banks to dump their toxic assets at the lenient central bank, to the potential benefit of taxpayers in states where policy is less lenient. Accordingly there is a strong case for co-ordination as regards liquidity interventions.

Recapitalization and Ownership

The nature of public recapitalization of banks can and did differ across countries. Apart from the scale of this intervention, there was variation in its form (preference shares versus ordinary shares) and the terms under which it was provided (for example, interest rates on preference shares, prices paid for ordinary shares). In the UK a specified scale of recapitalization (either public or private) was made a condition of access to some forms of liquidity support. There was significant consolidation of the banking sector, with public facilitation in various ways of the mergers and takeovers that took place.

As with liquidity, public recapitalization of a bank creates both positive and negative international spillovers. Risk is reduced for overseas creditors (non-bank depositors as well as other banks) and the bank's ability to lend is enhanced, conferring advantages to borrowers that are unlikely to be exclusively national. Against these benefits, to the extent that public recapitalization has a subsidy component, foreign banks will be placed at a competitive disadvantage.

Macroeconomic Policy

Both monetary policy (narrowly defined) and fiscal policy exhibit important international spillovers. As regards monetary policy, unilateral interest rate cuts are 'beggar-thy-neighbour', since their main effect is to cause currency depreciation and the diversion of demand from foreign goods to domestic goods. In a time of recession, therefore, there is a risk of self-defeating competitive depreciation, creating a strong general case for policy co-ordination to prevent excessive rate cuts.

Conversely, as discussed above, unilateral fiscal policy is likely to be insufficiently expansionary, creating a case for co-ordination to raise fiscal impulses. For the EU, Krugman (2008) made rough estimates of the 'bang per euro': the GDP rise for a given rise in the fiscal deficit. His estimates were 1.03 per cent for unilateral fiscal expansion and 2.23 per cent for co-ordinated expansion. If policy is unco-ordinated, therefore, the fiscal impulses are likely be too small. Moreover, co-ordination in the form of a broad agreement to act is likely to prove inadequate, since each country will face a temptation to free ride on the actions of others. For an efficient outcome, country-level actions need to be specified as precisely as possible and there needs to be the possibility that failure to act as agreed will be penalized in some way.

Regulation

Banking regulation is addressed in the following section. International spillovers are important in this area since the ability of banks to move between jurisdictions creates the conditions for a possible 'race to the bottom' in national policies. For our purposes regulation stands somewhat apart from the other three policy areas. While changes in, say, monetary or fiscal policy can and should sometimes be rapid, the more permanent character of changes in regulation means that a more deliberate response is appropriate, as has indeed been the case. So our assessment of the EU response will place particular emphasis on processes as opposed to actual changes in policy.

II. Crisis Prevention and Crisis Management:
The EU Policy Framework

Crisis Prevention Framework

Crisis prevention, narrowly defined, comprises *financial regulation* and *financial supervision*.[8] Financial regulation lays down the prudential rules with which financial institutions have to comply to ensure effective risk management as well as disclosure rules to promote market discipline. Financial supervision tries to ensure that financial entities apply those rules in practice and encompasses co-operation between supervisors, which is paramount in crisis management as discussed below (ECB, 2007).

In the EU, whereas financial *regulation* is largely carried out at the EU level, financial *supervision* is largely carried out at the national level. Moreover, even the EU directives regulating banking (the Capital Requirements Directive, CRD), securities (the four 'Lamfalussy directives', named after the legislative process through which they were agreed), insurance (the Solvency II Directive) and financial conglomerates (the Financial Conglomerates Directive) are often based on a minimum common denominator, as a result of convoluted compromises and trade-offs, as in the case of the CRD, and leave ample room for national discretion.

Many of the directives mentioned above incorporate rules agreed in international regulatory forums. The CRD, for example, incorporates into EU legislation the Basel II accord, which is a non-legally binding gentlemen's agreement issued by the Basel Committee on Banking Supervision (BCBS). There are also financial activities that are as yet neither regulated at the EU level (such as hedge funds and credit rating agencies), nor internationally.

Financial supervision is mainly carried out at the national level. Banking supervision is carried out either by the central bank or a separate banking supervisory authority. In many jurisdictions, however, the central bank remains responsible for, or involved in, financial stability, even if it is not responsible for banking supervision (for an overview, see Masciandaro and Quintyn, 2007).

There are EU committees of national supervisors such as the Committee of European Banking Supervisors (CEBS) across the main segments of the financial sector – banking, securities and insurance, plus financial conglomerates – in which the activity of national supervisors is co-ordinated.[9] The

---

[8] A broader definition would encompass appropriate frameworks for monetary and fiscal policies to promote financial stability.
[9] For the activities of these committees concerning the so-called levels 2 and 3 of the Lamfalussy framework see Quaglia (2008).

Banking Supervision Committee (BSC) of European System of Central Banks (ESCB) also acts as a co-ordinating forum.

Crisis Management Framework

Crisis management may entail actions across a wide range of policy areas as indicated earlier: liquidity, recapitalization and ownership, macroeconomic policy and regulation. As far as regulation is concerned, crisis management may, as in this case, go beyond mere implementation of pre-existing rules to encompass emergency changes to those rules. Of paramount importance in the EU is, or should be, co-operation between national governments, central banks and financial supervisors. The bases for such co-operation have been both bilateral and multilateral memoranda of understanding (MoU) together with ECOFIN Council conclusions, in both case non-binding.

Regarding liquidity, in the Eurosystem, market-level assistance is provided through open-market operations, with the collateral and any associated credit risk located at ECB level. In contrast, institution-level emergency liquidity is provided via standing facilities operated by the NCBs and in this case the collateral and credit risk remain at national level (ECB, 2008a, p. 21), just as in non-euro area countries. Regarding recapitalization and ownership, responsibilities lie with national governments acting within EU rules, which are primarily but not exclusively competition law. For macroeconomic policy, fiscal policy is the province of national governments, subject, in the case of the euro area, to the Stability and Growth Pact. Interest rate policies are set at euro area level or national level, depending on the degree of the state's participation in EMU. On regulation, crisis management can involve changes in regulations at national level as well as changes at EU level in the directives within which national regulations have to be framed.

The framework is summarized in a report from the Economic and Financial Committee (EFC)[10] in September 2007, which outlined 'common principles for cross-border crisis management' and 'burden sharing' (EFC, 2007, p. 10). 'Burden sharing' arises when in a financial crisis public resources must be used, in which case 'direct budgetary net costs will need to be shared among affected Member States on the basis of equitable and balanced criteria, which take into account the economic impact of the crisis in the countries affected and the framework of home and host countries' supervisory powers' (ECOFIN Council, 2008). The principles were subsequently endorsed by the

[10] This committee is composed of senior officials from the economic and/or finance ministries of the Member States, the central banks, the ECB and the Commission.

ECOFIN Council in October 2007 (ECOFIN Council, 2007) and were incorporated into the existing MoU signed in 2005. The main common principles for cross-border financial crisis management that can be extrapolated from the EFC/Council documents are the following (not all points are listed):

(1) 'The objective is not to prevent bank failures'.
(2) 'In a crisis situation, primacy will always be given to private sector solutions'.
(3) 'The use of public money to resolve a crisis can never be taken for granted and will only be considered to remedy a serious disturbance in the economy and when overall social benefits are assessed to exceed the cost of recapitalization at public expense'.
(4) 'Managing a cross-border crisis is a matter of common interest for all Member States affected'.
(5) 'Arrangements for crisis management and crisis resolution will be consistent with the arrangements for supervision and crisis prevention'.
(6) 'Any public intervention must comply with EU competition and state-aid rules'.
(7) 'The global dimension will be taken into account in financial stability arrangements whenever necessary. Authorities from third countries will be involved where appropriate'.

In the EU, there are a variety of MoUs designed to promote co-operation in crisis management. There are also regional and national MoUs, such as those among the central banks of the Nordic region and between the Dutch and Belgian authorities, motivated by the presence of large cross-border financial groups in these regions (the Nordea group in the Nordic countries and the Fortis group in the Benelux). An MoU on high-level principles of co-operation between the banking supervisors and central banks on crisis management was adopted in March 2003. In addition, in January 2001 an MoU on the co-operation between banking supervisors and central banks in their capacity as payment systems overseers was signed which contains provisions dealing with the exchange of information in the event of liquidity or solvency problems (ECB, 2007). An MoU on co-operation between the banking supervisors, the central banks and the finance ministries in financial crises was signed in May 2005, including arrangements for the development of contingency plans for crises, along with stress-testing and simulation exercises (ECB, 2007). These memoranda were revised in early 2008, in response to the crisis.

To summarize, some basis for co-operation over crisis management in the areas of liquidity and recapitalization was created, but it was vague and

Table 1: Who Does What in Crisis Management in the EU

Action	Authorities responsible
Liquidity	
Asset side:	
direct liquidity support	ECB and Eurosystem NCBs in the euro area
purchases of illiquid assets	NCBs backed by national treasuries in euro area or not
Liability side:	
deposit guarantees	National treasuries, partly unilateral, partly in response to changes in EU directives (see below)
non-deposit liability guarantees	National treasuries
Recapitalization and ownership	
Recapitalization	National treasuries + short-lived proposal for an EU fund European Commission (DG Competition) approval for state aids to banks
Mergers	European Commission in cross-border cases, otherwise national authorities
Macroeconomic policy	
Interest rate changes	ECB-Eurosystem in euro area NCBs in non-euro area
Fiscal measures	National treasuries Stability and Growth Pact for euro area, setting upper threshold for budget deficit
Regulation	
Deposit insurance	EU authorities via directive on deposit insurance minima National authorities for higher levels of insurance

Source: Authors' own data.

non-mandatory. In the area of fiscal policy, neither the Stability and Growth Pact nor the Broad Economic Policy Guidelines (which apply on a non-binding basis to non-euro area members) made any provision for crisis management. On regulation, the framework was primarily designed to prevent crises, rather than to provide mechanisms for their collective management. The IMF in its annual review of the euro area (IMF, 2007, p.18, see also 2006 and 2008) observed: 'The core problem, which is widely recognized, is that national authorities' fiduciary responsibilities are toward national treasuries and this limits their incentives to work towards a common EU-wide stability framework'. Table 1 summarizes how responsibilities for crisis management are divided among national and supranational bodies.

III. Policy Responses to the Crisis

This section provides a thematic account of policy responses to the crisis, although the classification of measures by theme is at times a bit arbitrary, for example, where banking rescues have fiscal implications.

Liquidity

It is useful first to distinguish between the function of lender of last resort *strictu sensu* and the provision of emergency liquidity to the system. The function of lender of last resort *strictu sensu* requires the provision of liquidity at a penalty rate to a specific financial firm that is illiquid, but solvent (Deutsche Bank, 2008). Should emergency liquidity assistance to solvent but illiquid operators be needed, national arrangements would apply. National central banks without supervisory power would get access to supervisory information and they would be responsible for intervention. In the case of a large amount of liquidity, the ECB Council would be involved (Padoa-Schioppa, 2004, pp. 177–218). The provision of (emergency) liquidity to the overall system, not to a specific bank, is a task that can only be performed at the Eurosystem level.

Significant injections of liquidity began in mid-2007. In Germany, the Bundesbank, with advice from the German financial supervisory authority, the BaFin, provided liquidity to illiquid financial entities (reportedly, German public banks were amongst the most exposed to the credit squeeze and liquidity crunch in Europe), as well as orchestrating rescues of two banks, one of which was experiencing solvency problems[11] – this was the function of lender of last resort *strictu sensu*. At the euro area level, the ECB intervened repeatedly in the market, injecting emergency liquidity into the system.[12] The ECB-Eurosystem's response to these events to some extent assuaged the concerns about the provision of emergency liquidity assistance in the euro area and the ECB's role therein, even though it raised other concerns, elaborated below.

Unlike the ECB, the Bank of England intervened belatedly, having previously indirectly criticized the ECB's interventions.[13] The Governor of the Bank of England (King, 2007) had argued that 'the provision of liquidity support undermines the efficient pricing of risk by providing *ex post* insurance for risky behaviour. That encourages excessive risk taking and sows the

---

[11] *Financial Times*, 22 and 28 August 2007.
[12] *Financial Times*, 15 August 2007.
[13] *Financial Times*, 12 September 2007.

seeds of a future financial crisis'. Only after the Northern Rock crisis erupted did the Bank of England change its stance. The different responses of the ECB and the Bank of England suggest that there were different regulatory philosophies in the EU and different approaches to maintaining financial stability, as elaborated below.

Wider international co-operation also took place. In December 2007, the ECB, the Federal Reserve, the Bank of England, the Bank of Canada and the Swiss central bank undertook a concerted action providing liquidity to tackle the credit squeeze.[14]

Following the bankruptcy of Lehman Brothers in the US on 15 September, unsecured inter-bank money markets froze in the euro area and banks became increasingly dependent on ECB liquidity operations and overnight borrowing (ECB, 2008b). On 15 October, the ECB expanded its list of assets eligible for use as collateral in its credit operations and increased the provision of longer-term liquidity by fully meeting banks' demand for liquidity at maturities of three and six months (ECB, 2008a). The list of eligible assets was subsequently tightened up, allegedly because some banks were gaming the system,[15] providing low-quality collaterals in credit operation with the ECB.[16] It should be remembered that where the ECB or the NCBs carry out what are considered normal open market operations the risks are pooled within the Eurosystem, but if NCBs bail out their own banks by buying illiquid assets or swapping them in some form for safe assets, the risk is borne by the Member State itself. In the event of losses by the Eurosystem there is no supranational fiscal authority behind them.[17]

Since the onset of the crisis, the ECB's liquidity management was evaluated as 'timely' and 'proactive' and its framework has been 'flexible' and 'robust' (IMF, 2008, p. 22). However, the limits of policy co-ordination were clearly revealed by the Summit of European G8 members on 4 October (Summit Statement, 2008) in that shortly after the end of one of the meetings, the German government unexpectedly and unilaterally issued a statement concerning the state guarantee on bank deposits in Germany, apparently without previously informing the other Member States, including those participating at the restricted meeting.[18] Ireland had previously undertaken a

---

[14] *Financial Times*, 13–14 December 2007.
[15] *Financial Times*, 5 September 2008.
[16] Spanish banks were indicated amongst the main culprits, see «http://uk.reuters.com/article/rbssFinancialServicesAndRealEstateNews/idUKL2760195720080527» and *The Daily Telegraph*, 29 January 2008.
[17] See Wilhem Buiter's *Financial Times* blog at: «http://blogs.ft.com/maverecon/2009/01/quantitative-and-qualitative-easing-again/».
[18] *Financial Times*, 25 November 2008.

similar course of action, which guaranteed almost all bank liabilities (not just deposits) and this was followed by actions in other Member States. The EU directive on deposit guarantee schemes set a minimum, not a maximum, for such schemes in the Member States and there was no collective action during the crisis either to set a maximum for deposit guarantees or to regulate guarantees in respect of non-deposit liabilities.

Recapitalization and Ownership

On 7 October 2008, the ECOFIN discussed a co-ordinated response to the financial crisis, relating in particular to support for systemic financial institutions and the definition of common principles for action (ECOFIN Council, 2008). The Member States committed themselves 'to take all necessary measures' (p. 6) to protect the stability of the banking system and the deposit of individual savers. Yet, more specific measures were not adopted. It should be noted that the possibility of creating a European stabilization fund, mainly for bank recapitalization, had briefly been considered by the French presidency and quickly dismissed due to the strong German opposition. Reportedly the Netherlands was the main proponent of the scheme, which was also supported by Italy and France, the latter with an ambivalent position.[19]

On 12 October 2008, the Heads of State or Government gathered in the Eurogroup, acting in agreement with the European Commission and the ECB, approved a concerted action plan and urged the other EU countries to adopt its principles. The plan provided for individual national governments to take co-ordinated measures to facilitate bank funding (by providing government guarantees for new medium-term debt issuance, which however did not include inter-bank lending) and recapitalization (government subscription of preference shares or other instruments) (Eurogroup, 2008). This framework was fully endorsed by the European Council on 15 and 16 October. Afterwards, the national governments adopted specific national plans, more or less following these guidelines.

Approximately €2 trillion was pledged by governments in the euro area to guarantee banks' new debt issuance, support their recapitalization or purchase their assets (ECB, 2008b). The US and UK governments also adopted national action plans.[20] In the US, up to US$2.5 trillion was committed to guarantee newly issued debt, purchase troubled assets and make capital

---

[19] *Financial Times*, 7 October 2008.
[20] Full details of all individual rescue packages can be found in the BIS Quarterly Review, December 2008. Available at: «http://www.bis.org/publ/qtrpdf/r_qt0812y.htm».

injections. In the UK, £300 billion was committed for recapitalization and guarantees of unsecured bank funding (ECB, 2008b).

Whereas the EU has very few positive rules on what the Member States must do to co-ordinate, the *acquis* are better developed in laying out what they cannot do, nowhere more so than in competition law. Accordingly, the Commission's Directorate General for Competition found itself having to rule on the acceptability of state aid to the banking system as well as bank mergers.

The Commission did not seriously attempt to resist the scale of assistance for and consolidation of banks but tried to modulate the distortionary consequences.[21] It issued two sets of guidelines on 13 October and 5 December (Commission, 2008a, 2009) stating how it would interpret the existing legislation.[22] Noting that Article 87(3)(b) of the Treaty provides that the Commission may allow state aid 'to remedy a serious disturbance in the economy of a Member State' (Commission, 2008a) it sought to insist that such aid respected key conditions such as non-discrimination and did not place aided banks at an undue advantage. With the latter in mind it sought to ensure that aids were appropriately valued and in particular that loans and preference shares were adequately remunerated with due allowance for risk. In this it was assisted by opinions issued by the ECB. It appears it approved, in essence, all schemes put to it.[23] Press reports suggested that the French plan was being rejected due to the 8 per cent coupon proposed but in the end it was agreed.[24]

The Commission has also to approve bank mergers with cross-border implications. The Lloyds TSB–HBOS merger was reviewed by the UK authorities alone, who decided that, despite possible competition concerns, it was in the public interest. DG Competition did not object to the UK decision. EU competition law does not have a public interest provision for mergers, but the Commission knew it should be pragmatic. The cross-border proposal for acquisition by BNP of Fortis Belgium was approved by DG Competition, subject to conditions for divestiture of some credit card activities in Belgium.[25]

---

[21] It should be noted however that the Commission's approval of the aid schemes was in principle temporary and subject to review after six months – a period which had not elapsed at the time of writing.
[22] For an excellent legal summary see Mayer Browne State Aid, *European Commission Issues Communication on Recapitalization of Financial Institutions 12 December 2008*. Available at: «http://www.mayerbrown.com/publications/article.asp?id=5941».
[23] See «http://ec.europa.eu/competition/sectors/financial_services/financial_crisis_news_en.html».
[24] See «http://berr.ecgroup.net/Publications/BusinessLaw/CompetitionMatters.aspx».
[25] *Le Monde*, 8 December 2008.

Fortis-Dexia

In late September 2008 Belgium's leading bank with operations in the whole Benelux area and Belgium's largest single employer, the Fortis financial group, began to face severe liquidity problems. Apart from the general financial situation Fortis had been fatally weakened by it joining RBS in a takeover of ABN-AMRO at a price that was clearly excessive. A private sector rescue proved impossible. On 28 September 2008 the governments of Belgium, the Netherlands and Luxembourg agreed a joint rescue plan which amounted to nationalizations separating the Dutch and Belgian operations. The scheme was rapidly agreed at a technical level and was initially judged a success. But further moves proved seriously problematic. There were immediate accusations of ill faith between Belgium and the Netherlands.[26] Belgium decided to sell its stake to BNP Paribas, but this was immediately challenged in the Belgian courts and the Belgian prime minister was forced to tender his resignation after accusations that he had tried to interfere with the case.

The case of Dexia, Fortis' main rival in Belgium, was simpler by contrast. It was adversely affected by its involvement in the US markets and above all problems with loans to the troubled German Hypobank. Dexia operated mainly in Belgium, Luxembourg and France and the three governments agreed on 30 September to inject additional capital. No political repercussions followed.

In all these operations the European authorities remained bystanders, authorizing the proposed interventions, though with conditions in the case of BNP-Fortis.

The 13 October announcement specifically stated that, since the banking sector is distinct, policy would not be as flexible for the rest of the economy, but subsequent action suggested a broader pragmatism. Overall, while its application of competition rules could not contribute positively to solving the problems the Commission seemed to have been quite successful in ensuring that the rules did not constrain recapitalization and restructuring, whilst minimizing the resulting competitive distortions.[27]

It is worth noting that the EU rules on disclosure (the Market Abuse Directive) which Bank of England Governor Mervyn King argued prevented a covert aid scheme for Northern Rock were not part of competition law but the internal market *acquis* and the Commission was reported as stating that if it had been consulted it would have expressed the view that there was scope for delaying announcements.[28]

---

[26] See NRC *Handelsblad*, 6 October 2008, «http://www.nrc.nl/international/Features/article2011684.ece/Belgians_angry_over_Fortis_deal».

[27] Brussels, 30 December 2008 'State Aid: Commission Approves First Real Economy Crisis Measures', available at: «http://europa.eu/rapid/pressReleasesAction.do?reference=IP/08/2063&format=HTML&aged=0&language=EN&guiLanguage=en».

[28] *The Times*, 22 September 2007.

Macroeconomic Policy

The bank rate was cut substantially in all advanced countries during the second half of 2008. How much co-ordination of policy took place is unclear. On 8 October, the US Federal Reserve, the Bank of England, the Bank of Canada, the Swiss National Bank and the *Sveriges Riksbank* enacted simultaneous half-point interest cuts in the bank rate. Perhaps this was no more than the co-ordinated announcement of actions that these central banks were minded to take in any case.

On 2 December, the ECOFIN council approved a European recovery plan prepared by the Commission (Commission, 2008b), subsequently endorsed by the European Council on 11–12 December. In particular, the Council supported an economic stimulus amounting to 1.5 per cent of EU GDP (€200 billion), made up of budgetary expansion by the Member States of €170 billion (around 1.2 per cent of EU GDP) and 'EU funding in support of immediate action of €30 billion' (approximately 0.3 per cent of EU GDP) (Commission, 2008b, p. 6). The plan called for Member States to 'co-ordinate their activities' allowing them to 'choose the most appropriate measures concerning expenditures and revenues, prioritizing those with a short term impact' (p. 1). Moreover, the plan asserted that the 'revised Stability and Growth pact, with all the flexibility it affords, is the appropriate framework for budgetary policy in Europe, consistent with the long-term sustainability of public finances' (p. 2).[29]

At the time of writing, it remains to be seen whether the European Council's decisions regarding both the size of the overall stimulus and the co-ordination of the activities of the Member States will be put into practice. Since no formal mechanism for such co-ordination was set up, it is not clear how, if at all, this will happen. What can be said is that the stimulus plans that were in place by December 2008 appear to have fallen a good deal short of the 1.2 per cent of EU GDP stipulated by the Council.

Estimating the magnitude of the fiscal stimulus is not straightforward, for example, because it is necessary to make judgements about the *additionality* of changes in spending and taxes over and above those generated by automatic stabilizers. According to one estimate, using a methodology that simply lumps together increases in government expenditure and tax cuts (i.e. making no allowance for a smaller impact on demand from the latter), the average stimulus across plans in the largest 13 of the EU economies amounted to no more than 0.57 per cent of GDP (Saha and von Weizsäcker, 2008). Adding in the EU-level component, which comprises additional loans from the European Investment Bank and an acceleration of Commission spending, would raise this to 0.64 per cent. Member States have insisted that the EU's total

[29] ECOFIN, press release, 2 December 2008.

budget be fixed and have refused to allow either uncommitted reserves to be spent or borrowing by the EU as such. The above numbers exclude the subsidy element contained in government measures to expand credit to both banks and non-banks.

As regards policies at national level, there was clearly parallel action, but no evidence of formal concertation on 'burden-sharing'. The Commission's recommendations left the timing and the relative scale of stimuli for the Member States to decide for themselves. Spain and the UK stood out as being towards the high end of fiscal stimuli. Italy by mid-December had declined to commit itself. German statements on fiscal policy were somewhat at odds with their actual policies. The German Finance Minister criticized UK policy as 'crass Keynesianism',[30] leading to a fierce response by economic commentators, and did not in fact appear to reflect Germany's own policy. This did include a fiscal stimulus, albeit one initially considered to be too small by critics and indeed eventually by the German authorities themselves.[31]

Regulation

The regulatory response to the financial crisis was co-ordinated in international forums, first and foremost, the Financial Stability Forum (FSF) and also at the EU level. Indeed, Angeloni (2008) argues that the former was at the forefront in the elaboration of the response to the crisis, not only internationally, but also within the EU. In the background there were tensions between national governments which wished to retain national discretion and which therefore preferred broad and consequently non-binding international co-operation and those which favoured EU-level co-operation, which was intrinsically more likely to be binding, thereby reducing national discretion. Moreover, irrespective of more general anti-federalist sentiments, the UK had economic reasons for favouring broader international co-operation, because of the strong presence in London of banks with a global reach.

The FSF comprises representatives from central banks, supervisory authorities and treasury ministries, senior officials from international financial institutions (IMF, Bank for International Settlements, Organization for Economic Co-operation and Development, World Bank) and international regulatory bodies (BCBS, International Organization of Securities Commissions, IOSCO, International Association of Insurance Supervisors, International Accounting Standards Board), as well as the Committee on Payment and Settlement Systems and the ECB. In 2008, it included representatives from G7

---

[30] See interview with Peer Steinbrueck published in *Newsweek* magazine, issue dated 15 December 2008, available at: «http://www.newsweek.com/id/172613».
[31] On the subsequent enlargement of the fiscal stimulus in January 2009, see Carare *et al.* (2008).

countries plus Hong Kong, Singapore, Australia and the Netherlands. It was asked by the Group of Seven (G7) to evaluate the causes of the turmoil and to put forward recommendations to address the existing weaknesses.

In April 2008, the FSF produced a report in collaboration with the other main international financial supervisory bodies. This suggested 'strengthening capital, liquidity and risk management', 'enhancing transparency and valuation' and reviewing the role of credit rating agencies (FSF, 2008). The 2008 G7 that met in the spring of 2008 endorsed the report produced by the FSF, highlighting the priorities for action in the short and medium term.

The principal EU measures taken were the following. The Deposit Guarantee Directive and the Capital Requirements Directive were revised. The revision of the latter directive was also tied up to the revision of the Basel II accord at the international level in the BCBS. In both these forums, the policy debate focused on the revision of risk weights for securitized products, the trading book review and new rules for liquidity risk management.

By December 2008, policy discussions concerning the revision of accounting standards, in particular the mark to market principle and how to evaluate illiquid assets, i.e. assets for which there is no liquid market, were still continuing in the EU as well as internationally.

A new legislative proposal for the regulation of credit rating agencies was put forward in November 2008 by the European Commission (Commission, 2008c), which would make legally binding several elements of the revised code of fundamentals for credit rating agencies, initially issued by the IOSCO in 2006 and revised in 2008.

As regards financial supervision, official discussions centred on 'strengthening' the existing system of colleges of supervisors for cross-border groups in the EU. Cutting across this, the Financial Stability Forum put forward proposals for the creation of *international* colleges of supervisors for cross-border groups. By December 2008, no new decisions had been reached in this area. Moreover it appeared that no consideration was given to the creation of an EU-wide supervisory authority, as advocated by a number of prominent commentators, including the ex-Chairman of the UK Financial Services Authority (Davies, 2009).

IV. Assessment

Our assessment of co-ordination in the EU response to the crisis is organized thematically using the classification introduced in section I. We then attempt to draw some more general lessons about the EU's ability to respond to new challenges.

Liquidity

ECB-Eurosystem liquidity injection into the system (emergency liquidity assistance, ELA) was carried out in a co-ordinated way and was more timely than the Bank of England's delayed action in the summer of 2007. However, there was some imprecision on the rules regarding the range of assets to be accepted as collateral in main refinancing operations and the 'haircuts'[32] (i.e. discounts) to be applied to different classes of asset. Since the ECB rules were relatively lenient, this created the risk that the ECB might end up taking a disproportionate quantity of low-quality assets. The substantial rise in the share of Spanish and Irish bank assets in the ECB's portfolio during 2008 suggests that this risk may possibly have materialized. Partly for this reason the ECB revised its collateral policy in December 2008.

LOLR operations, for which the responsibility lies at national level, potentially entail spillovers, especially when the institution supported has a significant presence in other EU countries, but since such operations are usually not publicized, we are unable to say more. Under current arrangements the ECB cannot take on the LOLR function, because it does not have the fiscal backing that assumption of this function would require.

Co-ordination of liquidity support via public guarantees of bank liabilities was a failure, as described earlier, especially as regards deposit guarantees, where unilateral action in Ireland triggered unco-ordinated, piecemeal defensive reactions in other EU members. Equally, the weak condition of markets for inter-bank lending might have been thought to justify co-ordinated action to guarantee such lending between banks in different national jurisdictions, but none was forthcoming.

Recapitalization and Ownership

Policy in the EU was kick-started by the UK's restructuring and recapitalization plan of 8 October 2008, which rejected the US approach at the time of simply buying up toxic assets from the banks in favour of partial public ownership with other support, notably loan guarantees, linked to acceptance of public capital (or the raising of equivalent private capital). Following the UK's initiative, a concerted action plan outlining broad guidelines on recapitalization/banking rescue was belatedly agreed at the Eurogroup/EU level. However, there was no concrete agreement on burden-sharing in the EU, beyond the general principles agreed in late 2007. Countries were left to implement the recapitalization plans as they chose, subject to approval by

---

[32] A haircut of 20 per cent means that if a bond with a redemption value of €100 is posted as collateral, only €80 will be lent against this.

DG Competition. As Nieto and Schinasi note (2008, p. 16), 'no single or collective entity devotes resources to safeguard the stability of the European financial system, or the amalgamation of these integrated national financial systems'.

Co-ordination was therefore ad hoc among the countries involved when it came to rescuing large cross-border banks. This seems to have worked quite well in the case of the rescue of Dexia, where the French and Belgian governments were involved, but the winding up of another large cross-border bank, Fortis, was politically and legally controversial, notwithstanding the multilateral MoU signed by the Benelux countries prior to the crisis and the established tradition of economic co-operation amongst them.

Macroeconomic Policy

There was one publicly announced co-ordinated interest rate cut, by seven central banks, in October 2008. Otherwise there was no overt co-ordination of interest rate policy, which does not prove that such co-ordination has not occurred.

On fiscal policy the EU failed to implement explicit and binding co-ordination on the magnitude and timing of fiscal impulses at national level. Theory suggests that in the absence of such co-ordination, national fiscal impulses are likely to be insufficient and on the basis of plans up to December 2008 this does appear to be the case. In this regard, the Breughel estimate of 0.64 per cent of EU GDP may be compared both with the EU target of 1.2 per cent and the IMF view that an impulse of about 2 per cent is required (Strauss-Kahn, 2008).

Regulation

The crisis exposed flaws in the regulation and supervision of financial institutions worldwide. In this area of policy it is not so much that the co-ordination of crisis *management* was at fault – as might be claimed, say, in the case of fiscal policy – but that the regulatory system itself was shown unequal to the task of crisis *prevention*.

So it was agreed that changes in regulation were needed, but by the end of 2008, change had been slow (for understandable reasons) and also uneven. To some degree, attempts to co-ordinate a regulatory response were hampered by disagreement among the Member States on where such co-ordination should take place (at the EU or international level). An example of a relatively rapid reform was the change to the Directive on Deposit Guarantee Schemes. An example of slow progress was the question of how supervision should be co-ordinated, perhaps because, far more than in the other cases, potential transfers of power from national to EU level were being mooted.

The one area where the EU has a binding supranational regulatory framework is competition law. Here in both state aids and merger policy the Commission acted in a politically sensitive manner, aiming only to limit the discrimination and the most serious anti-competitive effects.

Overall Lessons

It is too early to evaluate the EU's policy response to the crisis against outcomes. We simply do not yet know whether a mild recession or something akin to the Great Depression is in store for us. Recent experience suggests that the EU can respond quickly and collectively, but not necessarily adequately, to an unexpected crisis.

In terms of processes the question remains open whether European institutions provide strong enough incentives to provide the 'semi-public good' of financial stability on an adequate scale (Osterloo and Schoenmaker, 2005; Nieto and Schinasi, 2008). Policy actions were prompt and well co-ordinated when one or both of two conditions were satisfied: (a) the existence of a robust institutional framework for co-ordination; (b) the presence of a shared analytical framework (or policy paradigm). Both conditions seem to have been satisfied in the area of monetary policy. Not only were some actions automatically co-ordinated in the Eurosystem, but co-ordination between it and other central banks was facilitated by a shared professional culture. It is less apparent that either of these conditions is satisfied in other policy areas, such as fiscal policy. Here, national governments acted in parallel, but as we have shown there are grounds to doubt that the fiscal impulses by the end of 2008 were either sufficient in aggregate or appropriately distributed among Member States.

Although this article began with some reference to the impact of the financial crisis on trade flows, we have not discussed trade policy as such. At time of writing, the EU had not resorted to protectionism, but neither had it responded to calls for a binding moratorium on any such measures. This may be a good illustration of an area where condition (a) holds, but (b) does not. The contrast with monetary policy suggests how important a shared analytical framework can be. Our analysis of the relative successes and failures of EU policy in the crisis suggests that, in general, good policy-making can be achieved by robust institutions together with a shared analytical framework, even where there are strong conflicts of interest.

Correspondence:
Lucia Quaglia
Department of Politics and Contemporary European Studies
University of Sussex
Brighton BN1 9RG
Tel +44 (0) 1273 678496
Fax +44 (0)1273 673563
email l.quaglia@sussex.ac.uk

References

Angeloni, I. (2008) 'Testing Times for Global Financial Governance'. *Bruegel Essay and Lecture Series*, Brussels.

Baldwin, R. and Evenett, S. (eds) (2009) *The Collapse of Global Trade, Murky Protectionism and the Crisis: Recommendations for the G20*. Available at «http://www.voxeu.org/reports/Murky_Protectionism.pdf».

Bank of England (2008) *Financial Stability Report*, October.

Bank for International Settlements (BIS) (2008) *Quarterly Review*, December. Available at: «http://www.bis.org/publ/qtrpdf/r_qt0812y.htm».

Carare, A., Mody, A. and Ohnsorge, F. (2008) 'The German Fiscal Stimulus Package in Perspective'. Available at: «http://www.voxeu.org/index.php?q=node/2835».

Commission of the European Communities (2008a) 'Communication from the Commission – the application of state aid rules to measures taken in relation to financial institutions in the context of the current global financial crisis'. 2008/C 270/02. *Official Journal*, C270, 25 October, pp. 8–14.

Commission of the European Communities (2008b) 'Communication from the Commission to the European Council, a European recovery plan'. 26 November, Brussels.

Commission of the European Communities (2008c) 'Proposal for a regulation of the European Parliament and of the Council on credit rating agencies'. COM(2008) 704 final, Brussels, 12 November.

Commission of the European Communities (2009) 'Communication – Recapitalisation of financial institutions in the current financial crisis: Limitation of the aid to the minimum necessary and safeguards against undue distortions of competition'. *Official Journal*, C10, 15 January, pp. 2–10.

Crosby, J. (2008) *Mortgage Finance: Final Report and Recommendations* (London: HM Treasury), November.

Davies, H. (2009) 'Europe's Banks Need a Federal Fix'. *Financial Times*, 14 January.

De Grauwe, P. (2008) 'The Banking Crisis: Causes, Consequences and Remedies', University of Leuven and CESifo, November. Available at: «http://shop.ceps.eu/downfree.php?item_id=1758».

Deutsche Bank (2008) 'Price Stability *v.* Lender of Last Resort'. *EU Monitor*, No. 52, 26 March.

Economic and Financial Affairs Council (ECOFIN Council) (2007) 'Council Conclusions on Enhancing the Arrangements for Financial Stability in the EU'. Luxembourg, 9 October.

Economic and Financial Affairs Council (ECOFIN Council) (2008) 'Council Conclusions on the EU Supervisory Framework and Financial Stability Arrangements'. Brussels, 14 May.

Economic and Financial Affairs Council (ECOFIN Council) (2008) 'Council Conclusions', 7 October.

Economic and Financial Committee (EFC) (2007) 'Developing EU Financial Stability Arrangements'. 5 September, Brussels.

Eurogroup (2008) 'Summit of the Euro Area Countries: Declaration on a Concerted European Action Plan of the Euro Area Countries'. Available at: «http://www.ue2008.fr/PFUE/lang/en/accueil/PFUE-10_2008/PFUE-12.10.2008/sommet_pays_zone_euro_declaration_plan_action_concertee».

European Central Bank (ECB) (2007) 'The EU Arrangements for Financial Crisis Management'. *Monthly Bulletin*, February, Frankfurt.

European Central Bank (ECB) (2008a) *Monthly Bulletin*, December, Frankfurt.

European Central Bank (ECB) (2008b) *Financial Stability Review*, December, Frankfurt.

Financial Stability Forum (FSF) (2008) 'Report of the Financial Stability Forum on Enhancing Market and Institutional Resilience', 7 April.

Group of Seven (G7) (2008) 'Statement of G-7 Finance Ministers and Central BankGovernors', 11 April 2008.

International Monetary Fund (IMF) (2006) *Country Report Euro Area Policies: Selected Issues*, No. 06/288, August.

International Monetary Fund (IMF) (2007) 'Euro Area Policies: 2007 Article IV Consultation'. *IMF Country Report*, No. 07/260, July.

International Monetary Fund (IMF) (2008) *Country Report Euro Area Policies: Article IV Consultation*, No. 08/262, August.

International Monetary Fund (IMF) (2009a) *Global Stability Report: Market Update*, 29 January.

International Monetary Fund (IMF) (2009b) *World Economic Outlook Update*, 28 January. Available at: «http://www.imf.org/external/pubs/ft/weo/2009/update/01/index.htm».

Kindleberger, C.P. (1986) *The World in Depression, 1929–39* (rev. edn) (Berkeley, CA: University of California Press).

King, M. (2007) *Turmoil in Financial Markets: What Can Central Bankers Do?* Paper submitted to the Treasury Committee by the Governor of the Bank of England. Available at: «http://www.bankofengland.co.uk/publications/other/treasurycommittee/other/paper070912.pdf».

King, M. (2008) Evidence to the Treasury Select Committee (Examination of Witnesses), 28 November. Available at: «http://www.publications.parliament.uk/pa/cm200708/cmselect/cmtreasy/1210/8112503.htm».

Krugman, P. (2008) 'European Macro Algebra'. *New York Times*, 14 December.

Masciandaro, D. and Quintyn, M. (eds) (2007) *Designing Financial Supervision Institutions: Independence, Accountability and Governance* (Cheltenham: Edward Elgar).

Nieto, M.J and Schinasi, G.J. (2008) 'EU Framework for Safeguarding Financial Stability: Towards an Analytical Benchmark for Assessing its Effectiveness'. *Banco de España Occasional Paper*, No. 0801.

Padoa-Schioppa, T. (2004) *The Euro and its Central Bank* (London: MIT Press).

Pauly, L.W. (2008) 'Financial Crisis Management in Europe and Beyond'. *Contributions to Political Economy*, Vol. 27, No. 1, pp. 73–89.

Quaglia, L. (2008) 'Committee Governance in the Financial Sector in the European Union'. *Journal of European Integration*, Vol. 30, No. 3, pp. 565–80.

Saha, D. and von Weizsäcker, J. (2008) 'Estimating the Size of the European Stimulus Packages for 2009'. JVW/ DS, Bruegel, 12 December.

Schoenmaker, D. and Oosterloo, S (2005) 'Financial Supervision in an Integrating Europe: Measuring Cross-Border Externalities'. *International Finance*, Vol. 8, pp. 1–27.

Summit of European G8 members (2008) 'Statement'. Palais de l'Elysée, Paris, 4 October 2008. Available at: «http://www.ambafrance-uk.org/International-financial-situation.html».

Strauss-Kahn, D. (2008) 'The IMF and its Future'. Speech at the Banco de España, Madrid, Spain, 15 December.

JCMS 2009 Volume 47 Annual Review pp. 89–98

The Slovenian Presidency: Meeting Symbolic and Substantive Challenges

SABINA KAJNČ
Centre for International Relations, Ljubljana

I. Symbolic and Substantive Challenges

Slovenia took over the Presidency of the Council of the European Union (EU) as the first of the 2004/07 accession countries, as the last country to hold the first trio-arranged Presidency and as the smallest of the Member States with the exception of Luxembourg ever to hold the Presidency. A triple challenge is enclosed in these simple facts: firstly, a closing of the 2004/07 enlargement process by proving the aptness of the new Member States not only to belong to a club, but also to lead it; secondly, defending the system of (some form of) a rotating presidency by showing that size does matter and that small can be advantageous; and, thirdly, a justification of the trio team presidency system in terms of coherence and consistency in the EU policies, not only by carrying out the programme, but also by keeping the trio priorities high on the agenda.

The substantive challenges confronting the EU and ahead of the Slovenian Presidency in the first half of 2008 cut across the above rather symbolic challenges. The Slovenian Presidency set itself five particular priorities: the co-ordination of the ratification process of the Lisbon Treaty, the launch of the third cycle of the renewed Lisbon Strategy, advancing the climate-energy package further by seeking an agreement on further liberalization of the internal market for gas and electricity, intercultural dialogue and the top priority: bringing the countries of the Western Balkans one step closer to the EU. While the first three priorities largely form part of an inherited agenda and promoting intercultural dialogue was more of a symbolic effort, the focus on the Western Balkans was a true Slovenian priority.

Slovenia prepared well for the Presidency. Organizationally and logistically the preparations ran smoothly from 2005 onwards and the conduct of the Presidency was flawless in these respects. In terms of domestic politics the government of the centre-right coalition headed by Prime Minister Janša's Slovenian Democratic Party tried to secure 'domestic peace' by putting forward the so-called 'agreement on not attacking the Government in the period of holding the EU Presidency'[1] as early as May 2007. The agreement was signed by all but two opposition parliamentary parties and though it officially remained in place, its value can be questioned. Party politics was stirred up by the presidential elections in 2007 (in which the government's favourite candidate lost) and continued with the government accusing the opposition of early campaigning, during the period of the Presidency, for the September 2008 general elections (which the opposition won).

The third cycle of the Lisbon Strategy was to be launched at the March European Summit and the third internal market package for gas and electricity desperately needed to be politically agreed upon for the Union to turn from common market related energy issues to external energy security during the French Presidency in the second half of 2008. Though the Lisbon strategy package was overshadowed by the climate-energy package at the Spring Summit, both packages shared the Commission's struggle to act as a motor in the interest of the Union. The credit crunch, global financial instability and soaring food and oil prices called for an EU-wide immediate response and also opened up the chances for a systemic approach to the not-as-yet communitarized financial regulation in the common market. Another chapter of the 'Yugoslav' story was to unveil itself in the first half of 2008, putting the EU's foreign policy credentials once again to the test, demanding a careful balancing between the principles of its enlargement policy and instruments of its crisis management.

These are only four issues that occupied the EU in the first half of 2008.[2] Most broadly they cut across two overarching themes: leadership in the EU, more specifically, the role of the Commission and the (reach of the small) Member States, including the dilemmas surrounding the future of the rotating presidency and the will for further deepening and widening of the EU. An

---

[1] Officially 'Agreement on the Co-operation of Political Parties, the Group of Unconnected Deputies and Representatives of National Minorities in the National Assembly of the Republic of Slovenia for the Successful Implementation of the Preparation and Presidency of the EU' (for more on the agreement see Fink-Hafner and Lajh, 2008).

[2] The Irish 'no' on the Lisbon Treaty was expressed during the course of the Slovenian Presidency (see Dinan, this volume). Though 'co-ordination' of national ratifications of the Lisbon Treaty was among Slovenia's priorities it was formulated rather clumsily as a priority. This was quickly proven by the coldly received advice of Prime Minister Janša to the Portuguese government not to hold a referendum on the issue in January. From then on, ratification by the Member States was respected as their internal affair and Slovenia's government measured its success by achieving the goal of 20 Member State ratifications.

insight into how the above-mentioned four issues have been dealt with in the first half of 2008 offers arguments for wider debates on EU governance and the future of the EU.

II. Climate and Energy Package: Manoeuvring between the Interests of the Commission and the Larger Member States

The 2007 Spring European Council called on the Commission to prepare proposals to fight climate change and promote renewable energy in line with the EU's commitments. The originally planned Communication for December 2007 was postponed until 23 January 2008. The Communication (Commission, 2008a) confirmed the fears that there would be highly divergent and cemented interests over the 'unbundling issue' on the part of powerful actors, such as France and Germany on one side – opposing the full unbundling – and the Commission – advocating it – on the other side.

The short time between the publication of the Communication and the March European Council that was scheduled to debate the issue left little room for the countries to study the report in depth, voice their concerns, elaborate their arguments and place them into the hierarchy of the Council machinery. Instead, the European Council witnessed an open debate on the issue at the highest level of Heads of State or Government. The Presidency Conclusions on the entire climate-energy package were weak, inviting the Commission 'to take account of the situation' (Council, 2008a) in further developing policies for a fully functioning and interconnected internal energy market. They were criticized by all sides, including the European Parliament, whose co-operation was necessary in order for the measures to be adopted.

The main achievement of the European Council, however, was an open debate between the Heads of State or Government. It made the interests of each Member State transparent, marked a negotiating manoeuvring space and by doing so offered the Slovenian Presidency a chance to table a viable proposal. Slovenia had no particular interests in the matter. Having itself one of the most liberalized energy sectors in terms of providers and distributors of natural gas and electricity (Behrens and Egenhofer, 2008, p. 20) it was a credible mediator and acknowledged as such by those from all sides of the interest spectrum on the issue. Eventual compromise between the Member States was reached at the Transport, Telecommunications and Energy Council on 6 June. The compromise digressed considerably from the Commission's proposal for the full ownership unbundling. While it acknowledged that full ownership unbundling was the first best option, the compromise allowed for continued joined ownership for vertically integrated systems, with specific measures to assure independence of the transmission operators (Council, 2008b). The goal of reaching the political agreement by June 2008 set at the March European Summit was thus reached, but the issue was quickly back on the table as the European Parliament rejected the compromise, favouring the tougher Commission's initial proposal, at its plenary session on 18 June 2008.

III. The New Cycle of the Renewed Lisbon Strategy: Finding a Niche – the 'Fifth Freedom'

The Lisbon Strategy was another issue high on the Slovenian list of priorities, in which the Commission had strong interests. With the 2010 goal of becoming the most competitive market in the world quietly dropped (Armstrong *et al.*, 2008, p. 414) and the twist in the 2005 re-launch of the Strategy by which the Commission lost its ownership at the expense of partnership with the Member States, the Commission struggled to exert control and keep up the momentum.

The Commission worked closely with the Portuguese Presidency in the second half of 2007 on the formulation of the Presidency Conclusions of the December 2007 European Council in the field of economic and social matters, previously not a subject for the December European Councils. This in part prejudiced the Spring 2008 Conclusions, which caused unease and a feeling of mistrust about Slovenia's capabilities in Ljubljana. Slovenia's Presidency programme advocated continuity in the new cycle with the four priority areas identified at the 2006 Spring European Council[3] and pledged to focus on the implementation of the National Reform Programmes in line with the common strategy. The Commission emphasized the human dimension and labour markets whilst the European Parliament put more weight on strengthening the social and employment priority.[4] The Slovenian Presidency, however, put investment into knowledge and innovation at the forefront of its 'Lisbon strategy priority'.

This was in part backed by the Commission's positive 2007 strategic report on growth and employment issues, largely due to the favourable economic climate in the EU between 2005 and 2007, which lowered Member States' concern for more engagement in social and employment issues. On

---

[3] These are: (1) building an innovative and creative knowledge-based society; (2) creating the conditions for a competitive and dynamic business environment; (3) developing human capital and addressing demographic challenges to ensure greater participation in the labour market; and (4) responding to energy and environmental challenges.

[4] See Commission (2007a); the debate in the European Parliament after the Presidency presented the programme on 21 January 2008 (European Parliament, 2008); also the analysis of the Lisbon Strategy and the call for the strengthening of its social dimension and reviving the European Employment strategy in the third cycle by Zeitlin (in Armstrong *et al.*, 2008, pp. 413–50).

the other hand the reportedly lower R&D investment as well as the official announcement of some countries that the 3 per cent target had been postponed placed additional pressure for action in this field. A combination of an engaged minister for development, Žiga Türk, and close co-operation with DG Research, through better access, communication and improved personal ties with the Commissioner for Research and Technology, Janez Potočnik, resulted in the 'fifth freedom' – free movement of knowledge – being integrated into the Presidency Conclusions.[5] As a novelty to be operationalized through the 'Ljubljana process' of enhanced governance within the framework of the European Research Area, it is unlikely to reach the importance of the traditional four freedoms. Combined with proper funding schemes and joined-up (national and EU-level) R&D programming, it might, however, provide some coherence to the management of European R&D.

IV. Financial Stability: Beyond the Reach

The financial crisis resulting from the US subprime crisis was addressed by the Ecofin Council in October 2007, which adopted a road map based on four key areas of work: improving transparency, valuation of financial products, strengthening prudential requirements and making markets function better. Slovenia's Presidency committed itself to working on these issues. However, throughout the Portuguese Presidency and during most of the Slovenian Presidency there was a strong sense in the euro area that European economies would escape the crisis caused by financial instability of the markets. The Chair of the Eurogroup, Luxembourg Prime Minister Juncker, admitted at the beginning of February that growth would slow down in 2008, in comparison to 2006 and 2007, but that there was no need to launch an extensive programme to stimulate the economy.[6] Two months later, Minister Bajuk, presiding over Ecofin, said at the informal Ecofin Council on 4 April that the slowdown of the economy in 2008 and 2009 was expected, also as a result of the high oil prices and the strong euro, but that the 'European economy is in a good position due to its strong fundamentals and absence of principal macroeconomic and financial imbalances'.[7]

More nervousness was felt in the UK, which was hit harder and earlier by the crisis in the US, and in the European Commission. Prime Minister Brown

---

[5] The free circulation of knowledge as an idea was introduced in the Green Paper 'The European Research Area: New Perspectives' (Commission, 2007b), but not then labelled the 'fifth freedom'.
[6] 'Juncker: Growth in the EU will Slow Down, but there will be no Recession' (interview in *Les Echos*, quoted by Slovenian Press Agency, 4 February 2008).
[7] 'Financial Ministers of the EU with Several Calls Regarding Financial Markets' (quoted by the Slovenian Press Agency, 4 April 2008).

invited the leaders of Germany, France, Italy and, belatedly, the Commission's President Barroso, to discuss the challenges caused by the financial crisis, leaving out the current President of the European Council, the Slovenian Prime Minister Janša, making a clear statement as to where the competence for necessary solutions lies. The Commission, on the other hand, called upon the European Council to 'go one step further' from the adopted road map, and to endorse a series of lines of action both in terms of internal policy and in international forums. At the same time, the Commission also acknowledged that the European economy was responding 'relatively well to turmoil in financial markets' (Commission, 2008b). Though the Commission stressed that action was essential, it did not see it as a pressing issue to be dealt with immediately, but rather as a commitment to be tackled during the French Presidency during the latter half of the year.[8]

Thus the lack of a sense of urgency was combined with a lack of will on the part of major European economies to tackle the problems under the Slovenian Presidency as they were reluctant to see EU-level regulation of financial market operators and at the same time, joined by the European Commission, saw Slovenia as unfit to lead on the matter. Indeed, the Slovenian Presidency acted accordingly. It had only five people, four in Ljubljana and one based in Brussels working on narrow Ecofin issues. It did not attempt to seize the chance to gather the political will in times of financial insecurity and to push for long overdue and politically difficult legislation on the European internal financial market regulation. Instead, it saw the adoption of a memorandum on co-operation in the field of cross-border financial stability as having very little added value, as it left unclear how decisions – albeit non-binding ones – are to be adopted, and it only technically worked through the Solvency II directive, putting the most fraught political issues in the directive to one side for its time in office.

V. Western Balkans: The Main Priority

After the 2004 enlargement, amidst discussions on 'absorption capacity' and 'limits of enlargement' there was a sense of 'Balkan fatigue' developing in the EU.[9] That Slovenia would make the Western Balkans its utmost priority during the Presidency was clear from the outset. After almost a decade of (foreign policy) efforts 'to escape the Balkans' (Bojinović, 2005) by joining the Stability Pact for south-eastern Europe in 1999, as part of 'Europe' and as a provider of security, Slovenia's foreign policy focus had gradually shifted

[8] Author interview, European Parliament, Brussels, 11 September 2008.
[9] Author interview, Council General Secretariat, Brussels, 9 June 2008.

towards strong engagement with the rest of the former Yugoslavia. Slovenia set itself two main goals: to conclude the ring of Stabilization and Association Agreements (SAA) for all countries in the region and to begin a dialogue with all states on a visa liberalization regime. Its overarching goal was to bring the region back to the top of the EU agenda given the uncertainty over Kosovo.

Slovenia's Presidency coincided with another chapter in the disintegration of Yugoslavia. Talks on the Ahtisaari plan for the future status of Kosovo failed in December 2007 and Kosovo's declaration of independence was looming. The Netherlands (and Belgium) vetoed the SAA with Serbia in January 2008, postponing once again Serbia's European integration and destabilizing its government. Both events caused unease over the stability of the region, and the EU as a whole did not want to fail in its backyard again. It was long clear that unanimity on the question of recognition of Kosovo (clearly a Member State competence) was impossible. The European Community had failed to speak with a single voice over the issue of recognition of Slovenia (and Croatia) and Slovenia was determined to do everything in its power to avoid history repeating itself.

The Council Conclusions of 18 February on Kosovo, following the Kosovan parliament's endorsement of the Declaration of Independence, left it to the Member States to decide on their relations with Kosovo, in accordance with national practice and international law. This was the lowest common denominator, but Slovenia's Foreign Minister Rupel was deeply relieved. He commented: 'we managed to see a uniformed decision, a unified stance and [. . .] we protected the unity of the EU'.[10] However, most importantly, the inability to reach a common decision on recognizing Kosovo did not disrupt the general framework of European engagements in the area, though the deployment of an EULEX mission to Kosovo, agreed upon already at the Council meeting on 16 February (thus prior to Kosovo's declaration of independence), was delayed until an agreement on handover of assets between the UNMIK and EULEX was reached in August 2008.

After the failed attempt to sign the SAA with Serbia in January, an offer for a political agreement was put forward (initiated by the British and the Dutch governments, causing outrage in the Slovenian administration), but rejected (to the relief of many who feared a precedent being made)[11] by the Serbian government. A new compromise was reached within the EU that would allow for the signing of the agreement, but subjecting its ratification by the Member States to their acknowledgement of the satisfactory co-operation of Serbia

[10] Quoted in 'EU Fudges Kosovo Independence Recognition', available at: «http://EUobserver.com», 18 February 2008.
[11] Author interview, Council General Secretariat, Brussels, 11 June 2008.

with the Hague Tribunal (Fink-Hafner and Lajh, 2008, pp. 51–2). The SAA was finally signed on 29 April in Luxembourg, controversially as Serbia was only weeks away from general elections and the prime minister was opposing the agreement. The so-called 'European option' won the elections in Serbia and a pro-European government was formed.

Slovenia undoubtedly worked most on the Western Balkan dossier during its term in office, having started working on its strategy towards the region in mid-2005. It tried to balance its stance towards Serbia and Kosovo through several visits to the region by the foreign minister, in 2007, assuring Serbia that it would work hard on its approximation to the EU, but also making the conditions for such steps clear to all states: Serbia's co-operation with the Hague Tribunal, Bosnia and Herzegovina's adoption of police reform and Macedonia's compliance with the preset conditions for the opening of the accession negotiations. Prime Minister Janša appealed to the European Council and the Secretary-General of the Council, Javier Solana, in a letter of September 2007, to speed up the process for both Serbia and Bosnia and Herzegovina. The foreign minister pushed hard for the speedy signing of the SAA with Bosnia and Herzegovina, after the latter adopted an agreement on a (considerably weakened) police reform, and the wording of the Declaration on the Western Balkans attached to the Presidency Conclusions of the Brussels European Council in June. These targets at times appeared unachievable, but the end result in terms of the goals set was positive: the ring of SAAs was concluded, the visa liberalization road map talks began with all states and the Declaration was attached to the Brussels European Council Presidency Conclusions. In addition, the numerous sectoral initiatives and programmes launched or advanced during the Slovenian Presidency meant that the Western Balkans would not slide down the EU agenda after the close of the Slovene Presidency.

Conclusions: Symbolic or Substantive Achievements?

Did Slovenia live up to the three symbolic challenges? Yes. It managed to run EU business as smoothly as usual and it set its mark on the EU club, thus proving that it had learned the community game. Apart from the above issues, numerous projects on a smaller scale were initiated or brought forward. The common agricultural policies health check was well under way, the neighbourhood policy, including its migration aspect, balanced. The vast majority of the Member States ratified the Lisbon Treaty, but this achievement became less important after the Irish 'no'. The lead was clearly taken to reach unity over the negotiating mandate for the long overdue new agreement with the

Russian Federation and negotiations were formally launched at the EU–Russia Summit in June.[12] Slovenia kept relations with Africa and Asian regions on the agenda, thus ensuring continuity and acting in good faith with its partners in the trio team presidency.

The picture is rather different as regards the substantive challenges. The Slovenian Presidency clearly revealed that there were limits to its reach. It concentrated on one aspect of the Lisbon Strategy only and it did not engage with the financial instability. Whether the result of smallness or newness, Slovenia was not equipped to cope with several broader issues, to initiate big projects or to engage with complex policies and to push the integration agenda further when the opportunity arose. However, it never aspired or pretended that it could do all this. Where its potential as a small presiding Member State might have been best exploited is in the field of foreign policy. In its role of external representative, beyond questions of the Western Balkans, it was largely preoccupied with form, but close co-operation with the Council General Secretariat meant that it could be said that Slovenia did a good job, which should give some clues as to the future governance of the Union. The presiding state, no matter how big or small, old or new, inevitably has its own agenda and it pushes (with varying degrees of success) for the adoption of the legislative[13] or political decisions it deems important for its own sake, but the permanent leadership structures in place, such as the High Representative for Common Foreign and Security Policy, make sure that the EU as a whole carries on without digression.

References

Armstrong, K., Begg, I. and Zeitlin, J. (2008) 'JCMS Symposium: EU Governance After Lisbon'. *JCMS*, Vol. 46, No. 2, pp. 413–50.

Behrens, A. and Egenhofer, C. (2008) 'Energy Policy for Europe: Identifying the European Added-Value'. CEPS Task Force Report (Brussels: Centre for European Policy Studies).

Bojinović, A. (2005) 'Geographical Proximity and Historical Context as a Basis of Active Foreign Policy Strategy of Small European Sates – the Case of Austria and Slovenia Regarding the Western Balkans'. *Politics in Central Europe*, Vol. 1, No. 1, pp. 8–29.

Commission of the European Communities (2007a) 'Keeping up the pace of change – Commission's December 2007 Strategic Report'. COM (2007) 803 final, Brussels, 11 December 2007.

---

[12] For a detailed account of Slovenia's efforts into reaching the unity over the negotiating mandate see Kajnč (2008).

[13] For an analysis of the presiding state's influence over the legislative procedure, see Thomson (2008).

Commission of the European Communities (2007b) 'Green Paper: The European research area: New perspectives'. COM(2007) 161 final, 4 April 2007.

Commission of the European Communities (2008a) '20 20 by 2020: Europe's climate change opportunity'. COM(2008) 30 final, 23 January 2008.

Commission of the European Communities (2008b) 'Commission puts forward proposals to the European Council on sovereign wealth funds and financial stability'. (IP/08/13), 27 February 2008.

Council of the European Union (2008a) 'Presidency Conclusions'. Brussels European Council, 13–14 March 2008 (7652/1/08 REV 1).

Council of the European Union (2008b) '2875th Council Meeting, Transport, Telecommunications and Energy Council'. Luxembourg, 6 June 2008, 10310/08 (Presse 162).

European Parliament (2008) 'Slovenia takes over EU presidency: prime minister addresses European Parliament'. Post-briefing item, 21 January.

Fink-Hafner, D. and Lajh, D. (2008) 'The 2008 Slovenian EU Presidency. A New Synergy for Europe? A Midterm Report'. SIEPS 2008:2op. (Stockholm: SIEPS).

Kajnč, S. (2008) 'Slovenian Presidency: How the 16th Member State Performed'. ARI 105/2008, Real Instituto Elcano, Madrid. Available at: «www.realinstitutoelcano.org/wps/portal/rielcano_eng».

Thomson, R. (2008) 'The Council Presidency in the European Union'. *JCMS*, Vol. 46, No. 3, pp. 593–618.

The French Presidency

RENAUD DEHOUSSE
Sciences-Po, Paris

ANAND MENON
University of Birmingham

'In Paris, Nicolas, you are like the Sun King. But Europe is like Germany,
a coalition of diverging interests. You need a lot of patience and skill.'

Angela Merkel, quoted in *The Times*, 1 July 2008

Introduction

Patience is perhaps not the most prominent personal attribute of Nicolas
Sarkozy. Perhaps happily, therefore, the French Presidency of the second half
of 2008 was nothing if not eventful. Confronted immediately prior to its
formal launch with the Irish rejection of the Lisbon Treaty on 12 June 2008,
Paris subsequently had to deal not only with repercussions of the Russian
invasion of Georgia, but also the disintegration of the international financial
system following the collapse of Lehman Brothers on 15 September. And
crises, as it turned out, required a kind of leadership much more in keeping
with the style of the French President. As John Thornill suggested in the
Financial Times, 'France's six-month presidency of the European Union has
been declared a triumph, most vocally by Nicolas Sarkozy, but by a few others
as well'.[1] Indeed, the Presidency has attracted widespread praise from other
European leaders: Italy's Silvio Berlusconi labelled it 'extraordinary', Irish
Taoiseach Brian Cowen 'excellent'.

How, then, to assess this turbulent six-month period? A Presidency can, in
part, be judged in terms of its effectiveness when it comes to delivering its

[1] *Financial Times*, 24 December 2008.

programme. After all, considerable diplomatic and administrative skill is required to ensure that both the Council of Ministers and European Council function effectively and anticipated outcomes are secured. However, it is not enough simply, as previous observers have done, to focus on the administrative functions of the Presidency (Maurer, 2008), or its effectiveness in 'uploading' national preferences onto the EU agenda (Ferreira-Pereira, 2008). After all, and particularly since the advent of the 'trio' system, the tortuous pace of much EU decision-making means that a Presidency can only really accomplish objectives devised and set by others.[2] As one former French Minister for Europe put it, the Member State holding the Presidency 'reaps what others have sowed and sows what others will reap' (Lamassoure, 2008). Thus, in order to provide an overall assessment, we cast our net somewhat wider, taking into account the ability of a Presidency to respond to, and co-ordinate EU responses to, the unexpected.

Consequently, we divide our analysis into three parts. Section I explores the ability of the Presidency to achieve its stated objectives. Section II examines its success in dealing with the crises that beset it. The final section considers the potential impact of the French period in office on the EU governance structure and its longer-term implications for the Union.

Our conclusions are mixed. It is hard to deny either that the Presidency accomplished most of the objectives it set itself prior to July 2008, or that this required considerable diplomatic fleetness of foot. Moreover, both the personality of the French President and the resources at his disposal proved well suited to the demands of incipient crises. The Union proved itself capable of often frenetic action in the face of external challenges. Yet the implications of what was achieved are mixed at best, particularly if attention is paid not merely to the fact of EU activity but also to the nature, and ultimate consequences, of these actions.

I. Presidency Priorities

One of the declared priorities of Nicolas Sarkozy was the restoration of the credibility of France in Europe, which had been somewhat eroded by the 2005 referendum. To this end, Jean-Pierre Jouyet, former *chef de cabinet* of Commission President Jacques Delors, was appointed as Secretary of State for European Affairs. He was charged with two missions: to help find a solution to the constitutional *impasse* sparked by the Irish rejection of the Lisbon Treaty, and to lay the groundwork for a successful Presidency in 2008.

---

[2] On average, it takes some 18 months from the moment when a Commission proposal is transmitted to the Council to its eventual adoption by the Parliament and the Council; see Dehousse *et al.* (2006).

The first of these was achieved rapidly, as President Sarkozy managed to convince Angela Merkel (then president-in-office of the EU), that the draft constitution should be abandoned in favour of a seemingly more modest 'Reform Treaty', later signed in Lisbon. In terms of the second, Paris was mindful of the widespread criticism directed at the Presidency of 2000, which had culminated in what was widely regarded as a fiasco at Nice. The government therefore invested considerable time and resources in advance planning. This was visible, *inter alia*, in the intensive contacts maintained with European partners and in the increased governmental presence in Brussels – where Jouyet was instructed to spend two days a week. The priority areas highlighted by Paris also bore the hallmarks of this careful preparation. Several were prominent on the longer-term agenda of the EU: energy and climate have featured high on the list of EU priorities since clear emissions reduction objectives (the so-called three 20s) were agreed in 2007. The idea of carrying out mid-term 'health checks' on the common agricultural policy was approved during the bad-tempered nego-tiations culminating in the 2007–13 financial perspective. Finally, the need to enhance the ability of Member States to deploy troops abroad has been a central element of the discourse on European defence for a decade or more.

As we shall see, however, although Paris could argue with some justifi-cation that its stated objectives were largely long-standing European ones, this was not always the case. Moreover, French preferences were not always representative of the mainstream views of their partners.

Immigration

In terms of immigration policy, for instance, Paris initiated and directed a process culminating in the signing of a European Pact on Immigration and Asylum. Negotiations had been started by the French government several months prior to the Presidency, the idea of the pact having been floated by Nicolas Sarkozy at a meeting of Interior Ministers in September 2006. A draft text, presented to the Justice and Home Affairs Council on 7 July 2008, prioritized three areas: a refusal of *en masse* regularizations of illegal immi-grants, the harmonization of asylum policies and rules for the return of illegal immigrants. The text was approved by the JHA Council in September 2008 and by the European Council the following month.

The French proposals, however, did not elicit unanimous support. The Spanish government in particular voiced concerns at plans for compulsory 'integration contracts' under which immigrants would agree to adopt 'national and European values' and learn the national language. Ultimately, the proposal did not figure in the text finally approved. Moreover, the provisions of the pact are merely declaratory, having no legal force.

All this being said, however, and whilst in no way signalling our approval of the rather punitive and restrictive approach to immigration implied by the Pact, its ultimate adoption represented a clear success for the incumbent Presidency. That Paris managed to initiate, draft and secure unanimous consent over a policy that reflected so clearly the priorities of its President was no mean feat.

Defence

Strengthening the European Security and Defence Policy (ESDP) was another key priority of the Presidency (Dimitrakopoulos *et al.*, 2009). As early as September 2007, *Le Monde* was claiming that the President was planning a 'Saint Malo mark two'.[3] Explicitly stated ambitions included an impressive list of the kinds of operations the Union should be able to carry out simultaneously (Kouchner, 2008),[4] and the creation of a defence 'G6' that would take the lead in forging ahead in co-operation on defence matters (Lellouche, 2008).

Proposals for ESDP were, however, an early victim of the Irish rejection of the Lisbon Treaty, in that the G6 plan was premised on the treaty's provisions for Permanent Structured Co-operation. In other areas, however, Paris proved itself willing to compromise on traditional elements of French policy in order to achieve progress. President Sarkozy indicated, in an interview with the *New York Times*,[5] that he would be willing to consider a French return to the integrated military structures of Nato in return for real progress on the ESDP. Similarly, whilst frequently accused in the past of pursuing 'symbolic' progress in ESDP via, for instance, the creation of an EU operational Headquarters – which some claim was a central issue prior to July 2008 (Vinocur, 2008) – it is interesting to note that French negotiators did not pursue such an objective at the final European Council of the Presidency, preferring instead to focus on mechanisms for improving European military capabilities.

Ambitious statements of intent in terms of capabilities development have elicited positive assessments in the academic literature (Howorth, 2009); in particular, the December 2008 Presidency Conclusions marked another step

[3] *Le Monde*, 13 September 2007.
[4] Kouchner demanded that the EU be able, simultaneously, to carry out: two important military stabilization and reconstruction operations, with up to 10,000 men for a period of at least two years; two rapid reaction operations, using battlegroups (around 1,500 troops); an emergency evacuation of European nationals; a surveillance or maritime or air interdiction mission; a civilian-military humanitarian assistance operation lasting up to 20 days; all along with ten or so civilian missions (police/justice) of variable size, including a larger, longer one.
[5] *New York Times*, 24 September 2008.

on the path to the acceptance by all Member States of the necessity of accepting the pooling of some military hardware (Howorth, 2009). Yet the history of ESDP is replete with yawning chasms between stated intentions and practical outcomes (Menon, 2009; Witney, 2008). Moreover, and for all the stated attachment to a more effective ESDP, the French Presidency signally failed to persuade its partners of the need to intervene when renewed fighting broke out in the Democratic Republic of Congo in late 2008. This was despite the fact that the crisis seemed tailor-made for the deployment of the newly created EU battlegroups, not least as the UN Secretary General specifically requested intervention on this scale (Menon, 2009).

Energy and Climate Change

In January 2008, the European Commission presented a climate action and renewable energy package setting out its 'three 20' objectives: a reduction in greenhouse gas emissions, the improvement of energy efficiency and an increase in the share of renewable energy sources – all by 20 per cent. The following March, the European Council declared that the binding national targets required to allow the Union to meet its overall goals should be agreed upon by the end of that year.

This confronted the Member State holding the Presidency in the second half of 2008 with a problem, as it was responsible for securing agreement on how the work of meeting these targets would be divided between Member States. As if this were not enough, virtually all these Member States were dissatisfied with some aspect of the targets themselves.[6] Moreover, what had always promised to be a contentious set of negotiations was rendered all the more so by the global financial crisis. Central and east European states in particular expressed concerns about the implications of proposed reductions in greenhouse emissions for their economies and for their reliance on Russian energy exports. At the October 2008 European Council meeting, Italy and Poland threatened to veto the whole package.

Nevertheless, a deal was secured between Heads of State and Government in December 2008. Certainly, the agreement reached has been the object of much criticism, not least because those sectors deemed to be at significant risk of carbon leakage (that is, those in which the costs of the emissions trading scheme might lead firms to relocate outside the EU) will receive emissions permits free of charge, amounting, according to some estimates, to around 90 per cent of European manufacturing. Moreover, there is real doubt as to whether the Member State 'principals' really deserve credit for carrying off the negotiations. In a lively account of the negotiations in the European

---

[6] *EUobserver*, 30 June 2008.

Council, former Secretary of State Jean-Pierre Jouyet underlines how Heads of State and Government, unable to master the technicalities of the *dossier*, gave free rein to their experts to thrash out a deal (Jouyet and Coignard, 2009).

For all this, however, given the difficult economic climate and the public anxieties voiced by several Member States about the environmental package, the very fact that agreement was reached at all – swiftly followed by approval in the European Parliament – represented something of an achievement on the part of the Presidency which brokered the deal at, and immediately before, the summit.

Barcelona Process: Union for the Mediterranean

The idea of a new partnership with Mediterranean countries was launched by Nicolas Sarkozy in 2007 (this section draws heavily on Dimitrakopoulos *et al.*, 2009). However his initial plan for a Mediterranean Union was clumsy, divisive and poorly handled. The original proposals foresaw the new body being funded through the EU budget whilst not including all Member States. They also entailed the creation of a structure that would exist and operate alongside the EU's neighborhood policy and the Barcelona process, a notion the German government rejected outright.[7]

Ultimately, the fact that agreement was reached on a form of the French proposal was due largely to the skill of Merkel in brokering a compromise. Indeed, the final agreement was hailed in some quarters as her triumph.[8] In essence, what had originally appeared to be a French project aiming to associate Mediterranean states under French leadership was transformed into a European project involving these states and the EU in its entirety. The shift in emphasis was neatly encapsulated in the change of designation from Sarkozy's preferred Mediterranean Union to Barcelona Process: Union for the Mediterranean.[9]

II. Crises

The Lisbon Treaty

Immediately prior to the formal launch of the French Presidency, the Irish people rejected the Lisbon Treaty, creating a difficult situation for the

[7] *Le Monde*, 16 February 2008.
[8] *Les Echos*, 14 March 2008.
[9] Alfred Gusenbauer, then Austrian Chancellor, was quick to note, with a dose of irony, that 'It is important for this to be a European project. We're not in the habit of arranging things only for a few Member States' (*Le Monde*, 15 March 2008, p. 9).

French, whose own electorate had derailed the Constitutional Treaty only a few years previously. From the first, President Sarkozy made it clear that the Presidency would be closely involved in attempting to resolve the issue. While declaring that one country could not prevent ratification from going ahead, he announced that he intended to work closely with the Irish government to find a solution. Indeed he travelled twice to Dublin and met repeatedly with Irish leaders. In July, he announced to the European Parliament that the Presidency would come up with a solution 'in October or in December'.

Although the Irish government failed in its stated ambition to propose a solution to the October European Council, progress was made in December. Following the presentation of the views of the Irish government, the Member States agreed that legal guarantees would be given (probably in the form of a protocol to be ratified together with the Croatian Accession Treaty) in response to Irish concerns on issues such as neutrality and taxation, while ensuring that each Member State retained a European Commissioner. This subtle compromise made it possible to go ahead with the Lisbon Treaty without the need for re-ratification in states that had already approved it (an idea to which the British government among others was adamantly opposed). In return for these concessions, the Irish government committed itself to holding a second popular vote 'by the end of the term of the current Commission'.

Paris thus accomplished all that could reasonably have been expected of it in terms of dealing with an unforeseen problem that had initially threatened to blight the whole Presidency. Here again, though, the eventual agreement owed as much to the ability of technical experts in the Council Secretariat to carve out a compromise as to political leadership.

Georgia

During the night of 7 August 2008, Georgia launched a military attack on South Ossetia. In response, Russia invaded Georgia. The French President immediately signalled his resolve to play an active role in attempting to resolve the crisis. On 12 August he travelled to Moscow to negotiate a ceasefire on behalf of the Union. On 1 September he convened an extraordinary meeting of the European Council to discuss the crisis, returning to Moscow and Tbilisi a week later, where he managed to obtain a partial Russian withdrawal. Subsequently, he persuaded his partners to agree to the deployment of an EU force to monitor the Russian withdrawal within 20 days – a timetable that was respected as 200 monitors were dispatched.

Following the crisis, Sarkozy emphasized the leading role the EU had played in solving the crisis,[10] while Vladimir Putin himself stressed the great peace-making role the French President had played.[11] The Union's reaction to the war, spearheaded by Sarkozy himself, did illustrate an ability to act and undertake relatively effective damage limitation. Yet there are grounds for scepticism concerning claims that the crisis marked the birth of the *Europe politique* for which French leaders have long been yearning (Jouyet and Coignard, 2009). Certainly, the French President was quick to take responsibility for the handling of the crisis, and his activism ensured a leading role for the Union in helping bring an end to it. Whether this is really what stopped the Russian tanks 40 kilometres from Tbilisi is another matter entirely. At the same time, the invasion and *de facto* annexation of parts of a sovereign European state engaged in a partnership with the Union can hardly be seen as a triumph for the latter and were indicative of its inability to influence the actions of the most powerful states in matters of international security (Menon, 2009).

The Global Financial Crisis

The global financial crisis burst into the open with the collapse of American Bank Lehman Brothers on 15 September 2008 (Quaglia *et al.*, this volume). This was swiftly followed by the collapse of Fortis and calls for state intervention in support of the ailing banking sectors in France and the UK. Once again, the Presidency was quick to react. And once again, a succession of meetings were convened: Sarkozy summoned a meeting of the G4 (i.e. the four Member States represented in the G8), then a gathering of the leaders of euro area countries (with British Prime Minister Gordon Brown as a star guest), followed by an extraordinary meeting of the European Council in October. He then flew to Washington to convince US President George W. Bush to convene an unprecedented meeting of the world's largest 20 economies. At a further informal summit called for 7 November, European leaders reached broad agreement on a common position to adopt on that occasion. Later the same month, the European Commission proposed a stimulus package involving tax and infrastructure plans.

Clearly it is somewhat early to provide a definitive judgement on the effectiveness of the Union's response to the crisis. What is obvious, however, is that the high-profile activity of Sarkozy managed at least to give the impression that EU governments were engaged and intended to achieve a high

[10] *Le Figaro*, 18 August 2008.
[11] *Le Figaro*, 13 September 2008.

degree of co-ordination. Again, however, it is far from clear that all ths amounts to effective leadership. The initial reactions of the Presidency were far from convincing. Because of German reluctance, the G4 meeting failed to agree on a co-ordinated action plan and irritated a number of (not necessarily small) Member States that had not been invited. Inspiration for the action plan to rescue an ailing banking sector via a mixture of state guarantees and cash injections clearly came from the Brown Plan, rather from anything devised in Paris. Co-ordination, moreover, had its limits. Disputes between France, Germany and Britain over an EU stimulus plan effectively stymied attempts to go beyond purely national responses to the unfolding economic crisis. Not only did national assessments of the nature and scale of the crisis differ, but widely varying fiscal situations meant governments enjoyed differing margins of manoeuvre. Nevertheless, the presidency's energetic reaction at least prevented the development of 'beggar-thy-neighbour' policies – which could not have been ruled out as the crisis erupted.

Implications

Many commentators have concluded that the six-month period between July and December 2008 reaffirmed the potential benefits that a permanent President of the European Council would provide. Sarkozy himself echoed such claims, arguing in an article in *Le Figaro*[12] that the Union would have reacted more effectively to the Russian invasion of Georgia if the Lisbon Treaty had been in effect (as a permanent chair of the European Council he could have acted alongside Heads of State and Government).

Such claims are at best debatable. For one thing, the relative effectiveness of the Presidency in addressing the various crises that assailed it owed much both to the personality of its Head of State and to the significant political and diplomatic resources that France as a large Member State could bring to bear. Moreover, the experience of the Presidency does not suggest that powerful Member States would necessarily defer to EU institutions. Sarkozy himself largely ignored the EU's foreign policy chief, Javier Solana, during their trip to Moscow to finalize the ceasefire between Russia and Georgia. And the Commission, willingly or not, appeared only backstage during initial reactions to the financial crisis.

Indeed, a broader consequence of the Presidency was a slide towards further Member State dominance over the workings of the Union. The danger signs were there from the start, as the *Élysée* launched an unprecedented *ad hominem* attack on Commissioner Mandelson for allegedly selling out European farmers during WTO negotiations. Meanwhile, a spokesman castigated

[12] *Le Figaro*, 18 August 2008.

the ECB decision to raise interest rates as 'at best pointless, at worst totally counter-productive'.[13] Similarly, Sarkozy's original plan for a Mediterranean Union was premised on the idea that it could be funded out of the EU budget whilst being open only to certain Member States – indicative of a profound contempt for the working methods of European integration (not shared as it turned out by several of his partners).

In more substantive terms, for all the breathless praise of the EU's role in crafting continental and global reactions to the international financial crisis, many of the individual measures taken at national level – including bail-outs of banks and specific industries – also called into question core aspects of the *acquis* on state aids or the stability pact. Thus, in many respects, it can be argued that the events of the semester favoured an approach closer to the 'leadership of the large' model advocated by France than to the rules-based approach traditionally backed by Germany.

However, the Presidency is also meant to play a brokering role between Member States, fostering consensus rather than simply promoting its own interests. Early rhetoric by the Sarkozy administration made much of the fact that 'in Europe France is determined to be a team player!' (Sarkozy, 2008a). Actions, however, often contradicted such conciliatory rhetoric. Thus, although the French government chose to make the launch of its Mediterranean Union a central element of the presidency, Heads of State and Government were invited to participate in a launch planned to coincide with the celebration of Bastille Day, thus creating the impression of a French initiative with predominantly national objectives. Moreover, even before the start of the Presidency, Paris indicated clearly its willingness to ignore the sensibilities of particularly its smaller partners. The Slovenian government saw the launch of its Presidency overshadowed by a press conference (8 January) at which Sarkozy outlined the priorities of the French Presidency. The Slovenian prime minister was left to inform MEPs that his presidency would not be as 'grandiose as France'.

A suspicion that Paris could treat its smaller partners in particular with some arrogance was merely reinforced as Estonia, Latvia, Lithuania and Poland criticized Sarkozy's willingness to sign up to a ceasefire agreement between Moscow and Tbilisi that did not mention the inviolability of Georgian territorial integrity. Some months later, the French President was forced to apologize for having declared at the November EU–Russia summit that Czech and Polish plans to participate in the American anti-missile shield would contribute nothing to their security. Tensions between Paris and Prague continued to smoulder as Sarkozy hinted at his desire to continue to chair the

---

[13] *Financial Times*, 1 July 2008.

Eurogroup at Heads of State and Government level after the end of the French Presidency.[14] Meanwhile the decision to send a parallel French diplomatic mission to the Middle East during the Gaza crisis in early 2009 – as the Czech foreign minister was there representing the EU – provoked criticism from several Member States.

The sense of crisis that pervaded the French Presidency meant that France's partners tended to go along with its initiatives rather than protest at the heavy-handed manner with which Paris tended to pursue them. Yet the fact that several smaller Member States emerged from the Presidency with a sense of resentment against what was often seen as bullying behaviour by the large state in the chair will certainly not facilitate consensus-building in more representative periods of EU activity.

Conclusions

What, then, to make of this 12th French Presidency of the EEC/EC/EU? A first lesson to be drawn concerns the way that France approaches its relations with the European Union. The six months between July and December 2008 underline all too clearly that France and the French care more about the EU when they have a sense of leading it. This was particularly true of the French President, who made it clear that he relished his time chairing the European Council.[15] The flip side of this, of course, is the question as to whether Sarkozy's France will be as effective as simply one partner among 27. His Gaza trip served to illustrate the potential problems that can arise when more than one capital aspires to lead.

It was not only the position of EU President that suited Sarkozy. His style of governing is more attuned to crises than to the normal pace of EU governance. During the Presidency, even the supposedly routine work of managing initiatives launched by his predecessors – such as the completion of negotiations over the environmental package – took on something of a crisis feel. And he reacted with the frenetic activism that has come to be his hallmark. Arguably only he amongst all European leaders could have reacted with the energy that characterized the Presidency's responses to the various challenges that confronted it.

No one could accuse the Union of failing to put its head above the parapet during any of the successive crises that engulfed it. What the Presidency did accomplish were visible EU reactions. A solution was found to the 'Irish problem'. High-profile diplomacy was followed by the despatch of monitors

[14] *Le Monde*, 22 October 2008.
[15] 'I have very much enjoyed the work,' he told the European Parliament in December 2008 (Sarkozy, 2008b).

to Georgia. A series of summits were held to discuss reactions to the financial crisis. Moreover, the hectic agenda that developed during Sarkozy's six months in the chair meant that there was little time for discussion on those issues where there was real potential for discord, such as the future of the Turkish membership application or of the CAP.[16]

Yet whilst such activity was doubtless impressive, the common denominator of it all was reactive measures. The EU could not restore the *status quo ante* in Georgia and its reaction to the economic crisis amounted to little more than *ex post facto* attempts to co-ordinate between Member States that initially did their own thing. The Presidency thus proved better at organizing action than at solving the problems at hand. And indeed the fact that EU action gained such high profile at all was itself partly down to contingent factors in that the United States was far less active than usual, led by a lame duck President and increasingly preoccupied with its own election campaigns.[17] In contrast, Sarkozy operated within a highly permissive domestic political environment, with the centre right occupying the Presidency and having a legislative majority.

Some credit should certainly go to Sarkozy for inventiveness: organizing a Eurogroup meeting at the level of Heads of State and Government on 12 October and inviting Gordon Brown to attend were both original initiatives. The manner in which he chaired the European Council – with less time permitted for declaratory statement by participants – was largely perceived as an improvement. Yet it is hard to avoid the feeling that in a complex system such as the EU, long-term impact is at least as much a matter of careful preparation and systematic co-ordination with key partners as of flamboyant leadership. In other words, whether the French Presidency will have a lasting positive impact on the evolution of the Union remains to be seen.

References

Dehousse, R., Deloche-Gaudez, F. and Duhamel, O. (2006) *Elargissement: Comment l'Europe s'adapte* (Paris: Presses de Sciences Po).
Dimitrakopoulos, D.G., Menon, A. and Passas, A.G. (2009) 'France and the EU under Sarkozy: Between European Ambitions and National Objectives?' *Modern & Contemporary France*, Vol. 18, No. 4.

---

[16] In both cases, however, Paris did not hesitate to express its opinions. Sarkozy made it clear, in a speech to the European Parliament in July 2008 that, without ratification of the Lisbon Treaty, France would block further enlargement ('If we remain with Nice, it is a Europe of 27'). On agriculture, interviews with officials in both London and Paris revealed that the French government would have reacted strongly to any WTO deal in December 2008 that challenged the CAP.

[17] As the Economist put it 'it is easier to behave like an alpha-male leader with a lame-duck American president' (*The Economist*, 23 October 2008).

Ferreira-Pereira, L.C. (2008) 'Portugal and the 2007 EU Presidency: A Case of Constructive Bridge-Building'. *JCMS*, Vol. 46, s1, pp. 61–70.

Howorth, J. (2009) 'Quelles Avancées Pour la Politique Européenne de Sécurité et de Défense (PESD)?'. *Annuaire Française des Relations Internationales, 2009*.

Jouyet, J.-P. and Coignard, S. (2009) *Une Presidence de Crises* (Paris: Albin Michel).

Kouchner, B. (2008) 'EU–Nato seminar – Opening speech by Bernard Kouchner, Minister of Foreign and European Affairs (excerpts)'. Available at «www.ambafrance-UK.org/EU-NATO-seminar-Bernard-kouchner-s.html».

Lamassoure, A. (2008) 'Le Grand Retour de la France en Europe'. *La Revue Internationale et Stratégique*, Vol. 69.

Lellouche, P. (2008) 'Huit Propositions pour Donner à l'Union une Défense Commune'. *Le Figaro*.

Maurer, A. (2008) 'The German Council Presidency: Managing Conflicting Expectations'. *JCMS*, Vol. 46, s1, pp. 51–9.

Menon, A. (2009) 'Empowering Paradise? ESDP at Ten'. *International Affairs*, Vol. 85, No. 2, pp. 227–46.

Sarkozy, N. (2008a) 'Sixteenth Ambassadors' Conference, Speech by Nicolas Sarkozy, President of the Republic'. Paris.

Sarkozy, N. (2008b) 'Discours de Le Président de la République, Parlement Européen'. Strasbourg.

Vinocur, J. (2008) 'Sarkozy has a Chance to Leave a Big Mark on Europe through EU Slot'. *International Herald Tribune*.

Witney, N. (2008) *Re-energizing Europe's Security and Defence Policy*. European Council for Foreign Relations.

JCMS 2009 Volume 47 Annual Review pp. 113–132

Institutions and Governance: Saving the Lisbon Treaty – An Irish Solution to a European Problem

DESMOND DINAN
George Mason University

Introduction

The result of the June 2008 Irish referendum on the ratification of the Lisbon Treaty – 53.4 per cent against; 46.6 per cent in favour; with a turnout of 53.4 per cent – was another stunning rebuke of the European Union, comparable to the French and Dutch rejections of the Constitutional Treaty in 2005. Ireland's rejection of the Nice Treaty in June 2001 was a harbinger of the Lisbon result. In the event, not only did many more people vote in 2008 than in 2001, but also many more voted against the Lisbon Treaty than had voted against the Nice Treaty seven years earlier (the 'no' vote was 28 per cent larger). The outcome of the 2008 referendum could not be dismissed by claiming a low turnout or voter apathy. Instead, the result was additional, unambiguous evidence of deep-rooted dissatisfaction with the EU in Ireland and beyond. If nothing else, it confirmed the wisdom of not holding referendums in other Member States as part of the treaty ratification process.

The result of the referendum raised a number of questions. Why is the EU so unpopular? Why had eight years of discussion about treaty change and negotiation of reform, beginning with the debate on the future of Europe in 2000, left the public so far behind? Why would people whose country had benefited so much from EU membership reject a revision of the founding treaties, first in 2001, then in 2008? More concretely, given that it would have to be ratified by all Member States in order to come into effect, could the

Lisbon Treaty be saved? What effect would late ratification or, ultimately, non-ratification have on EU governance and institutions?

Few EU leaders – in national governments, the Commission and the European Parliament (EP) – had the opportunity or inclination to dwell on the fundamental question of the EU's deep unpopularity. Nor did they see the Irish result as having precipitated a crisis, although French President Nicolas Sarkozy could not refrain from using that word in his speech to the EP in July 2008 (Sarkozy, 2008). Rather, most saw it chiefly as having placed a large obstacle in the path to ratification of a treaty on which they had spent substantial time and political capital and which they were determined to implement. The referendum result posed a challenge – not necessarily 'one of the most difficult challenges in [EU] history', as EP President Hans-Gert Pöttering claimed, but a formidable challenge nonetheless.[1] Politics being the art of the possible, EU leaders would have to find a way to remove the Irish obstacle, prevent contagion to other 'high-risk' Member States, such as the Czech Republic, Poland and the United Kingdom, and ensure implementation of the treaty as soon as possible after the original target date of January 2009.

EU leaders were careful to say that they would not pressure Ireland; overt pressure to come up with a quick fix could easily have backfired, especially as 'Don't be Bullied' was a popular slogan of the 'no' campaign. However, pressing ahead with ratification in the eight other countries that had not yet ratified the treaty, in order eventually to isolate Ireland as the sole hold-out, constituted a subtle form of pressure.[2] So did statements to the effect that failure to ratify the Lisbon Treaty had put an end to enlargement, despite the fact that the Commission assured Croatia that its accession was still on track. So did frequent assertions by Sarkozy, Commission President José Manuel Barroso and others about the potential value of the Lisbon Treaty, particularly later in the year with reference to the war in Georgia and the financial crisis. So, too, did making clear from the outset that national leaders would not countenance renegotiation of the treaty. Clearly under pressure, it was up to the government in Dublin to find 'a specifically Irish solution to a European problem' (O'Brennan, 2008).

---

[1] Quoted in 'European Parliament: Ratification Must Continue'. *Europolitics*, 18 June 2008.
[2] Eight other countries had not ratified at the time of the Irish referendum: Belgium, Cyprus, Czech Republic, Italy, Netherlands, Spain, Sweden, UK; by the end of the year, apart from Ireland only the Czech Republic had yet to ratify the treaty. Although the treaty had passed through the Polish Sejm and Senate, the Polish President had not yet signed it either at the time of writing.

I. The Irish Solution

Many national leaders sympathized with Taoiseach Brian Cowen; after all, referendums on Lisbon would probably have turned out badly in several Member States. Nevertheless there were recriminations. By all accounts the Irish government had run a lacklustre campaign. Moreover, a recent change of leadership in Fianna Fáil, the main party in the ruling coalition, had distracted the government. In May 2008, only weeks before the referendum, Cowen took over as party leader and Taoiseach from Bertie Ahern, who left under a cloud of alleged financial impropriety. Ahern's lack of focus on the impending referendum and ensuing responsibility – however small – for the outcome contrasted sharply with his image in early 2004 as the man who, as president-in-office of the European Council, had rescued the Constitutional Treaty following the collapse of the Intergovernmental Conference in December 2003. The nature of Ahern's departure and his indirect contribution to the referendum result more than likely ended any hope that he might have had of becoming the first elected President of the European Council, should Lisbon be ratified.

The European Council would be instrumental in helping Ireland find a way out. Cowen had an opportunity to explain himself at the regularly scheduled meeting of the European Council in June 2008. There, EU leaders 'took stock of the situation on the basis of an initial assessment provided by the Taoiseach' and accepted Cowen's 'suggestion to come back to this issue at its meeting [in] October 2008 in order to consider [. . .] a common way forward' (Council, 2008a). The incoming French Presidency did not welcome the complication of the Irish 'no' vote. Sarkozy had been deeply involved in recasting the Constitutional Treaty in its Lisbon form; he seemed personally slighted by the Irish result. Given his voluble personality, it was difficult for Sarkozy not to let the matter rest until later in the Presidency semester. During a trip to Dublin on 21 July, he embarrassed the government and stirred up anti-Lisbon feeling by undiplomatically stating the obvious: Ireland would have to hold a second referendum.[3]

Post-referendum opinion polls identified several reasons for the success of the 'no' campaign.[4] The most prominent was lack of knowledge or understanding of the treaty, despite extensive media coverage and a vigorous effort

---

[3] *Irish Times*, 22 July 2008.
[4] See especially European Commission, 'Post-Referendum Survey in Ireland: Analytical Report', *Flash Eurobarometer 245*, July 2008; and the Irish government-sponsored survey by Millward Brown IMS, 'Post Lisbon Treaty Referendum Research Findings September 2008', available at: «http://www.dfa.ie/uploads/documents/Publications/Post per cent20Lisbon per cent20Treaty per cent20Referendum per cent20Research per cent20Findings/final per cent20- per cent20post per cent20lisbon per cent20treaty per cent20referendum per cent20research per cent20findings.pdf».

by the Referendum Commission, an independent body set up by law to ensure that voters were informed about the issues at stake.[5] Other reasons included nebulous concerns about Irish identity; apprehension that the alleged militarization of the EU would put an end to Irish neutrality; fear that the EU would somehow undermine Ireland's constitutional prohibition of abortion; worries about possible tax harmonization at high continental European levels, especially with regard to Ireland's competitive corporate tax rate of 12.5 per cent; distrust of politicians, particularly in light of persistent financial scandals and Ahern's recent resignation; and loss of influence and representation in Brussels because of a reduction in the Commission's size – a reduction already mandated by the Nice Treaty. The amount of misinformation and disinformation in Ireland about the Lisbon Treaty was staggering. There was little evidence that anyone opposed the treaty on its merits. An unlikely coalition of radical leftists, far-rightists, social conservatives, libertarians and neo-liberals, including, most notably, Libertas, a well-funded anti-Lisbon lobby group that later became a political party to contest the 2009 EP elections, preyed on the uncertainties of many of the electorate and blindsided the political and business establishment.[6]

The Lisbon Treaty was difficult to advocate because of its complexity and because it lacked a compelling rationale, such as the single market and structural funds in the case of the Single European Act, or economic and monetary union in the case of the Maastricht Treaty. It was far harder to argue for than against Lisbon, especially in short sound bites. Under the circumstances, 'If in doubt, vote no' seemed like good advice. Even with the best will in the world, which was not the case in Ireland in June 2008, 'asking a binary question about such a complex document [would] infallibly generate a profusion of doubts and objections' (Dehousse, 2008). This is a perennial problem with holding a referendum on such an issue. Voters tend to answer not the question asked but an unrelated question, such as whether they like the current government.

Regardless of the reasons for the 'no' vote, a growing realization among political and business elites that the outcome of the referendum was a disaster for Ireland helped concentrate the government's mind. A joint sub-committee of both houses of the Oireachtas (parliament) held a series of hearings in October and November 2008 'to analyse the challenges facing Ireland [. . .] following the Lisbon Treaty referendum result and to consider Ireland's future in the EU' (Oireachtas, 2008, p. 13). Testimony from Irish officials in Brussels about the extent to which the outcome diminished the country's

---

[5] See «http://www.lisbontreaty2008.ie/».
[6] For an assessment of the campaign, see Institute of International and European Affairs, 'Ireland's Future after Lisbon: Issues Options Implications', Dublin, November 2008, pp. 32–49.

standing there threw an interesting light on how governments perceive national influence within the EU. Catherine Day, as Secretary General of the Commission the most senior Irish person in the Brussels bureaucracy, claimed that 'Ireland's image in the EU has been tarnished by the "no" vote. I can see every day that it has reduced our ability to shape and influence events in the EU [. . .] Other Member States tend to view us now only through the prism of the Lisbon Treaty' (Oireachtas, 2008, pp. 23–4). According to Noel Dorr, a former Secretary General of the Department of Foreign Affairs, 'What we did has greatly weakened our influence among Member States. This matters because [. . .] influence and the ability to build alliances and coalitions within the Council have been the key to our success in the Union' (Oireachtas, 2008, p. 33). Bobby McDonagh, Ireland's Permanent Representative in Brussels, lamented that '[u]ntil earlier this year, people [thought] of Ireland as a small constructive country which has been helpful to them and so they wished only to be helpful to us. Now, without any ill-will, when they see us they think of Lisbon' (Oireachtas, 2008, p. 24).

Such testimony, not unexpected form the officials who gave it, added immeasurably to the pressure building on the government to find a way out of the morass. In its report, the sub-committee concluded that because the Lisbon result 'inhibits Ireland's ability to promote and defend its national interests at a European level [. . .] [and has caused] a sense of uncertainty about Ireland's future role in the EU [. . .] a solution must be found that keeps Ireland at the heart of Europe while respecting the democratic will of the Irish people by arranging for these concerns to be accommodated by the other Member States' (Oireachtas, 2008, p. 6).

At the October European Council, Cowen presented the results of the government's post-referendum assessment and asked for more time to propose a solution, not least because the Oireachtas sub-committee was still at work. The conclusions noted that the European Council would 'return to this matter at its meeting in December 2008 with a view to defining the elements of a solution and a common path to be followed' (Council, 2009). Nevertheless the contours of a solution were taking shape. Spurious though many of the arguments against Lisbon appeared to be, the Irish government had no choice but to take them seriously and attempt to change the minds of as many naysayers as possible by getting legally binding guarantees from the EU to allay their concerns. Cowen could not admit publicly what Irish officials conceded privately: if the European Council would agree to legally binding language in a treaty protocol to address issues raised by the anti-Lisbon side, and agree also to retain one Commissioner per Member State, the government would hold a second referendum. Irish officials began working out the details with the Council secretariat, which played a key role in resolving the problem, as it had after previous rejections of treaty change in national referendums.

The Irish government wanted a legally binding protocol rather than a political declaration in order to show that it was taking seriously the concerns of the 'no' side and also to strengthen its case that a second referendum would be substantively different from the first, even if its purpose was the same. The government was sensitive to opinion in Ireland that holding a second referendum merely because it disliked the result of the first was profoundly undemocratic. Indeed, such opinion seemed in the immediate aftermath of the June referendum to have strengthened opposition to the treaty. Other governments sympathized to some extent with Ireland and wanted the issue resolved as quickly as possible. However, none was willing to reopen the Lisbon Treaty, even by taking the seemingly innocuous step of attaching a protocol to it. Hence the decision to attach the Irish protocol not to the Lisbon Treaty but to the next amendment of the founding treaties – most likely Croatia's accession treaty. Even so, British Prime Minister Gordon Brown, under pressure from Euro-sceptics, sought clarification from the Council's legal service that the arrangement with Ireland would not in any way change the Lisbon Treaty.[7]

The 'road map' for resolving the Lisbon problem would involve a series of carefully choreographed steps. Thus, the European Council in December 2008 agreed that it would decide in due course, 'provided the Lisbon Treaty enters into force', to retain the Commission's size at one national of each Member State. The European Council also 'carefully note[d] the other concerns of the Irish people' as set out in an annex of the conclusions, and, provided the Irish government committed itself to 'seeking ratification of the Treaty of Lisbon by the end of the term of the current Commission [October 2009]', agreed that those concerns would 'be addressed to the mutual satisfaction of Ireland and the other Member States' (Council, 2009). Characteristically, Sarkozy took credit for finding the solution. In fact, the Irish government and the Council Secretariat negotiated the arrangement, albeit in close consultation with the French Presidency.

For all the political and legal manoeuvring leading up to the December summit, there could be no guarantee that a second Irish referendum would produce the desired result. Yet by the end of 2008 prospects for a successful outcome improved considerably, thanks to the global economic crisis, which hit Ireland particularly hard. Speaking in Brussels just before the December summit, Irish Foreign Minister Micheál Martin remarked that the financial

---

[7] See 'Having Obtained Legal Guarantees, Cowen Announces Second Irish Referendum'. *Europolitics*, 13 December 2008.

crisis, which 'underlined the critical value of [Ireland's] membership of the Union and the euro area', was turning Irish opinion firmly in favour of the Lisbon Treaty (Martin, 2008). The foreign minister would have been expected to draw such a conclusion from the country's sudden economic downturn. Yet anecdotal evidence buttressed his claim. According to a popular joke doing the rounds at the end of 2008, 'What is the difference between Ireland and Iceland? One letter and about six months'.[8] Although ratifying Lisbon would not make a material difference to Ireland's economic plight, it would provide some comfort by affirming the country's good fortune to be in a relatively safe port – the euro area – during a fierce financial storm. So much was opinion in Ireland changing by the end of 2008 that a second referendum seemed possible even before October 2009.

II. Institutional Implications of the Irish Solution

The conclusions of the December 2007 European Council proclaimed confidently that 'the Lisbon Treaty provides the Union with a stable and lasting institutional framework. We expect no change in the foreseeable future' (Council, 2008b). A year later, resolving the Irish problem would necessitate a number of institutional changes – some transitional, others permanent – to the Lisbon framework as originally understood by EU leaders. Regardless of unexpected developments that might require new institutional arrangements, any EU treaty would need institutional preparation before being implemented. That was especially the case for the Lisbon Treaty, whose provisions entailed considerable institutional adjustment. Accordingly, the European Council called in December 2007 for the 'necessary preparatory work [. . .] to ensure the full functioning of the Treaty as soon as it enters into force' (Council, 2008b).

Six months later, the European Council 'took note of the preparatory work carried out in line with its December 2007 conclusions' (Council, 2008a). In fact, there was little work to take note of, at least in the Council itself. Based largely on papers presented by the Council Secretariat, the Committee of Permanent Representatives had begun to consider a variety of legal-political points that needed clarification – ranging from the extension of the co-decision procedure (what to do with legislative proposals already in the pipeline?), to revised budgetary procedures, to the new procedure for appointing the Commission President, to the appointment of the new European Council President and the High Representative for Foreign Affairs and Security Policy, to the setting up and operation of the External Action Service

---

[8] Quoted in the *Financial Times*, 16 January 2009, p. 8.

– but had not progressed very far by the time of the Irish referendum in June 2008. Thereafter, preparation for implementing the Treaty became too sensitive in the Council to be conducted actively and openly.

The EP was somewhat less inhibited about planning for Lisbon. As in treaties past, the EP was a big winner in the Lisbon Treaty, which increased its legislative power (by greatly extending the scope and slightly changing the modalities of the co-decision procedure), gave it the formal right to elect the Commission President and enhanced its budgetary authority (by abolishing the distinction between compulsory and non-compulsory expenditure). Parliament relished the prospect of having more power and lost little time preparing to exercise it. In its resolution on the Lisbon Treaty, adopted by a large majority in February 2008, Parliament welcomed the treaty's institutional innovations, especially regarding co-decision. In future, the report opined, 'the public will clearly be able to see that European legislative acts are adopted by the chamber which represents them [the EP] and by the chamber which represents states [the Council of Ministers]' (European Parliament, 2008).

Because, under the terms of the Lisbon Treaty, its first reading would result in a 'position' (analogous to the Council's common position) rather than merely an 'opinion', the EP would have to ensure that all amendments adopted at that stage formed a consolidated text for incorporation into the Commission's proposal. Moreover, the applicability of co-decision to many additional policy areas, especially in Justice and Home Affairs, would mean a substantial increase in the responsibilities of several committees. Similarly, the marked addition in the number of issues over which Parliament would acquire the right of assent would increase the EP's workload.

Jean-Luc Dehaene, formerly Prime Minister of Belgium and Vice-President of the Constitutional Convention, a leading MEP in the 2004–09 parliament, began work early in 2008 on a report on the implications of the Lisbon Treaty for inter-institutional relations. Dehaene put his report on hold in June 2008, lest speculation about the institutional implications of the treaty interfere with efforts in Ireland to resolve the post-referendum problem. The Dehaene Report reappeared following the December 2008 European Council's agreement on the ratification road map and along with two others was adopted by the EP's Committee on Constitutional Affairs in March 2009 (European Parliament, 2009).

Uncertainty about the fate of the Lisbon Treaty in mid-2008 put a halt to preparations for the selection of individuals to fill the two new top-level positions stipulated in it: the standing President of the European Council, to be elected by the Heads of State and Government for a once-renewable two-and-a-half-year term, and the High Representative for Foreign Affairs, who would also be a Commission Vice-President. Despite provision in the treaty for electing the new European Council President, there was little doubt among the Heads of State and Government that the first incumbent would be chosen by consensus. Before the outcome of the Irish referendum threw implementation of the treaty off track, Sarkozy was looking forward to shepherding the selection of the European Council President and the newly designated High Representative at the December 2008 summit. As part of the package of top-level appointments, Sarkozy hoped as well to reach informal agreement in December 2008 on the nominee for next Commission President, although such an agreement is usually reached at the June summit immediately before the end of the Commission's mandate (in this case, June 2009). There was growing certainty throughout the year that Barroso would be re-nominated by the European Council and approved by the EP, unless the PES (Party of European Socialists) won a majority in the June 2009 elections and chose to confront the European Council by opposing Barroso, a centre-right politician.

During the negotiations that preceded the Constitutional Treaty, leaders of many of the small Member States, including Barroso when he was Prime Minister of Portugal, had complained about the new position of European Council President, lamenting the end of the rotating presidency and complaining that the presidency would become the preserve of the big Member States. Once the new position was included in the Constitutional Treaty and preserved in the Lisbon Treaty, Barroso, then the Commission President, changed his tune, arguing that continuity in the European Council Presidency would be 'useful' (Barroso, 2008). Yet speculation in 2008 about possible candidates suggested that the position would go to someone from a small Member State, perhaps Barroso himself, if he chose not to be reappointed Commission President, or Jean-Claude Juncker, Prime Minister of Luxembourg (although Gordon Brown reportedly strongly opposed Juncker's appointment).

In the intricate and contentious politics of EU appointment, the selection of the new High Representative came to be seen as a 'balancing item' with regard to the appointments of the Commission and European Council Presidents. Balance in the EU means not only between big and small Member States, but also between north and south, east and west, left and right, and men and women. Clearly, so many factors could not be juggled in three top-level appointments. Fortunately, there are plenty of high-level positions – such as President of the European Central Bank; directors-general in the Commission and Council secretariat; secretary-general in the Commission, Council, and EP – to even things out. As for big/small Member State balance, the likelihood of former prime ministers from small Member States filling the two top EU positions suggested that the position of High Representative would go to someone from a big Member State. Javier Solana, currently the High Representative for the Common Foreign and Security Policy, forerunner of the Lisbon Treaty position, seemed unlikely to seek appointment to it. There were no obvious alternative candidates by the end of 2008.

As Jean-Luc Dehaene pointed out, the delay in nominating the President of the European Council and the High Representative for Foreign Affairs, due to the outcome of the Irish referendum, at least had one beneficial effect. Presuming a second referendum took place and that the result was positive, the new incumbents, plus the next Commission President, would take office at about the same time in early 2010 – presuming that the European Parliament confirmed all three.[9] Had the Lisbon Treaty been implemented in January 2009, as originally planned, the High Representative who, as a Commission Vice-President, needs to be approved by the Parliament, would have had to serve on an interim basis until the new Commission took office in November 2009, the EP having made it clear that it would hold confirmation hearings in late 2008 on the High Representative to serve out the remaining months of the Barroso Commission, and then again in September or October 2009 to serve in the next Commission, even if the first incumbent was re-nominated. Needless to say, the ideal solution to the timing of these nominations and investiture proceedings would be for the second Irish referendum to take place *before* the June 2009 EP elections.

As it was, the road map approved by the European Council in December 2008 suggested that the Lisbon Treaty would be implemented in January 2010 at the earliest. Therefore, rather than have a new Commission take office, as planned, in November 2009 – a new Commission which, according to the Nice Treaty, would have fewer members than there are Member States – national leaders agreed to extend the life of the current Commission until the Lisbon-adjusted Commission could take office. There were two precedents for this: in 1992, the Delors Commission extended its term by two years in order to bring the term-in-office of the Commission into line with the five-year mandate of the EP; and in 2004 the Prodi Commission remained in office for an additional few weeks because of a delay in completing the investiture procedure for the incoming Barroso Commission.[10] These precedents demonstrated that the Commission could easily stay in office beyond its agreed term, with the Council's approval.

---

[9] See Dehaene's remarks in European Policy Center, 'The European Parliament: waiting for Lisbon'. Event Report, Brussels, 20 February 2008, available at: «http://www.epc.eu/en/er.asp?TYP=ER&LV=293&see=y&t=2&PG=ER/EN/detail&l=&AI=846».
[10] See 'Lisbon Treaty: Can Commission Extend its Mandate?' *Europolitics*, 4 October 2008.

The delay in implementing the Lisbon Treaty was far more consequential for the EP than for the Commission. Without the Treaty, which stipulated a Parliament of 750 members, plus the President (as agreed to by the European Council in October 2007), Parliament would shrink from its current 785 members – an unusually large number because the representatives from Bulgaria and Romania, which joined the EU in 2007, were added to the EP on a transitional basis – to the 736 permitted under the Nice Treaty. The EP and the 12 Member States whose parliamentary delegations were due to increase in size under the Lisbon Treaty were understandably unhappy about this. Accordingly, the European Council agreed in December 2008 to introduce the Lisbon allocation of seats as soon as possible after the treaty's implementation, following the June 2009 elections, although Germany, whose delegation was set to drop from 99 to 96 under the Lisbon Treaty, would be allowed to keep the extra three seats, thereby bringing the total number of seats for the 2009–14 Parliament eventually to 754 (Council, 2009).

Apart from its effect on the size of the institution, the EP fretted that a delay in implementing the Lisbon Treaty would mean that the procedure for appointing the Commission, a procedure that formally enhanced the power of the EP, would not be used in 2009. In particular, the EP wanted the European Council to take into account the results of the June 2009 elections when nominating the Commission President, who would then be elected by the Parliament. Confident of retaining a majority after the next election, and therefore of being able to elect Barroso to a second term, the EPP (European People's Party) eagerly championed parliamentary prerogatives and insisted that this provision of the Lisbon Treaty come into effect even before the treaty was ratified. Hopeful that they might win a majority, and equally insistent on parliamentary prerogatives, the PES pushed also for immediate implementation of the new procedure. The European Council agreed, and attached a declaration to the December conclusions stating that 'the appointment of the future Commission, in particular the designation of its President, will be initiated without delay after the European Parliament elections of June 2009' (Council, 2009).

Other institutional adjustments necessitated by the delay in implementing the Lisbon Treaty concerned transitional measures for the elected President of the European Council and the High Representative for Foreign Affairs, who would chair the newly configured Foreign Affairs Council. The European Council agreed in December 2008 that if the treaty entered into force in January 2010 or later, the country in the Presidency at that time would continue in office until the end of the semester, and that the country next in line for the rotating presidency would be responsible for changing to the new presidency arrangement and also for transitioning to the system for chairing the Foreign Affairs Council (Council, 2009).

The most important institutional implication of the Irish solution concerned the composition of the European Commission. The Commission's size has been a sensitive issue since the founding of the original Communities. In the mid-1990s, with numerous central and eastern European countries eager to join the EU, the question of the Commission's size assumed immense political importance in the run-up to the Amsterdam Treaty. National governments failed to resolve it then. After difficult negotiations they agreed three years later in the Nice Treaty that, once the EU enlarged to 27 Member States, the Commission would be limited in size to two-thirds of the number of Member States. The Lisbon Treaty seemed to put an end to the issue by stipulating that the European Council would agree on a rotation system (the 'fair rotation rule') to ensure that Member States would be represented equitably in the Commission over time. Instead of being reduced in size, however, the Commission would, according to the Irish solution, continue to include one national of each Member State. The Lisbon Treaty itself contained the legal basis for maintaining the status quo. Specifically, the treaty allows the European Council, acting unanimously, to alter the 'two-thirds' arrangement.

Given the time and effort that national governments spent trying to reach agreement on reducing the Commission's size, it was surprising how quickly the European Council discarded the idea and ideal of a smaller Commission. Many governments suddenly abandoned strongly held convictions that a Commission corresponding in size to an EU of 27 or more Member States was simply unworkable. France, which had long campaigned against a large Commission, abruptly reversed direction and instead championed the principle of maintaining the size of the College at one national per Member State.

The realization, however belated, that under the originally understood Lisbon arrangement France would not always have a Commissioner, and that this could diminish French influence in the EU while also weakening the Commission's legitimacy, may help to explain the French U-turn. So may the possibility that future Commission and European Council presidents would most likely come from small Member States, thereby depriving France, whenever it did not have a Commissioner under the fair rotation rule, of representation at the highest EU levels. Speaking to the press on 15 December, Sarkozy was 'convinced' that a Commission without a French or German representative would make 'no sense'. The French President ridiculed the original Lisbon formula: 'We stop Member States from having the [rotating Council] presidency and on top of that we take from them the possibility [of having] a Commissioner [. . .] It is a conception and vision of Europe which is not mine'.[11] Yet such a conception and vision of Europe had not prevented

---

[11] Quoted in *EUObserver.com*, 16 December 2008.

Sarkozy from endorsing the idea of a smaller Commission when he helped salvage the Lisbon Treaty from the wreckage of the Constitutional Treaty in 2007.

Ironically, it was three small Member States – the Benelux countries – that objected to abandoning plans to reduce the Commission's size. They pointed out that the reason for having fewer Commissioners was to improve the institution's efficiency and that the Nice agreement was an essential part of a complicated political deal on the EU's institutional balance – the other elements being the modalities of qualified majority voting and the size and allocation of seats in the EP. Scrapping the proposed arrangement for the Commission would therefore cause an institutional imbalance in the EU. In the event, the indirect legitimacy conferred on the Commission by always having a national of each Member State, as well as the big Member States' preference for always being able to nominate a Commissioner, trumped the principle of balance and rationale of efficiency.

Ever since the era of Jacques Delors, Commission Presidents, including Barroso, have lamented the growing size of the College. Like Sarkozy, Barroso abruptly changed his mind on the Commission's size in the aftermath of the Irish referendum. Now Barroso was willing to keep a large Commission if it helped Ireland ratify the Lisbon Treaty. Contradicting earlier statements about the unacceptability of a large Commission, Barroso claimed at the end of 2008 that 'It is not a problem to have a 27-member Commission or larger as it works more effectively than with fewer members [. . .] the Commission is more effective with 27 as the more numerous we are the more we push for a compromise, that's the paradoxical effect of numbers'.[12] Barroso's about-turn might also have been due to a realization that a large Commission requires a strong president in order to be efficient. Sarkozy made exactly that point when he opined that in a larger college the Commission President 'should be active, reactive and proactive', and must be strong in order to play a 'harmonizing role'.[13]

III. Life without Lisbon

Regardless of the Irish referendum, the EU would have operated in 2008 under the terms of the Nice Treaty. One of the rationalizations for the Lisbon Treaty and the Constitutional Treaty before it was the need to simplify the cumbersome decision-making arrangements contained in the Nice Treaty, especially in view of enlargement. Nevertheless the EU has operated

---

[12] Quoted in 'Barroso backs one commissioner per country principle'. *EUObserver.com*, 9 December 2008.
[13] Quoted in *EUObserver.com*, 16 December 2008.

remarkably efficiently since the Nice Treaty came into effect, notwithstanding the accession of ten Member States in 2004 and another two in 2007. Following the agreement in December 2008 on the road map for ratification of the Lisbon Treaty, Hans-Gert Pöttering remarked that the EU needed to end its 'current institutional paralysis'.[14] The EP President was venting his frustration with the ratification delay rather than accurately describing the state of EU inter-institutional relations and decision-making. Certainly, implementation of the Lisbon Treaty would help the EU institutionally, but the current arrangements work surprisingly well.

The ambitious and complex energy-climate package agreed to by the European Council and the EP in December 2008 is evidence of the effectiveness of decision-making in the enlarged, Lisbon-less EU, not least because of the agility and innovativeness of the individuals and institutions involved in the decision-making process. Although a fascinating case study, however, the energy-climate package is exceptional in many ways and is not necessarily a model of good decision-making. In particular, it highlights the limited influence of the Commission President, the prominence of the Council President, the willingness of the EP's leadership to cut corners for the sake of a grand bargain and the downside of rushing to reach agreement by a definite deadline.

Prompted by the European Council in March 2007, the Commission mulled over and finally introduced a raft of legislative proposals in January 2008 that aimed to reduce carbon dioxide emissions in the EU by 20 per cent by 2020, increase renewable energy use by 20 per cent and improve energy efficiency by 20 per cent (Commission, 2008). The Commission, Council and Parliament agreed to fast-track the legislative process with a view to wrapping up the package by December 2008. Barroso, whose signature policy upon becoming Commission President – the Lisbon strategy for economic modernization and reform – now seemed moribund, put the energy-climate package at the top of the Commission's agenda. Unlike the Lisbon strategy, the energy-climate package involved traditional legislative decision-making, in which the Commission has the exclusive right to introduce proposals. Accordingly, the Commission would be at the heart of the matter.

There was broad consensus within the EU on the goals of the package but not on how best to achieve them. Inevitably the issue would pit environmental organizations against business interests; divide political groups in the EP; and drive a wedge between Member States which saw themselves as environmental leaders and those seen as environmental laggards. Given the dependence of central and eastern European countries on highly polluting coal for

---

[14] Quoted in 'Freedom requires regulation, says Pöttering'. *Europolitics*, 12 December 2008.

electricity generation and the steep price of conversion to cleaner fuel – not least the security cost of switching to Russian gas – the energy-climate package risked exacerbating the east–west cleavage in the EU. The Commission's proposals were suitably circumspect and not entirely satisfactory to every Member State, business interest and non-governmental organization with a stake in the outcome. Steering such a far-reaching, momentous and potentially divisive package to completion within less than 12 months would be a Herculean task.

The French Presidency took up the challenge in July 2008 (Dehousse and Menon, this volume) and quickly eclipsed the Commission, whose influence in the co-decision procedure unavoidably diminishes once a legislative proposal leaves the Berlaymont. In this case, Sarkozy seized the initiative from Barroso, whose role was reduced to that of a cheerleader for the goal of 20-20-20 by 2020. While apparently acting in concert with Barroso, Sarkozy made it abundantly clear that he was completely in charge.

Given the sensitivity and urgency of the issue, a final agreement would have to be thrashed out in the European Council. By announcing that the European Council would supplant the relevant Council formation as the ultimate decision-making forum – in effect, that unanimity would replace qualified majority voting as the decision-making instrument – Sarkozy strengthened the hands of those Member States determined to make as many changes as possible to the Commission's original proposals. For the sake of wrapping up the package on time (December 2008), the Commission was happy to oblige.

Sarkozy suffered a setback in the European Council in October 2008 when other national leaders complained about inadequate consultation and pushed back against the proposed package. Two groups of countries demanded concessions. The first, consisting of old industrial countries such as Belgium, Italy and Germany, were primarily concerned about 'carbon leakage' – the possible relocation of energy-intensive firms to countries with less onerous and expensive climate change regulation. The second, the so-called 'Group of Nine' central and eastern European countries, wanted free allocation of emissions permits for their largely coal-fired electricity generators. By threatening, or threatening to threaten, a veto, Poland succeeded at the summit in having inserted into the conclusions a commitment that the eventual deal would '[have] regard to each Member State's specific situation' (Council, 2008c). In other words, Poland and other countries would get generous concessions in the final package.

Sarkozy spent considerable time and political capital in bilateral and plurilateral meetings with fellow national leaders in the run-up to the December European Council. The most noteworthy of these was a meeting in

Gdańsk, Poland, with the leaders of the Group of Nine. As expected, the outcome of the preparatory negotiations, and of the European Council itself, was a package that, although undoubtedly important and hailed as historic by Barroso and Sarkozy, was riddled with concessions, exemptions and transition periods, and was far less impressive than what the Commission and the Council Presidency had advocated.

Having secured a political agreement in the European Council, Barroso and Sarkozy looked to the EP for swift adoption of the package at the first-reading stage of the co-decision procedure. Needless to say, the Commission, Council and Parliament had engaged in numerous inter-institutional discussions (trialogues) on the package throughout the year, culminating in a final meeting immediately after the December European Council. The EP leadership, acting mostly through the Conference of Presidents of the political groups, generally supported the scope and schedule of the proposed legislation. The main political groups were firmly on board. In the event, most MEPs (members of the EP) seemed more susceptible to their national government position than to their political group affiliation. Not surprisingly, the Greens were the exception.

Regardless of where they stood on the final package, many MEPs expressed concern about the way in which the European Council, led by an aggressive French Presidency, appeared to have hijacked the co-decision procedure. As Avril Doyle, *rapporteur* for one of the draft directives, complained, there should be 'no question of the EP accepting a European Council diktat [. . .] There is no legal provision for heads of state to be involved in the co-decision process. That there was trialogue negotiation and COREPER approval underlines that this high-level consultation was exceptional and should not in any way be seen as setting a precedent for any other co-decision issue'.[15]

The EU's eagerness to be seen as the global leader on climate change, especially before a new, comparatively more environmentally friendly US administration came into power, accounts in part for the speed and the mode of decision-making on the energy-climate package. So does Sarkozy's determination to reach an agreement during France's Council Presidency, and Barroso's desire to reach an agreement well before the end of his Commission Presidency with a view to being reappointed for a second term. While undoubtedly a significant accomplishment, the final package might

---

[15] Quoted in 'Agreement for Energy-Climate Change Package is Victory for Climate but not for Democratic Procedures, Says Parliament'. *Europolitics*, 18 December 2008; see also 'Carbon Emissions Trading Report Agreed. Avril Doyle MEP, *Rapporteur* for the European Parliament', EPP-ED Group in the European parliament Press Release, 13 December 2008, available at: «http://www.epp-ed.eu/Press/showPR.asp?PRControlDocTypeID=1&PRControlID=8128&PRContentID=14123&PRContentLg=en».

nonetheless have benefited from more time and reflection during the decision-making process. The extent to which the quality of the package suffered from the haste and manner of its adoption will be apparent in due course, possibly to the detriment of the EU's credibility as a climate change leader.

IV. Looking Ahead

National leaders, Commissioners and MEPs were acutely aware in 2008 that EP elections were due to take place in June 2009 and that the current Commission was reaching the end of its mandate. Barroso cited the energy-climate package and his stewardship late in 2008 of the European Recovery Plan as the main accomplishments of his Presidency. Apart from the shortcomings of the energy-climate package, however, the European Recovery Plan, and Barroso's reaction more generally to the global financial crisis, left a lot to be desired. Some national leaders and many MEPs criticized Barroso for failing to appreciate the seriousness of the financial situation and for not responding sooner to it. Martin Schulz, leader of the PES, scored political points by criticizing Barroso and suggesting that his caution was due, in part, to excessive deference to President Sarkozy with a view to ensuring Barroso's nomination to serve a second term as Commission President. Motivated not by political interest but by concern about the Commission's waning influence, Etienne Davignon, a former Commission Vice-President and one of the most influential elder statesmen in Brussels, took the highly unusual step of castigating Barroso publicly and urging him to restore the Commission's political prominence (Friends of Europe, 2008).

Undoubtedly Barroso was angling for reappointment as Commission President, but his leadership in 2008 reflected the political reality of limited Commission influence more than inadequate personal initiative or undue deference to national leaders. The departure of several Commissioners in 2008 for ministerial positions in their home countries demonstrated both the approaching end of the Commission's mandate and the widely held view that holding national ministerial office conferred greater prestige and power than being a member of the Commission. The most prominent instance of that – the sudden return in October 2008 of Trade Commissioner Peter Mandelson to a cabinet position in London – was a big relief to Barroso, given Mandelson's policy disagreements with France and personal difficulties with Sarkozy.

As for the Parliament, there was much joking about the collapse of the ceiling of the Strasbourg hemicycle in August 2008. Was this a sign that the EP should stay permanently in Brussels? The EP's obligation to hold monthly plenary sessions in Strasbourg is enshrined in the treaties, but makes it difficult to improve the Parliament's public image, to which MEPs paid more attention as the 2009 elections approached. More than anything else, MEPs and other EU and national officials want to reverse the trend of declining voter turnout. To that end, the EP launched a public relations campaign in 2008 to apprise voters of the institution's importance. At the same time, leaders of the two main political groups, the EPP and the PES, sharpened their attacks against each other partly in order to generate some publicity and excitement among the electorate. One of the most obvious points of contestation between them, for which the elections should be decisive, concerns the Presidency of the EP. The winning political group should surely hold the Presidency for the five-year parliamentary term. Despite his sharp criticism of Barroso and the EPP, however, PES leader Schulz made it clear throughout 2008 that he hoped to perpetuate the cosy arrangement between the EP's two largest groups to take turns – two-and-a-half years each – in the Presidency. Schulz also hinted that he wanted to be President during the PES' turn.

Such posturing is endemic in EU politics, but does not help endear the EU to a wider public. Despite the EP's new public relations campaign, sporadic and uneven media coverage of the EP, which tends to highlight the institution's idiosyncrasy rather than its importance, almost guarantees that most Europeans know little about legislative and other important accomplishments in Brussels and Strasbourg. The Irish referendum generated far more interest at home and abroad than EP elections ever will. The second Irish referendum would most likely provoke a more reasonable discussion of the Lisbon Treaty and of the implications of rejecting it, but there was little to suggest in 2008 that either the Treaty's travails or the conduct of regular EU affairs had generated greater sympathy or support for the EU as a whole.

Key Readings

Hix, S. (2008) *What's Wrong with the European Union and How to Fix it* (Cambridge: Polity Press).

Houses of the Oireachtas (2008) Sub-Committee on Ireland's Future in the European Union, *Ireland's Future in the European Union: Challenges, Issues and Options*, November 2008, available at: «http://www.oireachtas. ie/viewdoc.asp?fn=/documents/committees30thdail/j-europeanaffairs/ Sub_Cttee_EU__20081127.doc».

Kurpas, S., Grøn, C. and Kaczyński, P.M. (2008) 'The European Commission after Enlargement: Does More Add up to Less?' CEPS Special Report (Brussels: CEPS).

Schout, A. and Jordan, A. 'The European Union's Governance Ambitions and its Administrative Capacities'. *Journal of European Public Policy*, Vol. 15, No. 7, pp. 957–74.

Tömmel, I. and Verdun, A. (eds) (2008) *Innovative Governance in the European Union: The Politics of Multilevel Policymaking* (Boulder, CO: Lynne Rienner).

Van den Berge, A. and Schout, A. *From Bending to Stressing National Interests? The Impacts of Reforms and Enlargements on EU Negotiation Between 1988–2008* (Clingendael: Netherlands Institute of International Relations, 2008), also available at «http://www.clingendael.nl/publications/2008/20081200_cesp_vandenberge.pdf».

References

Barroso, J.M. (2008) 'Mouvement Européen-Belgique, Débat en collaboration avec *Le Soir*', 9 April 2008. Available at: «http://www.mouvement-europeen.be/index.html?page=326».

Council of the European Union (2008a) 'Presidency Conclusions'. Brussels European Council, 19–20 June 2008, Brussels, 17 July 2008, 11018/1/08.

Council of the European Union (2008b) 'Presidency Conclusions'. Brussels European Council, 14 December 2007, Brussels, 14 February, 16601/1/07.

Council of the European Union (2008c) 'Presidency Conclusions'. Brussels European Council, 15–16 October 2008, Brussels, 16 October 2008, 14368/08.

Council of the European Union (2009) 'Presidency Conclusions'. Brussels European Council, 11–12 December 2008, Brussels, 13 February, 17271/1/08.

Dehousse, R. (2008) 'One No Too Many'. *EUSA Review*, Autumn. Available at: «http://www.eustudies.org/publications_review_fall08.php#forum-4».

Commission of the European Communities (2008) '20 20 by 2020: Europe's climate change opportunity'. Communication from the Commission to the European Parliament, the Council, the European Economic and Social Committee and the Committee of the Regions, COM/2008/0030 final.

European Parliament (2008) 'Report on the Treaty of Lisbon'. Committee on Constitutional Affairs, Rapporteurs Richard Corbett and Inigo Mendez de Vigo, 2007/2286(INI).

European Parliament (2009) 'Draft Report on the impact of the Treaty of Lisbon on the development of the institutional balance of the European Union'. Committee on Constitutional Affairs, 2008/2073(INI), 26 January 2009.

Friends of Europe (2008) 'Board of Trustees Meeting, 10 October 2008'. Available at: «http://www.friendsofeurope.org/Pressdesk/Trusteesspeakout/tabid/536/articleType/ArticleView/articleId/173/Friends-of-Europes-Board-of-Trustees-meeting.aspx».

Houses of the Oireachtas (2008) 'Ireland's Future in the European Union: Challenges, Issues and Options'. Sub-Committee on Ireland's Future in the European

Union, November 2008, pp. 6, 13, 23–3. Available at: «http://www.oireachtas.ie/viewdoc.asp?fn=/documents/committees30thdail/j-europeanaffairs/Sub_Cttee_EU__20081127.doc».

Irish Times (2008) 'Sarkozy Visit: "Useful, Very Enriching" Visit Satisfies President and Exhausts Everyone Else'. 22 July 2008.

Martin, M. (2008) 'Ireland and the Lisbon Treaty, Remarks by Minister Martin, European Policy Centre "60 minutes briefing" '. European Policy Centre, 8 December. Available at: «http://www.foreignaffairs.irlgov.ie/home/index.aspx?id=79645».

O'Brennan, J. (2008) 'Ireland and the Lisbon Treaty: Quo Vadis?' CEPS Policy Brief, No. 176, October, p. 2.

Sarkozy, N. (2008) 'Speech before the European Parliament'. Strasbourg, 10 July 2008. Available at: «www.elysee.fr/.../download/?mode=press&filename=Discours_strasbourg_version_anglaise_du_10.07.08.pdf».

JCMS 2009 Volume 47 Annual Review pp. 133–150

Greening the Internal Market in a Difficult Economic Climate

DAVID HOWARTH
University of Edinburgh

Introduction

2008 was a year of turmoil in the financial markets, rapid economic slow-down and the start of recession in several European economies, bank bail-outs and growing calls for protectionism (see Quaglia *et al.*, in this volume). We might expect the principal casualties of these developments to have been European market integration and liberalization measures, the rigorous application of EU Competition Policy rules and the adoption and application of environmental and other measures that impose costs upon European industry. EU fiscal policy rules have effectively been suspended and several bank bail-outs by national governments have verged on breaking EU competition policy rules. However, it is difficult to demonstrate that the internal market and environmental legislative and policy agenda of 2008 was altered significantly by reactions to the crisis.

As bankruptcies and unemployment rise in 2009, no doubt the negative impact of the recession on market integration and liberalization will be further felt. In 2008, one of the most significant policy developments concerning the internal market was the stalled liberalization of the energy sector. However, this was in no way linked to the economic slow-down: French and German governments have long dragged their heels on liberalization in these sectors and long opposed the unbundling of gas and electricity production and supply. More surprising was the success in adopting ambitious targets to cut EU carbon emissions over the next decade. Despite the inevitable watering down of the European Council's initial goals and the Commission's legislative proposals and the frequent disappointment of environmentalist groups, this represents a considerable achievement – if not the greatest legislative accomplishment for the EU in 2008. Following a brief analysis of the agreement on energy markets, the bulk of this article is centred upon the climate change package.

I. The Fudged Liberalization of Energy Markets

In 1996 and 1998, the EU adopted directives to liberalize, respectively, the electricity and gas sectors (96/92/EC and 98/30/EC, revised in 2003). Several Member States supported the Commission's push for liberalization and moved quickly to open their markets or, as in the case of the UK, had already largely done so. Other Member States, notably France and Germany, were sceptical if not hostile to full liberalization and the unbundling of production and supply (Andersen, 2001). German and French governments stuck to the minimum requirements of the 1996 and 1998 directives. The Commission took legal action against no fewer than 17 Member States (by 2006), including the UK, to force through some developments. The principal problems encountered were: price discrimination to the benefit of historical customers; lack of legal unbundling and insufficient managerial separation between electricity and gas transmission and distribution system operators to ensure that they were independent of each other; preferential access to networks for historical customers and insufficiently transparent tariffs; lack of free choice of supplier; and insufficient independence or competence granted to national regulators, in particular to set tariffs for accessing the networks. In addition to ideological opposition to liberalization there was persistent domestic political opposition, with strong trade union, party political and public hostility – stoked by the fear that gas and electricity prices would rise after liberalization. One of the most contentious issues, third-party access to transmission networks for electricity and gas, was blocked by several Member States through the discretion allowed in the 1996 and 1998 directives (Andersen and Sitter, 2006). The directive allowed Member States to choose between regulated and negotiated third-party access and to develop or maintain their national regulatory models. Germany opted not to establish a new regulatory authority for gas. A third 'single buyer' model was incorporated into the directive to allow France to maintain elements of its national electricity monopoly, although this option (in effect an opt-out) was never used. In several Member States, public take-up of alternative energy providers has been minimal and market access restricted. Homogeneous integration in the energy sector worked only with respect to a limited range of policy initiatives including price transparency for electricity and gas contracts.

The Commission continued to push for a complete unbundling of production and supply which would force energy producers to sell off transmission networks. It sought to break up large energy companies into production and supply entities, arguing that only this would effectively allow new entrants greater access to the market. The Commission argued that insufficient competition inside Member States hindered investment in infrastructure and kept prices artificially high. Giving competing energy companies access to Europe's pipeline and transmission networks would, it was claimed, reduce the scope for market abuse by integrated suppliers. Independent transmission businesses would have an incentive to install new pipes and wires to meet demand, rather than restrict capacity to protect parent companies.

The March 2006 European Council agreed a new 'Energy Policy for Europe' which set market liberalization among its top objectives, while the March 2007 European Council renewed its commitment to proceed with the liberalization of European energy markets, establishing a list of criteria with which to proceed. In response, the EU energy commissioner, Andris Piebalgs, renewed the Commission's efforts to push ahead with unbundling. However, eight Member States remained firmly opposed to forcing energy producers to sell off transmission networks – the Group of Eight: France, Germany, Austria, Bulgaria, Greece, Latvia, Luxembourg and Slovakia. Given this refusal but also the perceived need for a clearer EU legal framework, the Commission decided to change tack.

In January 2008, the Commission proposed a new directive on unbundling energy production. This directive would effectively allow Member States that had not decoupled to avoid doing so. Energy companies would not be required to sell grids and pipelines. However, they would face tougher regulation and a requirement for more independent management. The Commission proposed the establishment of an independent system operator (ISO). Big energy companies would retain ownership of the transmission lines, but hand managing control over networks to an entirely separate operator which would be required to have a different group of shareholders from the parent company.

Yet this compromise gesture was still rejected by the Group of Eight which argued that energy producers should be allowed to retain ownership of transmission and called for a less radical energy liberalization scheme. Opponents of unbundling argued that strong national champions were needed to square up to Gazprom, the Russian gas giant that supplied much of Europe. When one supplier was so dominant, they argued, the debate about asset ownership was an irrelevance. In an open letter to the Commission, the Group of Eight also argued amongst other points that unbundling violated private property rights, was incompatible with the free movement of capital and increased the risk of EU companies falling under the control of non-European firms (notably Gazprom).[1]

The Group of Eight presented their own proposal for a new EU directive which called for a third option involving the creation of a so-called transmission system operator (TSO). Energy companies would be allowed to retain their hold over both production plans and supply grids but the management would be kept separate as a way to satisfy the Commission's demand for the separation of energy companies' production and supply operations. While independent from one another they would be connected only by a common set of shareholders. Transmission system operators would be organized in the legal form of a joint-stock company, would have their own corporate identity, with separate branding, communication and premises. A strict regulatory regime would be established in order to guarantee the separation. The Commission challenged both the content and legal aspects of the Group of Eight's initiative. It argued that the proposal did not meet the criteria outlined by the EU leaders in March 2007 for liberalization of the energy sector and that it was illegal for Member States to initiate what was, in effect, a proposal for an EU directive.[2] The Commission insisted that only the two options outlined in the January version of the directive – full ownership unbundling and an independent system operator (ISO) – could be considered by the European Parliament.

In early May, members of the European Parliament's Industry Committee backed the Commission's two-choice solution and explicitly rejected the Group of Eight's third option. Yet the vote was close and MEPs split along national, rather than party, lines. Some 26 committee members voted against the third option, 22 MEPs were in favour, while three abstained, which suggested that a vote in plenary could see a different outcome. The German centre-right MEP Angelika Niebler, who chaired the Industry Committee, asserted that 'there will be a compromise, including the third way, or there will be nothing'.[3] Then, in a second vote on 19 May, the Industry Committee made a U-turn, calling for the Commission to take on board the objections of the Group of Eight.

In June 2008, Member State governments reached a compromise, agreeing to embed into EU law the right for individual governments to choose one of three different models of unbundling: full ownership unbundling, when a

[1] *EUObserver*, 31 January 2008.
[2] *EUObserver*, 20 February 2008.
[3] *EUObserver*, 7 May 2008.

parent company sells its transmission networks to a different firm; the independent system operator (ISO) option proposed by the Commission in January that allows big energy companies to retain ownership of the transmission lines, but requires them to transfer managing control over networks to an entirely separate operator (which would not share any shareholders with the parent company); and a third option – very close to the one preferred by the Group of Eight – the creation of a so-called independent transmission operator (ITO) which permits a parent company to retain ownership of transmission networks which would be heavily supervised by a national regulator. Under this new third option, the new directive imposes additional requirements upon the parent company and ITO to reinforce the independence of the latter, including a mechanism preventing top management from moving freely between a company's production and transmission wings. Management involved in transmission operations is not to be permitted to work three years before and four years after in the parent company. Furthermore, the national regulator is to examine the transmission operator's development and investment plans and could demand changes. While the new directive will bring about a change in national practice in the eight Member States which have to date opposed unbundling, the new directive in effect formally reinforces differentiation in the organization of national energy markets. Opponents to the directive have argued that it effectively endorses the anti-competition practices in certain Member States and undermines full market liberalization and European market integration.[4] In a 9 July vote in the Parliament, 579 MEPs voted in favour, while only 80 were against and 52 abstained.

II. Greening the Internal Market

Amongst the most significant EU legislative developments in 2008 was the adoption of the climate change package. Four directives were adopted, establishing targets that, if met, should result in a significant reduction of CO_2 emissions by the year 2020. Throughout the year, there were intense debates on the precise provisions to be adopted – within and between Member States governments, EU institutions, industrial interests and environmentalist groups. The EU needed new targets on climate change to cover the period following the Kyoto Protocol's 2008–12 target dates and to cover the newest 12 Member States. The Commission and Member States also sought to establish EU policies prior to international negotiations on Kyoto II to take place in Copenhagen in December 2009. The Commission argued that European economies should adopt higher targets and direct increased funding to

[4] *EUObserver*, 10 July 2008.

green technologies as a double incentive to establish first-mover advantage. The March 2007 European Council committed the EU to cutting carbon emissions by at least 20 per cent on 2005 levels by 2020 and to increasing energy security and requested the Commission to draw up necessary draft legislation and policy proposals.

The EU-15 were on track to meet their collective target of 8 per cent under the 1997 Kyoto Protocol of cutting greenhouse gas emissions by 8 per cent for the period 2008–12 from 1990 levels, the Kyoto agreement's baseline year (EEA, 2008). While Denmark, Italy and Spain were behind in reducing emissions, the performance of the other EU-15 nations was enough to compensate. As of 2006, four Member States – France, Greece, Sweden and the UK – had already apparently reached an emissions level below their Kyoto target and the eight other states were on track to meet their targets. Further reductions were to be achieved by a combination of domestic policies and measures, reforestation and buying 'carbon offsets' – permitted under the Kyoto Protocol – through which countries pay for other states to make the carbon reductions on their behalf. However, it was likely that several Member States would have to purchase more carbon offset credits than previously planned in order to achieve their target. At the start of 2008, renewable energy in the EU stood at 8.5 per cent of total production.

On 23 January 2008, the Commission presented an impressive climate change package, consisting of three directives to be adopted by the Member States. The package included three targets, known rather catchily as 20-20-20: a 20 per cent overall reduction in CO_2 emissions from a 2005 baseline, a 20 per cent increase in the share of renewable energies in energy consumption and a 20 per cent increase in energy efficiency, all to be achieved by 2020. The reduction in emissions would have to increase to 30 per cent by 2020 if an international agreement was reached committing other major economies to this higher target. The targets, for the period 2013–20 cover those industries not included within the existing carbon emissions trading scheme (ETS) – the EU's key method for reducing greenhouse gases under the Kyoto Protocol – notably agriculture, buildings and transport. The Commission also proposed fines to be imposed upon Member States which did not meet targets: an 'excess emissions penalty' – equivalent to those imposed under the ETS of around €100 per extra tonne of CO_2 emitted. If a Member State did not pay the penalty, the extra CO_2 emitted would then be deducted from the ETS allowances allotted to the Member State and sold instead by the European Commission. Member States that 'overachieved' by cutting greenhouse gases to below their targets would be able to sell that part of their emissions allocation to another Member State. But any money from the sale would have to be spent on 'green' investments such as renewable energy development or

Table 1: Member State CO_2 and Renewable Energy Targets (for 2020)

Member State	CO2 targets (percentage change from 1990 base)	Renewable energy targets (percentage of total energy consumed)
Austria	−16	34
Belgium	−15	13
Bulgaria	+20	16
Czech Republic	+9	13
Cyprus	−5	13
Denmark	−20	30
Estonia	+11	25
Finland	−16	38
France	−14	23
Germany	−14	18
Greece	−4	18
Hungary	+10	13
Ireland	−20	16
Italy	−13	17
Latvia	+15	42
Lithuania	+15	23
Luxembourg	−20	11
Malta	+5	10
Netherlands	−16	14
Poland	+14	15
Portugal	+1	31
Romania	+19	24
Slovakia	+13	14
Slovenia	+4	25
Spain	−10	20
Sweden	−17	49
United Kingdom	−16	15

Source: Commission (2008).

energy efficiency. The package also detailed how each Member State would contribute to meeting the targets by 2020 (see Table 1).

The package included a proposal to reinforce the ETS – in which high-polluting companies buy CO_2 emission credits from lower-polluting firms in order to meet national carbon output quotas. The existing ETS covered 11,186 energy-intensive installations throughout the EU – including power plants, oil refineries, steel mills and cement factories – which produced almost half of the EU's CO_2 emissions. Under the existing ETS, 90 per cent of credits were given out free. The Commission argued that the existing ETS was faulty because it was based on national emissions caps and did not provide enough guarantees to achieve the 2020 goal. In the new proposed ETS, Member States would no longer devise their own national allocation plans and grant pollution permits to companies. These plans would be replaced from 2013 by auctioning or free allocation through single EU-wide rules. The auctioning revenues would be delivered to Member State governments. Apart from the power sector which would be subject to full auctioning from the start of the new regime in 2013, industrial sectors and aviation would increase auctioning gradually, with the sale of one-fifth of pollution permits in 2013 rising by 10 per cent annually to 2020. In energy-intensive industrial sectors where the competitiveness of companies would be strongly undermined by the ETS, the free provision of ETS allowances could continue.

The Commission also proposed a directive on carbon capture and storage – a carbon emissions reduction method that involved storing underground carbon instead of releasing it into the atmosphere. The Commission announced an overhaul of the rules on granting state aid for environmental projects to permit an increased government subsidy of measures such as carbon capture and storage (CCS), public transport projects and emissions trading. Governments would be able to contribute up to 60 per cent of the cost of environmental projects co-ordinated by large enterprises – up from 40 per cent – and up to 70 per cent and 80 per cent for medium-sized and small businesses, respectively, and up to 100 per cent for projects awarded by competitive tender.

In a speech to the European Parliament on 15 January 2008, President Barroso promised not to bow to Member State and industry pressure to water down the Commission package. The Commission repeatedly argued that the EU, by acting quickly, would have a first-mover advantage in the green market. Furthermore, the EU's international reputation for being a flag-bearer for environmentally friendly proposals was at stake. In the months following the 23 January launch of the legislative package, the Commission had to resist intense Member State pressure to modify its directives and change its calculations on how much each Member State should contribute to CO_2 emissions reduction and renewable energy. Rich Member States criticized the methodology used to set national targets (GDP per capita and relative national wealth) but several poorer Member States also expressed their opposition to their targets.[5] BusinessEurope, Europe's main employers' association, and the European Round Table of Industrialists warned of the huge economic implications of the revised ETS, and the disadvantage for European firms if they had to comply with stricter environment rules than their American and

[5] *EUObserver*, 13 March 2008.

Chinese competitors.[6] Industry also feared that the new ETS would begin operation even if the 2009 international negotiations on a new climate change deal failed to reach an agreement. To address this concern, the March European Council agreed that 'appropriate measures' would be taken if international negotiations failed: energy-intensive industries could get free pollution permits – instead of having to buy them by auction – linked to technological benchmarks, while the EU could also seek to make foreign companies take part in the ETS.

By mid-2008, it became apparent that nine Member States would be obstructive on the climate change package: eight central and eastern European countries (CEECs) (Poland, Hungary, the three Baltic states, Romania, Bulgaria and Slovakia) and Italy, with the Poles and Italians posing the greatest potential threat to an agreement. In late May, seven CEECs (all the above with the exception of Poland) proposed a different distribution of carbon dioxide emission targets to those tabled by the Commission in January, arguing that the new regime should take into account previous national efforts in curbing climate change and future growth prospects.[7] This new proposal assigned the newest EU Member States lower targets on the grounds that they expected to see a more rapid rise in industrial output in the coming years. The seven CEECs also sought more generous emission quotas in the sectors not included in the existing ETS, beyond those already provided by the Commission in its January proposal which applied a solidarity principle (according to GDP per capita) in allocations of quotas in areas such as transport, waste, construction and farming, with richer countries receiving stricter targets than poorer ones. The seven CEECs argued that the Commission's proposal, which set 2005 as the new baseline year for setting new emissions targets, did not fully take into consideration the efforts made by EU countries in the fight against climate change from the early 1990s. The Commission challenged these claims, arguing that the new Member States underwent economic restructuring during the 1990s rather than real efforts to cut emissions, and that relative wealth levels were already taken into consideration in its proposal. The eastern Europeans claimed that there were serious investments made at the time in more modern, cleaner technologies, pointing to how emissions did not noticeably increase after their economies improved. Italy and Poland threatened to veto the EU's package to tackle climate change, saying their economies could not bear the added burden that emissions reductions would impose. They led efforts to block the launch of 'full

[6] See, for example, *Financial Times*, 21 January 2008.
[7] *EUObserver*, 28 May 2008.

auctioning' of CO_2 credits in heavy industry from 2013, pushing this back to 2020. With high-polluting coal plants producing 96 per cent of the country's energy, the Polish government feared that the introduction of the auction system from 2013 would see its energy firms outbid by richer western rivals, resulting in increased energy costs, hampered investment in new technologies and lower economic growth.

The French Council Presidency of the second half of 2008 placed an agreement on the climate change package at the top of its priorities and a key criterion by which the success of the Presidency should be determined (Dehousse and Menon, this volume). Italian and eastern European opposition prevented an agreement on a common text at the October European Council. In early December, President Nicolas Sarkozy met with eastern European leaders in Gdańsk to reach a compromise deal. Sarkozy offered the group of nine countries (the eight mentioned above and the Czech Republic) to phase in the CO_2 permits payments for existing power facilities, with the nine countries to receive 70 per cent of permits for free in 2013 dropping to zero by 2020. Sarkozy also offered to lift the threat of legal penalties for countries which did not meet their national CO_2 reduction targets by 2020. He proposed the organization of a 2016 climate change summit to introduce corrections to any package agreed at the December European Council, if the impact upon post-communist economies was too great. Sarkozy also promised to help the CEECs construct nuclear power plants in the coming years, while President Barroso offered the Polish government an extra €2 billion in energy infra-structure grants up to 2013. The nine eastern European countries continued to demand a CO_2 'compensation mechanism', which would assign them an additional 10 per cent carbon emissions allowances compared to wealthier EU states, allowing them to sell the credits to finance new power plants. In the lead-up to the December European Council there were further concerns about the impact of the financial crisis upon financing the climate change package.

The MEPs on the European Parliament's Environment Committee voted to reinforce the European Commission's legislative package on 7 October. The day was dubbed 'Green Super Tuesday' by environmental groups because of the committee's marathon session which involved voting on all three major laws in the Commission's climate package because the French Council Presidency sought to fast-track their adoption by Member States. Committee MEPs voted to support the Commission's national CO_2 emissions reductions but also voted to cut emissions still further in the future – by 50 per cent as of 2035 and between 60 and 80 per cent by 2050. The MEPs accepted the Commission's proposed ETS reform, its fines on Member States that did not meet their emissions targets and rules on selling excess emissions cut to another Member State. However, the committee also voted to ensure that power companies, which had benefited from profits as a result of earlier free allocation of permits, would be forced to pay for all their emissions permits from 2013. The committee ring-fenced 100 per cent of auction revenues from the ETS, a sum that could be worth as much as €50 billion a year by 2020, strictly for climate-related purposes. More controversially, the committee moved to decrease the Commission's original proposals for the amount of 'carbon offsets' that European Member States could use towards their carbon reduction targets. The December European Council reached an agreement on the energy and climate package which effectively eliminated all the reinforced measures sought by the Parliament's Environment Committee. The final package was nonetheless approved by the Parliament on 17 December.

The Inclusion of Aviation in the ETS

There was a running battle throughout the year on whether the aviation industry should be included in the ETS and, if so, from when. Although the aviation sector was responsible for just 2 per cent of global carbon dioxide (CO_2) emissions in 2008, its contribution to climate change was, according to some experts, growing faster than any other source, with greenhouse gas emissions from aviation in the EU increasing by 87 per cent between 1990 and 2006, according to the Commission.[8] In its January legislative package, the Commission proposed for the aviation industry to take part in the ETS from 2012. On 27 May, the European Parliament's Environment Committee voted for the aviation industry to be in the ETS from 2011, with the sector having to pay for 25 per cent of its permits to produce carbon dioxide in the first year and from 2013 falling into line with other sectors. The Environment Committee agreed to include business jets in the scope of the scheme but not small aircraft. Member States argued that only 10 per cent of pollution permits should be auctioned. In June, negotiators from the Parliament and the Council agreed that aviation should be included from 2012, with 15 per cent of pollution permits to be auctioned and 85 allocated for free. The measure would apply to all aircraft taking off or landing in the EU, including those of non-EU companies. In July, the Parliament voted overwhelmingly (640 to 30) for this and on 19 November, the Parliament and Council adopted the directive to include aviation activities in the ETS. The International Air Transport Association (IATA) was incensed, arguing that many airlines would collapse

---

[8] *EU Observer*, 6 February 2008.

especially in a context of skyrocketing fuel prices. For their part, environmental groups claimed that the measures approved would actually lead to
increased emissions on the grounds that the extra warming impact of aviation
emissions over ground-based CO_2 emissions was unaccounted for in the
agreed scheme.[9]

The EU has encouraged the construction of less-polluting airplanes
through the Clean Sky initiative, a joint public–private partnership to develop
'green' aviation technologies, confirmed by an EU regulation in December
2007. With €1.6 billion in funding, the initiative was to be one of the biggest
EU research funding programmes in history. Aeronautics manufacturers
Airbus, Dassault, Saab and Rolls Royce signed up to the initiative. Half the
money is to come from the EU's R&D funding programme with the other half
from industry. The aim of the initiative is to halve emissions of carbon dioxide
by 2020, cut nitrogen oxide by 80 per cent, halve noise pollution and set up
an eco-friendly life cycle for products – across design, manufacture, maintenance and scrapping or recycling. The Clean Sky project involves 86 organizations from 16 countries: 54 private companies, 15 research centres and 17
universities.

The Carbon Capture Debate

In its January legislative package, the Commission called for the promotion of
a controversial carbon emissions mitigation technology known as 'carbon
capture and storage' (CCS). CCS 'captures' carbon dioxide from power plants
and stores it in underground geological formations or in deep oceans instead
of releasing it into the atmosphere. The CCS was presented as one mechanism
to help achieve the long-term goal of halving greenhouse gas emissions by
2050. The January package included a series of revised guidelines on state aid
for environmental protection that would enable Member State governments to
support CCS pilot project plants, because the current cost of the technology
was much higher than the price of carbon. Carbon dioxide captured and
stored would not be considered as emitted under the ETS. There were many
critics of the scheme. The iron and steel industry was very sceptical of the
EU's schedule for the development of CCS prior to 2020. Environmental
groups also expressed concern as to the viability of CCS because it would
undermine efforts to cut back on fossil fuels usage. These groups argued that
the CCS process itself was very energy intensive and required the extra
extraction of fossil fuels and they noted the potential for leakage of CO_2 from
underground sites.

[9] *EUObserver*, 18 July 2008.

The Automobile Industry and CO_2 Reductions

Late in 2007, the Commission had proposed another EU directive (not part of its climate change package) that from 2012, the average carbon dioxide emissions of new cars would have to be reduced to 130 grammes per kilometre – a reduction of about 24 per cent on the average 158 grammes of CO_2 per kilometre cars emitted in 2008. Companies that did not meet the 130g target would be fined €20 per gramme per kilometre over the limit in 2012, an amount that would increase to €95 by 2015. In 2007, automobiles accounted for about 14 per cent of the EU's CO_2 emissions.[10] Environmentalists wanted to see a target of 120g/km by 2012, in line with an official EU target first proposed in 1994 by the then German environment minister, Angela Merkel. The 14-year-old target was supposed to have been achieved by 2005 but was postponed three times – in 1996, 1997 and 2007. The European Automobile Manufacturers' Association (ACEA) – which represents 15 major producers – also opposed the emission cap of 130 grammes per kilometre and insisted that any target should be based on an impact assessment,[11] estimating the new CO_2 legislation would cost the industry €25 billion while consumers would have to pay an extra €1,500 per car. The ACEA lobbied for amendments to the legislation to introduce a three-step phase-in of the emissions reduction targets, with 70 per cent of a company's car fleet having to meet the target in 2012, 80 per cent in 2014 and the full fleet only having to meet the target in 2015. The industry also proposed a considerable reduction in the fine imposed on car firms from €95 per gramme per kilometre to €50. Member States were divided on the new directive with some preferring to avoid making reference to any specific figure. Other points of disagreement included the calendar and penalties and as to whether revenues collected via penalties would be reverted to the EU's budget or be transferred to national coffers. It was also necessary to define how to share the burden between different car manufacturers. While Germany was the chief producer of large, heavy vehicles such as BMW, Daimler and Porsche, French and Italian carmakers produced lighter, more energy-efficient automobiles, such as Peugeot, Renault and Fiat.

There were significant divisions in the Commission on car emissions that surfaced repeatedly throughout the year, with the German Industry Commissioner, Günter Verheugen, adopting the more sceptical German position on the directive that was championed by the Environment Commissioner Stavros Dimas and formally approved by the College of Commissioners. In a 14 January speech to the European Parliament, for

---

[10] *Financial Times*, 25 September 2008.
[11] *EUObserver*, 5 June 2008.

example, Verheugen argued that the Commission's directive should be structured in a way that did not harm the competitive position of European carmakers on the world stage.[12] On 9 June, French President Sarkozy and German Chancellor Merkel agreed to support the Commission's proposal to limit average CO_2 emissions of new cars. Yet the two countries also called for a period of several years to introduce the cap and for a softer line on penalties imposed if industry failed. France further proposed that instead of all cars sold in 2012 being restricted to emitting a maximum of 130 grammes of CO_2 per kilometre, only 60 per cent of all new cars would have to meet the standard, with new cars having to meet the target by 2015. The proposal would effectively give car manufacturers an additional three years to implement CO_2 emissions reductions across the entirety of their fleets. The French proposal recommended giving car companies credit for 'eco-innovations' that produce cleaner vehicles or lower-emission cars. The French government also sought exemptions for manufacturers that did not sell many vehicles and credit offered to those that sold electric cars.

In a surprise vote, on 25 September, the European Parliament's Environment Committee endorsed the Commission's proposed directive on car emissions, rejecting the amendments agreed by Member States on a phase-in and industry pressure to extend the deadline to 2015. The committee also proposed a second, deeper target of 95 grammes of CO_2 per kilometre on average by 2020, subject to a review in 2014. The 46 MEPs voting in favour (versus 19) included Socialists, Liberals and Greens. The Commission's proposals had still however to win approval of the full sitting of the Parliament, where German MEPs across party lines would vote against it. On 6 October, the ACEA asked the EU for a €40 billion loan to maintain a 'level playing field' with the US car industry which the Bush administration had just provided a $25 billion support package.[13] On 15 December, an inter-institutional agreement was reached on car CO_2 emissions which accommodated Member State concerns. There would be a phasing-in of car volumes that needed to comply with the target, starting with 65 per cent in 2012 – only slightly more than the 60 per cent agreed by the Member States – rising to 100 per cent in 2015. The phasing-in of penalties would also be delayed with the €95 fine applying only from 2019. The second deeper target of 95 grammes of CO_2/km by 2020 would be non-binding and car manufacturers would be allowed to earn eco-innovation credits which could contribute up to seven grammes to their target until 2014.

---

[12] *EUObserver*, 15 January 2008.
[13] *Financial Times*, 6 October 2008.

The Directive on Renewables

The third element of the Commission's climate change package and third major directive to be adopted concerned the development of renewable energy sources with the target of 20 per cent renewables by 2020, with binding national targets for each Member State (see Table 1). The adoption of this directive was subject to comparatively little Member State discord, although the Italians temporarily delayed the final agreement by demanding that the 2020 target be subject to a review in 2014. Having been disappointed by the legislation adopted in the other areas, environmental groups were very supportive of the directive on renewable energy agreed by the Parliament, Commission and Council on 9 December, calling it 'historic' and 'the world's most important energy law'.[14] By June 2010, Member States will have to draw up national action plans describing how they will meet their 2020 targets, which the Commission will then assess. Member States will also have to report biennially on their progress. Central to the agreement are largely intact proposals from the Parliament's Industry Committee on greater co-operation between Member States to achieve the target, including joint projects on green electricity production, heating or cooling. Member States will also be able to transfer renewable energy 'statistically' between themselves. The new directive also permits the counting of green electricity consumed in a Member State but produced via newly constructed joint projects with countries beyond the EU.

The Biofuels Debate

The encouragement of biofuels as a source of renewable energy proved one of the most controversial elements of the Commission's climate change package. At the March 2007 European Council, Member States agreed that the EU should increase the use of biofuels in transport fuel to 10 per cent by 2020, up from the 5.75 per cent target to be achieved by 2010. However, expert attitudes were already shifting dramatically on biofuels. In September 2007, the Organization for Economic Co-operation and Development (OECD) pointed out the environmental and social risks created by biofuels. The World Bank and the United Nations World Food Programme produced similarly critical positions. In January 2008, the Commission's own scientific institute, the Joint Research Centre (JRC), leaked an unpublished internal report criticizing the sustainability and social costs of biofuels.[15] On 11 January, a group of 17 NGOs – including Oxfam and Friends of the Earth –

---

[14] *EUObserver*, 10 December 2008.
[15] *Financial Times*, 18 January 2008.

sent a letter to the EU Energy Commissioner, Andris Piebalgs, asking him to introduce much tougher standards on biofuel production or give up mandatory transport biofuel targets altogether.[16] Several international organizations and environmentalist groups saw increased production of biofuels as a major contributing source of the dramatic rise in world food prices in 2008.

As opposition to biofuels grew, the EU came under increasing pressure to develop a set of sustainability rules governing the fuel source. EU Member States disagreed on what constituted 'sustainable'. In April, President Barroso requested a study on whether there was any relationship between the recent jump in global food prices and biofuels. The move came amid speculation that there was a growing division within the Commission over the question. In mid-April, the Commissioner responsible for development, Louis Michel, said that biofuels were a 'catastrophe'.[17]

Most EU Member States also switched their position on biofuels. At the end of June, the French government came out against the EU's 10 per cent biofuels target and indeed any target, arguing that the EU had proposed things the wrong way round by setting targets prior to environmental and social criteria for the production of biofuels.[18] In early July, European energy ministers backed away from the EU's biofuels for transport target, admitting a gross confusion on their part in which they said they had been misreading policy documents since the target was initially proposed a year and a half earlier.[19] The ministers said that upon closer inspection, EU proposals that aimed for a target of 10 per cent of fuels for cars and lorries to come from biofuels by 2020 in fact only required 10 per cent of fuels to come from renewable sources which may or may not be biofuels. These sources could also include hydrogen fuel cells or electric cars using electricity from alternative sources.

In early July, the Parliament's Environment Committee voted to cut the EU's biofuels target in a unanimous 36-0 vote, with eight abstentions. The MEPs recommended that the EU should aim to make between 8 and 10 per cent of energy for transport come from renewable sources by 2020, with an interim target of 4 per cent by 2015. Of this latter target, at least 20 per cent would have to come from electric cars or the use of hydrogen fuel, or alternately biogas or second-generation biofuels made from algae or agricultural waste. The Commission responded with concern, while environmental campaigners welcomed the higher target, but repeated their insistence that biofuels should be excluded altogether. On 11 September, members of the

[16] *EUObserver*, 14 January 2008.
[17] *EUObserver*, 24 April 2008.
[18] *EUObserver*, 30 June 2008.
[19] *EUObserver*, 7 July 2008.

European Parliament's Industry Committee voted overwhelmingly to re-establish the original target of using renewable sources for transport fuel for 10 per cent of vehicles by 2020, but confirmed that these sources were not necessarily traditional biofuels, recommending that two-fifths of the 10 per cent target would have to come via cars that run on hydrogen or that use electricity from renewable sources such as solar and wind power, or from so-called second-generation biofuels. MEPs also voted for a major review in 2014 of biofuel impact on the environment and on food prices before Member States could continue with the 2020 goal.

The 9 December inter-institutional agreement supported the Commission's original target figure but also provided some non-binding encouragement to Member States to increase their use of renewable sources other than first-generation biofuels. According to the agreement, second-generation biofuels will be able to be counted twice towards the 10 per cent target and electric cars could be counted at two and a half times their real contribution towards the target. Binding sub-targets for forms of renewable transport such as electric cars or clean-energy trains which had been introduced by the Parliament were abandoned, leaving Member States free to choose whether to count these toward the 10 per cent target. In the inter-institutional agreement, biofuels will have to achieve a 50 per cent saving in greenhouse gas emissions by 2017 in order to be accepted under the 10 per cent target. This figure represented a compromise splitting the difference between the Commission's 35 per cent and the Parliament's Industry Committee's 60 per cent saving by 2015. The move to 50 per cent would be subject to a review. Yet the Commission's controversial and unverified new rules for calculating the greenhouse gas impact of different biofuels will apply – thus allowing European sugar beet to continue to be used in the production of biofuels. The Parliament gave in on most of its previous demands. Environmentalist groups were exasperated with the agreement which they said represented a major defeat on biofuels.[20]

Conclusion

There has been considerable criticism by many MEPs, environmentalist groups and others of the climate change package adopted in December 2008. Some have called the 20 per cent cuts by 2020 a 'mirage' given the extent to which Member States will be able to engage in carbon offsetting.[21] Even the

---

[20] *Financial Times*, 10 December 2008.
[21] *EUObserver*, 12 December 2008.

Financial Times bemoaned the concessions made to heavy industry,[22] which is to be shielded from much of the cost of buying tradeable permits in the ETS – the major concession made to principally Poland and Germany. The concessions fundamentally undermine efforts to make polluters pay for emissions, seen as an essential step in fighting climate change. However, that a deal was achieved on the verge of the worst recession faced by Europe since the 1930s should be celebrated as an accomplishment. The EU's climate change package agreed on 17 December is the world's most stringent and sets the benchmark for the international negotiations that are set to take place in 2009.

Key Readings

Knill and Liefferink's (2007) *Environmental Politics in the European Union* textbook provides an excellent introduction to the making, development and implementation of EU environmental policy.

Pedersen *et al.*'s (2008) *Energy Policy for Europe: Identifying the European Added-Value* is a CEPS Task Force Report prepared by a group consisting of industry, NGOs and EU officials and other experts examining the main direction, principles and added-value of EU energy policy and the key measures that will be crucial for a successful policy. The report focuses upon energy market and security issues as well as climate change.

Bibliography

Andersen, S.S. (2001) 'Energy Policy: Interest Articulation and Supranational Authority'. In Andersen, S.S. and Eliassen, K.A. (eds) *Making Policy in Europe* (London: Sage).

Andersen, S. and Sitter, N. (2006) 'Differentiated Integration: What is it and How Much Can the EU Accommodate?' *Journal of European Integration*, Vol. 28, No. 4, pp. 313–30.

Knill, C. and Liefferink, D. (2007) *Environmental Politics in the European Union* (Manchester: MUP).

Pedersen, K., Behrens, A., Egenhofer, C. (2008) *Energy Policy for Europe: Identifying the European Added-Value* (Brussels: CEPS).

EEA (European Environment Agency) (2008) *Greenhouse Gas Emission Trends and Projections in Europe 2008: Tracking Progress towards Kyoto Targets*. EEA Report, 5/2008 (Copenhagen: EEA).

[22] *Financial Times*, 14 December 2008.

JCMS 2009 Volume 47 Annual Review pp. 151–170

Justice and Home Affairs

JÖRG MONAR
College of Europe/University of Sussex

Introduction

While the Irish rejection of the Treaty of Lisbon – with its numerous reforms in the justice and home affairs (JHA) domain – cast a shadow over future development perspectives the year 2008 saw nevertheless a continuous growth of the Union's 'area of freedom, security and justice' (AFSJ). With a total of 144 texts adopted during the year[1] the annual output of the JHA Council was in numerical terms 12 per cent lower than in the record year before – but in substantive terms the year was marked by the adoption, especially in the field of judicial co-operation in criminal matters, of an impressive range of major legal instruments and, especially in the field of asylum and immigration policy, several major new initiatives.

I. Developments in Individual Policy Areas

Refugee Policy

The first phase of the establishment of the Common European Asylum System (CEAS) was completed in 2005 with the adoption of the 'Qualifications Directive'. Yet the implementation of the first-phase instruments has clearly shown that this emerging system is still far from meriting the term 'common' because of wide margins left to national implementation measures,

[1] Lists of texts provided by the General Secretariat of the Council and own calculations.

frequent cases of non-implementation, strongly diverging national practices and major differences regarding country of origin information. The persisting high degree of diversity means that refugees can still expect to be treated better in some Member States than in others – which encourages secondary movements – and goes against the fundamental principle of providing equal access to protection across the Union. The resulting 'asylum lottery' was again sharply criticized by the European Council on Refugees and Exiles (ECRE) which appealed in April to the JHA Council to urgently address the differences in quality of the national asylum systems (ECRE, 2008).

During 2008 the extent of the problems were highlighted in an unprecedented way in the case of Greece which has the lowest asylum-seeker recognition rate in the EU and has frequently been accused by Amnesty International, the European Council of Refugees and Exiles (ECRE) and other NGOs of violating the rights of refugees. On 31 January the Commission launched a treaty-infringement procedure against Greece because of the lack of sufficient legal guarantees for a substantive examination of asylum applications after the transfer of an asylum seeker from another Member State under the Dublin II Regulation. Legislative changes introduced in Greece made the Commission withdraw the case from the Court on 18 September, but concerns were not limited to the Commission: on 7 February Norway – which participates in the CEAS – suspended the return of refugees and asylum seekers who had entered Norway via Greece because of concerns about the possible violation of rights of asylum seekers and Germany temporarily suspended the return to Greece of unaccompanied minors (UNHCR, 2008).

These developments put additional pressure on the Commission, entrusted under the Hague Programme with the task of proposing a new set of 'second-phase' CEAS instruments based on an evaluation of the 'first-phase' instruments, with the new instruments to be in place by 2010. On 17 June the Commission adopted a new policy plan on asylum entitled 'An integrated approach to protection across the EU'. The Commission therein acknowledged the persisting major differences between the national systems, but also pointed to major evolutions of importance to future policy-making such as the historic low of asylum application numbers in the EU, the growing importance of subsidiary protection not covered by the Geneva Convention and the relative growth of the burden of EU border Member States because of their geographical position. The Commission announced a series of proposals aimed at improving and further harmonizing protection standards, the creation of a European Asylum Support Office (EASO) to support practical co-operation and measures to promote solidarity both inside the Union and in co-operation with third countries involving substantial financial measures.

The first set of legislative proposals for the second CEAS phase was then put forward by the Commission on 3 December and concerned the recasting of the 2003 Reception Conditions Directive, the 2003 Dublin and the 2000 Eurodac Regulations.

As regards the amendments to the Reception Conditions Directive the Commission proposed to extend its scope to applicants for subsidiary protection (i.e. those not eligible for Geneva Convention status on grounds of individual persecution but nevertheless facing a threat in their countries), to facilitate asylum seekers' access to the labour market (at the latest after six months, to make provision for comparable living conditions in all Member States – these currently still vary considerably) which should take into consideration social assistance levels available to nationals and to restrict the detention of asylum seekers to specified exceptional circumstances in need to be confirmed by a judicial authority within 72 hours (Commission, 2008b). In the case of the Dublin Regulation the Commission's proposals were aimed at both increasing the efficiency of the procedures determining the Member State responsible for processing an asylum application – mainly through the introduction of new deadlines and the clarification of humanitarian, sovereignty and cessation of responsibility clauses – and at strengthening the legal safeguards for persons falling under the procedure – mainly by providing for enhanced information rights, a right to appeal against any transfer decision from one Member State to another and a right to legal assistance (Commission, 2008c). The proposed recast of the Eurodac Regulation on the comparison of fingerprints of asylum seekers, finally, was aimed at tightening the deadlines for the transmission of data (in practice there are often huge delays which reduce the effectiveness of the system) and (for reasons of data protection) a more efficient management of the deletion of data and a better control of access to Eurodac data (Commission, 2008d).

These proposals addressed some of the most glaring deficits of the current instruments – as well as several inconsistencies (such as the non-inclusion of subsidiary protection which is not in line with the 2005 Qualifications Directive). They were broadly welcomed by the UNHCR and ECRE as a step forward for the protection of refugees' rights, but there were still concerns that the root problems of the 'asylum lottery' were not addressed, and initial reception of the proposals in the Council was mixed, especially as regards living standard guarantees and access to the labour market. As the Commission's other proposals for the second-phase instruments were still outstanding at the end of the year, it became clear that the CEAS would not be in place – as originally scheduled by the Hague Programme – by 2010 but 2012 at the earliest.

Migration Policy

The sphere of migration policy reached again the level of 'high politics' during the year as much political attention was given to the negotiation of the 'European Pact on Immigration and Asylum', an instrument which French President Nicolas Sarkozy had been advocating forcefully already during his election campaign in 2007. The French initiative, which dominated an informal meeting of the EU Justice and Home Affairs ministers in Cannes on 7–8 July, was aimed at extending key elements of the French government's attempts to better manage migration policy challenges at the national level by a combination of skill-selective legal immigration quota, new integration requirements for immigrants and higher expulsion rates of illegal immigrants. Yet already before the Cannes meeting French Immigration Minister Brice Hortefeux had to water down the original version of the Plan circulated in January as a 'tour of capitals' revealed strong opposition to some elements of the French approach.

Spain, in particular, raised major objections against the proposed 'integration contracts' which would have obliged migrants to learn their host country's language and become acquainted with its national identity and European values as well as to a proposed commitment for all Member States not to engage in large-scale 'regularizations' of illegal immigration (such as the one enacted by Spain in 2005) which the French government regards as a major 'pull-factor' of migration. With the 'integration contracts' causing uneasiness in several other Member States (including Austria) and Greece providing some support to the Spanish position on regularizations the first had to be taken out of the Pact and the second became subject to a rather vague formula of political intent. A further point of contention was initial French proposals to invest the planned EASO (see above) with the power to examine asylum applications and take decisions, which were strongly opposed by Germany which wanted to retain national control over asylum decisions and led to a limitation of the EASO's role to the facilitation of information and analysis exchange and the development of practical co-operation between national administrations.

After a watered-down version of the Pact had been approved at the end of the Cannes informal meetings and some further minor changes the 'European Pact' was then formally adopted by the European Council on 15–16 October – a further proof of the Heads of State and Government's now well-established role as strategic agenda-setters for the development of the AFSJ. The Plan (Council, 2008a) contains a strong endorsement of skill-selective legal immigration for highly qualified third-country nationals (very much in line with the ongoing negotiations on the EU 'blue Card' – see below) which should be accompanied by more national action to facilitate integration; all this, however, in accordance with the individual needs and approaches of the Member States, so that harmonization effects are likely to remain limited. As regards illegal immigration, it puts an emphasis on the Member States ensuring that illegal immigrants leave their territories, the encouragement of voluntary return, the mutual recognition of expulsion decisions, more effective procedures in the negotiation of readmission agreements with third countries and a case-by-case approach to regularization rather than 'generalized' regularizations. External border control capabilities are to be upgraded by a range of measures including more support for border Member States and – by 2012 – the introduction of biometric visas, electronic recordings of entry and exit. In the field of asylum the Pact commits the Union to establishing the EASO with the more limited functions mentioned above in 2009 and a completion of the second-phase asylum legislation 'at the latest' in 2012. A substantial section of the Pact is dedicated to a 'comprehensive partnership' with countries of origin and transit, providing, *inter alia*, for Member States 'as far as they are able' to offer possibilities of temporary 'circular' migration to nationals of eastern and southern neighbouring countries, a better targeting of development policy instruments at reducing immigration potentials in countries of origin and the facilitation of migrants' financial remittances to countries of origin for the purpose of investments and welfare insurance. In its final form the Pact ended up as a compromise document which left wide margins of manoeuvre to Member States, but it nevertheless set some strategic priorities which are likely to leave their mark on the 2010 to 2014 successor programme to the Hague Programme.

While the Pact was still under negotiation, on 17 June the Commission put forward a set of principles corresponding to the Pact's strategic objectives. In its Communication 'A Common Immigration Policy for Europe: Principles, Actions and Tools' the Commission started by highlighting the 'reality' of immigration into the EU by estimating that the third-country national share of the EU's total population had reached 3.8 per cent and that new net arrivals were of the order of 1.5 and 2 million per year (Commission, 2008e). The Commission also reiterated its argument that higher levels of legal immigration into the EU would be needed as by 2060 the working-age population of the Union would fall by almost 50 million, even with continued net immigration of current proportions. It then developed ten principles which combined largely uncontroversial elements – such as the need for more skill-selective channels for legal immigration – with some more controversial ones – such as the approximation of the status of legally resident third-country nationals to that of EU nationals. The most distinct points of focus of the Communication were on 'solidarity' and 'security', to each of which three of the principles were dedicated. Under the solidarity heading the Commission regrouped a rather wide array of different issues from information exchange over an improved use of EU financial instruments to co-operation with third countries. Yet the emphasis on financial solidarity was most noteworthy and was an early indication that the Commission might push for the earmarking of more EU budgetary means for this domain in the current and probably also the next financial perspective. No less noteworthy was the strong emphasis on the security dimension of migration management, sustained in spite of the 'fortress Europe' criticism this surely was to fuel, with the Commission advocating, amongst other measures, the tightening of visa security checks, reinforcing the operational dimension of the external border management agency Frontex and developing a range of measures against undeclared work and illegal employment as part of the overall effort against illegal immigration and trafficking in human beings.

The restrictive side of the EU's migration policy took a step forward with the adoption on 8 December, after three years of negotiation, of the Directive on common standards and procedures for returning illegally staying third-country nationals. This so-called 'Returns Directive' was heavily criticized by NGOs – some of which coined for it the term 'directive of shame' – and led to major controversies in the European Parliament. Arguing that the Directive failed to provide adequate protection to those subject to expulsion orders the Greens/EFA and GUE/NGL groups had proposed to reject the Directive – to be adopted under the co-decision procedure – outright. Yet on the basis of compromise proposals tabled by the EPP-ED group which partially strengthened the legal safeguards, the Directive was passed in the first reading by 369 votes to 197, with 106 abstentions, which was a further indication that the Parliament was becoming ever more 'pragmatic' in seeking compromises with the Council on sensitive justice and home affairs issues since the introduction of co-decision in 2005.

The Return Directive (European Parliament/Council, 2008a), which was finally adopted on 16 December, provides for any decision on 'return' (in the EP debates the less neutral term 'deportation' had been used) being followed by two different stages as follows: a first stage in which the person subject to the decision has an opportunity to depart voluntarily, lasting between seven and 30 days depending on national implementing legislation. This voluntary period can be reduced to zero, however, if there is a risk of absconding, an application for legal stay has been manifestly unfounded or fraudulent or a national security risk. After expiration of the voluntary period a removal order marks the start of the second stage, during which the person can be detained pending removal if there is a risk of absconding or hampering the removal process. The detention issue was one of the most controversial and the final compromise reached provides for a maximum of six months detention which can be extended by a further 12 months and is subject to judicial approval. The EP's LIBE Committee had advocated judicial approval at the latest within 48 hours, but the Council prevailed with the more vague formula 'as speedily as possible'. The length of detention had divided the Council, and in the end both the United Kingdom – where return detainees can be held indefinitely – and Ireland – where detainees can be held for a maximum of eight weeks – decided not to opt in. The Directive also provides for a re-entry ban into the Union of a maximum of five years. Passage in the European Parliament was helped by provisions for effective legal remedies, including legal advice, representation and linguistic assistance, although some Member States – including the UK – took the view that existing protection regimes provided already ample guarantees and that the Directive could make the return of illegally staying third-country nationals more difficult.

If the Return Directive showed the difficulties which Member States can also have in agreeing on the – usually more consensual – restrictive measures, negotiations on the EU 'Blue Card' Directive became a test-case for consensus-building on the legal immigration side. The Commission's proposal of October 2007 (see Monar, 2008) had already limited access to the Blue Card with its combined residence and work permit to third-country nationals highly quali-fied both in terms of professional qualifications and the above-average salary levels the work contracts offered to them would need to provide for. Unsur-prisingly the salary criterion – fixed by the Commission at three times the minimum wage in the respective EU country – proved controversial, this all the more so as some Member States do not have a minimum wage, a fact which the Commission had failed to take sufficiently into account. Consensus then emerged on using instead average wage levels, but positions in the Council varied between the Netherlands advocating 1.3 times the average wage and Germany 1.7 times. In November the European Parliament came out with a 388 to 56 majority in favour of 1.7 times average salary, Member States remaining free to decide on how many Blue Cards they want to issue per year and a stronger protection of the preference given to EU nationals, showing the Parliament not precisely on the forefront of liberalization of third-country legal immigration. With the Parliament only having consultation powers in matters of legal immigration this did not make much of an impact on the Council, and some Member States – in particular Germany – had anyway already secured provisions protecting existing national schemes in this field and national control of admissions. Final adoption of the Directive would have been possible at the end of the year, based on the requirement of a work contract offer of at least one year with a minimum of 1.5 times average salary (to be lowered to 1.2 times in case of a particular national need) and major restrictions on Blue

Card holders' rights to move to other EU countries (Council, 2008b). Yet adoption was delayed by the Czech Republic which insisted on the Blue Card Directive not entering into force before the lifting of all remaining restrictions on the free movement of workers rights of citizens of the new EU Member States by the old Member States.

Border and Visa Policy

In matters of external border policy the year saw only one major new initiative, the European Commission's proposals of 13 February regarding the creation of a European border surveillance system (EUROSUR) with an initial focus on the EU's southern maritime borders in the Mediterranean Sea and in the southern Atlantic. In its Communication (Commission, 2008f) the Commission highlighted the fact that surveillance of these border areas, which involve eight Member States, is currently carried out by 50 different authorities from 30 institutions – with the inevitable co-ordination problems and deficits such a fragmentation entails – and underlined that – because of technical (current performance of radar/optical sensors, limited availability of satellites) and financial limitations – the areas covered by surveillance are currently restricted to certain flat or coastal areas and those areas of the land border or open sea in which operations are carried out. The EUROSUR system should be set up to enable national authorities to counter more rapidly and effectively attempts to enter the EU illegally as well as cross-border crime such as trafficking in human beings and drug smuggling. The Commission proposed to establish the system in three phases up to 2013, starting with a phase of upgrading and extending national border surveillance systems around national co-ordination centres in each of the eight Member States which would be interlinked via a special communication network with the Union's border agency Frontex included for the purpose of better co-ordination of joint operations and common risk analysis. In the second phase targeted research and development would be carried out on the improvement and integrated use of surveillance instruments such as unmanned aerial vehicles (UAVs) and earth observation satellites which could ultimately be used to establish a 'common pre-frontier intelligence picture' allowing for an earlier identification of external border risks and a better targeting and earlier launch of operational reactions. In the third and final phase EUROSUR would result in the creation of an integrated network of reporting and surveillance systems for border control and internal security purposes involving all existing systems at the national and the European level ('a system of systems') covering the Mediterranean Sea, the southern Atlantic Ocean (Canary Islands) and the Black Sea.

With the EUROSUR initiative the Commission responded to the Member States' declared interest in the strengthening of external border surveillance as a key instrument for tackling illegal immigration. Yet the proposals inevitably fuelled critical reactions from NGOs and some political groupings about the EU's 'fortress Europe' rationale, now enhanced by an almost futuristic emphasis on advanced technology use. Perhaps in an effort to diffuse some of these accusations the Commission underlined that the planned new capabilities would also enhance the search and rescue capacity regarding the overcrowded and unseaworthy boats desperate migrants often use to try to reach the Union's shores (Commission, 2008f, p. 4). Apart from referring to the necessary research work being funded via the 7th EU Research Framework Programme the Commission was also vague about the full financial implications which the introduction and use of advanced instruments such as UAVs and observation satellites might have.

While the EUROSUR project appeared in part slightly futuristic Frontex continued to this year to expand its more concrete activities. Some of those were directly related to the EUROSUR objectives: in the field of maritime border surveillance progress was made with the putting into place of the European Patrols Network (EPN) in the Mediterranean. This comprises the creation of the National Co-ordination Centres also referred to in the EUROSUR initiative, enhanced information exchange, the development of common patrolling areas and the planning and implementation of joint operation with full involvement of Frontex.

Several Frontex-led common external border operations during the year were focused on the detection of illegal migrants at airports. In March LONG-STOP targeted inadequately documented passengers from the Indian subcontinent, in March/April ZARATHUSTRA focused on detection of illegal migrants from Iraq and Afghanistan and in May ZORBA had as its main objective the detection of illegal migration coming from Western Balkan and neighbouring eastern countries. The continued joint operation HERA to tackle illegal immigration from west African countries heading to the Canary Islands was, with nearly 6,000 migrants diverted back or deterred and a total of 360 facilitators arrested, amongst the most successful in terms of numbers. Yet HERA also showed the importance of co-operation with neighbouring third countries as the diverting back had only been possible on the basis of the agreements Spain had concluded with Mauritania and Senegal allowing for the diverting back of migrants' boats of departure to their points of departure, with Mauritanian or Senegalese law enforcement officers being present and in charge of the diversion operations onboard of the deployed EU vessels (Frontex, 2009a).

With Frontex appearing more and more as the linchpin of EU external border measures its effective functioning has a commensurate importance. An external evaluation during the year revealed that the strong prioritization of actual border management operations – mainly due to political pressure from the Member States – has gone hand in hand with a weaker development of the internal processes of the agency. This has meant, for instance, that the co-operation between the Risk Analysis Unit and the Operations Unit is underdeveloped, resulting in risk analysis outcomes not always being given due consideration when planning for joint operations. It was also noted that in terms of human resources Frontex was struggling to build up its absorption capacity in line with the massive increase of the budgetary resources assigned to it since its inception in 2005. With €70.4 million the 2008 budget of Frontex was nearly doubled with regard to the year before, another indication of how much it has become the instrument of choice of the Member States to respond to external border problems. The continuing difficulties with the Polish authorities regarding the still outstanding headquarters agreement and providing non-Polish Frontex personnel with an adequate status and papers was also identified as a problem – an interesting example of a Member State first insisting on being assigned the seat of an EU agency and then failing to provide a fully functional basis for its operation (Frontex, 2009b).

The multiple delays of the introduction of the second-generation Schengen Information System (SIS II), caused both by technical problems and poor initial management by the Commission, forced the Council on 24 October to adopt a new interim EC Regulation on the migration from the current system to the SIS II as the original transition instrument was to expire at the end of 2008 (Council, 2008c). The new Regulation extended the transition arrangements – and the necessary tests to be completed – to the planned completion in 2010, a delay of two years for the major functional upgrading of this instrument which the Council has repeatedly declared crucial both for external border controls and law enforcement co-operation within the EU.

Yet the year ended on a more positive note for the Schengen border system as the Council decided on 27 November that Switzerland had met all conditions for a full integration into the Schengen area (Council, 2008d). As a result internal border controls between Schengen and the surrounding EU countries were abolished on 12 December, with air borders to follow on 29 March 2009. Switzerland thus became the third non-EU Schengen member (after Iceland and Norway), highlighting again the peculiar situation of non-EU members participating in a substantial part of the EU's AFSJ while two EU Member States (Ireland and the United Kingdom) still maintain their op-out from most of this part.

Under the strain of the refusal of the US to extend bilateral visa waiver arrangement to all new EU Member States the EU's common visa policy continued to look much less 'common' during the year than provided for by the EC Treaty. On 26 February the Czech government signed a memorandum of understanding with the US in which it agreed to an enhanced transfer of data on passengers, suspected terrorists and migration-related matters to the US in exchange for access to the US visa waiver programme, thereby seriously undermining the common EU position on these issues as well as the common visa policy in general. As five other new Member States – Estonia, Latvia, Lithuania, Hungary and Slovakia – lost little time to follow this demonstration of coherence and solidarity in the enlarged EU, the Commission prefered not to – as initially indicated – take legal action against the 'bilateral' approach, focusing instead on a new round of negotiations with the US. Yet the divisions in the EU camp did obviously nothing to increase the US' willingness to compromise, so that in July the Commission felt compelled to announce retaliatory measures against the US in the form of a temporary restoration of the visa requirement for US nationals holding diplomatic passports if no progress would be achieved by 1 January 2009 (Commission, 2008g, p. 9). The transatlantic tension was then gradually defused by the US extending its visa waiver programme in October to the above-mentioned six 'bilateralists' and in December to Malta which, however, had more to do with the respective countries having given in to US demands than with the Commission's threats of retaliation. At the end of the year prospects looked good for the other five new Member States being soon included in the arrangement as well, but this surely without any gain for the Union's credibility as an international actor in this field.

Judicial Co-operation

In the domain of judicial co-operation in civil matters an important step forward was taken with the adoption on 17 June of the Regulation (EC) 593/2008 on the law applicable to contractual obligations, better known as the 'Rome I Regulation' (European Parliament/Council, 2008b). This legal instrument followed the adoption in 2007 of the 'Rome II Regulation' on non-contractual obligations and pursues the same fundamental objective, which is to contribute to the proper functioning of the internal market through enhancing cross-border legal certainty and the predictability of outcomes of cross-border litigation. The Regulation maintains the fundamental principle of the original 1980 Rome Convention (which it replaces) of the autonomy of contracting parties in terms of the choice of the applicable law. Yet it clarifies a number of rules which had led to different interpretations by national courts, especially as regards the law applicable if parties to a cross-border contract have not made an explicit choice of the applicable law. Faced with massive opposition from consumer businesses and several Member States the Commission had to give up its original proposal to mandatorily tie consumer contracts to the law of the Member State where the consumer is habitually resident. The elimination in the last negotiation phase of a controversial provision on the proprietary aspects of the assignment of debts – which would have made the application of the law of the assignor's habitual residence mandatory and might have had considerable implications for financial markets – contributed much to the British government reconsidering its original position not to participate in the measure (Monar, 2008) and to finally declare its (belated) opt-in on 28 July. This was done after a public consultation exercise (UK Ministry of Justice, 2008a) which was one of the relatively rare examples of a Member State's government inviting public reactions to Community legislation.

The pace of progress in the sphere of judicial co-operation in criminal matters accelerated sharply during the year, with the formal adoption of several legislative instruments which had been under negotiation for several years.

On 24 July the JHA Council adopted the Framework Decision on taking account of convictions in Member States in the course of new criminal proceedings (Council, 2008e). This instrument is aimed at ensuring that previous convictions handed down in other Member States are taken into account in case of criminal proceedings involving reoffenders. It obliges courts to take such previous convictions into account but does not harmonize the consequences attached to the existence of previous convictions which continue to vary considerably under the different national criminal law systems. It can therefore be regarded as a minimal(ist) mutual recognition measure.

Two closely interrelated mutual recognition instruments were adopted on 27 November. The first one was the Framework Decision on mutual recognition – for enforcement purposes – of judgments in criminal matters imposing custodial sentences (Council, 2008f). It defines the rules under which a Member State, with a view to facilitating the social rehabilitation of a sentenced person, is to recognize and enforce a sentence rendered by another Member State and is based on the assumption that serving the sentence in the Member State of nationality (or another Member State to which the person has strong links) will normally help with social rehabilitation and reintegration. The transfer to the enforcement authorities of the respective other Member State must be based on assessment of the issuing authority that the transfer will indeed serve this rehabilitation purpose. The executing authority can object against the transfer if it thinks that this purpose is not met, but not the sentenced person if the transfer is to the Member State of nationality or the one to which the person is to be deported after being released from the sentence. After the transfer the serving of the sentence will be governed by the law of the executing Member State, including potential decisions on early or conditional release. The Framework Decision applies – under abolition of the principle of double criminality – to the list of 32 serious offences which also applies to the European Arrest Warrant, but to other crimes only if they also constitute an offence under the law of the executing Member State. The executing state has to deduct any period of deprivation of liberty already served in the issuing state and cannot aggravate the sentence imposed by the latter in nature or duration. This measure was complemented by the Framework Decision of 27 November on the application of the principle of mutual recognition to judgments and probation decisions with a view to the supervision of probation measures and alternative sanctions (Council, 2008g) which is aimed at ensuring that the respect of probation obligations, such as, for instance, the obligation to avoid contact with certain persons or to carry out community services, can be properly supervised and enforced in another than the issuing Member State, making it again possible for the sentenced person to comply with probation conditions in another Member State which in most cases may be the Member State of origin.

Taken together these two Framework Decisions constitute significant building blocks for the construction of the EU's criminal justice area as they combine the predominating law enforcement rationale with one of rehabilitation. The fact that such measures can also entail practical problems for some Member States was underlined by the fact that Poland requested a temporary derogation from the custodial sentences Framework Decisions on grounds that it needed more time to 'face the practical and material consequences of transfer of Polish citizens convicted in other Member States, especially in the light of an increased mobility of Polish citizens within the EU' (Council, 2008f, p. 28).

On the mutual recognition side, the Council was also able, finally, to adopt on 18 December the much delayed Framework Decision on the European Evidence Warrant (EEW) giving a cross-border reach to judicial search or seizure warrants on the model of the European Arrest Warrant (Council, 2008h). The unanimity rule showed in this case again its full impact on the substance of this important measure: not only will the scope of the EEW be restricted to already available evidence in the form of documents, objects and data (not covering, for instance, DNA samples or the monitoring of bank accounts), but the Council also raised the condition for the abolition of the double criminality principle for 32 serious offences to them being punishable in the issuing state by a custodial sentence of at least three years. The effectiveness of the EEW is also likely to be affected by the introduction of a 'territoriality clause', allowing a Member State to refuse a Warrant for offences committed wholly or mainly within its territory. Germany, which had not played the most constructive role during the negotiations, reserved its right, under an opt-out mechanism, to issue a declaration making the execution of a European Evidence Warrant subject to verification of double criminality in cases relating to terrorism, computer-related crime, racism and xenophobia, sabotage, racketeering and extortion or swindling, if it is necessary to carry out a search or seizure for the execution of the warrant.

Significant progress was also achieved in the field of approximation of national substantive criminal law, although here the baseline remained minimal harmonization.

On 24 October the Council adopted Framework Decision 2008/841/JHA on the fight against organized crime which defines as a 'criminal organization' any structured association of persons acting in concert with a view to committing offences which are punishable by deprivation of liberty or a detention order of a maximum of at least four years to obtain, directly or indirectly, a financial or other material benefit (Council, 2008i). The key element of this EU instrument (which replaced a Joint Action of 1998) is that it obliges Member States to classify as a criminal offence the 'participation' in such a criminal organization even if a person does not take part in the actual execution of this activity, but favours knowingly the achievements of the organization's objectives through otherwise non-criminal activities such as providing information, financing operations or recruitment of new members. This is crucial for the fight against organized crime which often involves the 'services' of people of a variety of professional backgrounds (such as bankers, accountants and transport companies) which as such are clearly not criminal activities. Yet the Member States had to struggle when it came to agree on a common framework for sentencing, which in the end led to a tortuous and, in terms of its harmonization effect, quite minimalistic compromise on a maximum term of imprisonment of 'at least between two and five years'.

The negotiations on the Council Framework Decision 2008/913/JHA on combating certain forms and expressions of racism and xenophobia by means of criminal law (Council, 2008j), adopted on 28 November, had been plagued for seven years by fundamental differences between the Member States with regard to some of the acts in question, perhaps best highlighted by the example of the denial of the Holocaust which – for obvious historical reasons – is a crime punishable by imprisonment in Austria and Germany but covered by the freedom of expression in a range of other EU countries. During the negotiations the UK and the Nordic countries, in particular, resisted the pressure of Germany and Austria for a more far-reaching criminalization of acts relating to racism and xenophobia. In the end agreement was reached on making the incitement to violence and hatred for racist and xenophobic purposes a criminal offence subject to a penalty of at least between one and three years. Yet controversial terms such the Holocaust were left out of the instrument, and Member States may choose to punish only conduct which is 'either carried out in a manner likely to disturb public order or which is threatening, abusive or insulting' – which leaves quite a wide margin for national implementation.

Also on the harmonization side, finally, the Council amended on 28 November by Framework Decision 2008/919/JHA (Council, 2008k) the 2002 Framework Decision on Combating Terrorism by introducing three new categories of terrorism-related offences: public provocation to commit a terrorist offence, recruitment for terrorism and training for terrorism. Especially the first category had been controversial because of the potential restrictions it could entail for the freedom of expression, and the carefully crafted Article 2 was inserted to protect national traditions and frameworks regarding the freedom of expression and of the media.

On the institutional side negotiations in the Council based on an initiative submitted by 14 Member States on 7 January led already in July to a consensus on a range of measures to strengthening Eurojust: the definition of a common basis of powers for the National Members (until now diverging widely), the setting up of an emergency On-Call Co-ordination (OCC) mechanism to ensure around the clock availability of Eurojust, an enhanced role of the Eurojust College in cases of conflicts of jurisdiction, the speeding up of transmission of information to Eurojust, the setting up of Eurojust national co-ordination systems to improve co-ordination at the national level in view of a more effective interaction with Eurojust and an improved input into its case management system, the authorization of Eurojust to process certain (limited) categories of personal data, the strengthening of co-operation with third states by allowing Eurojust to post liaison magistrates in these countries and the reinforcing of co-operation with other bodies such as Europol, OLAF, Frontex and the Situation Centre (SitCen) in the Council (Council, 2008l). The respective Council Decision on the strengthening of Eurojust was adopted on 16 December, but its entry into force was delayed because it was tied to the prior finalization of the Europol Decision (see below). Yet the Council was able to adopt a Decision on the European Judicial Network on the same day, strengthening certain aspects of the functioning of this network of national contact points and its links with Eurojust (Council, 2008m).

Police Co-operation

By comparison with judicial co-operation the developments in the police co-operation domain were more modest. The delayed Council Decision on the stepping up of cross-border co-operation, particularly in combating terrorism and cross-border crime, providing, *inter alia*, for automated access to and transfer of DNA profiles, dactyloscopic data and certain national vehicle registration data (the so-called 'Prüm Decision' – see Monar, 2008), was formally adopted together with the technical implementation Decision on 23 June (Council, 2008n), this however without putting all concerns about the protection of personal data to rest. Yet with regard to the latter it clearly helped that the Council was able to finally adopt on 27 November the Framework Decision on the protection of personal data processed in the framework of police and judicial co-operation in criminal matters (Council, 2008o). This came as the first – and long overdue – horizontal data protection instrument in the 'third pillar' domain, and a barrage of criticisms from the European Parliament, the European Data Protection Supervisor and civil liberties organizations contributed to certain additional safeguards being retained in the final text. In his assessment of the Framework Decision the Data Protection Supervisor, Peter Hustinx, regretted that it only covers police and judicial data exchanged between Member States, EU authorities and systems, and not domestic data as well as the lack of consistency with the 'first pillar' data-protection Directive (95/46/EC) – which further restricts the purposes for which personal data can be used – and the absence of a common protection standard as regards the transfer of data to third countries (European Data Protection Supervisor, 2008).

The operational capabilities of EU police co-operation were (slightly) strengthened by the adoption on 23 June of Council Decision 2008/617/JHA on the improvement of co-operation between the special intervention units of the Member States of the European Union in crisis situations (Council, 2008p). This lays down general rules and conditions to allow for special law enforcement intervention units of one Member State to provide assistance and/or operate on the territory of another Member State. Such assistance can consist of providing the requesting Member State with equipment and/or expertise and/or of carrying out actions on the territory of that Member State, using weapons if so required. Yet operational activities operate under the responsibility, authority and direction of the requesting Member State and in accordance with the law of that Member State, and no role at all is provided for Europol or any other EU structure.

In May the Council was able to reach political agreement on the Council Decision establishing the European Police Office (Europol) but final adoption of the text was still delayed at the end of the year because of parliamentary scrutiny reservations. The Decision will replace the Europol Convention and transform Europol into an EU entity funded from the general budget of the EU (instead of from national budgets). While not transferring any executive law enforcement powers to Europol, the draft Decision would extend the agency's possibilities to assist national authorities, *inter alia*, by not any longer being bound by the current pre-condition of factual indications of involvement of organized crime structures, the facilitation of its participation – in a supportive function – in Joint Investigation Teams and the direct access of national authorities to the Europol Information System. The draft also provides for agreements to be concluded with other EU structures (including the European Central Bank) and improved procedures regarding Europol's relations with third countries (Council, 2008q). Yet in terms of its actual operational functions *vis-à-vis* national authorities Europol would even under the new Decision still appear weaker than Eurojust in the judicial sphere.

II. Further Development Perspectives

Developments during the year showed that the JHA domain continues to be one of the most dynamic policy-making areas of the Union, with a significant output even in the non-communitarized, unanimity-dominated fields of police and judicial co-operation in criminal matters. Although the potential non-ratification of the Lisbon Treaty was widely regarded as negative for the future development prospects, it is unlikely that this would lead to a standstill in this domain as Member States simply have to further develop common responses to key challenges as regards migration management and the fight against serious cross-border crime. The report to the Council of the informal high-level 'Future Group' (Monar, 2008) submitted in July – stronger on the analysis of current deficits than on a coherent vision for the future of the AFSJ – was significant in this respect as its key proposals were not tied to the fate of the Treaty of Lisbon (Council 2008r). At the end of the year there was widespread agreement that 2009 would become a key year for the AFSJ because of both the decision on the fate of the Lisbon Treaty and the scheduled adoption under the Swedish Presidency of the successor Programme to the Hague Programme, the 'Stockholm Programme'. Should the first be positive the second could well give a similarly strong impetus to further development of this domain as the Tampere Programme after the entry into force of the Amsterdam Treaty in 1999.

Key Readings

Brady, H. (2008) 'Europol and the European Criminal Intelligence Model: A Non-state Response to Organized Crime'. *Policing*, Vol. 2, pp. 103–9.

Plender, R. (2008) 'EU Immigration and Asylum Policy – The Hague Programme and the Way Forward'. In *ERA Forum*, Vol. 9, pp. 301–25.

Suominen, A. (2008) 'The Past, Present and the Future of Eurojust'. *Maastricht Journal of European and Comparative Law*, Vol. 15, pp. 217–34.

References

Commission of the European Communities (2008a) 'Communication [. . .] Policy Plan on Asylum: An Integrated Approach to Protection across the EU'. COM(2008)247, 16 June.

Commission of the European Communities (2008b) 'Proposal for a Directive [. . .] Laying Down Minimum Standards for the Reception of Asylum Seekers' (Recast). COM(2008)815, 3 December.

Commission of the European Communities (2008c) 'Proposal for a Regulation [. . .] Establishing the Criteria and Mechanisms for Determining the Member State Responsible for Examining an Application for International Protection Lodged in One of the Member States by a Third-Country National or a Stateless Person'. COM(2008)820, 3 December.

Commission of the European Communities (2008d) 'Proposal for a Regulation [. . .] Concerning the Establishment of "Eurodac" for the Comparison of Fingerprints [. . .]. COM(2008)825, 3 December.

Commission of the European Communities (2008e) 'Communication [. . .] A Common Immigration Policy for Europe: Principles, Actions and Tools'. COM(2008)359, 17 June.

Commission of the European Communities (2008f) 'Communication [. . .] Examining the Creation of a European Border Surveillance System (EUROSUR)'. COM(2008)68, 13 February.

Commission of the European Communities (2008g) 'Fourth Report [. . .] on Certain Third Countries' Maintenance of Visa Requirements in Breach of the Principle of Reciprocity'. COM(2008)486, 23 July.

Council of the European Union (2008a) 'European Pact on Immigration and Asylum'. Brussels, 23 November, 13440.

Council of the European Union (2008b) 'Proposal for a Council Directive on the Conditions of Entry and Residence of Third-Country Nationals for the Purposes of Highly Qualified Employment'. 16952, Brussels, 10 December.

Council of the European Union (2008c) 'Council Regulation (EC) No 1104/2008 of 24 October 2008 on migration from the Schengen Information System (SIS 1+) to the Second Generation Schengen Information System' (SIS II). OJ L 299, 8 November.

Council of the European Union (2008d) 'Council Decision of 27 November 2008 on the Full Application of the Provisions of the Schengen *acquis* in the Swiss Confederation'. OJ L 327, 5 December.

Council of the European Union (2008e) 'Council Framework Decision 2008/675/ JHA of 24 July 2008 on Taking Account of Convictions in the Member States of the European Union in the Course of New Criminal Proceedings'. OJ L 220, 15 August.

Council of the European Union (2008f) 'Council Framework Decision 2008/909/ JHA of 27 November 2008 on the Application of the Principle of Mutual Recognition to Judgments in Criminal Matters Imposing Custodial Sentences or Measures Involving Deprivation of Liberty for the Purpose of their Enforcement in the European Union'. OJ L 327, 5 December.

Council of the European Union (2008g) 'Council Framework Decision 2008/947/ JHA of 27 November 2008 on the Application of the Principle of Mutual Recognition to Judgments and Probation Decisions with a View to the Supervision of Probation Measures and Alternative Sanctions'. OJ L 337, 16 December.

Council of the European Union (2008h) 'Council Framework Decision 2008/978/ JHA of 18 December 2008 on the European Evidence Warrant for the Purpose of Obtaining Objects, Documents and Data for Use in Proceedings in Criminal Matters'. OJ L 350, 30 December.

Council of the European Union (2008i) 'Council Framework Decision 2008/841/ JHA of 24 October 2008 on the Fight Against Organized Crime'. OJ L 300, 11 November.

Council of the European Union (2008j) 'Council Framework Decision 2008/913/ JHA of 28 November 2008 on Combating Certain Forms and Expressions of Racism and Xenophobia by Means of Criminal Law'. OJ L 328, 6 December.

Council of the European Union (2008k) 'Council Framework Decision 2008/919/ JHA of 28 November 2008 Amending Framework Decision 2002/475/JHA on Combating Terrorism'. OJ L 330, 9 December.

Council of the European Union (2008l) '[Draft] Council Decision on the Strengthening of Eurojust and Amending Decision 2002/187/JHA Setting up Eurojust with a View to Reinforcing the Fight Against Serious Crime'. Brussels, 24 November, 14927.

Council of the European Union (2008m) 'Council Decision 2008/976/JHA of 16 December 2008 on the European Judicial Network'. OJ L 348, 24 December.

Council of the European Union (2008n) 'Council Decision 2008/615/JHA of 23 June 2008 on the Stepping Up of Cross-Border Co-operation, Particularly in Combating Terrorism and Cross-Border Crime'. OJ L 210, 6 August.

Council of the European Union (2008o) 'Council Framework Decision 2008/977/ JHA of 27 November 2008 on the Protection of Personal Data Processed in the Framework of Police and Judicial Co-operation in Criminal Matters'. OJ L 350, 30 December.

Council of the European Union (2008p) 'Council Decision 2008/617/JHA of 23 June 2008 on the Improvement of Co-operation between the Special Intervention Units of the Member States of the European Union in Crisis Situations'. OJ 1 210, 6 August.

Council of the European Union (2008q) '[Draft] Council Decision Establishing the European Police Office (Europol)'. 9 October, 8706/3/08 REV 3.

Council of the European Union (2008r) 'Report of the Informal High-Level Advisory Group on the Future of European Home Affairs Policy ("The Future Group")'. 9 July, 11657/08.

ECRE (2008) 'Memorandum to the JHA Council: Ending the Asylum Lottery – Guaranteeing Refugee Protection in Europe'. Brussels, April.

European Data Protection Supervisor (2008) 'EDPS Sees Adoption of Data Protection Framework for Police and Judicial Co-operation Only as a First Step'. Brussels, 28 November.

European Parliament/Council of the European Union (2008a) 'Directive 2008/115/EC [. . .] on Common Standards and Procedures in Member States for Returning Illegally Staying Third-Country Nationals', OJ L 348, 24 December.

European Parliament/Council of the European Union (2008b) 'Regulation [. . .] of 17 June 2008 on the Law Applicable to Contractual Obligations (Rome I)', OJ L 177, 4 July.

Frontex (2009a) 'HERA 2008 and NAUTILUS 2008 Statistics'. Warsaw, February 2009. Available at: «http://www.frontex.europa.eu/newsroom/news_releases/art40.html».

Frontex (2009b) 'External evaluation of the European Agency for the Management of Operational Co-operation at the External Borders of the Member States of the European Union'. Final Report, Warsaw, January 2009. Available at: «http://www.frontex.europa.eu/specific_documents/other/».

Monar, J. (2008) 'Justice and Home Affairs'. *JCMS*, Vol. 46, s1.

UK Ministry of Justice (2008a) 'Rome I – Should the UK Opt In'. Consultation Paper CP05/08, London, 2 April 2008.

UNHCR (2008) 'UNHCR Position on the Return of Asylum-Seekers to Greece under the "Dublin Regulation" '. Geneva, 15 April.

Legal Developments

MICHAEL DOUGAN
Liverpool Law School, University of Liverpool

Introduction

Another year, another cascade of rulings from Luxembourg. Some follow on from important cases discussed in previous editions of this *Review*: for example, *Rüffert* and *Commission v. Luxembourg* concerning the legal framework governing posted workers,[1] which together build on the controversial approach adopted by the European Court of Justice (ECJ) in *Laval un Partneri*;[2] and *Bartsch* on the enforceability of the general principle of Community law prohibiting discrimination on grounds of age,[3] which clarifies the implications of the notorious *Mangold* case.[4] Other judgments constitute significant developments across myriad additional fields of Community and Union law: for example, cases like *FIAMM* and *Masdar* exploring the extent to which the Community institutions may incur non-contractual liability under Articles 235 and 288 EC based on lawful acts;[5] the *Small Arms and Light Weapons* ruling concerning the demarcation of competences between development co-operation under the First Pillar and foreign policy matters falling within the Second Pillar;[6] *Cartesio* on the scope of the freedom of establishment where a company wishes to transfer its seat to another Member

---

[1] Case C-346/06 (3 April 2008) and Case C-319/06 (19 June 2008), respectively.
[2] Case C-341/05 [2007] ECR I-11767.
[3] Case C-427/06 (23 September 2008).
[4] Case C-144/04 [2005] ECR I-9981.
[5] Case C-120/06 (9 September 2008) and Case C-47/07 (16 December 2008), respectively.
[6] Case C-91/05 (20 May 2008).

State;[7] *Coleman* and *Maruko* on the scope and nature of protection against discrimination on grounds of disability and sexual orientation (respectively);[8] and *Sweden v. Council* concerning application of the right of access to documents to advice provided to a Community institution by its own legal service.[9]

In accordance with established practice, this article offers more detailed consideration of just a few of the other major rulings delivered by the Community courts during 2008.

I. Anti-Terrorism: The United Nations, the European Union and Fundamental Rights Protection

In its eagerly awaited ruling in *Kadi and Al Barakaat*, the ECJ addressed the scope of protection for fundamental rights under Community law, as regards EU implementation of the United Nations' (UN) system for imposing financial sanctions against persons and entities (allegedly) associated with Osama bin Laden and the Al-Qaeda network.[10]

It will be recalled that the UN Security Council established (by means of resolutions) a Sanctions Committee responsible for identifying and updating the list of affected persons and entities. Taking the view that implementation of the UN sanctions regime necessitated action at the Community level, the Council of Ministers adopted a series of common positions under the Second Pillar, together with implementing regulations under the First Pillar. Those measures provide for the freezing of assets across the Community territory of designated persons and entities, the list of which is updated by the Commission in the light of determinations made by the Sanctions Committee. The claimants in *Kadi and Al Barakaat*, who were among those listed, brought an action for annulment of the relevant Community measures, *inter alia*, on the grounds that they breached the claimants' fundamental rights (such as the rights of the defence and to property) as protected under Community law.[11]

In 2005, the Court of First Instance (CFI) dismissed the actions brought by Kadi and Al Barakaat.[12] It was held that, although not a member of the UN, the Community is nevertheless bound to respect the UN Charter. For their

---

[7] Case C-210/06 (16 December 2008).
[8] Case C-303/06 (17 July 2008) and Case C-267/06 (1 April 2008), respectively.
[9] Cases C-39 & 52/05 (1 July 2008).
[10] Cases C-402 & 415/05 (3 September 2008).
[11] The parties also alleged that the Community had no legal competence to adopt the contested measures imposing financial sanctions upon individuals and groups unconnected to the governing regime of a third country.
[12] Case T-315/01 *Kadi* [2005] ECR II-3649; Case T-306/01 *Yusuf and Al Barakaat International Foundation* [2005] ECR II-3533.

part, the Community courts have no jurisdiction to review the lawfulness of Security Council or Sanctions Committee decisions according to the fundamental rights recognized under Community law. In implementing the determinations of the Security Council and Sanctions Committee, as regards persons and entities associated with Osama bin Laden and the Al-Qaeda network, the Community institutions had acted under circumscribed powers and without any autonomous discretion. For the Community courts to review the lawfulness of those Community implementation measures would therefore be tantamount to calling into question, albeit indirectly, the actions of the Security Council and Sanctions Committee themselves. Nevertheless, the Community courts were entitled to determine whether decisions of the Security Council and Sanctions Committee were compatible with *jus cogens*, i.e. the body of higher rules of public international law binding on all subjects of the international legal order, including the UN, and from which no derogation is possible – though the CFI ultimately concluded that the UN sanctions regime did not in fact infringe any of the rights protected under *jus cogens*.

The CFI's finding that the Community courts have, in principle, no jurisdiction to review the internal lawfulness of Community regulations giving effect to UN Security Council resolutions was the focal point of the appeal in *Kadi and Al Barakaat*.[13] The ECJ began by asserting that the Community is based on the rule of law, inasmuch as neither the Member States nor the Community institutions can avoid review of the conformity of their acts with the basic constitutional charter provided by the EC Treaty. Furthermore, international agreements can affect neither the allocation of powers fixed by the Treaties nor the autonomy of the Community legal system. In particular, the obligations imposed by an international agreement cannot prejudice the principle that all Community acts must respect fundamental rights as a condition for their own lawfulness. However, the review conducted by the Community courts concerns only the Community act intended to give effect to an international agreement. It is not for the Community judicature to review the lawfulness of an international agreement as such, even (for example) on grounds of its compliance with the rules of *jus cogens*. Moreover, for the Court to find that a Community act giving effect to an international agreement is contrary to a higher rule of the Community legal order would not entail any challenge to the primacy of that agreement under international law.

Against that background, nothing in the principles governing the relationship between the international legal order under the United Nations (on the

---

[13] Unfortunately, space precludes consideration of the equally significant issues addressed by the CFI and ECJ concerning the nature of Community competences in cross-pillar cases, the scope of application of Article 308 EC and the principle of attributed powers under Article 5 EC.

one hand) and the Community legal order (on the other hand) excludes the possibility of judicial review of the internal lawfulness of a Community act in the light of the Community's own fundamental freedoms. After all, the UN Charter leaves the members of the United Nations a free choice among the various possible models for implementing Security Council resolutions into their domestic legal orders. Furthermore, nor can any such immunity from jurisdiction for a Community measure, based on the primacy at the level of international law of obligations under the Charter of the United Nations, find a basis in the EC Treaty itself. In particular, Article 307 EC, according to which the EC Treaty shall not affect rights and obligations arising from pre-existing international agreements between Member States and third countries, cannot be understood to authorize any derogation from the principles of liberty, democracy and respect for human rights as enshrined in Article 6(1) TEU and which form part of the very foundations of the Community legal order.

The ECJ also dismissed any idea that the Community courts should (voluntarily) decline to exercise their jurisdiction to review the legality of Community measures adopted to give effect to Security Council resolutions, on the basis that the UN had established its own administrative system offering relevant persons and entities an opportunity to be heard, thus ensuring that fundamental rights are adequately protected under the UN legal system in any event. After all, the relevant amendments to the system for adding/removing persons or entities to/from the UN list were adopted after the Community measures contested by Kadi and Al Barakaat. In any event, even the existence of an amended re-examination procedure before the UN Sanctions Committee could not give rise to a generalized immunity from jurisdiction within the Community's own legal order. In particular, the Court considered that the re-examination procedure remains essentially diplomatic and intergovernmental and clearly fails to offer guarantees of judicial protection to the relevant persons/entities.

The ECJ therefore found that the CFI had erred in law by denying its own jurisdiction to review the lawfulness of the contested Community regulations. In fact, the Community judicature must ensure the review – in principle, the full review – of the lawfulness of all Community acts in the light of fundamental rights as general principles of Community law, including review of Community measures which are designed to give effect to the UN Security Council resolutions concerned with the maintenance of international peace and security.

Applying that principle to the case at hand, the ECJ held that the Community had patently failed to respect the claimants' rights of the defence: it is true that the particular nature of financial sanctions implies that the

Community institutions cannot be required to communicate the grounds for their decision, or afford the person concerned a hearing, *in advance of* the initial listing; nevertheless, the contested Community measures made no provision for communicating evidence to, and hearing the relevant person, *at the same time as or after* his or her listing. In addition, the ECJ found that the Community had infringed the claimants' right to property: the restrictive effects of financial sanctions may be justified by a legitimate public interest, particularly having regard to the possibility for the competent national authorities to make available funds necessary for the relevant person's basic expenses, but the Community must still furnish guarantees enabling the relevant person to put his or her case to the competent authorities. Although in principle the disputed Community regulation should therefore be annulled so far as it concerned the applicants in *Kadi and Al Barakaat*, the Court decided to exercise its power exceptionally to maintain the legal effects of the relevant measure for a period of no more than three months, during which time the Council could take steps to remedy the specific infringements identified by the ECJ in its ruling.

The judgment in *Kadi and Al Barakaat* raises multiple and multifaceted issues, on which the journals will no doubt be replete with thorough scholarly analysis. For present purposes, some basic observations should suffice to give an indication of initial reactions to *Kadi and Al Barakaat* and of the ruling's potential implications.

Many EU lawyers see the judgment as one of the most powerful demonstrations to date of the Court's commitment to the protection of human rights and effective judicial protection within the Community legal order. The ruling in *Kadi and Al Barakaat* certainly endorses the rhetoric of placing fundamental individual freedoms at the very heart of the European integration process – an essential prerequisite for the validity and indeed legitimacy of Community action. The Court's stance is all the more striking given that, in a sphere such as anti-terrorism, it is not uncommon for political pressure to be heaped upon the judges to dilute or even disapply human rights safeguards on the basis of an allegedly existential threat to the public interest. Perhaps most significantly, the *Kadi and Al Barakaat* litigation involved one of the cornerstones of the global system of counter-terrorism co-operation instituted by the United Nations: the ECJ was therefore resisting not only internal political concerns raised by the other Union institutions and many Member States, but had to grapple also with the implications of its ruling for the broader system of international peace and security. Indeed, for the sake of maintaining the Union's own commitment to human rights, the Court was prepared to limit the effective authority of the UN Security Council within the Community legal order.

Of course, the latter aspect of the *Kadi and Al Barakaat* dispute provides fuel for certain more critical reactions to the ECJ's ruling. Concerns have been expressed about the potential implications of the judgment for the effectiveness of the sanctions regime and the battle to disrupt the international financing of terror groups – though it should not be forgotten that the Court temporarily upheld the legal effects of Kadi's and Al Barakaat's listing, so as to afford the political institutions time to correct their previous (essentially procedural) infractions without endangering the public interest. More seriously, many international lawyers seem worried about the potential damage done by the *Kadi and Al Barakaat* ruling to the credibility of the United Nations – an organization whose reputation has already suffered repeated serious blows over recent years, yet which remains for both the Union and its Member States the key to an international system of governance and law orientated around peaceful multilateral co-operation. Indeed, some commentators have suggested that the *Kadi and Al Barakaat* ruling marks an unfortunate turn towards introspection by the ECJ and an uninspiring example of unilateralism by the Union itself: even if the Court was at pains to stress that its ruling concerned only the internal lawfulness of the Community's implementing regulations, not the status of the UN Charter and/or of Security Council resolutions for the purposes of the international legal order, the *Kadi and Al Barakaat* ruling might nonetheless give the impression of a Union concerned above all else to ring-fence the autonomy of its own legal system.

However, such criticisms should not be exaggerated. No sovereign legal order surrenders itself completely to the influence of an external entity, even to the point of sacrificing the basic values which express and authenticate that legal order's fundamental identity and define its own sense of purpose. The ruling in *Kadi and Al Barakaat* affirms the autonomy of Community law in the sense of an irreducible core – respect for human rights – which cannot be traded away through the contracting of international agreements or in the desire to fulfil certain diplomatic commitments. If anything, the ruling in *Kadi and Al Barakaat* should focus the UN Security Council's attention, more closely and more urgently, on its own *modus operandi* for imposing financial sanctions upon named persons and entities, particularly as regards the Sanctions Committee's evident shortcomings when it comes to safeguarding individual rights; or at least force the UN Security Council to acknowledge that there are inherent limits to how far its counter-terrorism regime can be treated as authoritative and unconditionally binding, specifically, at the point where Sanctions Committee decisions come to be translated into the domestic legal systems of states and regional organizations possessed of significantly more advanced standards of fundamental rights protection.

From that point of view, the ECJ's ruling in *Kadi and Al Barakaat* could even be interpreted as a plea for constructive dialogue between the Union institutions and the United Nations, with a view to gradually improving the Sanctions Committee's own procedures for compiling its counter-terrorism lists – a mutually beneficial interaction, precisely of a pluralistic nature, not unfamiliar to EU lawyers already (for example) from relations between the ECJ and various national constitutional courts, or between the ECJ and the European Court of Human Rights. In that regard, it is interesting to note that, according to the ECJ, the deficiencies of the Sanctions Committee's existing procedures ruled out any 'generalized immunity' from scrutiny for the Community's implementing regulations. Does that leave the door open for a future revision of the *Kadi and Al Barakaat* ruling, were the Sanctions Committee to adopt a more satisfactory approach to individual rights, along the lines of the doctrine of equivalent protection practised *vis-à-vis* the ECJ itself by those national constitutional courts and the Strasbourg judges? Yet even if the Court indeed intended to leave open such a possibility in principle, the prospects for any 'equivalent protection' approach in practice seem rather remote, for the time being at least, given that it would presuppose a genuinely radical over-haul of the entire United Nations sanctions regime.

Such issues provide a useful cue for highlighting some of the other questions opened up by the ruling in *Kadi and Al Barakaat*. To start with, the Court's assertion that the Community judicature must ensure the review, and in principle the full review, of the lawfulness of Community acts concerning counter-terrorism sanctions invites speculation about how far such judicial scrutiny will indeed develop in future cases. For example, how would the ECJ respond to a claimant who argued that the substantive evidence relied upon by the Sanctions Committee, and thus of necessity by the Community institutions, was actually insufficient to justify his/her listing for financial restrictions? Indeed, for those purposes, what weight might the ECJ give to the fact that the substantive evidence is almost invariably treated as highly confidential, allegedly for security purposes, so that many governments are reluctant to make disclosure, even *in camera*, to the competent judicial authorities? In that regard, there may be room for the fruitful cross-fertilization of jurisprudence between the case law on the judicial protection of those listed by the UN Sanctions Committee (such as *Kadi and Al Barakaat* itself) and that concerning the treatment of persons and entities subject to financial restrictions imposed by the EU of its own initiative (as in the *OMPI* cases).[14] After all, the CFI in *OMPI III* (also delivered in 2008) seemed to signal a more

---

[14] Case T-228/02 [2006] ECR II-4665; Case T-256/07 (23 October 2008); Case T-284/08 (4 December 2008).

robust approach to judicial scrutiny of the substantive decision to implement an EU-own listing, particularly in situations where the relevant Member State or Union institution refuses to make the relevant evidence available to the Community courts.[15] Is what's good for the EU goose also good for the UN gander? If so, *Kadi and Al Barakaat* may have laid the ground for many and more intractable clashes between the findings of the Sanctions Committee and the expectations of the ECJ.

Another line of enquiry concerns the potential implications of *Kadi and Al Barakaat* beyond the specific issue of counter-terrorism sanctions, for the status of fundamental rights protection within the EU as a whole. Might the Court's strong vindication of the central importance within the Union legal order of the basic values expressed in Article 6(1) TEU lead the judges to adopt a more adventurous approach to human rights issues in other fields where the current position is considered less than satisfactory, for example, as regards standing for natural and legal persons to bring an action for annulment under Article 230(4) EC? However, it might be hoping too much to expect that the Court's commitment to fundamental freedoms will evolve into a *truly* irreducible core of constitutional principles, providing the basis for judicial protection even in the face of the primary Treaty provisions themselves, for example, in fields such as the Third Pillar where the system of access to justice in the particularly sensitive field of criminal law has been deliberately hamstrung. We might therefore find that affirming the autonomy of the Union's internal legal orders in cases like *Kadi and Al Barakaat* is in fact a double-edged sword, safeguarding respect for fundamental freedoms against the depredations threatened by external actors, but also reinforcing the authority of the Member States themselves to undermine human rights guarantees in their capacity as 'masters of the Treaties'.

II. Residency Rights for Third Country National Family Members of Migrant Union Citizens

Regulation 1612/68, while the relevant provisions were in force, granted rights of residence not only to migrant Community nationals falling within the scope of the free movement provisions, but also to certain of their family members.[16] Such family rights are particularly valuable for third-country nationals (TCNs) who would otherwise be governed by national immigration rules alone, the latter usually being substantively less generous and/or administratively more onerous than Community law. However, in its 2003 ruling in

---

[15] Case T-284/08 (4 December 2008).
[16] OJ Special English Edition 1968 (II), p. 475.

Akrich, the ECJ held that Member States were entitled to reserve the benefit of Regulation 1612/68 to those TCN family members already lawfully resident in one Member State at the time of moving to another Member State with, or to join, the relevant Union citizen.[17] It thus seemed clearly established that merely being or becoming a qualifying family member of a migrant Union citizen is not necessarily enough to trigger the protection of Community law, if the claimant has not already otherwise gained lawful entry into the Union territory, and does not of itself serve to regularize the immigration status of a TCN currently unlawfully resident within the Union. The relevant provisions of Regulation 1612/68 were subsequently repealed and replaced by Directive 2004/38,[18] but it was generally assumed that Member States continued to be entitled to restrict the residency rights of TCN family members in accordance with the *Akrich* ruling.

However, the law took a dramatic and surprising turn in the *Metock* dispute.[19] *Metock* concerned Irish rules adopted on the basis of the *Akrich* ruling, requiring TCN family members of migrant Union citizens to satisfy a condition of prior lawful residence in another Member State, before being able to rely on the domestic regulations implementing Directive 2004/38 into Irish law. On that basis, the Irish authorities refused to issue residence cards to a number of TCN family members of migrant Union citizens. The High Court sought guidance as to whether the Irish prior lawful residence requirement was compatible with Directive 2004/38. It is important to note that the ECJ dealt with the reference by a special accelerated procedure, and thereby delivered its judgment in a matter of four months, having heard the Advocate General but without the latter's Opinion being made publicly available.[20]

The Court began by observing that Directive 2004/38 did not expressly make the application of Community law conditional upon prior lawful residency in a Member State. In fact, the relevant provisions of Directive 2004/38 confer rights of entry and residency upon TCN family members without any reference to the latter's place or conditions of residence before arriving in the host state. True, the ruling in *Akrich* had held that Member States were entitled to insist that TCN family members must be lawfully resident in another Member State in order to benefit from Regulation 1612/68, but that conclusion must now be reconsidered: the enjoyment of rights to entry and residence under Regulation 1612/68 cannot depend on the prior lawful residence of the relevant TCN family member in another Member State. On that

---

[17] Case C-109/01 [2003] ECR I-9607. Though Member States are not *required* by Community law to do so: Case C-1/05 *Jia* [2007] ECR I-1.
[18] [2004] OJ L 158/77.
[19] Case C-127/08 (25 July 2008).
[20] Article 104a of the ECJ's Rules of Procedure.

basis, a more generous interpretation must also apply to the new provisions of Directive 2004/38, which is designed to strengthen the rights of Union citizens, who cannot therefore derive fewer rights from Directive 2004/38 than from previous Community secondary legislation.

The Court continued to assert that that interpretation of Directive 2004/38 is consistent with the division of competences between the Community and the Member States. The Community institutions enjoy the power to enact the measures necessary to bring about free movement for Union citizens. For those purposes, if Union citizens were unable to lead a normal family life in the host state, the exercise of their fundamental right to free movement under Community law would be seriously obstructed and that is true even if his/her TCN family members are not already lawfully resident in another Member State. On that basis, the Community legislature was entitled to regulate, by means of Directive 2004/38, the entry and residence of TCN family members in the host state, including where those family members were not already lawfully resident in another Member State. Conversely, to recognize the exclusive competence of each Member State to grant or refuse entry based on a criterion of prior lawful residency would mean that the free movement rights of Union citizens would vary from country to country – a prospect incompatible with the Treaty's objective of creating an internal market characterized by the abolition, as between Member States, of obstacles to the free movement of persons.

Ireland (and several other intervening governments) argued in favour of maintaining the ruling in *Akrich* on the grounds that, given strong pressures of migration, it was necessary to control immigration at the Community's external borders. To that end, national requirements based on prior lawful residency enabled Member States to examine the circumstances of every individual's first entry into the Union territory; conversely, to prohibit such requirements would undermine the ability of Member States to control immigration at their external frontiers and could facilitate a great increase in the number of persons able to benefit from residency rights within the Union. The ECJ was unmoved: residency rights would still be limited to qualifying family members of migrant Union citizens (not just open to every TCN); Community law still entitles Member States to refuse entry even to TCN family members on grounds of public policy, security or health; and Member States remain competent to refuse residency rights in cases of abuse or fraud (such as marriages of convenience).

The ECJ therefore held that Directive 2004/38 precludes national legislation from requiring TCN family members to have previously been lawfully resident in another Member State before arriving in the host state in order to benefit from the rights conferred by Community law. The Court concluded by clarifying that the spouse of a migrant Union citizen benefits from the protection of Directive 2004/38 irrespective of when and where the marriage took place and of how that spouse entered the host state. In particular, qualifying TCNs enjoy the right to join a migrant Union citizen, even where the family was founded only after the latter's arrival in the host state. Similarly, TCNs may benefit from the protection of Community law, even where they had already entered the host state before becoming a qualifying family member of a migrant Union citizen.[21]

It falls beyond the scope of the present article to express any opinion on the merits as such of the Court's latest foray into the political and social maelstrom of immigration into the Union by third-country nationals. Suffice to say that even though the group in question may be restricted by the need for and nature of their relationship to a migrant Union citizen, the ruling has still seriously antagonized various national actors – not only in Ireland, but in other countries too, most notably Denmark – keen to control or restrict the numbers of foreigners settling in the territory of their own Member State. Such controversy stems partly, of course, from the proposition that the simple fact of a qualifying relationship to a migrant Union citizen can now translate into rights of entry into and residence within the Union territory. As regards such TCNs, the Member State's ability to exercise gate-keeping functions at the Union's external frontiers has been virtually suppressed;[22] the powers of the national authorities to deal with individuals guilty of a whole range of immigration irregularities have also been significantly curtailed. Particularly at a time of serious economic recession, when immigration debates tend to acquire an even more venomous tone than usual, such developments are fuel for the stoking of populist anxieties and resentment. Nevertheless, the controversy is further aggravated by the fact that *Metock* will benefit the family members not only of foreign Union citizens moving to another Member State, but also of own nationals whose past movement entitles them to invoke Community law against their country of origin so as to facilitate the entry and residence of a qualifying TCN (even if such past movement was undertaken solely for that very purpose). Indeed, the moral pressure, or in some cases, a domestic constitutional obligation, to extend comparable rights to the TCN family members of purely static own nationals may further expand the range of potential beneficiaries from, and further ratchet up the political tension consequent upon, the ruling in *Metock*.[23]

---

[21] See also Case C-551/07 *Sahin* (19 December 2008).

[22] Unsurprisingly, other than in situations involving fraud or abuse; and as regards the relatively extreme cases falling within the concepts of public policy, security or health.

[23] A problem entirely disowned by the ECJ: see paras. 76–79 of the ruling in *Metock*.

Setting the irresolvable acrimonies of the immigration debate aside, the ruling in *Metock* remains susceptible to criticisms of a more legally tangible nature. A good starting point is the task of ascertaining the essential rationale underpinning the Court's reasoning in *Metock*: two main possibilities arise, each bringing their own problems.

In the first place, it could be argued that the primary method of analysis in *Metock* was textual, focusing on the proposition that Directive 2004/38 does not expressly impose any sort of prior lawful residency requirement. Against the background of that apparent legislative blank canvas, the Court first overruled *Akrich* so far as concerns Regulation 1612/68, then projected that overruling of *Akrich* onto Directive 2004/38 itself, on the grounds that the latter measure should only expand (not restrict) the Union citizen's rights. However, if the text of Directive 2004/38 does hold the key to *Metock*, such reasoning can be criticized as entirely disingenuous. One can safely assume that the only reason the Community institutions, when drafting Directive 2004/38, did not expressly incorporate a prior lawful residency requirement was precisely because *Akrich* had only just previously affirmed the competence of the Member States to impose one. Why feel obliged to refer expressly to a competence which was assumed already to exist? Viewed in that light, there is a strong argument for saying that the silence of Directive 2004/38 as to prior lawful residency should properly have been construed as a tacit reflection of *Akrich*; the Court's overruling of that judgment and its reinterpretation of Directive 2004/38 could therefore be considered a frustration of the legitimate understandings and expectations of the Member States.

In the second place, however, it is possible to argue that the initial textual element of the Court's analysis in *Metock* was actually less important to its overall judicial reasoning in the case than its subsequent reliance on the underlying principles of free movement as derived from the primary Treaty provisions. After all, whether one believes that Directive 2004/38 was actually intended to reflect the previous *Akrich* judgment, or (being more generous towards the Court) one is prepared to accept that the silence of Directive 2004/38 as to prior lawful residency can be interpreted as effective indifference to the status of the *Akrich* ruling, the challenge remains of how to justify the Court's decision to overrule *Akrich* as regards Regulation 1612/68, and then suppress its application to Directive 2004/38. That decision simply cannot be explained by the supposed intentions of the Community legislature alone, and its true motivation must lie elsewhere in the Court's analysis, for which purpose the only viable way of explaining *Metock* must be the Court's conviction that, to uphold the possibility of prior lawful residency conditions as sanctioned in *Akrich*, would both perpetuate certain obstacles to free movement resulting from an actual or potential interference with the migrant Union citizen's right to family life, and tolerate differences in the quality of free movement of persons across the Single Market, depending on the approach to the entry and residence of TCN family members adopted by each individual Member State. In other words: *Metock* involved a simple change of judicial mind about the underlying compatibility of prior lawful residency requirements with the free movement of Union citizens under the Treaty.[24]

Yet if that reasoning provides the real key to *Metock*, then it has serious implications for the competence of the Community legislature to respond to the Court's judgment. After all, if the rationale of *Metock* lay in a purely textual analysis of Directive 2004/38 – the idea that that measure did not expressly permit the imposition of prior lawful residency requirements – then it would at least remain open to the Community legislature to amend Directive 2004/38 at some point in the future, so as quite consciously to reinstate the legal effects of the *Akrich* ruling. However, if the basis for *Metock* consists not in the text of Directive 2004/38, but rather in the underlying demands of free movement law – based on the primary Treaty provisions and the fundamental rights of Union citizens – then the effect of the judgment could be effectively to tie the hands of the Community legislature: the preclusion of prior lawful residency requirements, uniformly across the Single Market, becomes *the only* permitted solution to the problem of regulating the entry and residency rights of TCN family members.

Arguably, therefore, it is not only the Court's willingness to meddle in that most politically and emotionally charged of public debates, but also its choice of legal tools for achieving its own particular policy preferences, that could adversely affect reactions to the *Metock* ruling. The Court should perhaps be more judicious about when it invokes the authority of the primary Treaty provisions, in a way that effectively entrenches judicial leads on sensitive policy issues that are by no means self-evident and justifiable by reference to hermeneutic techniques alone, and by so doing, risks emasculating the power of the Community's accountable political institutions subsequently to strike out along a different – not necessarily inferior or illegitimate – policy pathway. What might seem doubly damaging to the Court's credibility in *Metock* is the fact that such an important ruling, involving such an abrupt change in the existing law, was delivered by means of an accelerated procedure which permits little time for proper scrutiny, debate and reflection among all interested stakeholders. Even the opinion of the Advocate General was not (and at the time of writing has still not been) made publicly available – hardly a triumph for judicial transparency and accountability, and a far cry

---

[24] A hesitation which arguably was already hinted at in *Akrich* itself (at paras. 58–60 of the ruling).

from the sentiment of open access to institutional legal advice set out in *Sweden v. Council*.[25] Indeed, one might well query whether the accelerated (and now urgent) preliminary reference procedures before the ECJ, in their current form,[26] are really well suited to deciding cases like *Metock* involving such delicate issues and complex points of principle.

III. Equal Treatment of Migrant Students as regards Educational Grants: A Turning Point for Union Citizenship?

Readers of this review will be well aware that the ECJ has grappled several times in recent years with the issue of how to allocate responsibility for the financial costs associated with migrant education. In the 2007 case of *Morgan and Bucher*, the ECJ explored the extent of financial support that migrant Union citizens are entitled to expect from their home country in respect of university education in another Member State.[27] But in 2005, the Court had delivered the equally important ruling in *Bidar* concerning the liabilities of the host state itself.[28] In that case, the Court found that English rules which sought to restrict access to state-subsidized student loans by economically inactive migrants – by requiring at least three years' residency prior to attending university, and by imposing a requirement that claimants be 'settled' in the UK which in practice was virtually impossible for migrant EU students to satisfy – were incompatible with the claimant's right to equal treatment under Article 12 EC.

The dispute in *Förster* gave the ECJ a fresh opportunity to consider the relationship between migrant students and their host state when it comes to the provision of maintenance assistance.[29] The case concerned a German national who moved to the Netherlands in 2000 and began studying for a university degree at the College of Amsterdam in 2001. Upon completion of that degree in 2004, she entered employment as a social worker in the Netherlands. Throughout her studies, Förster had undertaken various kinds of paid employment and also received maintenance assistance for her university studies from the Dutch authorities. However, an investigation into her employment record showed that Förster had in fact been out of work for a period of six months during 2003 and the Dutch authorities therefore sought recovery of that portion of her maintenance grant. Under Dutch law, migrant Community nationals who are not in employment are only entitled to student

---

[25] Cases C-39 & 52/05 (1 July 2008).
[26] See Articles 104a and 104b of the ECJ's Rules of Procedure (respectively).
[27] Cases C-11-12/06 [2007] ECR I-9161.
[28] Case C-209/03 [2005] ECR I-2119.
[29] Case C-158/07 (18 November 2008).

grants if they have been lawfully resident in the Netherlands for at least five years. No such residency requirement was imposed upon students of Dutch nationality. Relying directly on the authority of *Bidar*, Förster challenged the Dutch rules under Community law: she had exercised her right as a Union citizen to move and reside in the territory of another Member State under Article 18 EC; as a lawfully resident migrant, she also enjoyed the right to equal treatment with Dutch nationals under Article 12 EC as regards all matters falling within the scope of the Treaty, including access to student financial assistance.

In principle, the Court agreed that Förster was entitled to benefit from the principle of equal treatment as regards access to the Dutch maintenance grant. In particular, even though Article 3 Directive 93/96 on the free movement of students expressly states that that measure shall not establish any entitlement to the payment of maintenance grants by the host state,[30] such a provision cannot preclude claimants from instead relying directly upon the rights conferred by Articles 18 and 12 EC. The key task was therefore to identify what restrictions could be imposed on the rights of foreign students to claim maintenance grants, without the different treatment of such migrants in comparison to Dutch nationals being considered discriminatory and consequently prohibited by Article 12 EC.

In this regard, however, the Court in *Förster* chose to distinguish *Bidar* and uphold the validity of the Dutch rules. According to the Court, the English rules at issue in *Bidar* were fatally flawed not so much by the three-year residency requirement, but rather because of the condition that claimants had also to be 'settled' in the UK, the latter being virtually impossible for any migrant student to fulfil, regardless of their actual degree of integration into the host society. However, the ruling in *Bidar* also affirmed that the host state may ensure that the grant of maintenance assistance to foreign students does not become an unreasonable burden which could have consequences for the overall level of assistance granted by that Member State. It is legitimate for a Member State to grant maintenance assistance only to students who have demonstrated a certain degree of integration into the host society, evidenced by the fact that the student in question has resided in the host state for a certain length of time. Here, the Dutch requirement of five years' residence within the Netherlands should be considered appropriate and proportionate to that objective – provided that the residence requirement was applied by the national authorities on the basis of clear criteria known in advance, so as to guarantee a significant level of legal certainty and transparency in the context of the award of maintenance grants to students.

---

[30] [1993] OJ L 317/59.

The change between *Bidar* and *Förster* is, in its own way, just as unexpected as that from *Akrich* to *Metock*. Moreover, *Förster* is a very difficult judgment to interpret and its implications for Union citizenship are unclear, though potentially highly significant.

Part of the difficulty stems from the fact that, as was the case with *Metock*, the Court's reasoning is in places unclear or even downright confused. Consider, for example, the fact that the disputed Dutch residency requirement seemed to apply only to foreign students, not to own nationals. Orthodox legal analysis tells us that such a rule can be examined in one of two ways under Community law: either the Court may find that the foreign and own nationals in question are not in comparable situations, so that no expectation of equal treatment in fact arises, and the relevant rule does not actually breach the Treaty at all or therefore need to be justified by reference to any public interest; or instead the Court may find that comparability exists and the relevant rule amounts to direct discrimination on grounds of nationality, in which event it is a well-established principle of Community law that justification can be found (if at all) only in the express Treaty derogations, not in the broader category of imperative requirements recognized in the case law itself. The Court itself explicitly adverted to that clear choice between two discrete analytical models in its judgment in *Förster*,[31] but then continued to dispense with any pretence of serious doctrinal rigour, by subjecting the disputed Dutch rule to the process of objective justification (thereby implying that comparability existed and the Treaty had indeed *prime facie* been infringed), then holding that valid justification lay in the Member State's legitimate desire to reserve financial assistance only to those foreign students considered sufficiently integrated into its society (an imperative requirement which should not have been available even in principle for a directly discriminatory rule).

Is that just sloppy judicial reasoning? Or was there a conscious judicial decision to save the disputed Dutch rules by hook or by crook, if necessary simply by bending the relevant legal principles, though without intending to set any broader precedent? For example, the Court may have silently assumed that own nationals automatically demonstrate a 'real link' to the relevant Member State, such that the disputed Dutch rules could, for all practical purposes, be treated as equally applicable though indirectly discriminatory.[32] If so, such reasoning makes considerable demands on the doctrinal imagination, and also runs counter to existing jurisprudence, which interrogates even

[31] At para 45 of the ruling.
[32] Note the advice of AG Mazák at para 134 of the Opinion delivered on 10 July 2008.

own nationals for evidence of their 'real link' to the relevant Member State.[33] Or should *Förster* be given a more radical reading, as the latest in a growing list of cases[34] which tend gradually to break down the once watertight distinction between direct and indirect discrimination, express derogations and imperative requirements, thus pushing Community law towards a unified test for objective justification? In any case, the Court's unconventional approach in *Förster* suggests the need to handle the ruling with a degree of caution when it comes to identifying its potential contribution to the legal framework governing the rights of migrant students or indeed of Union citizens in general.

With that warning in mind, it will be recalled that the case law on Union citizenship prior to *Förster* had crystallized around two major principles, originally established in *Grzelczyk* and *Baumbast*,[35] but increasingly applicable to all questions of residency, equal treatment and barriers to movement affecting migrant Community nationals. First, Community secondary legislation which itself purports to restrict the migrant's opportunities for free movement is nevertheless amenable to a form of 'indirect judicial review', whereby Member States are obliged to apply the relevant provisions in accordance with the general principles of Community law, especially the principle of proportionality, so that those provisions may not be enforced against an individual where that would exceed what is necessary to protect the Member State's legitimate interests.[36] Secondly, even though Member States may limit access to social benefits by imposing qualifying criteria intended to demonstrate the existence of a 'real link' between the claimant and the relevant welfare community, the necessary evidence cannot be gathered exclusively on the basis of generalized criteria, without giving due consideration to the 'personal circumstances' of each individual claimant.[37]

The problem is that the Court refused to apply either of those core tenets of its own case law on Union citizenship to help resolve the dispute in *Förster*.

Consider, in the first place, the principle of 'indirect judicial review'. Many commentators had identified a direct tension between the *Bidar* ruling, which concerned a national requirement of three years' lawful residency before qualifying for access to student loans; and Article 24 Directive 2004/

---

[33] Consider, e.g. Case C-224/98 *D'Hoop* [2002] ECR I-6191; Case C-287/05 *Hendrix* [2007] ECR I-6909; Cases C-11-12/06 *Morgan and Bucher* [2007] ECR I-9161; Case C-499/06 *Nerkowska* (22 May 2008).

[34] Consider, in particular, Case C-379/98 *PreussenElektra* [2001] ECR I-2099.

[35] Case C-184/99 [2001] ECR I-6193 and Case C-413/99 [2002] ECR I-7091 (respectively).

[36] Consider, e.g. Case C-406/04 *De Cuyper* [2006] ECR I-6947; Case C-287/05 *Hendrix* [2007] ECR I-6909; Case C-228/07 *Petersen* (11 September 2008).

[37] Consider, e.g. Case C-224/98 *D'Hoop* [2002] ECR I-6191; Case C-138/02 *Collins* [2004] ECR I-2703; Case C-209/03 *Bidar* [2005] ECR I-2119; Case C-287/05 *Hendrix* [2007] ECR I-6909; Cases C-11-12/06 *Morgan and Bucher* [2007] ECR I-9161; Case C-499/06 *Nerkowska* (22 May 2008).

38, which states that migrant students who do not also qualify as workers should only be entitled to equal treatment as regards maintenance assistance after five years of lawful residency within the host state.[38] Several academics had argued that that tension could be resolved precisely through recourse to the technique of 'indirect judicial review', i.e. requiring the Member States to offer equal treatment, despite the express provisions of Directive 2004/38, where required by the principle of proportionality. Indeed, exactly such an approach was recommended to the Court in *Förster* by Advocate General Mazák.[39] The ECJ, however, refused to follow suit. On the contrary, even though Article 24 Directive 2004/38 had not yet entered into force at the time of the dispute in *Förster*, the Court nevertheless directly referred to that provision in support of its relatively accommodating approach towards the disputed Dutch residency requirement.

Förster therefore implies that national rules on access to student financial assistance, adopted in compliance with the 'five year test' contained in Article 24 Directive 2004/38, will be enforceable as such; for its part, the *Bidar* ruling seems to have been confined to its own facts (based on the additional and indisputably disproportionate requirement in that case for students to be 'settled' in the UK). In itself, that makes *Förster* a rather poor manifestation of the principle only just enunciated in *Metock*, that Directive 2004/38 was intended to strengthen the legal status of Union citizens and should not be interpreted so as to confer fewer rights than existed before its adoption.[40] More importantly, however, if that interpretation of *Förster* is correct, it could have reverberations well beyond the specific problems associated with student financial assistance. After all, the tension between *Bidar* and Article 24 Directive 2004/38 was not the only apparent contradiction between the Court's case law and Community secondary legislation: consider rulings such as *Collins* on equal treatment for migrant workseekers,[41] *De Cupyer* and *Petersen* on the exportation of unemployment benefits[42] and *Hendrix* on access to disability benefits[43] – each of which supported (or at least pointed towards) the same principle that Community secondary legislation restricting the rights of Union citizens should only be enforced by the national authorities if justified on proportionality grounds. Does the Court's more conservative approach in *Förster* suggest that that technique of 'indirect judicial review' will henceforth be restricted or even suppressed, to be replaced by

---

[38] [2004] OJ L 158/77.
[39] See paras. 131–133 of the Opinion delivered on 10 July 2008.
[40] See above.
[41] Case C-138/02 [2004] ECR I-2703.
[42] Case C-406/04 [2006] ECR I-6947 and Case C-228/07 (11 September 2008), respectively.
[43] Case C-287/05 [2007] ECR I-6909.

greater judicial deference towards the parameters of welfare support for Union citizens set out by the Union's political institutions?

Consider, in the second place, the requirement for Member States to undertake a 'personal circumstances' assessment of each individual migrant Union citizen before refusing access to any given social benefit. It is particularly striking that the Court in *Förster* made no effort whatsoever to require the Dutch authorities to examine the claimant's personal circumstances, with a view to establishing whether her 'real link' to Dutch society could be verified by reference to factors other than the generalized requirement of five years' continuous lawful residency within the national territory. Yet if her personal circumstances had indeed been taken into account, the claimant would surely have had a strong case for arguing that the blanket application of the disputed Dutch rule was entirely disproportionate in her case, since she had clearly become fully integrated into Dutch society at an educational, professional and personal level.[44]

Does *Förster* therefore indicate that the Court has begun to retreat back, not just from the principle of 'indirect judicial review' over Community secondary legislation, but also from an interventionist approach to the justification of national rules hindering the free movement or equal treatment rights of migrant Union citizens, based on the 'personal circumstances' assessment? If so, that would seem to vindicate O'Brien's recent argument that Union citizenship, as it is evolving in the case law, seems more concerned with procedural fairness and the appearance of justice than with promoting any particular substantive vision of transnational solidarity or guaranteeing any given standard of welfare support to the individual (O'Brien, 2008). It may also reflect the political and social uncertainties of what it actually means to be a Union citizen, and of what (as the Court would say) the 'fundamental destiny' of Union citizenship itself might be, in the deeply troubled constitutional world of European integration created by the negative results in the referendums on Treaty reform held in France, the Netherlands and Ireland. But one must admit that, if *Förster* was indeed intended to be thus interpreted, it would amount to a remarkably sudden, as well as extreme, *volte face* by the Court: after all, only a few months separate the ruling in *Förster* from previous rulings, such as *Nebrowska* and *Grunkin and Paul*,[45] that clearly and strongly affirm the need for Member States to undertake an assessment of each individual Union citizen's 'personal circumstances' before restricting the exercise of his/her fundamental Treaty freedoms.

---

[44] Again, see paras. 128–130 of the Opinion delivered by Advocate General Mazák on 10 July 2008.
[45] Case C-499/06 (22 May 2008) and Case C-353/06 (14 October 2008), respectively.

The challenges of interpreting *Förster* should by now be clear. The case law on Union citizenship – for all its faults – had at least developed a relatively coherent and predictable methodology for addressing all manner of restriction on the rights to free movement and equal treatment. At the very least, the Court seems to have decided upon a more restrictive approach to the legal rights specifically of migrant students as regards relations with their host state. Left at that, *Förster* would suggest the beginning of a serious fragmentation in the case law. Yet the ECJ may find it difficult (in policy terms) to justify why one particular class of Community national should be signalled out for such (non-)special treatment; or (in doctrinal terms) to construct highly differentiated and even mutually incompatible legal tools for extrapolating the basic rights derived from Union citizenship. The ruling in *Förster* – either by design or by necessity – might therefore signal a more fundamental turning point in the entire case law on Union citizenship, by reining in some of the more exuberant judicial experiments in manufacturing novel expectations of cross-border social solidarity based on the principle of 'indirect judicial review' and the 'personal circumstances' assessment. If *Förster* indeed marks the start of a wholesale retreat in the case law on Union citizenship, that would at least preserve the values of coherence and predictability between different classes of claimants and of restrictions – but the life of Community lawyers in the field of free movement would surely lose a little of its recent lustre.

Conclusion: On Accusations of 'Judicial Activism' Levied Against the ECJ

As usual, it would be unwise to draw any general conclusions about the current state or future trajectory of Community law based simply on the judgments discussed in this chapter (however significant each of those rulings might be for their respective fields of legal scholarship). But 2008 did in fact witness an outpouring of political and academic debate over broader questions concerning the nature and functioning of the Community legal order – prompted in large part by the very public allegations of 'judicial activism' levied against the ECJ by Roman Herzog (the former German Federal President) and Lüder Gerkin (Director of the Centre for European Policy).[46]

The consensus among legal commentators is that many of the specific allegations made by Herzog and Gerkin fall apart upon closer scrutiny, being based upon an incomplete understanding, or a rather selective analysis, of Community law. Nonetheless, Herzog and Gerkin's campaign to 'Stop the

---

[46] *Frankfurter Allgemeine Zeitung*, 8 September 2008.

European Court of Justice' should remind us of two important points. First, even if the Court deserves to be defended against ill-founded attacks, of course that should not inhibit objective debate about and substantiated criticism of the judicial function. As rulings such as *Metock* and *Förster* illustrate, the Court's reasoning can indeed be found wanting and its choices sometimes appear questionable – but to say so is hardly to side with the forces of ideological Euro-scepticism. Secondly, although one might be tempted to dismiss the critique of Herzog and Gerkin as unworthy of serious scholarly engagement, the fact remains that high-profile political attacks upon the Court – however unfair – can still do much damage to the institution's authority. And unfortunately, Herzog and Gerkin have hardly been alone in launching stinging political assaults upon the Community judiciary in recent years: besides the reaction in Member States such as Denmark to the *Metock* ruling, consider the furore in Austria following the *Access to University* case,[47] or among trades unions across Europe after *Viking Line* and *Laval un Partneri*.[48]

Such episodes cumulatively create a difficult dilemma for the ECJ. On the one hand, there is surely an understandable desire not to let the administration of justice be held captive to often groundless political attacks. On the other hand, the development of Community law cannot take place in a vacuum, protected from the vicissitudes of the wider political debate – warts and all – about the nature, extent and implications of European integration. It is not merely a matter, therefore, of the ECJ remaining aware of and responsive to serious critical analysis of its jurisprudence; there is also the thorny problem of deciding how far the judicial development of Community law should swim either along with or against the tide of wider political and social events. Nor should we forget that, in resolving such dilemmas, the stances adopted by other judicial actors will inevitably play a highly influential role: particularly as the German Federal Constitutional Court gears up to revisit the delicate balance between Union and national competences, in disputes over the ruling in *Mangold*,[49] and German ratification of the Treaty of Lisbon, 2009 will surely witness yet more soul-searching over the constitutional role, legitimacy and accountability of the Union judiciary.

Key Reading

2008 saw the appearance of several detailed legal analyses of and reflections upon the Treaty of Lisbon, which despite its current state of suspended animation, may nevertheless be of interest to many readers, for example:

[47] Case C-147/03 *Commission v. Austria* [2005] ECR I-5969.
[48] Case C-438/05 [2007] ECR I-10779 and Case C-341/05 [2007] ECR I-11767 (respectively).
[49] Case C-144/04 [2005] ECR I-9981.

Craig, P. (2008) 'The Treaty of Lisbon: Process, Architecture and Substance'. *European Law Review*, Vol. 33, pp. 137–66.

Dougan, M. (2008) 'The Treaty of Lisbon 2008: Winning Minds, Not Hearts'. *Common Market Law Review*, Vol. 45, pp. 617–703.

Snell, J. (2008) ' "European Constitutional Settlement" and Ever-Closer Union and the Treaty of Lisbon: Democracy or Relevance?' *European Law Review*, Vol. 33, pp. 619–42.

Among the significant new contributions to the burgeoning literature on Union citizenship published in 2008, one might single out the following pieces:

Borgmann-Prebil, Y. (2008) 'The Rule of Reason in European Citizenship'. *European Law Journal*, Vol. 14, pp. 328–50.

O'Brien, C. (2008) 'Real Links, Abstract Rights and False Alarms: The Relationship between the ECJ's "Real Link" Case Law and National Solidarity'. *European Law Review*, Vol. 33, pp. 643–65.

Spaventa, E. (2008) 'Seeing the Wood Despite the Trees? On the Scope of Union Citizenship and Its Constitutional Effects'. *Common Market Law Review*, Vol. 45, pp. 13–45.

JCMS 2009 Volume 47 Annual Review pp. 193–212

European Union's Relations with the Wider Europe

RICHARD G. WHITMAN
University of Bath

ANA E. JUNCOS
University of Bristol

Introduction

Relations with the wider Europe in 2008 were marked by a set of contradictory developments. Enlargement of the EU made minimal progress in the last year with Turkey's accession negotiations operating at slow speed and Croatia's path to membership running into obstacles. There was an attempt to breathe new life into the relationship with neighbouring states in the European Neighbourhood Policy (ENP) with the French government's proposals for a Mediterranean Union and a counterbalancing set of proposals from other Member States for an Eastern Partnership. Armed conflict between Russia and Georgia in August, and the Israel military intervention in Gaza in late 2008, saw the Union struggling with the role of conflict manager within its neighbourhood. Further crisis in the form of the global recession also impacted on the wider Europe with Iceland experiencing a financial crisis and the prospect of an unanticipated membership application.

I. Enlargement

General Developments

2008 was hailed as a key year for enlargement. Five years after the launch of the Thessaloniki Agenda, Serbia and Bosnia finally signed their Stabilization and Association Agreement (SAA) with the EU. Croatia, Turkey and Macedonia were also hoping to move further in the integration process, the latter with its eye on the opening of accession negotiations. In February, the new Regional Co-operation Council took over from the Stability Pact signalling increased ownership of the process of regional co-operation. In March 2008, the European Commission presented a Communication with new initiatives aiming to further people-to-people contacts and to make the prospect of membership more concrete for the citizens in the region. Visa liberalization was put on the table for the first time, with negotiations on the liberalization of the visa regime beginning at the end of May 2008. The Commission's Communication also proposed an increase in the number of scholarships for students from the Balkan region and new initiatives were announced aimed at supporting civil society development and regional co-operation (Commission, 2008a).

Despite some positive signs, progress has generally been disappointing. This is due to several factors: the slow pace of domestic reforms, the continuing failure to adopt institutional reforms at the EU level and standing bilateral issues (see Vachudova, this volume). First, the Commission's Enlargement Strategy yet again identified lingering problems in the candidate and potential candidate countries, specifically regarding weak institutional and administrative capacity, the enforcement of rule of law, the fight against corruption and organized crime, high unemployment and inflation, a highly confrontational political climate and ethnic related tensions (Commission, 2008c). Ethnic politics remained one of the main stumbling blocks for progress towards membership. Political, economic and social reforms fell hostage to recalcitrant nationalist politicians in Bosnia and threatened the European perspective of Serbia, Kosovo and Macedonia. European integration imposes high adoption costs for politicians in the candidate countries. In some cases, EU integration not only threatens their power base, but also their private economic interests as many of them profit from weak legal and regulatory frameworks and are involved in organized crime.

Second, uncertainty about the ratification of the Lisbon Treaty continued to haunt enlargement, particularly after the rejection of the Lisbon Treaty in Ireland's June referendum. At the December European Council, the Irish government agreed to hold a second referendum in the autumn of 2009 after having secured a series of concessions by the other EU Member States. However, failure to ratify the treaty by the 27 Member States could endanger the next round of enlargement. Third, bilateral issues also threatened to hold up enlargement, with some EU Member States using their privileged position inside the EU to put pressure on candidate countries in the hope that they would make concessions. Thus, Turkey's accession continued to be delayed over the conflict with Cyprus; the name dispute between Macedonia and Greece jeopardized Macedonia's Nato accession; and a long-standing border dispute with Slovenia got in the way of Croatia's path toward membership. Although not related to a bilateral grievance, the Netherlands has also blocked the implementation of the Serbia's SAA until the country delivers war criminal Ratko Mladic to the International Criminal Tribunal for the former Yugoslavia (ICTY).

By the end of 2008, the financial crisis had yet to bite fully in the Balkans and Turkey. Although its impact could be expected to be more limited in the region than in western Europe given the low levels of foreign investment and credit extension, the financial crisis might still have an impact on the enlargement process more generally. In the current economic climate, EU Member States might be more cautious about taking more members on board especially if that means increasing economic competition and budgetary disbursements. All in all, the prospects for enlargement look rather bleak.

Candidate Countries

Croatia

Croatia made some progress towards membership in 2008. By the end of 2008, 22 out of 35 negotiation chapters had been opened and seven chapters had been provisionally closed. In its enlargement package, the Commission presented a timetable for the technical conclusion of negotiations. Provided that certain conditions were met, Croatia was expected to reach the final phase of negotiations in 2009. Yet, some areas for improvement were identified in the last Commission's Progress Report (Commission, 2008d). As regards political criteria, some problems remained regarding the reform of the judicial system and public administration and the fight against organized crime and corruption – two Croatian journalists were murdered in connection with corruption cases in 2008. Another challenge related to the implementation of the legislation on minority rights and refugee return. Concerns were also raised regarding Croatia's co-operation with the ICTY and access by the Court to certain documents.[1] Furthermore, public opinion remains a matter of concern. According to a Gallup survey conducted in September and October 2008, only 29 per cent of Croats think that Croatian EU membership would be a good thing.[2]

A border dispute with Slovenia has become a new hurdle in Croatia's path towards membership. The 18-year-old grievance concerns a bay in the Adriatic Sea, close to the Slovenian city of Piran, and the rights of access to international waters of Slovenian ships. At the accession conference in

---

[1] *EUobserver.com*, 6 February 2009.
[2] *Gallup Balkan Monitor*, accessible at: «http://www.balkan-monitor.eu/files/BalkanMonitor-2008_Summary_of_Findings.pdf», p. 15.

December, Slovenia blocked the opening of nine new chapters and the closing of two more chapters. The dispute threatened to delay Croatian EU accession, with the Slovenian government mentioning the possibility of holding a referendum on Croatian accession if the dispute is not resolved.

Turkey

Although Turkey's technical negotiations made some progress in 2008, the process has moved very slowly since the opening of negotiations in 2005. In December 2008, the EU decided to open two more chapters out of the 35-chapter negotiation package, which brings the total of open chapters to ten. However, the opening of new chapters is held up by the conflict over Cyprus and Turkey's continued refusal to allow Greek Cypriot ships and airplanes entry to its seaports and airports. The re-launch of negotiations on the re-unification of Cyprus in September 2008, following the election of the new Greek-Cypriot President Dimitris Christofias in February, generated some moderate optimism, but an agreement is still far off. Indeed, tensions continued in late 2008, when the Turkish navy challenged two Greek Cypriot oil survey ships in international waters off Cyprus.

As regards domestic politics, in July 2008 the EU sighed with relief when the Turkish Constitutional Court decided not to ban the country's ruling party, the Justice and Development Party (AKP), which had been accused of undermining the country's secular system. However, internal tensions between the AKP and the Kemalist secularist establishment continued. In its annual progress report, the European Commission reminded Turkey of the essential reforms that needed to be tackled, including the reform of the constitution, protection for minority rights, civil–military relations and the implementation of reforms on freedom of expression (Commission, 2008e).

In the area of energy policy, the Commission's Enlargement Strategy stated that 'Turkey's geo-strategic position gives the country a vital role in the EU's energy security, particularly diversification of energy sources' (Commission, 2008c, p. 5). The report also highlighted the need for closer energy co-operation between the EU and Turkey, as well as other countries in the region. An example of this co-operation lies in the new EU-backed initiative Nabucco, a new gas pipeline which will connect the Caspian region, Middle East and Egypt – via Turkey, Bulgaria, Romania, Hungary – with Austria with the aim of reducing dependence of central and western European gas markets on Russian gas. The Commission's report also acknowledged the constructive role played by Turkish diplomacy in regional stability. After the war in Georgia, Turkey proposed a regional initiative in the South Caucasus to promote dialogue among the countries of the region; Turkish diplomacy was also actively involved in the mediations between Syria and Israel, between Israel and Hamas and in negotiations with Iran over its nuclear policy. Moreover, the historic visit of Turkish president Abdullah Gul to Armenia, who attended a World Cup qualifying football match in September, was hailed as a first step in the normalization of relations between the two countries. Turkey and Armenia have had no diplomatic relations since Armenia became an independent country in 1991 and since Turkey has refused to recognize the mass killing of Armenian civilians during World War I as genocide.[3]

Public support for EU membership has continued to decline in Turkey. The percentage of Turkish citizens that would see EU membership as a good thing decreased from 49 per cent in 2007 to 42 per cent at the end of 2008 (Eurobarometer, 2008b, p. 32). For its part, public opposition to Turkish membership within the EU, in particular in Austria, Germany and France continued to be strong: 55 per cent of EU citizens were against the integration of Turkey (Eurobarometer, 2008a, pp. 29–30). However, some positive political developments have to be noted in France. A constitutional amendment that would have made it compulsory to hold referendums on EU membership of large countries was rejected by the French Senate in June. According to the latest version of this clause, it will be up to the French President to decide how to ratify a country's EU accession, either by a parliamentary vote or referendum.[4]

Macedonia

Macedonia saw the possibility of opening accession negotiations slip by once again in 2008. Some progress was recorded on police and judicial reform and the implementation of the Ohrid Agreement. However, according to the Commission's annual progress report, Macedonia does not yet meet the political criteria (Commission, 2008g). For instance, corruption remains a serious problem, in spite of recent legislation. The opening of negotiations was also severely disrupted by the violent incidents in Albanian-populated areas that were reported during the parliamentary elections held in June. The incumbent Prime Minister Nikola Gruevski's centre-right party won the election by a strong majority. After the election, Gruevski pledged to accelerate the pace of reforms. It was not enough, however, to secure a recommendation by the Commission to open negotiations at the end of the year.

On another front, the dispute with Greece over the country's name was again the object of heated exchanges between the two states. Greece refused to support Macedonia's aspirations to join Nato until the name dispute had

[3] *BBC News*, 6 September 2008.
[4] *EUobserver.com*, 24 June 2008.

been resolved.[5] As a result, only Albania and Croatia were invited to join Nato at the Bucharest summit in April 2008, while Macedonian officials walked out of the summit as a protest against the Greek blocking. The quarrel may also have implications for further progress towards EU membership. The June Council Conclusions stressed, at the request of Greece, that 'maintaining good neighbourly relations, including a negotiated and mutually acceptable solution on the name issue, remains essential' for Macedonia's EU integration process (European Council, 2008a, p. 15).

Potential Candidate Countries

Serbia and Kosovo

When Serbia and Kosovo failed to reach an agreement on Kosovo's final status before the 10 December 2007 deadline, the EU managed to prevent an open division between those Member States that wanted to recognize the imminent independence of Kosovo and those who did not.[6] The deal in December meant that those Member States that so wished could proceed with recognition – as of March 2009, 22 Member States had recognized Kosovo's independence.[7] In spite of reassurances that 'resolving the pending status of Kosovo constitutes a *sui generis* case that does not set any precedent' (European Council, 2007, p. 20), Romania, Spain, Greece, Slovakia and Cyprus refused to recognize Kosovo on the grounds that it could set an important precedent for other territories seeking independence. In the short term, this deal prevented an internal EU crisis; in the medium and long term, however, the arrangement seems unsustainable.

At the European Council of 14 December 2007, the EU also agreed to launch a rule of law mission, EULEX, to support the police, judiciary and customs services in Kosovo. However, its deployment was delayed for a year due to Russia's opposition in the Security Council to the transfer of power from the UN to the EU mission. Further delays occurred in November when the Kosovan authorities rejected a preliminary six-point agreement between Serbia and UN negotiators.[8] A final agreement was reached by all parties that EULEX would remain neutral regarding Kosovo's status and that it would operate under UN Security Council Resolution 1244 as requested by Serbia. EULEX was finally deployed in December 2008.

---

[5] *EUobserver.com*, 6 March 2008.
[6] Kosovo declared its independence on 17 February 2008.
[7] In total, 51 countries had recognized Kosovo on 1 March 2009, see: «http://www.president-ksgov.net/?id=5,67,67,67,e,749».
[8] *EUobserver.com*, 17 November 2008.

As far as relations with Serbia are concerned, the December European Council also expressed its confidence that progress towards EU membership could be 'accelerated' (European Council, 2007, p. 20). However, this move was strongly opposed by Prime Minister Kostunica's Democratic Party of Serbia, which rejected any deal with the EU, including the signing of the SAA unless the EU committed to support Serbia's territorial integrity. For its part, the Democratic Party of President Tadic, who won the presidential elections in January, was willing to move closer to the EU in spite of Kosovo's declaration of independence. These disagreements led to the collapse of the governmental coalition and early parliamentary elections on 11 May. As had been the case in January, the elections became a referendum on Serbia's European perspective and the Serbian electorate again confirmed their support for the European path. The pro-European government led by Mirko Cvetkovic, that emerged out of the May elections, consisted of a coalition between Tadic's Democrats and the reformed Socialists (SPS) – the party of late President Milosevic. A few days before the election was due, the EU decided to sign the SAA with Belgrade, a move intended to boost pro-European forces. However, the implementation of the trade agreement proved to be more difficult than expected as the Netherlands refused to move forward until Serbia demonstrated full co-operation with the ICTY.

Only two weeks after the arrival of the new government, Serbian security forces arrested Bosnian Serb war crimes suspect Radovan Karadzic who was living and working in Belgrade under a new identity. The Union hailed this development as a historic step in Serbia's path towards EU membership. The arrest did not unblock the implementation of the trade agreement, but the EU used this opportunity to call on Serbia to deliver the remaining war criminals, Ratko Mladic and Goran Hadzic. In Serbia, the arrest and transfer to the Hague of Karadzic was received with both indifference and hostility. According to a Gallup survey, more than two-thirds of Serbs sees the ICTY as biased.[9] The verdict that acquitted former prime minister of Kosovo Ramush Haradinaj in April 2008 also contributed to undermining the image of the ICTY among the Serbian population.

Bosnia and Herzegovina, Albania and Montenegro

For the last four years, the political situation in Bosnia and Herzegovina has deteriorated due to increasing tensions between the main ethnic parties, which has led to a stalemate in the process of reform. When the High Representative decided to modify the majority necessary to pass a decision in the federal institutions in 2007 this prompted a major political crisis, but open

---

[9] *Gallup Balkan Monitor*, available at: «http://www.balkan-monitor.eu/dashboard.php».

conflict was averted following concessions from all parties. While the local political leaders made a last-ditch effort to find a solution to the long, drawn-out negotiation on police reform at a meeting in Mostar in October 2007, the EU agreed to initial the SAA on 4 December 2007 without the conditions having been met in full.

Expectations for 2008 were thus high. Indeed, some progress was made during the first quarter of the year with the passing of legislation regarding the implementation of police reform. The reform package adopted by the House of Peoples in April foresaw the establishment of several state-level co-ordinating bodies, although it did not centralize the competencies on policing issues at the state level.[10] This step, which constitutes one of the main 'European conditions', could only take place after a new Bosnian constitution had been agreed, a process which, as of March 2009, had not yet begun.

The new laws on police reform finally paved the way for the signing of the long-awaited SAA on 16 June. However, this has confirmed what many suspected: the signing of the agreement, although a significant milestone on the path towards EU membership as it might be, has not substantially transformed the political dynamics in Bosnia. One year on, the country is still a long way from being a functioning state. Although Kosovo's independence has not led to serious instability in the country, it has contributed to already inflammatory nationalist rhetoric. The victory of nationalist parties at the October local elections confirmed the underlying ethnic divisions and the fragility of the Bosnian state. As in previous election campaigns the run-up to the election was characterized by increased political turbulence and nationalist demagogy. With some commentators warning of Bosnia being on the brink of collapse (Ashdown and Holbrooke, 2008), the Council expressed concerns about the deterioration of the political situation in the country (Council, 2008b, p. 24). In spite of the political instability, it was believed that the security situation was stable enough to allow for a withdrawal of the military operation in Bosnia. In October, the EU Defence Ministers agreed to phase out EUFOR Althea, although they did not set a specific date for the withdrawal.

According to the Commission's annual report, Montenegro needed to improve its administrative capacity and the performance of the judiciary, as well as to tackle widespread corruption. Despite these recommendations, Montenegro filed a formal application for EU membership under the French Presidency in December 2008.[11] This move also encouraged preparations in Serbia and Albania to present applications in 2009. However, the Commission

[10] *Euroactiv.com*, 17 April 2008.
[11] Euroactiv.com, 16 December 2008.

has made clear to the Albanian authorities that it is still too early to move towards candidate status.[12] For the country to achieve this status, it will have to implement several reforms identified in the Commission progress reports, in particular regarding the fight against corruption and organized crime as well as improving its judiciary and its administrative capacity. On the other hand, Albania's accession to Nato is now a certainty after being invited to become a member of the Alliance at its Bucharest summit in April 2008.

II. European Neighbourhood Policy

General Developments

Union for the Mediterranean

President Nicolas Sarkozy first announced his intention to establish a 'Mediterranean Union' during his Presidential election campaign in a speech on 7 February 2007 (Soler i Lecha, 2008, p. 19). According to his original plan, the Mediterranean Union would bring together all the Mediterranean coastal states to revitalize and strengthen co-operation across the Mediterranean basin, but outside the EU framework. The initiative constituted a major attempt to reshape not only French foreign policy, but also European foreign policy. It openly recognized the fact that the Barcelona Process had failed to further economic and democratic reforms in the EU's southern neighbours, and to close the widening gap between the northern and southern coasts of the Mediterranean. Many also saw in this initiative an attempt to frustrate Turkey's membership aspirations.

By July 2008, a change of name to the 'Barcelona Process: Union for the Mediterranean' signalled a scaling back of ambitions and significant changes to the initial project (Dehousse and Menon, this volume). Sarkozy's initiative had to overcome severe opposition and criticisms from both its EU partners and southern Mediterranean countries.[13] Fierce opposition to the original Mediterranean Union came from France's traditional ally, Germany. Chancellor Merkel rejected the idea of a Union restricted to Mediterranean coastal states. It was feared that such a project would lead to the establishment of different spheres of influence in EU foreign policy. Spain and Italy were concerned about the impact of this initiative on the Euro-Mediterranean policy. Other Member States feared an unnecessary duplication of institutional arrangements. Turkey, for its part, rejected any suggestions that the Mediterranean Union would provide an alternative to EU membership. Libya

---

[12] EUobserver.com, 6 May 2008.
[13] *International Herald Tribune*, 6 July 2008.

was also very critical of the project, while other southern Mediterranean countries did not openly oppose the initiative, but were far from enthusiastic about it.

As a result of this opposition, particularly from Germany, the original French plan was watered down. A new Franco–German proposal in the form of a 'Barcelona Process plus' was presented to the European Council on 13 March 2008. The Commission was then entrusted with fleshing out the proposal. The Commission Communication of 20 May spelt out the main elements of this initiative. The 'Barcelona Process: Union for the Mediterranean' aims to complement rather than replace existing EU policies (the Barcelona Process and the European Neighbourhood Policy). Unlike Sarkozy's plan, it has been launched under the EU umbrella and is open to all EU Member States, the members and observers of the Barcelona Process and other Mediterranean states (Croatia, Bosnia and Herzegovina, Montenegro and Monaco). The new initiative is expected to give a new impulse to the Barcelona Process in three ways: (1) by upgrading the political relations between the EU and its Mediterranean partners with a biannual summit of Heads of Government; (2) by increasing co-ownership of the process (a co-Presidency will be established with this end in mind); and (3) by launching regional and sub-regional projects relevant to the citizens of the region (Commission, 2008b). A number of initiatives dealing with energy, environment, civil protection and transport are currently being discussed.

At the Paris Summit for the Mediterranean on 13 July 2008, the Union for the Mediterranean was officially launched. In November 2008, foreign ministers decided that Barcelona would be the Union for the Mediterranean's Headquarters.[14] While this initiative brings more flexibility and a fresh impetus to a stricken Barcelona Process, it has failed to seriously rationalize EU external policies, adding a new framework to an increasingly complex network of regional policies. One might also wonder how this renewed partnership will succeed in promoting political and economic reforms where the Barcelona Process has previously failed.

Eastern Partnership

The proposal for an Eastern Partnership (EaP) was presented jointly by Poland and Sweden at the GAERC on 26 May 2008. The EaP was a well-prepared diplomatic initiative by the Polish government led by Donald Tusk and represented a significant departure in substance and style from the 2005–07 Law and Justiceled coalition government (Cianciara, 2008). As

---

[14] *EUobserver*, 4 November 2008.

with the Union for the Mediterranean the initiative was intended to reinvigo-
rate the relationship between the EU and a sub-group of countries, in this
instance eastern Europe and the Southern Caucuses, covered by the ENP. The
countries covered by the EaP are Ukraine, Moldova, Armenia, Azerbaijan,
Georgia and Belarus. The latter's participation is conditional upon an
improved human rights record and moves towards democracy. Belarus'
formal inclusion was debated at length by the Member States because of
long-standing EU opposition to the governing regime and the leadership of its
president Alexander Lukashenko. The debate over the inclusion of Belarus
illustrates that the EaP is an uneasy compromise between its stated objectives
of promoting 'commitments to the rule of law, good governance, respect for
human rights, respect for and protection of minorities, and the principles of
the market economy and sustainable development' and the more naked realities of geopolitics with any exclusion of Belarus viewed as advantageous to
Russia's interests (Commission, 2008f).

That the EaP was counter-balancing and linked eastern initiatives to the
southern-focused Mediterranean Union was illustrated by both proposals
being debated at the 19–20 June meeting of the European Council. The
Commission was invited to prepare a proposal on the EaP for spring 2009 and
then, at the 1 September 2008 Extraordinary European Council called in
response to the fighting in Georgia, encouraged to accelerate its work and
report by the end of the year (European Council, 2008a, b).

The Commission's proposals to realize the Partnership are to embed the
EaP within the wider ENP (Commission, 2008f). They are also to give the
EaP a multilateral framework but with the bulk of its implementation pursued
bilaterally with the participating states. The multilateral framework is for four
'policy platforms' on democracy, good governance and stability; economic
integration and convergence with EU policies; energy security; and contacts
between people.

Bilaterally each of the participants are offered the prospect of an Association Agreement with the EU but with no commitment to that these agreements
hold out any prospect of future full membership of the Union. The Association Agreements would provide for the creation of individual deep and comprehensive free trade areas (DCFTA) with each partnership country and
which, in turn, could be joined together to form a Neighbourhood Economic
Community. 'Mobility and Security Pacts' are also envisioned to ease cross-
border movement and as part of a 'phased approach' via visa facilitation
negotiations with partners and 'in the longer term' opening dialogues on
visa-free travel with all the partners. No new institutions or secretariat or
dedicated funding initiative is proposed for the EaP. Activities envisioned are
being covered under the existing European Neighbourhood Policy Instrument

(ENPI) and the Neighbourhood Investment Facility (EIF). The formal launch of the Partnership took place at an 'Eastern Partnership Summit' in May 2009.

The arrangements proposed for the EaP by the Commission have faint echoes of the Stabilization and Accession Process for the Western Balkans and with the same intended benefit for the EU of creating a road map for the development and deepening of relations. However, the significant difference is that the EaP is not intended to hold out the prospect of EU accession as the final destination.

Bilateral Relations – Belarus, Ukraine

The existent bilateral relationships with the EaP states were not subject to significant alteration in 2008. The EU's most difficult bilateral relationship remained that with Belarus. The EU had promised to consider an easing of visa restrictions and other sanctions if the Parliamentary elections scheduled for September 2008 were more free and fair than their predecessors in 2006. Although the OSCE electoral observer mission declared that the elections were 'undemocratic' there was a subsequent mini-thaw in EU–Belarus relations. Following its decision not to recognize the independence of Abkhazia and South Ossetia and the release of three political prisoners, a visa ban, introduced in 2006, following the earlier parliamentary elections that the EU viewed as unfree and unfair, was suspended in October 2008 for a period of six months. The ban had covered over 30 officials and Belarusian president Alexander Lukashenko. Other sanctions including an arms embargo and assets freeze remain in place.

Ukraine's domestic political disfunctionality and the ongoing internecine war within the governing 'Orange' coalition retarded the development of EU–Ukraine relations in 2008. Real substantive progress was not made in the negotiations for a replacement of the Partnership and Co-operation Agreement which has been in force since 1998 and with an intended ten-year duration. As noted in last year's review, the negotiation of a New Enhanced Agreement (NEA) started in March 2007 and is intended to go beyond the Partnership and Co-operation Agreement and the existing Joint Action Plan which was for a three-year duration from 2005.[15] The New Enhanced Agreement is intended to be a comprehensive and cross-pillar agreement introducing a contractual basis for integration, convergence and co-operation in various fields such as political reforms, rule of law, human rights, border management, migration and the Common Foreign and Security Policy, and will lead to a deep and comprehensive free trade area between Ukraine and

---

[15] «http://ec.europa.eu/world/enp/pdf/action_plans/ukraine_enp_ap_final_en.pdf».

the EU. Further rounds of negotiations on the NEA took place after Ukraine joined the World Trade Organization (WTO) in February 2008, but have moved at a slow pace to date.

The EU–Ukraine summit which was held at the Elysée Palace (rather than the scheduled venue of Evian because of President Sarkozy's shuttle diplomacy on the Georgia conflict) on 9 September 2008 yielded few tangible results. This was not entirely due to the actions of Ukraine, as Member States still remain divided as to whether an EU membership perspective should be offered to Ukraine. Member States were willing to concede the promise of an opening of a dialogue on a visa-free regime for Ukraine (a key issue for Ukraine) as improvements are being sought in the way that the current Visa Facilitation Agreement is being implemented by some EU Member States. President Sarkozy put the best possible gloss on the meeting by presenting the Union's offer of an Association Agreement for Ukraine and there was a certain desperation in the wording of the summit *communiqué* that stated that the EU 'leaves the door open to progressive further developments' (Council, 2008a, p. 3).

The year ended with Russia threatening to cut gas supplies to Ukraine on 1 January 2009 if a dispute over a $2 billion gas debt was not resolved. As EU Member States remain heavily reliant on Russian gas transiting through Ukraine, as was the case during a similar dispute in early 2006 which resulted in a curtailment of supply, the bilateral relationship between Russia and Ukraine remains of key importance to the Union.

Georgia–Russia War

The Georgia–Russia war in August 2008 illustrated vividly the potential that the so-called 'frozen conflicts' in the post-Soviet periphery have to threaten security and stability in the European Union's eastern neighbourhood. Although the EU had appointed a Special Representative for the South Caucasus in February 2006 with a mandate to resolve the conflicts over South Ossetia and Abkhazia the EU's diplomacy did not make significant headway. The EU has found it difficult to seek resolution of the conflict because of the weakness of the Georgian state, the turbulent transition of power during the Rose Revolution, the instability and violence in the wider Caucasus region as a whole, especially in relation to Chechnya, and significant deterioration of Georgian–Russian relations in recent years.

In two rounds of mediation, the French Presidency of the EU achieved first a ceasefire agreement between Tbilisi and Moscow under the six-point settlement plan of 12 August 2008. Then on 8 September 2008 the EU brokered another agreement that detailed the mechanics for how to realize the settlement of the conflict on the basis of the 12 August ceasefire. As a part of the 8 September Russian–Georgian agreement, talks were chaired by a troika of the EU, UN and OSCE, with support from the US, and with an agreement that these should be held in Geneva. Subsequently, the conflict parties further agreed that two working groups would be established, one focusing on security and stability and another on Internally Displaced Persons (IDPs) and refugees. The first session of these so-called Geneva talks took place on 15 October amidst controversy over the participation of delegates from Abkhazia and South Ossetia, and eventually broke down over procedural issues. Initially envisaged to be held on a fortnightly basis, a second meeting was postponed until 18 November 2008. This second meeting was more constructive, and even though there was no breakthrough on substance, this meeting was significant because it was for the first time since the August war that Georgian and Russian officials met and discussed the situation. Moreover, despite initial resistance from Georgia, discussions in the working groups included delegates from South Ossetia and Abkhazia. A further meeting took place on 17 and 18 December 2008 which reached no concrete agreement, with the consequence that the incoming Czech Presidency inherited a significant foreign policy challenge from its French predecessor.

While the French Presidency can take some considerable credit for its role in brokering a ceasefire it also complicated the arrangements for the EU's diplomacy in the region. The role of the existing Special Representative for the South Caucasus, Peter Semneby, was undermined by the French EU Presidency when President Sarkozy insisted on, and pushed through, the appointment of a separate EU Special Representative for the crisis in Georgia in the person of Ambassador Pierre Morel (who was also serving as EU Special Representative for Central Asia) on 25 September.[16] While this has allowed France to keep some control over the EU's engagement in Georgia after the end of its EU Presidency, it has created an unnecessary overlap of mandates and competences.

As a further contribution to managing the conflict the GAERC decided, on Monday 15 September, to establish an unarmed civilian ceasefire monitoring mission in Georgia for an initial 12-month period.[17] The ESDP EUMM mission of 200 monitors was deployed on 1 October and with the personnel drawn from 26 of the 27 Member States.

---

[16] Council Joint Action 2008/760/CFSP.
[17] Council Joint Action 2008/736/CFSP.

South Caucasus: Armenia, Azerbaijan

The EU's efforts to achieve a settlement of the conflict over Abkhazia and South Ossetia are a reminder that there is another frozen conflict that falls within the South Caucuses: Nagorno-Karabakh. In the case of the ENP Action Plans in the Union's eastern neighbourhood where they do make specific reference to conflict settlement, they are often vague and lack the kind of specificity necessary to tie them credibly to incentives that are only conditionally available to partner countries. Moreover, Action Plans, as they are based on a consensus between the EU and the partner country, are not automatically indicative of the EU's own priorities. Thus, for example, in relation to the Nagorno–Karabakh conflict, the Action Plan with Azerbaijan mentions conflict settlement as the number one priority; the Action Plan with Armenia has it listed as seven in a list of eight areas of priority action. Conditionality is problematic in the case of Azerbaijan, a country benefiting from its hydrocarbon wealth and playing on the EU's declared intention to diversify its energy supplies and decrease its dependency on Russia in terms of both supply and transit.

Middle East

During 2008 the EU held a series of meetings with the Palestinian Authority, including political dialogue at the ministerial level, aimed at deepening bilateral relations. It continued work on the implementation of the Interim Association Agreement and contributed to the strengthening of the Palestinian security forces through the activities of its ESDP mission EUPOL COPPS. The mission continued to support the training of Palestinian police and co-ordinating the provision of equipment in the territory controlled by the Palestinian Authority. The Council also agreed to extend the mission's supporting activities to the judiciary, the prosecutors and penitentiary services.

Talks with Israel to upgrade its relations with the EU continued throughout 2008. At the EU–Israel Association Council, a decision was made to offer Israel advanced status. This would mean increased diplomatic co-operation with the EU, participation in European agencies and programmes and the establishment of a working group with a view to examining the integration of Israel into the European single market. However, despite having the approval of the Commission, the Council and the European Parliament Foreign Affairs Committee, the plenary of the European Parliament decided to postpone the vote on this proposal in December, to pressure Israel to stop all settlement building activities and end its siege of the Gaza Strip.

The Middle East Peace Process suffered a new reverse in 2008. Throughout the year, the EU had urged the parties to return to the negotiating table with a view to concluding a peace agreement before the end of 2008 as agreed at Annapolis in November 2007. However, EU declarations failed to have any impact on the ground. The Israeli blockade of all crossings into and out of the Gaza Strip led to a major humanitarian disaster (Tocci, 2009, p. 7). After a short-lived Egyptian-mediated truce, Hamas militants resumed the firing of rockets against Israel. Israel responded with the launch of a three-week military offensive against Hamas. The level of destruction caused by the Israeli offensive and the number of civilian casualties prompted large mobilizations around the world against the war.

On 27 December, the French Presidency responded to the violence in Gaza with a declaration condemning Israeli bombings and the rocket attacks by Hamas. It also called for an immediate ceasefire (Presidency of the EU, 2008). An EU delegation travelled to the region to participate in the mediation efforts on 4 January (Tocci, 2009, p. 7). At the same time, EU Member States were also active in the negotiations taking place in the UN context. Despite these efforts, the Gaza crisis showed the limitations of the EU's foreign policy in the Middle East once again. The EU failed to influence either side in the conflict. In keeping with tradition, Israel showed distrust of the EU and only responded to US pressures; as for Hamas, the EU itself had refused to engage with this party in the conflict. Moreover, the system of rotating Presidencies not only constituted a disruption in the mediation efforts started by the French Presidency, but it also showed the problems when a small and inexperienced Presidency is at the helm.

North Africa

Among the countries of the region, Morocco maintains the closest relationship with the EU. This was confirmed at the EU–Morocco Association Council meeting of 13 October, which granted Morocco advanced status. At the meeting, the parties agreed to implement a series of measures designed to strengthen the partnership. Morocco's advanced status should lead to increasing co-operation in political and security matters and a comprehensive free trade agreement, as well as the integration of Morocco into a number of EU sectoral policies. In sum, the focus of EU–Morocco bilateral relations continues to be trade, investment and security co-operation, primarily in the areas of migration and anti-terrorism, while issues of democratization, human rights or participation of civil society feature little on the agenda.

Other countries in the region such as Tunisia and Egypt also expressed their interest in a stronger partnership with the EU for 2009. An agreement on EU financial assistance to Egypt for the period 2007–10 was signed in March 2008, under the new European Neighbourhood and Partnership Instrument that replaced MEDA. The financial package of €558 million aims at supporting the implementation of the ENP Action Plan adopted in 2007. A preliminary agreement was also reached to further liberalize trade in agricultural and fishery products. In December, the EU and Egypt signed a Memorandum of Understanding to enhance energy co-operation. Egypt is not only the sixth largest natural gas supplier to the EU, but also a key transit country between the EU and the Middle East. In the political domain, concerns were expressed by the European Parliament about human rights abuses in Egypt (European Parliament, 2008).

Improvement of EU–Libya relations continued in 2008, following Libya's recent moves to reintegrate in the wider international community. In July, the Council adopted a decision authorizing the Commission to negotiate a Framework Agreement, opening the way for the establishment of contractual relations between the EU and this Mediterranean country for the first time. The Agreement should also strengthen political dialogue and promote an increase in trade and investments between Libya and the EU. The negotiations, launched in November 2008, have focused on a wide range of issues of common concern for both parties, including migration, the establishment of a free trade area, co-operation on foreign policy and security issues and energy.

III. EEA and Switzerland

Iceland

The global financial crisis which unfolded in 2008 had one of its most dramatic manifestations within the wider Europe. The collapse of the banking system in Iceland and the dramatic depreciation of the Icelandic króna brought crisis to a member of the European Economic Area (EEA) and associate member of the Schengen area. Iceland was required to seek financial assistance from the IMF. The EU was not directly involved in the attempt to resolve Iceland's financial difficulties. Rather, there was the emergence of a bilateral dispute between the UK and Iceland over the handling of depositors' money in the British subsidiaries of the Icelandic banks Landsbanki and Kaupthing.

The Icelandic financial and banking crisis generated considerable domestic debate in Iceland on EU and euro area membership and with opinion polling indicating a significant shift in public opinion in favour of membership. Debate within the Independence and Progressive Parties, which had been opposed to EU accession, appeared to be shifting in favour of the position of the Social Democratic Alliance which favours a referendum on whether to seek membership of the EU. Enlargement Commissioner Olli

Rehn stated that the Commission was 'mentally preparing' for an application for EU membership following a general election anticipated for spring 2009.[18]

Switzerland

The Member States agreed on 12 December 2008 that Switzerland would be permitted to join the Schengen zone. Participation was approved by the Swiss public in a referendum in 2005. Joining Schengen will also require Switzerland to enhance border controls with Lichtenstein as the latter will remain outside the zone. Switzerland has also scheduled a referendum for 8 February 2009 on the extension of free movement of labour for citizens of Bulgaria and Romania and a further referendum is anticipated when the latter two states accede to Schengen, which is unlikely to occur before 2011.

Conclusions

Events in the wider Europe in 2008 demonstrated the extent to which the EU faces a set of ongoing challenges within its near abroad. The EU's capacity to manage, shape and structure the international relations of the continent through a combination of the enlargement process and the ENP are uncertain.

The current atrophy of the enlargement process raises questions about the extent to which the EU's strongest foreign policy tool is losing its purchase. A diminishing enthusiasm on the part of the Member States for future enlargements is translating into a reduced perception of the prospects for membership in the applicant states. Furthermore, Member State divisions over Kosovo have diminished the Member States' previously largely cohesive collective policy in the Western Balkans.

The emergence of both the proposals for the Mediterranean Union and the EaP in 2008 also demonstrate the ongoing problems of the ENP as a policy that is sufficiently calibrated to accommodate all of the EU's bordering states. Whether the Mediterranean Union and the EaP represent a 'hollowing out' of the ENP remains to be seen. Furthermore, the difficulty encountered by the EU in brokering an end to the Israeli intervention in Gaza reinforced the impression that the EU's ambitions to remodel the wider Mediterranean Union remain hostage to the travails of the Arab–Israeli conflict.

The EU can take some credit for its role in bringing a ceasefire to the war in Georgia, but it has now also taken on a direct responsibility for the resolution of one of the conflicts in Europe which has previously proved to be intractable. Increasingly, the EU's ambitions for the eastern half of the

[18] *Reuters*, 11 December 2008.

continent are being complicated by a more assertive Russian foreign policy. Russia appears to be increasingly treating the EU as a direct competitor for the exercise of influence within the wider Europe and this is creating an additional complication for the EU in the pursuit of its policies within the neighbourhood.

Key Reading

Epstein and Sedelmeier (2008) and the articles in the Special Issue of *Journal of European Public Policy*, Vol. 15, No. 6, provide an excellent discussion of conditionality in the post-accession context. In particular, see articles by Schimmelfennig (2008) on the Western Balkans and Turkey, and Lavenex (2008) on the European neighbourhood policy. See Gillespie (2008) and Bechev and Nicolaidis (2008) for an overview of the Mediterranean Union and analysis of both the potential and pitfalls inherent in this initiative.

References

Ashdown, P. and Holbrooke, R. (2008) 'A Bosnian Powder Keg'. *The Guardian*, 22 October.

Bechev, D. and Nicolaidis, K. (2008) 'The Union for the Mediterranean: A Genuine Breakthrough or More of the Same?'. *The International Spectator*, Vol. 43, No. 3, pp. 13–20.

Cianciara, A.K. (2008) 'Eastern Partnership – Opening a New Chapter of Polish Eastern Policy and the European Neighbourhood Policy?' *Analyses and Opinions* 4, June 2008, Institute of Public Affairs, Warsaw. Available at: «http://www.isp.org.pl/files/8679201040703671001213792577.pdf».

Commission of the European Communities (2008a) 'Communication from the Commission to the Council and the European Parliament. Western Balkans: Enhancing the European Perspective'. COM(2008) 127 final, Brussels, 5 March 2008.

Commission of the European Communities (2008b) 'Communication: Barcelona Process: Union for the Mediterranean'. COM(2008) 319(final), 20 May.

Commission of the European Communities (2008c) 'Communication from the Commission to the Council and the European Parliament. Enlargement Strategy and Main Challenges 2008–09'. COM(2008) 674 final, Brussels, 5 November 2008.

Commission of the European Communities (2008d) 'Croatia 2008 Progress Report'. SEC(2008) 2694, Brussels, 5 November 2008.

Commission of the European Communities (2008e) 'Turkey 2008 Progress Report'. SEC(2008) 2699, Brussels, 5 November 2008.

Commission of the European Communities (2008f) 'Communication from the Commission to the Council and the European Parliament. Eastern Partnership'. COM(2008) 823 final, Brussels, 3 December 2008.

Commission of the European Communities (2008g) 'The Former Yugoslav Republic of Macedonia 2008 Progress Report'. SEC(2008) 2695, Brussels, 5 November.

Council of the European Union (2008a) 'EU–Ukraine Summit'. Doc. 12812/08, Paris, 9 September.

Council of the European Union (2008b) 'Council Conclusions'. 2903rd General Affairs and External Relations Council, Doc. 15396/08, 10–11 November.

Epstein, R. and Sedelmeier, U. (2008) 'Beyond Conditionality: International Institutions in Post-communist Europe after Enlargement'. *Journal of European Public Policy*, Vol. 15, No. 6, pp. 795–805.

Eurobarometer (2008a) 'Eurobarometer 69, The European Union Today and Tomorrow'. Available at: «http://ec.europa.eu/public_opinion/archives/eb/eb69/eb69_part3_en.pdf».

Eurobarometer (2008b) 'Eurobarometer 70, Public Opinion in the European Union, First Results, Autumn 2008'. Available at: «http://ec.europa.eu/public_opinion/archives/eb/eb70/eb70_first_en.pdf».

European Council (2007) 'Presidency Conclusions'. Brussels European Council, 14 December 2007, Brussels.

European Council (2008a) 'Presidency Conclusions'. Brussels European Council 19–20 June 2008, Brussels.

European Council (2008b) 'Presidency Conclusions'. Brussels European Council 1 September 2008, Brussels.

European Parliament (2008) 'European Parliament Resolution of 17 January 2008 on the Situation in Egypt' (Strasbourg: European Parliament).

Gillespie, R. (2008) 'A "Union for the Mediterranean" [. . .] or for the EU?' *Mediterranean Politics*, Vol. 13, No. 2, pp. 277–86.

Lavenex, S. (2008) 'A Governance Perspective on the European Neighbourhood Policy: Integration Beyond Conditionality?' *Journal of European Public Policy*, Vol. 15, No. 6, pp. 938–955.

Presidency of the European Union (2008) 'Déclaration de la présidence du Conseil de l'Union européenne sur les violences à Gaza'. Available at: «http://ue2008.fr/PFUE/lang/fr/accueil/PFUE-12_2008/PFUE-27.12.2008/PESC_Gaza_27_decembre_2008».

Schimmelfennig, F. (2008) 'EU Political Accession Conditionality after the 2004 Enlargement: Consistency and Effectiveness'. *Journal of European Public Policy*, Vol. 15, No. 6, pp. 918–37.

Soler i Lecha, E. (2008) 'Barcelona Process: Union for the Mediterranean Genesis, Evolution and Implications for Spain's Mediterranean Policy'. *CIDOB Documento de Trabajo* 28/2008, Barcelona.

Tocci, N. (2009) 'Lessons from Gaza: Why the EU Must Change its Policy'. *CFSP Forum*, Vol. 7, No. 2, pp. 7–9.

JCMS 2009 Volume 47 Annual Review pp. 213–232

Relations with the Rest of the World

DAVID ALLEN and MICHAEL SMITH
Loughborough University

Introduction

2008 was the year in which concerns about both energy security and the environment began to make a significant impact upon all aspects of the EU's external activities along with a growing anticipation that the result of the US presidential election was likely to mark a real change in the EU–US relationship. The most significant politico-military challenge came from events in Georgia in the summer but, inevitably, by the end of the year there was also a major focus on the impact of the growing global economic and financial crisis on EU external relations.

One of the results of these co-existing pressures and forces was a continuing uncertainty about the extent to which the EU could play a leading role in key international processes. The international role of the Union has long been a subject of commentary and analysis (Elgström and Smith, 2006) and two aspects of the new international conjuncture are likely to be especially demanding in this context. First, the politicization and securitization of areas in which the EU has been able to lead because of its role as a 'civilian power' might make further progress for the Union less uncontroversial and might lead to questions of legitimacy and accountability. Second, the impact of a revitalized United States will also create new challenges for the EU, by rendering less practical the differentiation between EU and US positions that was characteristic during the George W. Bush administrations. As we shall see, a number of areas in European external policy illustrate the kinds of uncertainty that might thus result.

I. General Themes

Foreign, Security and Defence Policy

In 2008, preparations to implement the foreign policy provisions of the Lisbon Treaty were put on hold once the negative outcome of the Irish referendum was known. Although there has been some discussion about what might be feasible without the Treaty (Federal Trust, 2009, pp. 36–41) there was also a reluctance to provoke further adverse comment from those opposed to the Treaty in a number of Member States. In December, the European Council, as part of a package designed to reassure Ireland, agreed to give a legal guarantee that 'the Treaty of Lisbon does not prejudice the security and defence policy of the Member States including Ireland's traditional policy of neutrality, and the obligations (to Nato and the UN for instance) of most other Member States' (Council, 2009). In return, Ireland committed itself to seeking ratification of the Lisbon Treaty by the end of the term of the current Commission. The European Council also agreed interim arrangements should the Treaty of Lisbon enter into force after a six-monthly Presidency has begun. In that event the Council Presidency, not the High Representative or the elected President of the European Council, will continue to chair the Foreign Affairs Council and European Council respectively (Council, 2009, Annex 1), with the new Lisbon Treaty arrangements entering into force under the following Presidency.

The major foreign policy challenge to the EU came in August with the crisis in Georgia (see Juncos and Whitman, this volume, for details of the crisis itself). The French Presidency, assisted by Washington's preoccupation with the financial crisis and the presidential election, moved swiftly under President Sarkozy's active leadership to mediate a ceasefire, the delivery of humanitarian aid and (eventually) the withdrawal of Russian military forces. All this was recorded and discussed further at an Extraordinary European Council meeting held on 1 September (Council, 2008b) but the subsequent follow-up (EU fact-finding mission, appointment of a special representative, development of a Black Sea Synergy initiative and an 'Eastern partnership') (Council, 2009) was perhaps more in the CFSP procedural tradition than an indicator of substantive progress.

As 2008 progressed it became clear that most EU Member States were attracted by the possibility of a major change for the better in the transatlantic relationship, should Barack Obama secure the US presidency. However as the aspiration became a reality there was a growing realization in EU foreign policy circles that a co-operative Obama administration might present almost as many challenges to the Europeans collectively as the abrasive Bush administration had done. Although 2008 was seen by many as a time to take stock of the evolution of the ESDP since its inception in 1999 (Menon, 2009; Federal Trust, 2009), the French Presidency gave a high priority to its further development. Whilst Irish sensitivities forced the French to backtrack a little on their initial ambition both to return France to Nato and then consolidate ESDP as the European arm of Nato, efforts were still made to develop the EU's military planning and headquarters capability, to get 'more bangs per euro' from the combined EU defence expenditure and to encourage the High Representative (HR) to review the 2003 European Security Strategy (ESS) (see De Vasconcelos, 2009; and Security and Defence Agenda, 2009 for academic reviews of the ESS). HR Solana formally presented his ESS Review to the December 2008 European Council. The Review itself (Solana, 2008) is a rather conservative account of the EU's security-related activities since 2003. It recognizes that the EU perhaps has to react less and do more strategically to command the world agenda, but it essentially calls for more of the same whilst recognizing that climate change, energy security, defence against cyber attacks, piracy on the high seas and a better working relationship with Nato all need to be added to the original 2003 list of EU security challenges.

The Presidency Conclusions for the December European Council include a significant declaration on the enhancement of ESDP (Solana, 2008). There is mention in the declaration of the need to enhance both military and civilian capabilities. The European Council stated that beyond 2010 it expected the EU to be capable of planning and conducting simultaneously two major military/civilian stabilization operations, each with a maximum of 10,000 men for at least two years, two rapid response operations of limited duration using EU battlegroups, an emergency operation for the evacuation of European civilians in less than ten days, a maritime or air surveillance interdiction mission, a civil military humanitarian operation lasting up to 90 days and around a dozen ESDP civilian missions, which could last several years and which could include a major mission of up to 3,000 experts.

To achieve this, the European Council declaration calls for greater resources to be provided (at present only five of the 27 EU Member States spend over the agreed Nato target of 2 per cent of GNP on defence), more specialization and less duplication of capability, a restructuring of the EU defence technological and industrial base guided by the European Defence Agency and the development of a new single civilian/military strategic planning structure for ESDP operations. The European Council called for continued and enhanced co-operation with the UN (where the EU already has increased its financial contribution from $200 million to $1 billion in recent years), the African Union and, in particular, Nato with whom co-ordination problems have been well recorded[1] (Toje, 2008). The Council backed a proposal to establish an informal EU–Nato high-level group to improve co-operation.

In 2008 the EU used its Instrument for Stability for the first time to spend €135 million on crisis prevention and crisis management matters. The EU formally agreed 59 new joint actions, decisions and common positions. Eleven of these related to the Western Balkans, six to the South Caucasus, six to Asia, two to the Indian Ocean, nine to the Middle East, two to eastern Europe and five to ESDP-related activities (full details of each action can be found at Commission, 2009, pp. 201–6). Three new ESDP operations were begun in Chad, Guinea Bissau and against pirates off the Somali coast, and two new operations in Kosovo and Georgia were agreed where also two new Special Representatives were appointed. The decision to launch Operation Atalanta against Somali pirates is the EU's first joint naval operation[2] although it had been co-ordinating the surveillance and protection activities of its Member States since September (EU NAVCO). Atalanta is co-ordinated by a British admiral based at the UK joint operations HQ in Northwood outside London and the force (Navfor) drawn from France, Germany, Greece, the Netherlands, Spain, the UK, Sweden and Norway is under the command of a Greek commodore. In January the EU agreed an ESDP training programme for the period 2009–10 to be run by a European Security and Defence College, which was established via a joint action in June and the European Police College. Part of the work of the two Colleges will be to identify and implement lessons learned from ESDP operations and there is also to be a European young officers exchange scheme which will be modelled on the university Erasmus scheme.

The Common Commercial Policy

As in most of the period since 2001, the EU's energies in commercial policy at the global level were largely concentrated on the continuing Doha Development Round negotiations within the World Trade Organization (WTO). These had been bedevilled in previous years by disputes over agricultural market access, with India and China especially resisting efforts by the US and the EU to achieve significant market opening without strong safeguard mechanisms. The year opened with renewed efforts to achieve progress, partly at least through a new 'quartet' of WTO members – the US, the EU, Brazil and India (a contrast to the 'quartet' that had operated since the early 1990s, of the US, the EU, Canada and Japan). Later in the year, these four

---

[1] *European Voice*, 31 July 2008 and 9 October 2008.
[2] *The Guardian*, 8 December 2008.

were joined by Australia and India in efforts to inject momentum into the process. The problem was that the underlying differences simply could not be wished away, and when the process came to a head in July, the Indians and the Americans were once again at the centre of the stand-off.[3] In the build-up to this climax, the US and the EU had worked closely together on a number of issues,[4] and the EU itself had made a number of significant concessions, for example on export subsidies for agricultural products,[5] to such an extent that the French especially harboured severe doubts about Trade Commissioner Peter Mandelson's capacity to defend their interests. But all was eventually in vain: the collapse of the July talks was followed by attempts to resuscitate the Doha Round as part of the G20 response to the international financial crisis, but these remained unfulfilled by the end of the year, not least because of congressional opposition in the US and the hiatus caused by the US presidential election followed by the transition period between the Bush and Obama administrations.

Alongside these efforts to push forward multilateral trade negotiations, the EU pursued its own inter-regional and bilateral agenda. In some ways, this push for free trade arrangements on the more limited level is a response to the difficulties of achieving global trade reform – and also to the efforts by the US and others to negotiate free trade agreements with a wide range of international partners. The EU in 2008 pursued negotiations with India, South Korea, ASEAN countries, the Gulf Co-operation Council, Central American countries and the Andean Community, but none of these produced final agreements during the year. The EU also opened negotiations with Ukraine, immediately following that country's accession to the WTO, which are designed to lead to a closer Association Agreement.[6] One of the problems attending all of these negotiations is that the EU finds itself dealing with increasingly assertive partners, who see the opportunity to extract significant concessions and to defend their own national interests; this seems to some to be a source of significant limitations on the EU's often-vaunted 'soft power' in the global trading system.[7]

Aside from the challenges of global, inter-regional and bilateral trade negotiations, 2008 also saw challenges to the EU's institutional and policy-making capacity in commercial policy. At the beginning of the year, Commissioner Mandelson had to abandon the reform of the EU's anti-dumping policy framework, recognizing that there was major opposition from a

[3] *Financial Times*, 30 July 2008.
[4] *European Voice*, 15 May 2008.
[5] *European Voice*, 28 July 2008.
[6] *European Voice*, 21 February 2008.
[7] *European Voice*, 20 December 2007.

number of key Member States; this opposition was backed up by suspicions on the part of EU producer interests that the proposed reforms would limit their capacity to claim injury and thus to obtain judgments against their rivals abroad.[8] The EU was able to undertake a review of its Generalized System of Preferences (GSP) and also to apply a new scheme known as 'GSP+', which gave additional preferences to countries abiding by certain standards of governance (Commission, 2009). The Commission also retained its core focus on competitiveness and market access, but as noted above this could often be resisted by key partners in the global arena. As the year wore on, things became markedly more worrying, with the financial crisis spawning protectionist pressures from within the Union and the threat of 'economic nationalism' abroad – a threat which was countered in several sharply worded speeches from Mandelson, but which did not go away.[9] By the end of the year, Mandelson was gone. Whilst his commitment to the defence of free trade had been consistent, the verdict on his tenure as Commissioner was qualified at best.[10]

Development Co-operation Policy and Humanitarian Aid

The global financial crisis raised real concerns in 2008 that the EU would not be able to meet its commitment to the Millennium Development Goals (MDG), especially as total EU development aid dropped by 3 per cent in 2007. In 2008 the EU contribution (that is the EU and its Member States) remained above an impressive 60 per cent of total global development aid and the Member States recommitted themselves to meeting their targets of contributing 0.5 per cent of EU GNP by 2010 (a total of €66 billion) rising to 0.7 per cent of EU GNP by 2015 (Council, 2008a). As world food prices rose and created concerns about both food availability and future production in the poorest of developing countries, the European Commission attempted a spectacular initiative when the Agricultural Commissioner, enthusiastically supported by President Barroso, proposed diverting €1 billion from the underspent CAP budget towards immediate food aid for the countries most in need.[11] The proposal was made in April and the Commission produced a legislative proposal by July, but when it was eventually agreed in November the result differed significantly from what had originally been planned. The Member States refused to allow money to be taken from the CAP allocation and instead found the €1 billion from the EU's emergency aid reserve, existing unspent development funds and from money allocated to the

[8] *Financial Times*, 12 January 2008.
[9] See, for example, *Financial Times*, 9 February 2008.
[10] *European Voice*, 16 October 2008.
[11] *European Voice*, 27 November 2008.

Instrument for Stability with an additional contribution of €240 million from the national budgets of the Member States. Worse, this was no longer aid for immediate consumption but to be spent over the 2008–11 period, whereas the original idea had been that a significant amount of the money would be available almost immediately to ensure that affected farmers had the funds to prepare the land and sow crops for the next harvest.

In 1993 the World Trade Organization ruled that the EU's preferential trade agreements with the African, Caribbean and Pacific (ACP) states were illegal and since 2002 the EU has been trying to conclude replacement regional economic partnership agreements (EPAs) with its ACP partners. This has been a long and painful process, but in 2008, by which time all the EPAs were meant to be in place, the first EPA agreement was signed with the 14 Caribbean countries that make up Cariforum. Elsewhere progress has been even slower, and in many cases has had to be made at the national rather than the preferred regional level. Apart from Cariforum, after the 1 January deadline, interim regional agreements during 2008 only were signed with the South African Development Community, the East African Community, the Pacific Countries and the East and Southern African Community as well as a host of individual agreements with 42 ACP countries. A number of the very poorest countries who lost their preferential agreements at the start of 2008 have continued to gain access to the EU via the *Everything but Arms* programme, but the others lost their trade preferences in January 2009 and will not regain them until their EPAs are concluded. The agreements that have been signed so far only cover trade in goods and not, as was anticipated when the process began, trade in services and investment as well. Nevertheless, in 2008 the European Development Fund allocated €4.88 billion to the ACP countries of which €3.9 billion went to Africa.

In 2008 the EU distributed €936 million in humanitarian aid for 90 projects in 60 countries assisting 118 million people, which included €363 million in Food Aid, assisting 25 million people. The European Commission's distribution of development aid and humanitarian assistance continued to attract critical scrutiny from the Court of Auditors, in particular for the way that the current (10th) European Development Fund implements the principle of country ownership, whereby large amounts of aid are handed over directly to the governments of recipient countries.[12] In November the Court described the Commission's interpretation of the eligibility criteria for this form of direct budgetary transfer as creating a 'high fiduciary risk'. The Court, the European Parliament and critics in the Member States all feel that the Commission does not apply its good governance criteria rigorously enough when

[12] *European Voice*, 13 November 2008.

it distributes EU development aid; this could become a more serious challenge to the present levels of aid as the Member States experience their own economic difficulties and as criticism of the EU and its policies becomes more widespread.

On related issues, 2008 saw an increased determination to consider climate change and energy security factors in all aspects of development policy as well as maintaining conditionality in the form of a variety of human rights dialogues and *démarches*. The EU spent €143 million via its Instrument for the Promotion of Democracy and Human Rights on ten electoral assistance missions, four election expert missions and 47 country-based support schemes. The EU played a major role in the International Conference on Financing for Development in Doha and recommitted itself to its 2007 EU Strategy on Aid for Trade in which it promised to spend €2 billion annually on EU trade-related assistance by 2010.

II. Regional Themes

Russia

At the first EU–Russia summit of 2008 in Khanty-Mansiysk (the first following the election of President Medvedev in March), negotiations for a new EU–Russia agreement to replace the 1994 Partnership and Co-operation Agreement were at last begun after no progress had been made in the previous year (Allen and Smith, 2008, p. 171). At the summit the EU and Russia also reached agreement on seven cross-border co-operation programmes to which the EU will contribute €307 million and Russia €122 million. The conflict in Georgia however (see Juncos and Whitman, this volume) meant that on 1 September an Extraordinary Meeting of the European Council (Council, 2008b) postponed all further meetings about the new EU–Russia agreement although the withdrawal of Russian troops from zones close to South Ossetia and Abkhazia was noted with satisfaction at the October European Council (Council, 2008c) and negotiations were formally resumed after the second EU–Russia summit in Nice in November.

The Georgian crisis inevitably impacted on EU–Russia relations beyond the question of negotiating a new agreement. Russia's concern about the prospect of Ukrainian and Georgian membership of the EU and NATO was further demonstrated in a renewal at the end of the year of the ongoing dispute with Ukraine over the pricing (for Ukraine) and transit (to western Europe) of Russian natural gas. Russia views EU attempts to assist Ukraine and Georgia and to reduce its own exposure to potential Russian retaliatory action over the supply of gas and oil as hostile and the atmosphere at the Nice summit was affected by the announcement, just before the meeting, by the European Commission of an energy package which stated that two absolute priorities for the EU were the linking of the three Baltic States to European power grids along with the creation of a southern gas corridor to transport gas from the Caspian to Europe bypassing both Russia and Iran.[13]

The Georgian crisis did serve to unite an EU which has become famously divided and indecisive over how to deal with a resurgent Russia. It was possible to discern a new firmness of purpose in the EU's friendly dealings with Ukraine at a summit in Paris in September, in its offering of a 'new and ambitious' agreement to Moldova as well as the lifting of sanctions against Belarus and Uzbekistan. These moves along with the energy package have been described[14] as the beginnings of a new strategy designed to undermine Russia's own position in relation to its 'near abroad'. However the major problem that the EU faced at the end of 2008 was the likelihood that the newly elected President Obama might soon be seeking the basis for a new relationship between the United States and Russia and that this would in all probability place further strains on attempts by the major EU Member States to maintain a common position towards Moscow. The UK, for instance, disappointed both Poland and Lithuania when it suddenly reversed its previously strongly argued objections to resuming negotiations on a new agreement with Russia just before the Nice summit. The UK's reversal had much to do with its concern that France (supported by Germany) was beginning to take the lead in defining the EU position towards Russia. Immediately after the Nice summit, President Sarkozy, on behalf of the EU, and President Medvedev together backed plans for a pan-European security summit to be held in 2009 in order to ease tensions raised by the Georgia crisis, by the energy supply issues and by the ongoing issue of missile defence in Europe.

Africa

The expansion of the EU's political and security involvement in Africa, which is designed to complement its already intense economic involvement, continued in 2008 (Pirozzi, 2009) with operations in Sudan, Chad, the Central African Republic (CAR), the Democratic Republic of the Congo (DRC), Guinea Bissau and Somalia. The EU also monitored human rights and the democratic situation in Zimbabwe, Guinea, Kenya, Mauritania, Burundi, Côte d'Ivoire and the DRC and sent an electoral observation mission to Ghana. Under the EDF framework the African Union received €300 million to enhance its capacity for peace support and peacekeeping missions in

---

[13] *The Guardian*, 14 November 2008.
[14] *European Voice*, 16 October 2008.

Africa. In July the first ever EU–South Africa summit was held in Bordeaux although no progress was made on South Africa's uncertainty about participation in the EPA between the EU and the Southern Africa Development Community (SADC). In October the EU announced an initiative designed to build up trilateral co-operation between the EU, Africa and China in recognition of China's expanding role in Africa and of the growing concern of the European Parliament about Chinese arms sales to African countries with poor human rights records (see below).[15]

Over Darfur, the EU responded to the indictment of Sudanese President Omer al-Bashir on genocide charges by the International Criminal Court (ICC) and the subsequent decision to issue an arrest warrant, by withdrawing European Community Humanitarian Office (ECHO) staff from Darfur whilst leaving some in the Sudanese capital Khartoum. However, faced with the problem of who might apprehend Bashir the EU went no further than to pledge an additional €300 million in aid over the following five years and to repeat its desire to see the UN–AU peacekeeping force in Darfur succeed. The EU was criticized for not offering much-needed military helicopters to the UN–AU force.[16]

In Zimbabwe, an EU offer to send election monitors to observe the much-criticized presidential election was unsurprisingly rejected; after the election the EU found itself still having to deal with a re-elected President Mugabe. In the face of a Russian and Chinese veto of further UN sanctions, Brussels renewed and widened its own restrictive measures, later extending them to include a number of European companies on its Zimbabwe blacklist.[17] The EU did not make any progress in persuading South Africa to be more proactively supportive of its positions on both Darfur and Zimbabwe at the EU–South African summit.

In December the EU resisted UN pressure to send troops to the eastern part of the Congo to ensure that humanitarian aid got through to those who had fled the fighting between the DRC government and rebel forces.[18] The UN wanted the EU to make use of its two available battlegroups but these are under the leadership of the UK and Germany who were and remain determined to resist a French desire to send them to the Congo because they are both overstretched in Afghanistan and elsewhere. After the coup in Mauritania the EU at first refused to make scheduled payments under its fisheries agreement with Mauritania but in the end backed off out of concern that EU fishermen would lose their rights in Mauritanian waters.

[15] *European Voice*, 25 April 2008.
[16] *European Voice*, 31 July 2008.
[17] *The Guardian*, 27 January 2009.
[18] *Financial Times*, 9 December 2008.

Asia

Asia has come to loom large in any discussion of EU external strategies, primarily because of the presence in the region of two of the most challenging emerging powers, China and India, but also because of the shifting balance of forces in key regions such as Central Asia. The EU has designated both China and India as 'strategic partners', but it is open to question how much strategy is reflected in its policies towards them and how much partnership is achieved (Smith and Xie, 2009). The longest-standing and most comprehensive engagement is with China and this continued to dominate EU policies towards Asia during 2008. Early in the year, the Commission sent what was described as its highest-powered delegation ever to Beijing – President Barroso, accompanied by nine Commissioners – to further the high-level dialogue that had emerged during the previous two or three years (Allen and Smith, 2008), and there was a consistent attempt to develop new areas of co-operation. But this was constrained by a number of non-economic factors, among which Tibet came to assume a central position. The EU expressed itself strongly when Chinese troops suppressed riots in Tibet during the early part of the year, and there were threats by several EU Member States to boycott the Beijing Olympics due to take place in August. Among those threatening a boycott was President Sarkozy of France, and although he eventually did attend, he was also at the centre of a serious diplomatic disagreement with Beijing later in the year when he planned to meet the Dalai Lama at a Nobel prize winners' meeting in Poland. The net result of this was that China called off the EU–China summit scheduled for December. The Chinese also took an increasingly assertive line in climate change negotiations, most obviously in relation to the Poznań conference which was held in November, calling for the EU and the US to bear their share of adjustment by the emerging economies.[19] Reference has been made above to the EU's response to greater Chinese assertiveness in Africa: the Commission presented a Communication on this 'trilateral' relationship in October, but did not escape criticism for its general tardiness and lack of positive action to resist the Chinese advance in an area long considered to be amenable to EU 'soft power' (Commission, 2008a).[20]

In addition to these strategic aspects of the EU–China relationship, there was a long list of more or less serious disputes arising from the growth and intensification of the EU–China trade relationship. It is inevitable that the 'deepening' of the relationship – together with a persistent and large trade

---

[19] *Financial Times*, 29 October 2008.
[20] *European Voice*, 16 October 2008.

deficit – will produce frictions across an ever-widening range of sectors,[21] and a key test for the EU is how effectively these are managed. Management itself is made more difficult by the tensions within the EU between different groups of Member States and between producer and consumer interests. During 2008, these tensions manifested themselves especially in the continuing story of shoe imports from China (and also Vietnam). Anti-dumping measures had been taken against these in 2006, but were due to expire in 2008. Most Member States wanted this to happen, but a vociferous minority, supported by shoe producers, demanded a review (and thus continuation of the measures) before they were ended. As a result, despite a majority vote in the Council to remove the measures, they were eventually extended to cover what was promised to be a compressed review period.[22] Other EU actions were directed towards the import of cheap candles and air compressors, whilst at the end of 2008 the monitoring process for Chinese textile imports, set up as a result of the 'bra wars' in 2005, was due to come to an end. Alongside these bilateral issues, the EU was also involved with the US and Japan in two disputes that went to the WTO: first, a formal dispute about tariffs imposed on imported car parts;[23] and second, a potential dispute about the way in which the reporting of financial information was restricted by the Chinese (by forcing all non-Chinese agencies to channel their reporting via a single Chinese agency, rather than providing it directly to firms).[24] As noted above, by the end of the year, concern about 'economic nationalism' in China was part of the policy context, and reflected the broader global financial crisis and its implications.

The 'strategic partnership' with India is at an earlier stage of development than that with China. Whereas with China the EU has a fairly long history of relations and of 'problem solving', with India the agenda is still developing and there is plenty of room for differences of perspective and priorities to become disabling.[25] Whilst in 2008 there were specific disputes about items such as the Indian liquor tax – which had been changed at the federal level as a result of EU pressure, only to re-emerge in some individual states within the Indian federation – more important were the tensions that emerged within the broader global context, and particularly within the Doha Round of WTO negotiations (see above). As a result of these and of other tensions emerging within the global financial crisis, slow progress was made during the year on the negotiations for an EU–India free trade agreement, although the EU–India

[21] *Financial Times*, 2 October 2008.
[22] *European Voice*, 11 September 2008.
[23] *Financial* Times, 19 April 2008.
[24] *European Voice*, 10 April 2008.
[25] *European Voice*, 2 October 2008.

summit held in Marseille on 29 September adopted a revised joint action plan.[26]

One key feature of the EU's engagement with Asia is what might be called 'complex inter-regionalism' (Hardacre and Smith, 2009): the multilayered approach which brings together broad multilateral, more limited 'mini-lateral' and bilateral relationships into a complex set of linked approaches to dealing with the continent. During 2008, the existence of this phenomenon was again in evidence, as the EU pushed forward its contacts at a variety of levels and also found that managing them was not as easy as might be imagined. The primary multilateral forum for EU–Asia relations is the Asia–Europe Meeting (ASEM), and in 2008 this held its seventh biennial meeting, in Beijing. At this Heads of State and Government meeting, 43 countries were represented, including (for the first time) India, Mongolia and Pakistan on the Asian side and Bulgaria and Romania on the EU side. Given the time at which it was held – 24 to 25 October – it was inevitably dominated by the global financial crisis, but it did also manage to issue a formal declaration about sustainable development. The ASEM is not just about Heads of State and Government, and in June 2008 there was also the first meeting of the Asia–Europe Social Partners Forum in Brussels, bringing together 150 representatives from the ASEM member countries. This is just the latest addition to the large network of public and private networks surrounding ASEM. Meanwhile, the EU played its part as an observer in the meetings of the South Asian Association for Regional Co-operation (SAARC) and of the Association of Southeast Asian Nations (ASEAN), thus demonstrating its commitment to more 'mini-lateral' processes, whilst also pursuing bilateral association agreements with members of ASEAN especially. When it came to the crisis caused by Hurricane Nargis in Burma (Myanmar) during May 2008, the EU found itself frustrated partly by the refusal of the Burmese junta to allow access for aid organizations, but also partly by the bilateral interests of China and the collective interest of ASEAN, which set out to lead the aid effort. Nonetheless, €2 million were dedicated to the cause, distributed through NGOs and not the Burmese government.

In 2007, the EU had agreed a strategy for a 'new' part of Asia – central Asia – and in 2008 it started to implement the policy. €63 million were spent and, despite the opposition of various human rights groups, it was proposed that the European Investment Bank (EIB) be allowed to extend the range of its activities to include central Asia. The EU–Central Asia Security Forum met for the first time in Paris under the French Presidency and discussed

---

[26] *European Voice*, 25 September 2008.

counter-terrorism and non-proliferation, human and drugs trafficking and issues related to the environment and energy security.

With regard to Uzbekistan, the EU decided not to renew the travel restrictions on government officials but did renew the arms embargo (both of these measures were initially imposed in 2005 following the Andijan massacre). Critics of this decision to ease the sanctions blamed Germany which has a military base in the Uzbek city of Termez.[27] In a similar vein the European Parliament was urged to agree an interim trade agreement with Turkmenistan despite the lack of progress on improving its human rights record. The EU has clearly been concerned to maintain and further its influence in a region which is both energy rich and an important staging post for military operations in Afghanistan but, as in other regions, its role is likely to be strongly shaped by the involvement of other major powers such as the US or China.

Latin America

Latin America displays some of the characteristics of Asia as a partner for the EU. There are key bilateral relationships, a growing web of inter-regional links and a range of issues around which these forces can gather and in respect of which they need to be managed. Thus, Brazil has been designated a 'strategic partner' by the EU, but it actually exists in a setting where a wide range of other institutional contacts between the EU and Latin America take place (Hardacre and Smith, 2009).[28] During 2008, the partnership with Brazil began to take a more concrete form: the second EU–Brazil summit, held on 22 December, adopted an Action Plan designed to shape co-operation over a three-year period and covering a wide range of policy areas. But as with other 'strategic partnerships', it had to be viewed in the context of tensions and linkages arising from global trade negotiations and the global financial crisis. Thus, Brazil along with India was one of the leading 'resisters' in the WTO Doha Round negotiations (see above); it is also a key member of the G20 of the world's largest economies, and thus of the principal forum for discussing the financial crisis. At the same time, in Latin America, the EU has a host of other points of contact: during May 2008, the EU–Latin America Summit was held in Peru, and adopted the 'Lima Agenda for Joint Action', whilst there were also meetings with other key regional actors and organizations. By the end of the year, Brazil was no longer alone as a 'strategic partner' in Latin America: in July, the Commission proposed that Mexico be added to the list (Commission, 2008b) and this was endorsed by the Council in October.

---

[27] *European Voice*, 30 April 2008.
[28] *European Voice*, 18 December 2008.

During June 2008, the EU also made an important diplomatic opening towards Cuba, which has long had an uncertain status in the Union's external relations because of the US embargo and associated policies towards the Castro regime. With the ascendancy of Fidel Castro's brother, Raul, some loosening of the Cuban regime's economic and political stance has taken place and the EU sees openings for economic and other contacts. Louis Michel, the Development Commissioner, visited the island during 2008 and it is clear that aid and development policy is a key area in which the EU feels it can make progress. This is also another area of policy where the Obama administration in the US might well have important effects on the potential for EU engagement.

The United States, Japan and Other Industrialized Countries

One way of summing up the EU's external relations in 2008 might be 'waiting for Obama'. From the beginning of the year, with the onset of the US presidential campaign, the coming change in US administrations and foreign policies was a preoccupation of Europeans far beyond the Brussels 'beltway', and the implications of a new president – whether Barack Obama, Hillary Clinton or John McCain – were exhaustively worked over in the press and in policy circles (Zaborowski, 2008; De Vasconcelos and Zaborowski, 2009). At the broadest strategic level, there was a key concern with the EU's potential role in the new era and this was given additional force by the actions of the Bush administration in its final year. At an early stage, the US Ambassador to Nato made it clear that the US was thinking in terms of the 'EU/Nato family' for security issues and that the EU was now accepted as a valid component of the transatlantic security relationship.[29] President Bush himself took an active role in his two visits to Europe during the year, and on the occasion of the EU–US summit in Brdo, Slovenia (10 June) the agenda covered a number of issues such as climate change and energy on which there had already been significant shifts in US positions. This, however, might be characterized as a 'phoney war' before the real business of the elections and a new president took over. In fact, this happened at an early stage, with Barack Obama's July speech in Berlin in which he set out his approach to Europe.[30] Significantly, although there was much in it to delight the EU, there was also a clear sense that Europe would be asked to do more on key policy areas – a new 'burden-sharing' argument which would undoubtedly be central to Obama foreign policy. It was clear by the autumn that despite Obama being 'Europe's candidate', the Europeans' expectations were almost bound to be

[29] *European Voice*, 13 March 2008; *Financial Times*, 3 April 2008.
[30] *Financial Times*, 25 July 2008.

disappointed.[31] Another key factor in shaping EU responses to the US during 2008 was the French Presidency, and especially Nicolas Sarkozy taking over as EU President for the second half of the year. Sarkozy adopted a clearly Atlanticist policy orientation at national and EU levels and promised a French return to the Nato integrated military command. But all of these political factors also have to be seen in the context of the deepening international financial crisis, which dominated the second half of the year and created a string of new demands for governments on both sides of the Atlantic. For some, this created a new role for the euro and for European collective action; for others, it created the likelihood of European embarrassment as fissiparous tendencies inevitably set in.[32]

At the same time as change was in the air, the existing agenda of EU–US concerns demanded attention. On the security side of the ledger, the EU, through the High Representative and the EU-3 (France, Germany and the UK), continued to play an active role regarding the question of Iran's nuclear weapons potential. Indeed, as the summer wore on and new proposals were put to Tehran, the High Representative came to be the chief carrier of messages and initiatives. Whilst the Iranian response to new offers was decidedly equivocal, it seemed not to be a total rejection; but by the autumn, the mood had hardened and an extension of United Nations sanctions was again being sought.[33] As noted elsewhere in this contribution, the prospect of additional demands for involvement by EU Member States in Afghanistan, in the context of the coming Obama foreign policy, further raised the stakes around what is seldom now called the 'global war on terror'.

Alongside these items of 'high diplomacy' or security policy, a number of other issues displayed the tensions created both across the Atlantic and within the EU by the demands of the 'new security agenda'. The EU and the US moved towards conclusion of agreements on extradition, but this did not dispose of the lingering doubts among many Europeans that suspects should not be extradited to the US where they might face the death penalty.[34] There was tension throughout the year because of US demands that EU Member States should sign bilateral Memorandums of Understanding about passenger security, in which they would undertake to provide extensive information to the US authorities in return for the prospect of being able to enter (or to continue in) the 'visa waiver' scheme; the Commission tried desperately to retain some control over what was negotiated and decided, but to little avail. By the end of the year, seven 'new' Member States had been added to the list

---

[31] *Financial Times*, 30 October 2008.
[32] *Financial Times*, 24 March and 3 April 2008.
[33] *European Voice*, 12 June 2008; *Financial Times*, 14 June 2008 and 7 August 2008.
[34] *European Voice*, 7 February 2008.

of those making the undertakings, with more on the way.[35] The EU continued to engage the US administration on issues of environmental and energy security, with more hope of making an impact than previously given the Bush administration's new-found multilateralism – but again, with the prospect of a new dawn in early 2009.

Security issues went alongside persistent economic issues in EU–US relations, and during 2008 there were several testing disputes to keep EU and US trade negotiators on their toes. The US, along with Japan and others, threatened the EU with WTO action in relation to a dispute over interpretation of the 1996 Information Technology Agreement (ITA); whilst the Europeans persisted in their view that new products such as flat-screen monitors could be subject to tariffs because they were not mentioned in the agreement, their opponents took the opposite view. Another set of frictions continued around the issue of biodiesel imports into the US; the Europeans insisted that US subsidies were driving their producers out of business, whilst the US insisted they were not. Online gaming, a sector in which the EU had banned international activity and thus was seen by the EU as discriminating against European providers, was another focus of recriminations, whilst the potential for another dispute arose when EADS, the European defence company, won a contract for provision of tanker aircraft to the US Air Force only to be the subject of congressional action designed to give Boeing a second chance. One small victory could be registered, not for either party but for the Transatlantic Economic Council (Allen and Smith, 2008), which provided the channel for an agreement to lift duties on US poultry treated with anti-microbial solutions – even this was surrounded by suspicions and complaints from EU producers, who feel US standards are lax.[36] Finally, the 'open skies' agreement between the EU and the US came into force in March 2008, allowing new entrants onto many transatlantic routes, but even this held the promise of disputes; the second phase of negotiations, which began in summer 2008, would open up many very sensitive areas such as ownership of US airlines and the prospect of US airlines being forced to comply with the EU's emissions trading system if they wished to fly into EU airports.[37]

EU relations with Canada saw interesting developments during 2008, with the Canadians pressing throughout the year for a deepening of the EU–Canada partnership, potentially through a free trade agreement.[38] The EU was less interested, partly because Canada as a member of the Organization for Economic Co-operation and Development was not a natural partner in any

[35] *European Voice*, 2 October 2008.
[36] *European Voice*, 7 February 2008, 3 April 2008, 8 May 2008.
[37] *Financial Times*, 14 May 2008.
[38] *European Voice*, 3 April 2008.

free trade agreement that might emerge – and in any case, Canada accounts for less than 2 per cent of overall EU trade. A Canadian general election also disrupted any negotiations, but at the EU–Canada Summit on 10 October new momentum was apparent, to such an extent that an agenda was set for negotiations on an economic partnership.[39] The EU and Canada also signed an 'open skies' agreement which – significantly in light of the EU's negotiations with the US – contained provisions on ownership of airlines.

The EU's relations with Japan and South Korea were relatively untroubled during 2008, although Japan was subjected to one of Peter Mandelson's attacks on 'economic nationalism' and barriers to investment.[40] The EU–Japan summit was held in Tokyo on 23 April, and focused especially on issues such as climate change and energy security; the Japanese hold a somewhat ambiguous position on climate change issues, having signed up both to the Kyoto Protocol and to other efforts sponsored by the US under the Bush administration. With South Korea, the EU has entered a period of negotiations: as well as updating the EU–Korea Framework Agreement, there is an ongoing push for a free trade agreement. The latter is viewed with some suspicion by the European automobile industry, which feels that its interests might well not be defended adequately by the Commission.[41]

Conclusion

By the end of 2008, the EU faced a challenging context for its external policies at the global level. A period of considerable activism over the previous five or six years had created new involvements, new partnerships and new commitments for the Union. At the same time, processes of change in the global arena had posed new challenges and risks as well as producing new opportunities. As the year ended, three challenges in particular seemed likely to shape the Union's role in a changing world: first, the challenge of emerging political and economic forces in Asia and elsewhere, underlined by the need to respond to the global financial crisis; second, the related need to respond to a more engaged (and thus arguably more challenging) administration in Washington; and finally, the need to confront the implications of expanded involvement in questions of global security, whether these took regional form, such as in Africa or central Asia or whether they were felt in key sectors of international life such as those of climate change and energy security. Combined with lingering uncertainty about the future of 'European foreign policy'

[39] *European Voice*, 23 October 2008.
[40] *European Voice*, 26 June 2008.
[41] *European Voice*, 7 February 2008.

as expressed in the Lisbon Treaty, these factors presented a demanding context for the further evolution of the EU's international role(s).

Key Readings

Commission (2009) provides a good review of the external activities of the EU along with footnoted links to all the relevant EU documentation. *European Voice* (2008a) provides a useful summary of recent ESDP developments and *European Voice* (2008b) does the same for Development Policy, whilst the same source provides periodic special reports on major 'strategic partners', including Brazil, India and China. *CFSP Forum* is published bi-monthly by FORNET («http://www.fornet.info»), and contains numerous articles on current CFSP and ESDP activities. Federal Trust (2009) provides a thoughtful response to the foreign policy situation following the rejection of the Lisbon Treaty. The propsects for a new EU–US relationship under Obama are well covered in De Vasconcelos and Zaborowski (2009) and Zaborowski (2008).

References

Allen, D. and Smith, M. (2008) 'Relations with the Rest of the World'. *Journal of Common Market Studies*, Vol. 46, s1, pp. 165–82.

Commission of the European Communities (2008a) 'The EU, Africa and China: Towards Trilateral Dialogue and Co-operation'. COM(2008)654 Final, Brussels, 17 October.

Commission of the European Communities (2008b) 'Towards an EU–Mexico Strategic Partnership'. COM(2008)447 Final. Brussels, 15 July.

Commission of the European Communities (2009) 'General Report on the Activities of the European Union, 2008'. Brussels, European Commission.

Council of the European Union (2008a) 'Presidency Conclusions'. Brussels European Council, 19–20 June 2008, 11018/1/08, CONCL.2.

Council of the European Union (2008b) 'Presidency Conclusions'. Brussels Extraordinary European Council, 16 October 2008, 14368/2/08, CONCL.4.

Council of the European Union (2008c) 'Presidency Conclusions'. Brussels European Council, 1 September 2008, 12594/2/08, CONCL.3.

Council of the European Union (2009) 'Presidency Conclusions'. Brussels European Council, 11 and 12 December 2008, 17271/1/08, CONCL.5.

De Vasconcelos, A. (ed.) (2009) *The European Security Strategy 2003–2008: Building on Common Interests*. ISS Report No. 05, February (Paris: EU Institute for Security Studies).

De Vasconcelos, A. and Zaborowski, M. (eds) (2009) *European Perspectives on the New American Foreign Policy Agenda*. ISS Report No. 04, January (Paris: EU Institute for Security Studies).

Elgström, O. and Smith, M. (eds) (2006) *The European Union's Roles in International Politics: Concepts and Analysis* (London: Routledge).

European Voice (2008a) 'Security and Defence: Special Report'. 10 July, pp. 16–24.

European Voice (2008b) 'Development Policy and Aid; Special Report'. 13 November, pp. 18–24.

Federal Trust (2009) 'A More Coherent and Effective European Foreign Policy?' Federal Trust Report, February 2009.

Hardacre, A. and Smith, M. (2009) 'The European Union and the Diplomacy of Complex Inter-regionalism'. *Hague Journal of Diplomacy*, forthcoming.

Menon, A. (2009) 'Empowering Paradise? The ESDP at Ten'. *International Affairs*, Vol. 85, No. 2, pp. 227–46.

Pirozzi, N. (2009) 'EU Support to African Security Architecture: Funding and Training Components'. EU Institute for Security Studies, Occasional Paper 76, February.

Security and Defence Agenda (2009) 'Assessing the Value of Security Strategy Reviews'. SDA monthly roundtable, February.

Smith, M. and Xie, H. (2009) 'The EU's Strategic Partnership with China: How Much Strategy? How Much Partnership?' Paper presented at the UACES Annual/ Research Conference, Angers, France, September.

Solana, J. (2008) 'Report on the Implementation of the European Security Strategy – Providing Security in a Changing World'. Brussels, December 2009, S407/08.

Toje, A. (2008) 'The EU, NATO and European Defence – A Slow Train Coming'. EU Institute for Security Studies, Occasional Paper 74, December.

Zaborowski, M. (2008) 'Bush's Legacy and America's Next Foreign Policy'. Chaillot Paper 111, September (Paris: EU Institute for Security Studies).

JCMS 2009 Volume 47 Annual Review pp. 233–257

Economic Developments in the Euro Area

AMY VERDUN
University of Victoria

On 1 January 2008 Cyprus and Malta adopted the euro; thus the euro area is now made up of 15 Member States. However significant that might seem, the euro area expansion will of course not be the main event for which the year 2008 is remembered. Severe turmoil and spreading of the scope and impact of the global financial crisis characterized economic developments in the euro area in 2008.

The financial difficulties that struck European markets in 2007 worsened dramatically and exponentially and developed into a fully fledged global financial crisis started by the so-called subprime mortgage crisis in the United States (US). The eventual global financial crisis including a stock exchange meltdown and a near breakdown of the banking system was triggered by a few events in late summer with the ultimate catalyst being the collapse of the US investment bank Lehman Brothers on 15 September 2008. In the days, weeks and months that followed, Europe and the rest of the world experienced a drying up of credit and falling asset prices on stock exchanges across the globe (see Quaglia *et al.*, this volume; Enderlein and Verdun, 2009) and subsequently economic recession. The response by euro area governments (as was that of all other countries of the Organization of Economic Co-operation and Development, OECD) was to offer rescue packages and to increase government spending. Also central banks, with the European Central Bank (ECB) as one of them, took swift and often co-ordinated action by simultaneously lowering interest rates and increasing liquidity to the banking sector. As a result of the credit crisis the economy during the autumn of 2008 experienced a severe contraction. In January 2009 the outlook of the International Monetary Fund (IMF) for the year 2009 suggests that the contraction of the advanced economies would amount to an unprecedented 2 per cent (IMF, 2009a), a forecast which was down by 1.7 per cent from the IMF autumn forecast (IMF, 2008b) (see Table 1a below). The size of the change in this forecast change over a period of just a few months is an indicator of the speed with which the recession took place and its size. By April 2009 this forecast was further revised downwards, with the IMF at this point projecting a contraction of 3.8 per cent for the advanced economies for the year 2009 (IMF, 2009b) (see Table 1b below). All these rapid changes in the forecast clearly indicate the unprecedented nature of the implosion of the economies and the extent of the uncertainty surrounding the forecasts.

In the countries of the euro area, economic growth in 2008 for the year ended at 1.0 per cent of gross domestic product (GDP) even though the euro area economy was in technical recession from the third quarter of 2008 (Commission, 2009b, p. 7), a figure further adjusted downwards to 0.9 per cent by April 2009. The overall growth rate for the world as a whole for 2007 was 5.2 per cent and 3.4 per cent for 2009 further adjusted downwards to 3.2 by April (see Table 1a and Table 1b below).

Though economic growth in the euro area collapsed in the course of 2008, the existence of the euro seemed to have protected euro area countries from speculative attacks that other European countries, not in the euro area, were suffering from at this time (such as the three 'outs' Denmark, Sweden, the United Kingdom and also new Member States such as Poland as well as non-EU European countries, such as Iceland). Many of these countries experienced significant depreciations of their currencies against the euro (Poland 11 per cent over the year, but 20 per cent since mid-September; United Kingdom 25 per cent over the year and 16 per cent since mid-September) and the central banks of some countries (for example, Denmark and Sweden) spent a considerable amount of their reserves and had to increase their interest rates to protect their currency. The Danish monetary authorities tried to keep the exchange rate of the Danish krona to the euro stable, and managed better than Sweden, but paid the price of raising interest rates substantially. Sweden let its currency depreciate (see also Jones, 2009). In currency markets the US dollar responded to the insecurity of the autumn months of 2008 by strengthening against other currencies, even the euro. Whereas the euro had been at historical highs against the US dollar throughout the seven months of 2008 reaching an all-time high just below \$1.60 in July, by 27 October 2008 it was

Table 1a: World Economic Outlook Update Projections (Annual % Change)

	2007	2008	Projections 2009	Projections 2010	Difference from November 2008 WEO Projections 2009	2010
World Output	5.2	3.4	0.5	3.0	-1.7	-0.8
Advanced economies	2.7	1.0	-2.0	1.1	-1.7	-0.5
of which						
United States	2.0	1.1	-1.6	1.6	-0.9	0.1
Euro area (15)	2.6	1.0	-2.0	0.2	-1.5	-0.7
Japan	2.4	-0.3	-2.6	0.6	-2.4	-0.5
Other advanced economies	4.6	1.9	-2.4	2.2	-3.9	-1.0
Emerging market and developing economies	8.3	6.3	3.3	5.0	-1.8	-1.2
Africa	6.2	5.2	3.4	4.9	-1.4	-0.5
Central and eastern Europe	5.4	3.2	-0.4	2.5	-2.6	-1.3
Commonwealth of Independent States	8.6	6.0	-0.4	2.2	-3.6	-2.3
Developing Asia	10.6	7.8	5.5	6.9	-1.6	-1.1
of which China	13.0	9.0	6.7	8.0	-1.8	-1.5
Middle East	6.4	6.1	3.9	4.7	-1.5	-0.6
Western Hemisphere	5.7	4.6	1.1	3.0	-1.4	-1.0
European Union	3.1	1.3	-1.8	0.5	-1.6	-0.8

Source: IMF (2009a).
Note: Real effective exchange rates are assumed to remain constant (8 December 2008–5 January 2009).

Table 1b: World Economic Outlook Update Projections (Annual % Change)

	2007	2008	Projections 2009	Projections 2010	Difference from January 2009 WEO Projections	
					2009	2010
World Output	5.2	3.2	-1.3	1.9	-1.8	-1.1
Advanced economies	2.7	0.9	-3.8	0.0	-1.8	-1.1
of which						
United States	2.0	1.1	-2.8	0.0	-1.2	-1.6
Euro area	2.7	0.9	-4.2	-0.4	-2.2	-0.6
Japan	2.4	-0.6	-6.2	0.5	-3.6	-0.1
Other advanced economies	4.7	1.6	-4.1	0.6	-1.7	-1.6
Emerging market and developing economies	8.3	6.1	1.6	4.0	-1.7	-1.0
Africa	6.2	5.2	2.0	3.9	-1.4	-1.0
Central and eastern Europe	5.4	2.9	-3.7	0.8	-3.3	-1.7
Commonwealth of Independent States	8.6	5.5	-5.1	1.2	-4.7	-1.0
Developing Asia	10.6	7.7	4.8	6.1	-0.7	-0.8
of which China	13.0	9.0	6.5	7.5	-0.2	-0.5
Middle East	6.3	5.9	2.5	3.5	-1.4	-1.2
Western Hemisphere	5.7	4.2	-1.5	1.6	-2.6	-1.4
European Union	3.1	1.1	-4.0	-0.3	-2.2	-0.8

Source: IMF (2009b).
Note: Real effective exchange rates are assumed to remain constant (25 February 2009–25 March 2009).

at a low of $1.25 against the US dollar and then fluctuated considerably for the remainder of the year.[1]

This article looks at the economic developments in the euro area by highlighting a few core characteristics of the euro area as a whole and those of the largest five economies of the euro area (Germany, France, Italy, Spain and the Netherlands). Section I provides some key economic performance indicators such as economic growth, employment, inflation and public finances. Sections II and III briefly discuss, respectively, ECB decisions in 2008 and the external dimension of the euro. Section IV looks at the five selected countries. Section V offers a reflection on the developments with economic and monetary union (EMU) over the reviewed time period with special attention paid to the global financial crisis and national government responses to the crisis. The final section closes with a brief summary and outlook for 2009.

I. Economic Developments in the Euro Area: Main Economic Indicators

Economic Growth

In January 2009, the International Monetary Fund (IMF) reported that the average rate of economic growth for advanced economies in the year 2008 was projected to be 1.0 per cent, which is down from 2.7 per cent the year before (IMF, 2009a, p. 6) and is projected to worsen in 2009. The crisis of 2008 is continuing the break in the overall trend of the euro area countries performing differently than other advanced economies in Europe and beyond. As was already mentioned in last year's review (Verdun, 2008) the performances of euro area countries were in sync with those of the other advanced economies in 2007 and this situation repeated itself more or less in 2008. With the onset of recession the euro area went into a period of synchronized recession caused by the financial crisis. The April 2009 IMF report which had as its theme 'crisis and recovery' and deals among other things with synchronization of business cycles suggests that such a recession is likely to be deeper and last longer (IMF, 2008a, 2009b). The economic performance in 2008 of the euro area countries was similar to that of the US and the same as the average of the advanced economies (see Table 1a and Table 1b). However, as was the case in previous years, the EU as a whole performed better than the countries of the euro area, again still largely due to the catch-up of central and

---

[1] Throughout this article (see also in sections below) exchange rates and the percentage change of exchange rates have been calculated using the ECB exchange rate calculator that can be found at: «http://www.ecb.int/stats/exchange/eurofxref/html/eurofxref-graph-usd.en.html».

eastern European countries (CEECs) that joined the EU in 2004 and 2007. While in November 2008 the IMF forecast that CEECs might still grow in 2009, the revised forecast of January and April 2009 suggests that these countries too will show negative growth (see Table 1b).

Statistical information about the performance of the economy changed dramatically during the course of 2008. In fact, compared to the forecast made in 2007 (see Verdun, 2008) the adjustments were major. Indeed, even at the time of writing it is clear that the figures that this Annual Report typically works with (Commission, 2008b) will be updated considerably in the spring forecast, which was not yet published at the time of writing.

The euro area economies that performed well in 2008 included the catch-up countries of the euro area – countries that have a GDP per capita that lies below the euro area average. In other words, the countries that had the fastest-growing economies per capita in 2008 were Cyprus, Greece, Malta and Slovenia. To this list should be added three other countries with the same sort of growth rates but that do not fit the regular profile of being a 'catch-up' country, namely Finland, Germany and the Netherlands. These countries have a broadly similar profile, as they have had above-average growth since 2006. Countries that performed poorly in 2008 were France, Ireland, Italy, Portugal and Spain (see Table 2). Ireland in particular was experiencing a real 'bust' after having 'boomed' for two decades. As was the case in 2007, in 2008 it is no longer as clear-cut that the old Member States, not part of the euro area ('the EU-15 euro-outs'), did better than the average of the euro area countries. Whereas last year it was only Denmark that performed markedly poorer, in 2008 all three countries, Denmark, Sweden and the UK, were no longer performing better than the euro area countries (in contrast to earlier years). Based on the autumn forecast, their GDP per capita rate for 2008 is comparable to the performance of Portugal and France (see Table 2).

Employment

The employment situation in the euro area further improved from its already excellent situation in 2007 (see Table 3). During the first half of 2008 unemployment fell to levels not seen in 25 years (ECB, 2009, p. 18) which is a further indication that the period prior to the onset of the autumn 2008 global financial crisis had been remarkably good. The year 2007 showed an average unemployment of 7.5 per cent, whereas 2008, based on the autumn forecast and including the downturn, is projected to reach 7.6 per cent. These employment statistics for 2008 thereby are still a marked improvement over the situation in 1992–2006 (Commission, 2008b, p. 153) during which time unemployment was never below 8.0 per cent on average in the countries of the

Table 2: GDP Per Capita (Percentage Change on Preceding Year, 2004–09)

	2004	2005	2006	2007	2008	2009
Belgium	2.5	1.3	2.3	2.0	0.7	−0.6
Germany	1.2	0.8	3.1	2.6	1.9	0.1
Ireland	2.9	4.1	3.1	3.5	−3.4	−1.8
Greece	4.6	2.5	4.1	3.8	2.8	2.2
Spain	1.6	1.9	2.3	1.8	0.0	−1.4
France	1.8	1.3	1.6	1.6	0.4	−0.5
Italy	0.5	−0.2	1.3	0.8	−0.2	−0.2
Cyprus	1.8	1.5	2.1	2.7	2.0	1.3
Luxembourg	3.1	3.6	4.8	3.6	1.6	0.3
Malta	0.4	2.9	2.3	3.0	1.9	1.5
Netherlands	1.9	1.8	3.2	3.2	2.1	0.2
Austria	1.8	2.1	2.8	2.6	1.6	0.3
Portugal	0.9	0.5	1.0	1.7	0.3	−0.1
Slovenia	4.2	4.2	5.5	6.2	3.7	2.7
Finland	3.4	2.6	4.6	4.1	2.0	1.0
Euro area	1.5	1.1	2.3	2.1	0.9	−0.2
Bulgaria	7.2	6.8	6.6	6.2	7.0	5.0
Czech Rep	4.4	6.0	6.4	5.4	4.2	3.4
Denmark	2.1	2.2	3.6	1.2	0.4	−0.1
Estonia	7.5	9.8	10.6	6.5	−1.2	−1.1
Latvia	9.3	11.2	12.9	10.9	−0.3	−2.2
Lithuania	7.9	8.5	8.5	9.5	4.2	0.2
Hungary	5.1	4.2	4.3	1.2	1.9	0.8
Poland	5.4	3.7	6.3	6.7	5.4	3.8
Romania	8.7	4.4	8.4	6.3	8.8	5.0
Slovakia	5.1	6.5	8.4	10.3	6.9	4.8
Sweden	3.7	2.9	3.5	2.0	0.2	−0.7
United Kingdom	2.3	1.4	2.2	2.7	0.5	−1.4
EU-27	2.0	1.5	2.7	2.4	1.1	−0.1
USA	2.7	2.0	1.8	1.0	0.6	−1.4
Japan	2.7	1.9	2.4	2.1	0.4	−0.3

Source: Commission (2008b) Autumn forecast, Table 4, p. 143).

euro area. In 2004 and 2005 euro area average unemployment was 9.0 per cent, dropping to 8.3 per cent in 2006. The finalized statistics for 2007 showed unemployment in the euro area at 7.5 per cent, which was without doubt the lowest. Once the finalized numbers come in for 2008, unemployment may well have increased above the forecast 7.6 per cent. The forecast figures for 2008 suggest that the euro area's employment performance is at 7.6 per cent – which is about half a percentage point above the EU employment average (the gap has been similar over the past four years, although it

Table 3: Percentage of the Civilian Labour Force Unemployed in the EU-15 (2004–09)

Euro area Member States	2004	2005	2006	2007	2008 expected	2009 projected
Belgium	8.4	8.5	8.3	7.5	7.1	8.0
Germany	9.8	10.7	9.8	8.4	7.3	7.5
Ireland	4.5	4.4	4.5	4.6	6.1	7.6
Greece	10.5	9.9	8.9	8.3	9.0	9.2
Spain	10.6	9.2	8.5	8.3	10.8	13.8
France	9.3	9.2	9.2	8.3	8.0	9.0
Italy	8.1	7.7	6.8	6.1	6.8	7.1
Cyprus	4.7	5.3	4.6	4.0	3.9	3.8
Luxembourg	5.0	4.6	4.6	4.1	4.0	4.3
Malta	7.4	7.2	7.1	6.4	5.9	6.2
Netherlands	4.6	4.7	3.9	3.2	3.0	3.4
Austria	4.9	5.2	4.8	4.4	3.9	4.2
Portugal	6.7	7.7	7.8	8.1	7.7	7.9
Slovenia	6.3	6.5	6.0	4.9	4.5	4.8
Finland	8.8	8.4	7.7	6.9	6.3	6.5
Euro area	9.0	9.0	8.3	7.5	7.6	8.4
Non-euro area Member States						
Denmark	5.5	4.8	3.9.	3.8	3.1	3.5
Sweden	6.3	7.4	7.0	6.1	6.0	6.8
UK	4.7	4.8	5.4	5.3	5.7	7.1
EU-27	9.0	8.9	8.2	7.1	7.0	7.8

Source: Commission (2008b, p. 153, Table 23).

appeared to have widened slightly in 2008). The reduction in unemployment both in the euro area and the EU at large over the past years has been caused by an increase in employment (the number of jobs is growing relative to the number of jobs that are disappearing). However the forecast for 2009 is grim. As had been the case in 2007, the Member State with the lowest unemployment in 2008 was the Netherlands; again, as in 2007, the other Member States with low unemployment rates were Austria and Luxembourg. Now that Cyprus is a member of the euro area it also appears on the radar of low-unemployment countries, sitting among the best performers. A country that has lost its low unemployment rate since 2007 was Ireland, which in 2008 faced dire straits regarding the economy, which at this time was translated into a serious increase in unemployment. In 2007 it had a level of unemployment of 4.6 per cent. By 2008 this percentage had gone up to 6.1 per cent (and was rapidly rising). Unemployment in Germany was on a downward trend and in 2008 was at 7.3 per cent, which was still slightly below the euro area average for this year (7.6 per cent). Belgium, Italy and Portugal had similar levels of unemployment to Germany. The Member States outside the euro area still had markedly lower levels of unemployment than either the euro area average or the EU average (see Johnson and Turner, this volume).

Inflation

In the year 2008 the inflation rate in the euro area was starting to increase somewhat to an average of 3.3 per cent, after having been at 2.1 per cent or 2.2 per cent during the previous five years (see Table 4). The performances of individual countries, however, diverged a lot this year, thereby breaking the trend of previous years. In 2008 the countries that had recently joined the euro area (and had experienced higher growth rates) were also showing higher inflation rates: Slovenia (5.5 per cent), Malta (4.7 per cent), Cyprus (4.4 per cent), followed by Greece (4.2 per cent), Luxembourg (4.1 per cent) and finally Finland (3.9 per cent) (last year still one of the best performers). The lowest inflation, as in 2007, was the Netherlands at 2.2 per cent. Note that the country with the lowest inflation rate was this year at the same level as the average of the previous year – another indicator of the increase in inflation during 2008. Of course, the whole inflation situation changed dramatically with the onset of the financial crisis. The updated statistics may well show a smaller increase in inflation over the full year 2008 once those statistics are available.

If we compare the inflation performance of the euro area countries with those in the rest of the EU we find quite a wide divergence between the euro area Member States and the three old Member States outside on the one hand and the new Member States on the other, although the average inflation rate for the EU-27 was still close to that of the euro area.

Public Finances

In 2008, public finances in the euro area had a positive outlook. In June 2008 Excessive Deficits Procedures (EDPs) were closed for the Czech Republic, Italy, Portugal and Slovakia. It left only two non-euro area countries in EDP (Hungary and Poland). It meant that by the second half of the year no euro area Member State was in excess of the 3.0 per cent budgetary deficit ceiling laid down in the Treaty on European Union and further clarified by the Stability and Growth Pact (SGP), which was reformed in 2005 (see Heipertz and Verdun, 2006; 2010; and see Table 5). Otherwise the improvements in public finances can be traced to higher tax revenues, so whether there may be problems with meeting the stipulations of the SGP will remain to be seen in future years during and after the economic downturn.

Table 4: Inflation: HCPI (Annual % change 2002–08)

	2002	2003	2004	2005	2006	2007	2008
Belgium	1.6	1.5	1.9	2.5	2.3	1.8	4.5
Bulgaria	5.8	2.3	6.1	6.0	7.4	7.6	12.0
Czech Republic	1.4	−0.1	2.6	1.6	2.1	3.0	6.3
Denmark	2.4	2.0	0.9	1.7	1.9	1.7	3.6
Germany	1.4	1.0	1.8	1.9	1.8	2.3	2.8
Estonia	3.6	1.4	3.0	4.1	4.4	6.7	10.6
Ireland	4.7	4.0	2.3	2.2	2.7	2.9	3.1
Greece	3.9	3.4	3.0	3.5	3.3	3.0	4.2
Spain	3.6	3.1	3.1	3.4	3.6	2.8	4.1
France	1.9	2.2	2.3	1.9	1.9	1.6	3.2
Italy	2.6	2.8	2.3	2.2	2.2	2.0	3.5
Cyprus	2.8	4.0	1.9	2.0	2.2	2.2	4.4
Latvia	2.0	2.9	6.2	6.9	6.6	10.1	15.3
Lithuania	0.3	−1.1	1.2	2.7	3.8	5.8	11.1
Luxembourg	2.1	2.5	3.2	3.8	3.0	2.7	4.1
Hungary	5.2	4.7	6.8	3.5	4.0	7.9	6.0
Malta	2.6	1.9	2.7	2.5	2.6	0.7	4.7
Netherlands	3.9	2.2	1.4	1.5	1.7	1.6	2.2
Austria	1.7	1.3	2.0	2.1	1.7	2.2	3.2
Poland	1.9	0.7	3.6	2.2	1.3	2.6	4.2
Portugal	3.7	3.3	2.5	2.1	3.0	2.4	2.7
Romania	22.5	15.3	11.9	9.1	6.6	4.9	7.9
Slovenia	7.5	5.7	3.7	2.5	2.5	3.8	5.5
Slovakia	3.5	8.4	7.5	2.8	4.3	1.9	3.9
Finland	2.0	1.3	0.1	0.8	1.3	1.6	3.9
Sweden	1.9	2.3	1.0	0.8	1.5	1.7	3.3
United Kingdom	1.3	1.4	1.3	2.1	2.3	2.3	3.6
Euro Area-15	2.3	2.1	2.1	2.2	2.2	2.1	3.3
EU-27	2.5	2.1	2.3	2.3	2.3	2.4	3.7
EU-25	2.1	1.9	2.1	2.2	2.2	2.3	3.5
EU-15	2.1	2.0	2.0	2.1	2.2	2.2	3.3

Source: Commission (2009).

The onset of the global financial crisis in autumn 2008, however, triggered a major turn in public finances. All governments started to spend more to reduce the severity and length of a likely recession and to avoid depression. The European Commission let it be known that although the global financial crisis would qualify as what is referred to in the SGP as 'an exceptional circumstance', the EDPs would be started if a Member State ran a deficit that was outside the parameters of the SGP. In other words, the Commission would start EDPs if the temporary circumstance no longer existed and if the size of the excessive deficit were not close to the 3.0 per cent reference value

Table 5: Net Lending (+) or Net Borrowing (−) General Government as a Share of GDP in EU-15 2004–09

	2004	2005	2006	2007	2008 estimated	2009 projected
Euro area Member States						
Belgium	−0.2	−2.6	0.3	−0.3	−0.5	−1.4
Germany	−3.8	−3.3	−1.5	−0.2	0.0	−0.2
Ireland	1.4	1.7	3.0	0.2	−5.5	−6.8
Greece	−7.5	−5.1	−2.8	−3.5	−2.5	−2.2
Spain	−0.3	1.0	2.0	2.2	−1.6	−2.9
France	−3.6	−2.9	−2.4	−2.7	−3.0	−3.5
Italy	−3.5	−4.3	−3.4	−1.6	−2.5	−2.6
Cyprus	−4.1	−2.4	−1.2	3.5	1.0	0.7
Luxembourg	−1.2	−0.1	1.3	3.2	2.7	1.3
Malta	−4.7	−2.8	−2.3	−1.8	−3.8	−2.7
Netherlands	−1.7	−0.3	0.6	0.3	1.2	0.5
Austria	−4.4	−1.5	−1.5	−0.4	−0.6	−1.2
Portugal	−3.4	−6.1	−3.9	−2.6	−2.2	−2.8
Slovenia	−2.2	−1.4	−1.2	0.5	−0.2	−0.7
Finland	2.4	2.9	4.1	5.3	5.1	3.6
Euro area	−2.9	−2.5	−1.3	−0.6	−1.3	−1.8
Non-euro area EU-15 Member States						
Denmark	2.0	5.2	5.2	4.5	3.1	1.1
Sweden	0.8	2.4	2.3	3.6	2.6	0.4
UK	−3.4	−3.4	−2.7	−2.8	−4.2	−5.6
EU-27	−2.9	−2.4	−1.4	−0.9	−1.6	−2.3

Source: Commission (2008b, p. 160, Table 37).

(for a discussion of the way the SGP will be affected by the global financial crisis see Heipertz and Verdun, 2010, chapter 9).

II. Policies of the European Central Bank

As had been the case in 2007 the Governing Council of the ECB continued to face a challenging year given the financial turmoil that first started in August 2007 and that continued and worsened dramatically in autumn 2008. Looking back on the financial turmoil ECB President Jean-Claude Trichet acknowledged that the start of the financial turmoil (9 August 2007) had been the most challenging period, as the ECB had to decide what stance to take. Yet, the follow-through and the developments of 2008 turned out to produce truly exceptional circumstances and were challenging to central banks and governments across the globe (Trichet, 2008).

The role of the ECB Governing Council was to set the key interest rates for the euro area (for a general discussion of ECB policy see Verdun, 2006). The

ECB interest rate policies need to secure price stability and without prejudice to that objective seek to promote economic growth and employment in the EU (as per the EU Treaty provisions). This year posed a challenge because of the severity of the economic implosion in the autumn of 2008 and the anticipated deep recession that was expected to follow in 2009. These developments implied that inflation would no longer be a major concern. The policy choices for the ECB were particularly difficult as prior to the last quarter of 2008 inflation in the euro area was at high levels, averaging out at 3.3 per cent over the whole year (see Table 4). In May the inflation rate as measured by the Harmonized Index of Consumer Prices (HICP) stood at 3.7 per cent but by December 2008 the HICP had dropped to 1.6 per cent (ECB, 2009, pp. 16–18).

The ECB left interest rates unchanged for more than a year and first changed interest rates with effect on 9 July 2008: due to the concern over inflation, rates were *raised* by 25 basis points but then following the major financial fall-out the ECB responded by bringing interest rates down in three stages by a total of 175 basis points by the end of the year, ending at 2 per cent.

One of the rate reductions, the one announced on 8 October, was a very high-profile co-ordinated action of many of the world's leading central banks: the Bank of Canada, the Bank of England, the Federal Reserve, the Sveriges Riksbank and the Swiss National Bank all participated in this co-ordinated effort.[2] It was the first clearly co-ordinated action of major central banks to change interest rate cuts collectively. It was also a strong signal on the part of the central banks that this crisis needed to be dealt with in a co-ordinated fashion. In Trichet's end-of-year interview, he also explained that the year 2008 featured many emergency meetings of the Governing Council via tele-conferencing (Trichet, 2008). That tool was used at various times throughout 2008 to deal with the crisis.

III. External Dimension of the Euro

Developments regarding the euro exchange rate can be divided into two parts. During the first part of the year the euro was high in foreign exchange markets, reaching a historical peak in April (ECB, 2009, p. 78). The euro reached high levels also *vis-à-vis* the US dollar (USD). In the first six months its exchange rate against the USD started around the $1.47 mark and then gradually went up to around $1.56 and oscillated there, never quite reaching the $1.60 mark (the maximum, which was also the all-time high against the

[2] See «http://www.ecb.int/press/pr/date/2008/html/pr081008.en.html».

USD was $1.5990, reached on 15 July 2008). From that mid-summer high, the euro came down and the low of the year was at $1.2460 on 27 October 2008 and stayed around the $1.27 mark until mid-December then climbed up again to end the year at $1.3917 (exchange rates are all taken from the ECB website).

The story of the euro decline in the latter half of 2008 against the USD, however, gives a distorted view. What was happening was that many currencies were depreciating *vis-à-vis* the USD and the euro as a result of the credit crunch, the banking crisis and the stock exchange crashes. In this situation of extreme volatility and uncertainty, currency investors fled into the USD whilst selling currencies from smaller EU countries, those of emerging economies and currencies of EU countries outside the euro area. Thus, over this period the USD was stronger than most other currencies, but *vis-à-vis* the USD the euro did not depreciate as much as other European currencies did, including the sterling and the Swedish krona. After having been stable for many years, both sterling and the Swedish krona lost 12–13 per cent from September through December 2008 against the euro. Even the Danish krona, which did better over the same time period (September–December), still lost 16 per cent between 7 October and the end of the year.

Another remarkable development was the image formation of the euro as a beacon of safety. During the turbulent autumn months the Icelandic krona went into freefall, because the Icelandic financial sector was collapsing. The result was that government officials and public opinion became more favourable towards the idea of joining the EU, in part to have the option of joining EMU. The Icelandic case is remarkable because even before these dramatic events, Jürgen Stark of the ECB had delivered a speech on 15 February 2008 to the Icelandic Chamber of Commerce, announcing that euroization (the unilateral adoption of the euro) in Iceland was not favoured by the ECB.[3] Similarly in Denmark and Sweden support for joining the euro increased over the course of 2008 in response to the havoc that financial markets had wreaked on currency markets (EUObserver, 2008; *The Guardian*, 2008).

IV. Developments in Selected Member States of the Euro Area

As has been the case over the past years, this section reports on developments in the various Member States of the euro area, which in turn are based on documents that – when published – had not yet reflected on the complete data of the year under review. Usually the difference between the projected outcome for the year under review, and the actual outcome once finalized, is

[3] See «http://www.ecb.int/press/key/date/2008/html/sp080213.en.html».

not that large. However, this year I expect there to be considerable difference in the review of the year 2008 (based on finalized statistics and effects of policies) as well as the outlook for 2009. At the time of writing the most up-to-date account has been used, but I nevertheless caution that the results may well differ considerably once the full statistics are known.

The reason this overview looks at individual Member States in the euro area is that the institutional design of EMU features a central authority responsible for monetary policy and a decentralized fiscal policy in the hands of national governments. Thus, more than in mature federations, its success depends on the economic performance of its constitutive states. Also, many will still equate the performance of the euro area with that of its main states. The performance of the larger Member States is particularly important as the ECB sets monetary policy based on a weighted average of the economies of the euro area. This section therefore discusses some economic developments in the largest five Member States of the euro area and assesses the differences in their performances on a number of characteristics, such as economic growth, investment and consumption, employment, public finances, inflation and considers the forecasts for 2009.

Germany

Economic growth in Germany in 2008 started off very strong in the first quarter, following a very strong few years of growth but due to the financial crisis started to decelerate in the last three quarters of the year (Commission, 2008b, p. 66). Calculated as an annual percentage change in GDP at previous year prices growth in 2006 was 3.0 per cent; 2.5 per cent in 2007; 1.7 per cent in 2008 and was forecast to be 1.8 per cent for 2009 (Commission 2008b, p. 68). Economic growth was boosted at the start of 2008 due to favourable weather conditions that boosted the construction sector. Yet the slower growth in the rest of the year was largely due to the effects of the global downturn. The German economy is heavily dependent on exports. With the slowdown of economic activity in neighbouring countries, Germany felt the effects of it. Export growth was expected to decrease from 4.5 per cent in 2008 to 1 per cent in 2009 (and recent data will see those figures reduced downwards). The other major factor was the tightening financial conditions following the credit crunch. Though investment in infrastructure might offer a little push-back, it will be insufficient to offset the effects of the crisis.

Private consumption in 2008 was not as strong as expected in the preceding year. Wages and the creation of employment in Germany should have increased private consumption substantially. However, this effect was partially offset by the increase in inflation in 2008 that led to another year of reduction of private consumption. The outlook for 2009 is still very uncertain. Overall it is felt that Germany is in a better position than others to weather the financial storm, in part due to its improved macroeconomic conditions. It had moderate wage increases in recent years, which enabled it to improve its overall competitiveness, as well as reforms in the labour market and reduction in unemployment (Commission, 2008b, p. 67). Yet wages increased significantly in 2008. Inflation in 2008 was on the rise with a number of factors contributing to higher wages as well as the delayed effects of increases in food and energy prices. Compared to 2007 employment in Germany rose in 2008 and unemployment came down (from 8.4 per cent in 2007 to 7.3 per cent in 2008) and there was a growth in the employment rate (which added up to an annual percentage change of 1.2 over the year).

Public finances in Germany were still healthy in 2008 after having been in order the preceding year for the first time in several years. The deficit had been at 0.2 per cent in 2007, whereas the government budget was projected to be in balance in 2008 for the first time since 2000 (Commission, 2008b, p. 68). The main reason behind the balanced budget was the rise in revenue, collected from direct taxation, which was up because of the increase in wages as well as the increase in employment overall. As a corollary, the government did not have to pay as much on unemployment insurance. It had been feared that company tax reform might negatively affect tax revenues, but that did not materialize.

Though inflation in Germany over the past years has been lower than in other euro area countries, in 2007 it was similar to the average in the euro area and in the EU-27, although by 2008 Germany is back to having a slightly lower inflation than the others (in 2007 German inflation stood at 2.3 per cent compared to 2.1 per cent in the euro area and 2.4 per cent in the EU-27; in 2008 these statistics had changed to 2.8 for Germany versus 3.3 in the euro area and 3.7 in the EU-27; see Table 4). Although Germany's large economy has the greatest impact on ECB policies, euro area interest rates do not normally exactly reflect economic conditions in Germany. So once again, ECB monetary policy was not exactly appropriate for Germany insofar as inflation rates in that country were concerned (for a long-term analysis of monetary policy appropriate for each Member State, see Lee and Crowley, 2009). Of course, the effects of the credit crunch, the drop in oil prices and the economic contraction mean that the situation in 2009 will differ dramatically compared to that in 2008 or what was forecast for 2009 (as of autumn 2008).

The forecast for Germany in 2009 is highly uncertain due to Germany's reliance on exports. All things remaining equal, public finance and macroeconomic conditions in Germany are probably fairly favourable for weathering the storm.

France

In last year's review it appeared that economic developments in 2007 diverged much between France and Germany. In the end, however, the differences were not that profound. Based on the *European Economy* autumn forecast (Commission, 2008b), economic developments in Germany and France will end up differing substantially in 2008. France witnessed a disappointing performance with subdued economic growth. Measured as the annual percentage change of French GDP at previous year prices, 2006 and 2007 each saw 2.2 per cent growth, whereas 2008 was projected to see growth in this country at 0.9 per cent and forecast to be at 0.0 per cent in 2009 (Commission, 2008b, p. 80) or worse (see Table 2 above). This stagnation, particularly after the first six months, was attributed to a decrease in domestic demand, in particular weak private consumption and a reduction in investment (Commission, 2008b, p. 78). As uncertainties grew throughout 2008 the housing market was weakening. Both imports and exports weakened in 2008 and, contrary to last year, imports were no longer growing faster than exports.

Taken over the whole year, the employment situation in France still showed an improvement in 2008. In 2007 job creation was about 1.4 per cent, whereas the projected increase in jobs in 2008 was 0.7 per cent. Similarly, whereas the rate of unemployment was 8.3 per cent in 2007, the forecast for 2008 is still only at 8.0 per cent, although given the crisis the prospect is no longer good for the years to come (Commission, 2008b, p. 80). As was the case in previous years, the unemployment rate in France is still high compared to other EU Member States, although in 2008 the gap was closing. The financial crisis, the credit crunch and subsequently the recession in 2009 will change the prospect on unemployment.

Public finances in France rapidly deteriorated in 2008. The budget deficit was due to increase to 3.0 per cent of GDP in 2008 up from 2.7 in 2007 and was projected to deteriorate further in 2009 (Commission, 2008b, p. 80; see also Table 5 above). Most of the increase in the budget deficit was higher expenditure and lower revenue due to the decline in economic growth. One of the reasons that expenditures was up was due to the higher cost of servicing the sovereign debt that was caused by the unexpected inflation. Other causes of higher expenditures were health care and social security (Commission, 2008b, p. 79). Revenues were slightly down as a result of the coming into effect of tax reforms of previous years. However, recent tax changes also had their effect (a professional tax rebate was partially offset by a tax on dividends). The public debt-to-GDP ratio has been at 64 per cent in 2006 and 2007 but is forecast to rise slightly to 65.5 in 2008 and increase further in subsequent years. As for the French government's budget deficit, although it stabilized in 2007, in 2008 it was at the threshold of 3.0 per cent and was likely to exceed this ceiling significantly in 2009 and 2010 given the deteriorating economic conditions, the increase in expenses and the drop in revenues.

Inflation in France was steady and marginally lower than elsewhere in the euro area and was forecast to be low in the next years. But the one exception was the year 2008 during which inflation surprisingly peaked at 3.3 per cent, causing other expenses to increase (see the above-mentioned inflation-indexed cost of servicing of sovereign debt; social security is also indexed to inflation). Inflation in 2006 was at 1.9 per cent, in 2007 was at 1.6 per cent and in 2009 projected to end up at 1.8 per cent without a clear view yet on the economic downturn (Commission, 2008b, p. 80). Thus the inflation of 2008 was clearly an outlier year. Because inflation in France was relatively close to that of the euro area as a whole, the ECB's interest rate policy is appropriate for France insofar as inflation was concerned.

The economic forecast for France for 2008 was by no means as favourable as it was last year. Growth was expected to drop below 1.0 per cent (Commission, 2008b, p. 80; see also Table 2 above). The prospect for 2009 has changed dramatically since last year because of the economic crisis. It was expected that 2009 will see a contraction but 2010 might witness a tentative recovery. The French government was very aggressive in seeking to offer stimulus packages to the French economy, but it was expected that some of these stimulus packages would only have an impact later on in 2009.

Italy

Economic growth in Italy in 2008 continued the poor performance that was already visible in 2007, a year in which other euro area countries were still experiencing high growth. Economic growth was close to zero in 2005 (0.6 per cent as a percentage of growth at previous year's prices (Commission, 2008b, p. 83), but negative as a measure of per capita growth (see Table 2 above). In 2006 and 2007 the situation was a little better, even if well below the euro area average, but the prospects for 2008, 2009 and 2010 were very gloomy. According to the *European Economy* autumn forecast (Commission, 2008b) Italy was looking worse than many other euro area countries (a trend already noticed in the spring forecast, Commission, 2008a, and the previous forecast, Verdun, 2008). The lack of domestic demand was seen as the main cause of poor growth in 2008. Demand was lagging behind in part because of rapid price increases in particular of goods that were frequently purchased. Households responded to it by cutting consumption, further aggravating the poor economic circumstances that Italy is in. It is expected, however, that the price increase will dramatically end after the third quarter of 2008 because of the exceptional circumstances in that quarter. The effects of the global financial crisis are expected to have first a negative effect on Italian GDP growth but gradually enable Italy to return to growth through lower commodity prices. Italy continued to lose market share. Thus, as in previous years (Verdun, 2006, 2007, 2008), Italy was not able to maintain competitiveness. Note, however, that one expert has calculated Italian competitiveness over a longer time horizon and finds that Italian competitiveness improved dramatically during the 1990s and has only been declining over the past decade but had not quite returned to the level of the early 1990s (Jones, 2009, pp. 44–6).

After a spectacular employment growth of 1.7 per cent in 2006, 2007 did not see growth of the same magnitude (1.0 per cent) and employment was projected to grow only by 0.7 per cent in 2008 (Commission, 2008b, p. 83). The same report forecast that unemployment would increase from 6.1 per cent in 2007 to 6.8 and 7.1 per cent in 2008 and 2009, respectively, but these statistics were likely to be adjusted upwards as the result of the economic recession in 2009 became clear.

The dramatic change in Italy's budget deficit in 2007 continued to look fairly good in 2008. After having had excessive deficits for years in a row, Italy returned to sound budgetary deficits in 2007 and was still seen to remain below the ceiling in 2008. The recession may of course change this prospect. Even though Italy has such a poor performance on growth and competitiveness its budgetary deficit was still looking to stay below the reference for 2008, even though the structural budgetary position was worsening in 2008. The relatively good position was in part the result of measures taken by Parliament in summer 2008 to achieve the medium-term objective of a balanced budget in 2010 (Commission, 2008b, p. 82). The public debt to GDP ratio was still above 100 per cent, but had been gradually dropping from 107 per cent in 2006 to 104 per cent in 2007 and is projected to remain at this level in subsequent years (Commission, 2008b, p. 83).

Inflation in Italy over the past few years had been around 2.2 per cent and in 2007 came to 2.0 per cent. However, as was the case in France, Italy in 2008 was an outlier with an inflation rate of 3.3 per cent. The figures for 2009 and 2010 are expected to come down significantly. Italy, like France, has an inflation rate that is close to that of the euro area as a whole. Thus, the ECB's interest rate policy was appropriate for Italy as far as price stability is concerned. Following a year of zero growth (2008) the economic forecast for Italy for 2009, coupled with constant downward adjustment of statistics in recent months, did not suggest any improvement next year in the case of Italy.

Spain

The year 2008 marked a break from a long period of strong economic growth in Spain – a country which had been growing faster than most Member States of the euro area for a dozen years or more. In these good years, Spain benefited from sustained credit expansion, strong immigration and sound monetary and fiscal policies (Commission, 2008b, p. 75). However, this long period of economic good times ended abruptly in the latter half of 2008 when the government was called back from holidays to address the serious state in which the economy and public policy found itself in. Over the year 2008 there was still positive growth, but this outcome was the result of the first two quarters showing growth, even though the last two quarters already showed a contraction of GDP. Measured as annual percentage of change at previous-year prices, 2006 saw 3.9 per cent growth, 2007 had 3.7 per cent growth, 2008 was forecast still to have 1.3 per cent, but growth in 2009 was projected to drop to −0.2 per cent (Commission, 2008b, p. 77). Table 2 shows that the growth per capita in 2008 was 0.0 per cent whereas the forecast for 2009 was 1.4 per cent – both figures were well below the euro area and EU averages (see Table 2 above). The severe downturn was the result of a number of factors: lack of consumer confidence, higher oil and food prices, tighter credit conditions, thus lower household private consumption, contraction of the housing market and investment in housing and equipment (Commission, 2008b, p. 75).

In 2008, the employment situation in Spain changed for the first time. Even employment is due to decline in Spain in 2008 by −0.2 per cent but the forecast for 2009 is bad (−2.0 per cent in Commission, 2008b, p. 77). Similarly, whereas the rate of unemployment had been 9.2 per cent in 2005, 8.5 per cent in 2006 and 8.3 per cent in 2007, the forecast was that by the end of 2008 the number would have jumped to 10.8 per cent and would be going up sharply in the years following (the autumn forecast that Spain's unemployment would be 13.8 per cent in 2009 and a whopping 15.5 per cent in 2010 – even before all the adjustments made to the statistics because of the 'worse-than-expected' economic recession).

Public finance in Spain had been in line with the EMU requirements on deficits and public debt. The Spanish government ran a surplus in the years 2005–07 but was forecast to be −1.6 per cent of GDP in 2008 and increasing to and beyond the reference value in the years ahead.

Over the past years, inflation in Spain tended to be relatively high: 3.4 per cent and 3.6 per cent in the years 2005 and 2006, respectively. In 2007, inflation came down to 2.8 per cent. As was the case in other euro area countries such as France and Italy, 2008 was an outlier year with inflation in this case as high as 4.2 per cent, mainly as a result of higher food and oil prices. However, this looked likely to be a one-off statistic, as growth has slowed, prices come down and the economy experienced a hard landing.

So in 2008 the economic forecast for Spain for 2009 was grim. Inflation looked set to come down. With Spain's economic performance overshooting into the negative, ECB monetary policy was once again not really suitable for Spain.

The Netherlands

The cases of Spain and the Netherlands were similar in a number of ways, even if there were also clear differences. Both countries had gone through a period of strong growth that in 2008 was coming to an end. The situation in the Netherlands is not as dire per se as the case of Spain. But the global financial crisis, in particular the banking crisis, hit the Netherlands disproportionally hard compared to the average EU country. The year 2008 still looked very good for the Netherlands, with growth likely to add up to 2.3 per cent at the end of the year. The forecast for 2009 in the *European Economy* autumn forecast was set at 0.4 per cent but had more recently been majorly revised downwards. The performance of the Netherlands in 2008 came on the back of strong economic growth in 2006 and 2007. Measured as an annual percentage change of the previous year's prices, 2006 featured 3.4 per cent growth, 2007 had a growth of 3.5 per cent whereas growth in 2008 was projected to end up at 2.3 per cent (Commission, 2008b, p. 98). In the Netherlands there were multiple drivers of growth, including private consumption, higher gas consumption and a reform in the health care system from public to private. The dampening effects were the increases in taxes and social premiums, the drop in consumer demand, the tightening of credit conditions and the reduction in wealth as a result of the worsening financial crisis in autumn 2008, including the dramatic fall of prices on the stock exchanges throughout the world (Commission, 2008b, p. 96).

The employment situation in the Netherlands was unique. Nowhere in the euro area has the labour market been tighter than in the Netherlands. In 2008 young women entering the labour market (offering their labour often part-time) were still replacing older women who had not been represented in the labour market to the same extent. The activity rate thereby was still going up in the Netherlands. Even though the market was so tight, trade unions were responsible in not setting too-high wage demands. As mentioned in last year's review, the Netherlands is a little different in that the average number of hours worked per person is relatively low – at just below 1,400 hours per person per year it has the lowest rate of all OECD countries (compared to an average of

1,625 hours per person in the EU-15 or the OECD country average of 1,775, OECD, 2008, p. 153). Most of the variance between the Netherlands and other EU and OECD countries is, however, attributable to the large number of part-time workers and the low number of people who work more than 45 hours a week. The unemployment rate in 2007 was about 3.2 per cent (down from 3.9 per cent in 2006). At the same time there still remained a high rate of unfilled vacancies. The ageing population is also going to cause a slow-down in the growth of employment.

The Netherlands has performed admirably lately with regard to the SGP's budget deficit criterion. In 2006 the budget was in surplus (0.6 per cent of GDP), as was the case in 2007 (0.3 per cent) and was forecast to be 1.2 per cent in surplus in 2008 (see Table 5 above). It is perhaps worth mentioning here that the public debt in the Netherlands was due to rise. In the autumn of 2008 the Dutch government purchased Fortis bank (at a cost of approximately 2.75 per cent of GDP). Also the government made funds available to ING bank, an amount equivalent to 1.75 per cent of GDP. These amounts, according to the *European Economy* autumn edition, will end up in the public debt calculation (subject to final approval by Eurostat). They do not affect the deficit criterion but will affect only the debt criterion. As a result, debt was forecast to rise from 45.7 per cent of GDP in 2007 to 48.2 per cent in 2008 and all things remaining equal was scheduled to come down again in subsequent years.

Inflation in the Netherlands dropped between 2002 and 2006, but was due to show a slight increase in 2007 and 2008. Thus, in 2008, different from previous years (but in line with other euro area countries) inflation in the Netherlands was increasing. With the forecast increase, however, one could conclude that the ECB's relatively tight interest rate policy was fine for the Netherlands. The 2009 economic forecast for the Netherlands was however grim.

V. An Assessment of Economic and Monetary Union in 2008 and a Response to the Global Financial Crisis

What started off as a financial crisis in 2007 visible mostly to banks, investors and those interested in financial matters, soon became a fully fledged financial implosion everyone became confronted with. The financial meltdown had some impact on EMU. Even though it is as yet unclear to what extent EMU will prevent the economy from falling further, it is clear that EMU has protected the various national economies from going into a tailspin and not being able to meet their obligations.

The financial meltdown in autumn 2008 also featured all European currencies (except the euro itself) in a downward spiral. The existence of EMU enabled these countries to be more protected against the speculative attacks on the part of currency traders.

The autumn 2008 events also showed how difficult it is to co-ordinate among national governments in times of stress. At first the aim was to come up with a joint agreement. But it soon became apparent that Member State governments had to produce something fast and thus did not co-ordinate. In the end their plans were reviewed and subsequently were approved, but not before various national Member States governments already made interventions.

Conclusion

The financial turmoil that started in August 2007 extended into the year 2008 with a climax in September/October 2008 when companies went bankrupt and many banks all but collapsed leading to stocks plummeting. The response by the countries of the euro area was in the first instance to try to co-ordinate their efforts, then to offer separate national solutions; subsequently the European Commission suggested a package that was eventually approved by the Council that again signalled co-ordination. Major central banks also co-ordinated their efforts on a couple of occasions and beefed up their communication with one another.

The year 2008 in its own way was very unbalanced: the first part of the year showed an increase in inflation, solid growth and employment, which all came tumbling down in the second half of 2008. The turmoil of the autumn of 2008 in itself was unprecedented and parallels were drawn with the crash of 1929. Governments on both side of the Atlantic responded by making stimulus packages available to avoid a depression reminiscent of the 1930s.

What have we learnt from these developments? First, EMU is a pretty strong edifice that – to date – appears able to deal with economic turmoil quite well. The euro seems sufficiently large and important that it did not go into a tailspin, as was the case with the currencies of a number of European countries. A second lesson is that even if the institutional structure of EMU was asymmetric (Verdun, 1996), to date it has been able to offer venues for communication and is an important symbol of political willingness to weather the storm together. Even though the EU is not a federal state and compared to mature federations it does not have a co-ordinated centralized federal budget, compared to some non-European countries each of the European Member States has large public budgets. As a result, public expenditure offers a vehicle for automatic stabilizers – even if a federal-type government is absent.

Whether or not the countries in the euro area will do well or not in the aftermath of the crisis is unclear. One thing that is apparent, however, is that Member States are continuously seeking to find a better way to co-ordinate, make rules and support their own economy as well as that of others.

The prospect for 2009 is extremely uncertain. The most recent forecasts by any agency state in their prefaces that any forecast is based on assumptions that may well prove to be incorrect. Those forecasts suggest a deep recession for 2009 with the advanced economies seeing their worst year in decades. What will happen after that year is even less predictable. But, as the Danish physicist Niels Bohr famously said, 'Prediction is very difficult, especially about the future'.

Key Readings

Issing (2008) offers an overview of the creation of EMU, the current workings of the ECB and the issues surrounding the institutional design of EMU. Written by a practitioner, a German central banker who spent numerous years first at the German Bundesbank, then at the ECB, offers excellent insights into how EMU works in practice and the issues at stake. Another very short book focusing on central banking issues is Geraats *et al.* (2008). Written by leading economists in the field, this book deals with the concern surrounding low credibility of the ECB and what can be done to enhance it.

Dyson (2008) assesses the first decade of the euro area from the perspective of the extent to which, and ways in which, the creation of the euro has affected EU Member States, 'insiders' and 'outsiders' alike.

A special issue of the *Review of International Political Economy*, 'At Home Abroad? The Dollar's Destiny as a World Currency', contains a number of articles that deal explicitly with the role of the dollar as the world's leading currency and how, when and under what conditions the euro may challenge dollar supremacy (see in particular Helleiner, 2008; Kirshner, 2008; McNamara, 2008).

Finally, on the global economic crisis there are various recent publications and websites that offer excellent background analyses and up-to-date information. An early analysis was provided in the September 2008 edition (special issue) of one of the online Berkeley Electronic Press journals, the *Economists' Voice*, 'Financial Regulation, Financial Crisis, and Bailouts' (Vol. 5, No. 5). Websites on the global economic crisis include: «http://www.voxeu.org/» (on which leading economists offer short and punchy analyses) and the website of Nouriel Roubini, available at: «http://www.rgemonitor.com/» that monitors the global financial crisis.

References

Commission of the European Communities (2008a) 'Economic Forecast'. *European Economy*, No. 3, Spring.

Commission of the European Communities (2008b) 'Economic Forecast'. *European Economy*, No. 6, Autumn.

Commission of the European Communities (2009) 'Harmonized Consumer Price Index'. Provided to the author by the Commission services, 7 April 2009.

Commission of the European Communities (2009b) 'Interim Forecast', *European Economy*, 19 January. Available at: «http://ec.europa.eu/economy-finance/pdf/2009/interimforecastjanuary/interim_forecast_jan_2009_en.pdf».

Dyson, K. (ed) (2008) *The Euro at Ten: Europeanization, Power, and Convergence* (Oxford: Oxford University Press).

Enderlein, H. and Verdun, A. (2009) 'EMU's Teenage Challenge: What Have We Learned and Can We Predict from Political Science?' *Journal of European Public Policy*, Vol. 16, No. 4, pp. 490–507.

EUObserver (2008) 'Denmark Re-thinks Euro Adoption amid Financial Crisis'. Available at: «http://euobserver.com/9/27023».

European Central Bank (2008) *Annual Report 2007* (Frankfurt: ECB).

European Central Bank (2009) *Annual Report 2008* (Frankfurt: ECB).

Geraats, P., Giavazzi, F. and Wyplosz, C. (2008) *Transparency and Governance: Monitoring the European Central Bank* 6, CEPR and Brookings.

The Guardian (2008) 'Opposition to Euro Wanes in Sweden and Denmark'. 27 November, available at: «http://www.guardian.co.uk/business/2008/nov/27/euro-currencies-sweden-denmark».

Heipertz, M. and Verdun, A. (2006) 'The Dog that Would Bark but Never Bite? Origins, Crisis and Reform of Europe's Stability and Growth'. In Torres, F., Verdun, A. and Zimmermann, H. (eds) *EMU Rules: The Political and Economic Consequences of European Monetary Integration* (Baden-Baden: Nomos).

Heipertz, M. and Verdun, A. (2010) *Ruling Europe: The Politics of the Stability and Growth Pact* (Cambridge: Cambridge University Press) (in press).

Helleiner, E. (2008) 'Political Determinants of International Currencies: What Future for the US Dollar?' *Review of International Political Economy*, Vol. 15, No. 3, pp. 354–78.

IMF (2008a) *World Economic Outlook. Housing and the Business Cycle* (Washington, DC: International Monetary Fund), April.

IMF (2008b) *World Economic Outlook: Financial Stress, Downturns, and Recoveries* (Washington, DC: International Monetary Fund), October.

IMF (2009a) *World Economic Outlook Update: An Update of the Key WEO Projections* (Washington, DC: International Monetary Fund), 28 January.

IMF (2009b) *World Economic Outlook: Crisis and Recovery* (Washington, DC: International Monetary Fund), April.

Issing, O. (2008) *The Birth of the Euro* (Cambridge: Cambridge University Press).

Johnson, D. and Turner, C. (2009) 'Developments in the Economies of Member States Outside the Euro Area'. *JCMS*, Vol. 47, s1.

Jones, E. (2009) 'The Euro and the Financial Crisis'. *Survival*, Vol. 51, No. 2, April–May, pp. 41–54.

Kirshner, J. (2008) 'Dollar Primacy and American Power: What's at Stake?' *Review of International Political Economy*, Vol. 15, No. 3, pp. 418–38.

Lee, J. and Crowley, P. (2009) 'Evaluating the Stresses from ECB Monetary Policy in the Euro Area'. *Bank of Finland Research Discussion Papers*, 2009 No. 11.

McNamara, K.R. (2008) 'A Rivalry in the Making? The Euro and International Monetary Power'. *Review of International Political Economy*, Vol. 15, No. 3, pp. 439–59.

OECD (2008) *OECD Factbook 2008: Economic, Environmental and Social Statistics* (Paris: Organization for Economic Co-operation and Development).

Quaglia, L., Eastwood, R. and Holmes, P. (2009) 'The Financial Turmoil and EU Policy Co-operation in 2008'. *JCMS*, Vol. 47, s1.

Trichet, J.-C. (2008) 'Interview with Financial Times'. Conducted by Lionel Barber, FT Editor, and Ralph Atkins, FT Frankfurt Bureau Chief, on Wednesday, 10 December 2008 in Frankfurt, published on 15 December 2008. Available at: «http://www.ecb.int/press/key/date/2008/html/sp081215.en.html»

Verdun, A. (1996) 'An "Asymmetrical" Economic and Monetary Union in the EU: Perceptions of Monetary Authorities and Social Partners'. *Journal of European Integration*, Vol. 20, No. 1, pp. 59–81.

Verdun, A. (2006) 'Economic Developments in the Euro Area'. *JCMS*, Vol. 44, s1, pp. 199–212.

Verdun A. (2007) 'Economic Developments in the Euro Area'. *JCMS*, Vol. 45, s1, pp. 213–30.

Verdun A. (2008) 'Economic Developments in the Euro Area'. *JCMS*, Vol. 46, s1, pp. 215–31.

Developments in the Economies of Member States Outside the Euro Area

DEBRA JOHNSON
Hull University

COLIN TURNER
Heriot Watt University

Introduction

The rapid deterioration in international financial markets during autumn 2008 reinforced and accelerated the slowdown and uncertainty that was already marring prospects for many of the world's economies. In the US, bankruptcies, bail-outs of mainstream financial institutions and broader initiatives to support the financial system and the economy as a whole tell their own story about the scale of the problems (see also Quaglia *et al.*, in this volume). Such events were not confined to the US and quickly spread to Europe and beyond. The banking system in Iceland collapsed. Several EU countries, including the UK, France, Germany, Belgium, Ireland and Luxembourg took measures to support troubled financial institutions and/or to give their economies a fiscal boost. The crisis also led Hungary and Latvia to approach the EU, the IMF and World Bank for financial assistance in 2008.

As a consequence, global economic growth fell from the 5 per cent average prevailing in 2004–07 to 3.3 per cent in 2008 and is forecast to slow to 0.5 per cent in 2009 (Commission, 2008, 2009). By the end of 2008, there were signs that the economic downturn was precipitating a collapse in world trade. Although world trade growth was 2 per cent in 2008, it slowed dramatically during the second half of the year and is forecast by the World Trade Organization (WTO) to fall 9 per cent in volume terms in 2009 (WTO, 2009). Some recovery is anticipated for 2010, an expectation fuelled by confidence, which may be misplaced, that the macroeconomic measures undertaken by

Journal compilation © 2009 Blackwell Publishing Ltd, 9600 Garsington Road, Oxford OX4 2DQ, UK and 350 Main Street, Malden, MA 02148, USA

national governments will be sufficient to mitigate the worst effects of the problems within the global financial system.

The US economy faced severe problems in 2008: unemployment rose, investment was scaled back; banks sought to restore their balance sheets and major industries like motor manufacturing teetered on the brink of collapse. This pattern was mirrored in Japan. Many emerging economies seemed initially resilient to these pressures but the severity of the downturn within the US also led these economies to downgrade their growth expectations substantially. Indeed China followed western economies and announced a substantial fiscal stimulus to mitigate the effects of the global downturn on domestic demand. Elsewhere in Asia, growth held up but this is expected to be temporary. Overall, 2009 is expected to be a year of economic stagnation around the world with the slowing growth rate of 2008 turning into outright recession in 2009.

This article addresses the issue of how those EU economies outside the euro area fared in the early stages of the international economic and financial crisis. Their 2008 experiences were wide-ranging: the Baltic states demonstrated the most dramatic turnaround in economic fortunes whereas the Balkan states continued to grow. In the latter case, these countries are not unaffected by the crisis but the timing of its impact has varied.

I. Overall Economic Performance of the EU Member States outside the Euro Area

By the end of 2007, economic uncertainty had begun to affect Europe but there was by no means a consensus that a severe economic crisis was on the way. A year later, following a succession of financial crises in major economies, which at times seemed to herald collapse of the banking system, few doubted that the world was in for a prolonged and deep recession.

What was remarkable was the speed of change in Europe's economic fortunes, a factor demonstrated by the extent of the European Commission's downwards revision of its November economic forecast in its interim forecast of January 2009 (Commission, 2009). Within two months, estimates for the 2008 out-turn outside the euro area were reduced by amounts ranging from 0.2 (United Kingdom) to 1.6 (the Czech Republic) percentage points. The biggest adjustments, however, were for 2009 when significant reductions in growth were forecast for most countries (see Table 1). The greatest reductions took place in the Baltic states: the outlook was adjudged to be 4.2 percentage points lower for Latvia, 4 percentage points for Lithuania and 3.5 for Estonia. Bulgaria and Romania, with reductions in their forecast growth reduced by

Table 1: Real GDP Growth (% Annual Change) – Non-Euro Area

	2002	2003	2004	2005	2006	2007	2008 (e)	2009 (f)
Bulgaria	n/a	5.0	6.6	6.2	6.3	6.2	6.4	1.8
Czech Republic	1.9	3.6	4.5	6.3	6.8	6.0	4.2	1.7
Denmark	0.5	0.4	2.3	2.4	3.3	1.6	−0.6	−1.0
Estonia	8.0	7.2	7.5	9.2	10.4	6.3	−2.4	−4.7
Latvia	6.5	7.2	8.7	10.6	12.2	10.3	−2.3	−6.9
Lithuania	6.9	10.3	7.4	7.8	7.8	8.9	3.4	−4.0
Hungary	4.3	4.2	4.8	4.0	4.1	1.1	0.9	−1.6
Poland	1.4	3.9	5.3	3.6	6.2	6.7	5.0	2.0
Romania	n/a	5.2	8.5	4.2	7.9	6.2	7.8	1.8
Slovakia	4.1	4.2	5.2	6.5	8.5	10.4	7.1	2.7
Sweden	2.0	1.7	4.1	3.3	4.2	2.5	0.5	−1.4
UK	2.1	2.8	2.8	2.1	2.8	3.0	0.7	−2.8
Euro area	0.9	0.8	2.5	2.0	3.1	2.9	1.0	−1.8

Source: Commission (2009).

2.7 and 2.8 percentage points, respectively, also saw a major turnaround in their economic outlook. Such sharp revisions over such a short period were highly unusual and reflect the rapid economic deterioration that occurred at the end of the year.

No country is immune from the downturn but the change in fortunes is most marked in the Baltic states, the leading countries in the growth tables in recent years. Much of the growth in both the Baltic and the Balkans had been funded by loans in foreign currencies, such as the euro and the Swiss franc, which have become increasingly difficult to service and could threaten financial stability in those western European states that have lent heavily to their eastern neighbours.

These lenders include Austria, Italy, France, Belgium, Germany and Sweden. In early 2009, public concern about the economy in several European countries manifested itself in public demonstrations, which have degenerated into violence in some cases, and played a role in the destabilization of some governments. As economic conditions are likely to get worse before they get better, the region could be in for a bumpy ride politically as well as economically.

Labour markets will be hit hard by the recession (see Table 2). It has taken many years for central and eastern European economies to reduce significantly the high levels of unemployment that accompanied their transition from command to market economies. The current recession will undo some of this good work. Unemployment is a lagging indicator: given the costs and time involved in recruitment, employers tend to release workers only when it

Table 2: Unemployment (% of the Civilian Labour Force) – Non-Euro Area

	2002	2003	2004	2005	2006	2007	2008 (e)	2009 (f)
Bulgaria	n/a	13.7	12.1	10.1	9.0	6.9	6.0	6.3
Czech Republic	7.3	7.8	8.3	7.9	7.2	5.3	5.0	5.7
Denmark	4.6	5.4	5.5	4.8	3.9	3.8	3.5	4.5
Estonia	10.3	10.0	9.7	7.9	5.9	4.7	5.1	8.8
Latvia	12.2	10.5	10.4	8.9	6.8	6.0	6.5	10.4
Lithuania	13.5	12.4	11.4	8.3	5.6	4.3	5.4	8.8
Hungary	5.8	5.9	6.1	7.2	7.5	7.4	7.7	8.8
Poland	19.9	19.6	19.0	17.8	13.9	9.6	7.4	8.4
Romania	n/a	7.0	8.1	7.2	7.3	6.4	6.2	7.0
Slovakia	18.7	17.6	18.2	16.3	13.4	11.1	9.8	10.6
Sweden	4.9	5.6	6.3	7.4	7.0	6.1	6.2	7.9
UK	5.1	4.9	4.7	4.8	5.4	5.3	5.7	8.2
Euro area	8.3	8.7	9.0	9.0	8.3	7.5	7.5	9.3

Source: Commission (2009).

is clear that the downturn is sustained. In the recovery phase, the initial impact on jobs is minimal as the resumption of growth focuses on utilizing underused capacity, including labour, before new jobs are created. The loosening of labour markets began towards the end of 2008 but the biggest increases in unemployment are forecast for 2009 with changes being most marked in the Baltic states and the United Kingdom. Improvements in labour markets will only occur after recovery is well established which could be in 2010 or beyond.

One consequence of the economic crisis is that several countries outside the euro area reassessed their position and began to consider bringing their possible entry into the eurozone forward. This is true of Denmark, and to a lesser extent Sweden, and of several states in central and eastern Europe. These smaller countries have seen their currencies buffeted about in the current economic maelstrom and envisage greater stability within the shelter of a major currency like the euro. Inflation is likely to be less of an obstacle to euro accession than seemed likely in 2008. The acceleration in inflation, clearly apparent in the statistics for 2008, peaked in the autumn and was already on its way down by the end of the year (see Table 3). The recession, helped by lower food and fuel prices – major factors in the recent upturn in prices – is helping to contain and reduce inflation. The biggest obstacle to quick expansion of the euro area will be the recession-induced deterioration in public finances and the requirement for applicant currencies to remain in ERM2 for two years at a juncture when the currencies have proven to be

Table 3: Inflation Rate^a (%) – Non-Euro Area

	2002	2003	2004	2005	2006	2007	2008 (e)	2009 (f)
Bulgaria	n/a	2.3	6.1	6.0	7.4	7.6	12.0	5.4
Czech Republic	1.4	−0.1	2.6	1.6	2.1	3.0	6.3	2.6
Denmark	2.4	2.0	0.9	1.7	1.9	1.7	3.6	1.6
Estonia	3.6	1.4	3.0	4.1	4.4	6.7	10.6	3.2
Latvia	2.0	2.9	6.2	6.9	6.6	10.1	15.3	6.8
Lithuania	0.3	−1.1	1.2	2.7	3.8	5.8	11.1	5.6
Hungary	5.2	4.7	6.8	3.5	4.0	7.9	6.1	2.8
Poland	1.9	0.7	3.6	2.2	1.3	2.6	4.2	2.9
Romania	n/a	15.3	11.9	9.1	6.6	4.9	7.9	5.7
Slovakia	3.5	8.4	7.5	2.8	4.3	1.9	4.0	2.9
Sweden	1.9	2.3	1.0	0.8	1.5	1.7	3.3	0.7
UK	1.3	1.4	1.3	2.1	2.3	2.3	3.4	0.1
Euro area	2.3	2.1	2.3	2.3	2.3	2.4	3.7	1.2

Source: Commission (2009).
Note: ^{a} Harmonized index of consumer prices.

unstable. Hitherto, the euro area has shown no inclination to relax the entry requirements. Indeed, insistence on the eligibility criteria seems resolute.

II. Economic Developments in the Old Euro-Outsiders

United Kingdom

The uncertainty that began to dog the hitherto buoyant UK economy by the end of 2007 turned into a complete reversal of fortune by the end of 2008. Following a sharp slowdown in the first quarter of 2008, economic growth was at a standstill in the second quarter before turning negative in the third quarter, the first shrinkage in the economy in 16 years. Following a second consecutive quarter of decline in the final quarter, the economy officially entered recession. The economy grew by a modest 0.7 per cent in 2008, compared to 3 per cent in 2007, but the biggest fall in UK growth is forecast for 2009 at −3 per cent for 2009. Recession could also easily spill over into 2010 and delay the slow recovery anticipated for that year.

Weaknesses in financial markets precipitated problems in the broader economy. The UK banking system first experienced problems in 2007 but these really snowballed in autumn 2008. In September, the government took over the mortgages and loans of Bradford and Bingley (the rest of the bank became part of the Spanish banking giant, Santander). In October, the government announced a rescue package for the banking sector worth at least £50 billion and up to a further £200 billion in short-term lending support. It also pumped £37 billion into three major banks – RBS, Lloyds TSB and HBOS – in one of the country's biggest nationalizations. This unprecedented banking crisis contributed to tense conditions in equity markets and the FTSE 100 fell 31 per cent during the year, further undermining business confidence and investment.

In addition to the bank bail-outs, crisis management has taken the form of a large fiscal stimulus and historically low interest rates. Consequently, public borrowing and debt are set to reach levels not seen for many years and will require difficult decisions once the economy starts to recover. As interest rates rapidly approach zero, there was discussion about switching the focus of policy to 'quantitative easing' – that is, measures to boost money supply.

Domestic demand, especially household consumption, for a long time the economy's main driving force, weakened throughout 2008.The consumption boom was rooted in easy credit and high levels of indebtedness as households borrowed against the rising equity in their property. The exposure of the UK financial system to the US subprime crisis had already shaken consumer confidence in late 2007. Tighter credit and the non-appearance of the normal spring house-buying spree further dented confidence as 2008 unfolded. After years of seemingly inexorable rises, house prices were at least 15 per cent lower at the end of 2008 than at the beginning. Further substantial falls were expected in 2009. Consumer confidence was hit further by progressive weakening of the previously strong labour market. In the final quarter of 2008, 203,000 jobs disappeared and unemployment rose to 1.86 million, the highest level since 1997. The bleak employment outlook helped moderate wages. Lower levels of disposable income plus tighter credit and attempts to build precautionary savings (after years of a falling savings ratio) looked set to continue to rein back domestic demand.

Business confidence also plummeted throughout 2008. After strong growth in 2007, both residential and business investment fell in 2008, although government investment did hold up. The tight credit conditions in terms of availability rather than cost (interest rates were 2 per cent in December compared to 5.25 per cent in January and fell even lower in early 2009) contributed to falling investment levels.

Most economic trends were decidedly negative in 2008 but some mildly positive developments took place. The slower import growth arising from falling domestic demand reversed the negative impact of net exports on economic growth. In 2008, the net export balance was largely neutral but was forecast to turn positive in 2009. The large depreciation of sterling under way since the middle of 2007 improved the competitiveness of Britain's exports, but the global recession has moderated export growth. The economic slowdown, however, restrained any inflationary pressure coming from the depreciation.

Denmark

The Danish economy began to falter before the rest of the EU. Its growth rate had already halved between 2006 and 2007, falling from 3.3 per cent to 1.6 per cent, before registering growth of −0.6 per cent in 2008. Thus, Denmark, Estonia and Latvia were the only non-euro area EU economies to decline in 2008. Domestic demand growth remained positive (just) in 2008: although there was some growth in both private and public consumption, falling investment, driven by falling construction demand, offset this. Some rebuilding of stocks did, however, help restrict the overall fall in GDP. The weakness of domestic demand was more than matched by the deteriorating contribution of net exports to GDP growth as a result of the weakness of Denmark's major export markets.

However, the full extent of the correction and its effects remained uncertain. Given the deflation of the over-inflated housing market, it was forecast that domestic demand would continue to fall throughout 2009 as the negative wealth effects of house price falls started to feed through into consumption patterns. Indeed, private consumption was expected to fall by 0.8 per cent in 2009. To some extent, these effects have been mitigated by tax changes, real wage increases and a relatively resilient labour market. Unemployment – which has been at historically low levels – will start to rise and by 2010 is forecast to reach 4.5 per cent. This is still relatively low, by Danish standards and compared to most other European economies.

One potentially significant change in Denmark as a result of the economic and financial crisis was the softening of its position to membership of the euro area that became apparent towards the end of 2008. The battering of the economy led to an increase in support for the euro, reflected in opinion polls and by politicians. In October, Prime Minister Rasmussen stated: 'the euro ensures political and economical stability in Europe and the current financial turmoil makes it evident that Denmark has to join the euro'. This followed government intervention to support the krone, which is pegged to the euro, and which resulted in higher interest rates at a time when the economy would benefit from lower rates. Rasmussen suggested that a further referendum on euro area membership could be held in 2011.

Sweden

Initial optimism that Sweden would avoid the worst of the economic downturn evaporated in early 2008. The annual average growth rates of 3.5 per cent enjoyed from 2004 came to an abrupt halt in 2008 when growth fell to 0.5 per cent. A contraction of 1.4 per cent was anticipated for 2009. This weaker economic performance was driven by the deteriorating external environment, which was forecast to continue its decline throughout 2009.

To some extent, the weakening external position was compensated by domestic demand which, despite slowing somewhat, held up relatively well. However declining consumer and business confidence eroded some of this mitigating factor. This has been driven not merely by less favourable labour markets but also by sharp erosion in household disposable income as interest rates rose (then fell) and borrowing conditions tightened. This has been compounded by rising production and financing costs which have (alongside falling exports) significantly dented business sentiment.

Whilst Swedish households did not have the weak balance sheets of other EU nations, there was still a risk that difficult credit conditions and rising unemployment would act as a drain upon this core driver of the economy. Less buoyant domestic demand plus falling asset prices (both in terms of stock market and house prices) threatened to be a significant drag on the Swedish economy over the next two years by lowering investment and diminishing the ability of the government to alleviate the worst effects of the downturn as a result of its eroding fiscal surplus.

The krona experienced a bumpy ride in 2008 as investors abandoned it in favour of larger, allegedly safer currencies. The depreciation of the currency looked set to help Swedish goods retain price competitiveness in a tricky trading climate. The weakness of the national currency in difficult economic times also weakened the resistance of the Swedish population to euro area membership: opinion polls, although not demonstrating a majority in favour of euro area membership, were at least showing a significant softening of the public's anti-euro position towards the end of 2008.

III. Economic Developments in the New Euro-Outsiders

Poland

In 2008, Poland experienced the main impact of the global slowdown through lower growth rather than outright recession. At the time of writing, high rates of domestic demand growth have thus far allowed the Polish economy to shrug off the worst of the global credit crisis. Private consumption has been sustained by a combination of personal tax cuts, indexation of pensions and real wage increases. However, the fall in investment growth from 17.6 per cent in 2007 to 8.2 per cent in 2008 has weakened domestic demand somewhat. Consequently, Polish GDP growth fell from nearly 6.7

per cent in 2007 to 5 per cent in 2008 and is forecast to slow further in 2009 to 2 per cent.

Exactly how far the Polish financial sector will be affected by the credit crisis is unknown. Whilst many of its 'universal' banks have a strong deposit base and were relatively unexposed to broader financial market developments, many small and medium-sized banks have come to rely on foreign financing. Thus, in some areas, the absence of credit has started to take effect. This has been most evident in the housing market where demand is clearly faltering.

Another cloud on the horizon for Poland is unemployment. After falling from nearly 19.6 per cent in 2003 to 7.4 per cent in 2008, the worsening economic outlook means that unemployment started to rise again by the end of 2008. However, the less favourable labour market conditions are not expected to be so great that the country will return to the double-digit unemployment of a few years ago. This claim is based on a belief that the fundamentals of the Polish economy are sound and that it does not suffer from the imbalances exhibited by some other central and eastern European economies.

Slower growth elsewhere in Europe is likely to be the main drag on Polish growth. Export growth almost halved in 2008 and was forecast to decline slightly in 2009. Imports fell as a result of lower domestic demand. The overall impact was a slight decline in the negative impact of net exports on growth and a continuing increase in the current account deficit to 5.6 per cent of GDP. Although representing a significant deterioration since 2005, Poland's current account deficit does not pose the same challenges as the equivalent deficits in the Baltic and Balkan states.

The slowdown in the Polish economy helped increase the government deficit to 2.5 per cent of GDP by 2008, a situation that is forecast to deteriorate further in 2009. The increasing deficit was generated by pre-existing measures, falling revenue and counter-cyclical measures agreed in the light of the crisis.

Hungary

Hungary was perhaps the most exposed of the central and east European economies to the international financial crisis. It was certainly the first to exhibit signs of a major economic slowdown. GDP growth had already fallen to 1.1 per cent in 2007, before sinking further to 0.9 per cent in 2008. The economy was forecast to contract by 1.6 per cent in 2009 before resuming modest growth in 2010. Growth was arrested by a sharp deceleration in domestic demand with all components remaining suppressed.

A primary cause of the rapid turnaround in Hungary's economic fortunes was the high exposure of its financial system to the global credit crisis. Both the household and business sectors hold high levels of foreign debt after taking out loans in euros to take advantage of favourable interest rates. By the end of 2008, the debt to western European banks stood at 88 per cent of GDP. This imbalance fed through into a sharp fall in the government bond and stock markets and depreciation of the forint.

The most evident impact of the financial crisis upon the real economy came through lower demand in Hungary's main export markets and increased and widespread credit rationing. As the ability to borrow is further curtailed, so private consumption will fall further. In turn, this will feed through into looser labour markets: employment had already started to fall and unemployment to increase in 2008 but the main impact of the crisis will not be felt until 2009.

The crisis provoked Hungary to seek financial support from the EU, the IMF and the World Bank. These three institutions together offered Hungary a €25 billion credit line to help it through its economic troubles. However, assistance has come with clear conditions relating to banking regulation and government spending cuts. Prior to the current crisis, the government deficit had been on a downward trajectory with the deficit falling from 9.3 per cent of GDP in 2006 to 3.3 per cent in 2008 following a programme of austerity measures as the government sought to balance its books. However, the financial crisis and the overseas borrowing undertaken by the government to cushion itself against the crisis threatened to undermine these efforts, leading to the above request for external support.

The credit crunch can be expected to have a sustained impact on the Hungarian economy and conditions will worsen as corporate profits fall and unemployment rises. Modest improvements can be expected in 2010, although the risks all remain on the downside.

Czech Republic

Given the open nature of the Czech economy, a sharp decline in its growth rate was to be expected in the face of international economic meltdown. Indeed, growth slowed to 4.2 per cent in 2008 (down from 6 per cent in 2007) with the impact of the global crisis intensifying from the final quarter of 2008. The slowdown in the main driver of growth – domestic demand – was the major factor behind the Czech slowdown. Domestic demand benefited from relatively robust labour markets, which are not expected to feel the effects of the downturn until 2009, but was adversely affected by the fiscal implications of the government's stabilization package and the reduction in real incomes generated by sharp rises in commodity and fuel prices. These trends fed through into lower investment flows, further accentuating the downturn. On the positive side, the Czech financial sector is not as heavily exposed to the subprime crisis as some other Member States but the economy is unlikely to escape the consequences of tighter credit conditions.

On the external side, export growth almost halved as the outlook for the Czech Republic's main export markets declined but imports fell even faster in response to slowing domestic demand. The net result was an increase in the contribution of the external balance to growth in 2008. However, the contribution of net exports was forecast to become negative in 2009 as the impact of struggling export markets started to take hold, despite weakening of the koruna.

The budget deficit was 1.2 per cent of GDP in 2008. This was expected to grow to 2.5 per cent in 2009 as the lower revenues and increased spending associated with the slowdown start to take effect. This will be compounded, to a limited degree, by the counter-cyclical measures introduced to mitigate the effects of the slowdown.

Compared to some central and eastern European economies, the Czech economy was forecast to be relatively lightly affected by the financial crisis. Unemployment was forecast to reach 5.7 per cent in 2009, an increase on 2008 but significantly below the average unemployment levels both inside and outside the euro area. Consumer spending growth was forecast to remain firm as a result of real wage increases. This relative optimism depended on assumptions about employment and credit conditions not being undermined and was not shared by all.

Slovakia

Following double-digit growth in 2007, the expansion of Slovakia's economy fell to a still healthy 7 per cent in 2008. A much sharper fall in the growth rate to 2.7 per cent is forecast for 2009 with a small recovery anticipated for 2010. Growth has been sustained by domestic demand – private and public consumption and investment – which although forecast to fall in 2009, will remain the main contributor to growth.

Unlike elsewhere in the region, at the time of writing, the financial crisis has had little impact on the domestic economy and credit conditions. The main impact, therefore, has been on trade and the slowdown has its roots in the external sector. Although import growth declined slightly in 2008, the biggest change on the external side has been the big fall in export growth which occurred as a result of the severe downturn in the outlook for the euro area, the location of Slovakia's main export markets. Consequently, the contribution of net exports to growth was minimal in 2008, rather than significant as in 2007. By 2009, the contribution of net exports to GDP growth is forecast to be neutral. However, there is a downside risk to this forecast: following the commencement of production from the major FDI automotive projects in Slovakia, the country's exports have become heavily reliant on this one sector which is itself highly sensitive to recession as consumers delay the purchase of new cars until confidence returns.

Overall, Slovakia's economy appears to be relatively well-placed to face the downturn. This optimism is supported by lower inflation and real wage growth, which supports domestic demand but which is not so great that it rules out small increases in productivity. A mildly expansionary fiscal policy will also help Slovakia withstand the downturn but could result in Slovakia's budget deficit breaching the 3 per cent ceiling of GDP early in its euro area membership. The economic slowdown, however, will arrest the improvements in Slovakia's unemployment rate which fell to 9.8 per cent in 2008, its lowest level for many years and almost half the level of 2002.

Estonia

In less than two years, Estonia has been transformed from one of the EU's star performers into an economy in deep crisis. The growth slowdown that began in the second half of 2007 with the downturn in Russian trade became a contraction by the second quarter of 2008. By the fourth quarter, the economy had declined by 9 per cent compared to the same period in 2007. Overall, Estonian GDP growth fell by 2.4 per cent in 2008.

Estonia has been badly affected by the global financial and economic crises. Domestic demand, especially private consumption and investment, had been the mainstay of Estonia's growth but was badly hit by deteriorating credit conditions and plummeting business and consumer confidence. This was reflected in the steady slide in retail sales from their February peak and was not helped by double-digit inflation. Fears of unemployment also damaged private consumption and diverted funds towards greater precautionary saving.

Decline in the previously booming real estate and construction sectors, which began in 2007, accelerated in 2008. Downturn in these sectors sent business confidence falling and contributed to big falls in industrial output. Some export industries, such as chemicals and precision instruments, continued to expand but most suffered from contraction of their major export markets. However, the impact of the economic crisis was relatively greater on imports, which were hit by falling domestic demand. Consequently, there was a significant decrease in the current account deficit in 2008 with an accompanying decline in the need for international borrowing.

Labour markets have been relatively slow to react to economic decline. Wage increases in 2008 averaged almost 15 per cent, far below 2007 levels, but were still significant in real terms and exceeding productivity growth. Employment started to decline in 2008 and there was a small increase in unemployment. Given the tendency for labour market indicators to lag growth, the impact of the recession on Estonian labour markets is expected to be at its most severe in 2009.

The recession will also undermine Estonia's public finances which have been in surplus for some years but which registered a deficit in 2008. Consequently the 2009 budget contained revenue-raising measures and proposals to restrain public spending. The success of these measures plus the anticipated fall in inflation are crucial to what Märten Ross, deputy governor of Estonia's central bank, described in December 2008 as 'the most significant short-term objective' – the adoption of the euro. He claimed this would become possible in 2011 or 2012 and was Estonia's 'primary guarantee for stability'. In early 2009, Estonia's prime minister proposed 2010 as a potential entry date – a target that relies on an early recovery in Estonia.

Latvia

During 2005–07, Latvia registered double-digit growth. By late 2008, the economy was in freefall with GDP shrinking by 10.5 per cent in the final quarter of the year compared to the same period in 2007. For 2008 as a whole, GDP fell 2.3 per cent. The 'soft landing' widely forecast for Latvia's economy had instead become a hard and bumpy one.

The roots of this sharp turnaround lie in reversal of the domestic property boom and falls in domestic demand, the driving forces behind the extraordinary growth. The first signs of trouble were already apparent towards the end of 2007 but things deteriorated significantly in the second half of 2008 when the international financial crisis started to take hold and reinforced the tightening of credit availability in Latvia.

Events took a further turn for the worse in November when the government took over the country's failing second largest bank, Parex banka. The combination of a severe economic downturn, the near impossibility of gaining credit, the lack of budgetary reserves and the need to support Parex banka led the government to seek financial assistance from the EU, the IMF and neighbouring states. Agreement was reached on a €7.5 billion loan which came with stringent conditions attached. The resulting economic stabilization package adopted in December resulted in the slashing of local government budgets and big cuts in public sector salaries. In early January 2009, popular resentment spilled over into rioting.

At first, the impact of the recession fed through only slowly into labour markets but this changed by the end of the year: in January 2009, unemployment, restrained initially by migration and an increased retirement rate, reached 8.3 per cent compared to less than 6 per cent only three months earlier. This deterioration in labour markets will continue in 2009 in the form of falling wages in both the public and private sectors and rising unemployment.

The crisis hit the external sector. Export growth lost momentum following the downturn in Latvia's major export markets. However, the 8.6 per cent fall in imports in 2008 accompanying the fall in domestic demand was even more marked. Consequently, the external balance turned positive in 2008. This also resulted in a significant improvement in the current account balance which fell to 15 per cent of GDP in 2008 from 23 per cent in 2007.

Despite, indeed because of, the economic uncertainty and instability facing it, the Latvian authorities, including Ilman Rimserics, the governor of the Bank of Latvia, regard meeting the Maastricht criteria and thus qualifying for euro membership as 'a top strategic goal'. Euro membership is seen as a way of enhancing macroeconomic stability and of supporting economic recovery and a target date for entry of 2012 has been suggested. The authorities see fiscal issues as being the biggest obstacle to achieving this goal.

Lithuania

Following almost a decade of extraordinary growth, Lithuania's economy hit the buffers. Although GDP growth registered 3.4 per cent in 2008, growth slowed considerably during the year, quashing hopes that Lithuania would be spared the sharp downturn of its Baltic neighbours. Domestic demand remained the main contributor to growth, albeit at a much lower level, but the global economic and financial crises led to deteriorating business and consumer confidence and lower industrial output and retail sales.

Private consumption (boosted by income tax cuts, wage increases and increases in social transfers) held up reasonably well in early 2008. However, slower credit growth and accelerating inflation began to undermine domestic demand as the year unfolded. Inflation peaked at 11.1 per cent for 2008 as a whole following food and fuel price increases and continuing pressure from domestic demand. Recessionary pressures should result in inflation below 6 per cent in 2009. Investment growth, in double figures for some years, turned negative in 2008 as the real estate and construction boom began to unravel; credit conditions tightened and residential and infrastructure construction and business investment continued to be hit by declining sentiment.

The turnaround in economic fortunes was reinforced by weakening labour market conditions during the second half of the year when unemployment started to increase and vacancy rates and employment to fall. Nominal wage increases remained high during 2008, suggesting a lag between the beginning of the economic downturn and full-blown labour market adjustment. However, unemployment is forecast to grow considerably in 2009–10 as the full impact of the recession takes effect.

Lithuania's external demand has declined in line with the outlook for its main trading partners. However, given that imports have dropped further as a result of falling domestic demand, the external balance has improved and some narrowing of the current account deficit has taken place. However, the latter remains substantial and prospects for further improvement will be hit by the scheduled 2009 closure of the Ignalina nuclear power plant, the supplier of 70 to 80 per cent of Lithuania's electricity which will need to be replaced by imports.

Earlier expansionary measures (such as direct tax reductions, higher social transfers and public sector wage increases) and weaker domestic demand led to a budget deficit approaching 3 per cent in 2008. In an attempt to keep public spending under control, in December the government introduced a budget package which proposed major cuts in spending and extensive tax changes. The population's response to these austerity measures was a peaceful demonstration which quickly degenerated into violence in January 2009.

Bulgaria

For most of 2008, Bulgaria's economy was in danger of overheating. Thanks to buoyant domestic demand, driven by strong investment and private consumption, boosted in turn by a tightening labour market, easy credit and an almost runaway growth in wages, GDP registered a robust 6.4 per cent growth in 2008. However, signs of troubled times ahead became apparent by the end of the year.

In the run-up to and immediately after EU accession, Bulgaria experienced big increases in capital inflows, which reached 27 per cent of GDP in 2007 (IMF, 2009). The global crisis has restricted capital inflows and hence the flow of credit. Consequently, the erstwhile booming residential property and construction markets encountered serious problems in autumn 2008 after banks virtually ceased extending loans for new projects and insisted on much larger deposits for mortgages.

Financial constraints and lower returns also began to impact negatively on FDI and investment generally. Bulgaria's current account deficit (equivalent to one-quarter of GDP) could no longer be covered by FDI and the country accumulated significant short-term liabilities. However, import growth will decline following the downturn in domestic demand and, although hit by a slowdown in their major markets, exports benefited from the impact of large FDI stocks and held up relatively well in 2008. As a result, the current account deficit is forecast to decline – but will remain at uncomfortably high levels.

Much-needed improvements in the external balance will depend on Bulgaria's competitiveness, challenged in recent years by the tightness of labour markets. Employment grew by 3.2 per cent in 2008 whilst unemployment fell by almost 1 percentage point, resulting in average wage increases of 19 per cent. Such trends pushed up unit labour costs to a level which outstripped improvements in labour productivity, thereby undermining price competitiveness. Rigid adherence of the currency board to pegging of the lev to the euro, and the consequent inability to adjust interest rates, has removed the option of devaluation to restore competitiveness. Some loosening of labour markets and lower wage increases are forecast for 2009. This will help reduce inflation, which peaked in 2008 at 12 per cent but which had started to weaken towards the end of the year.

In weathering the current economic crisis, Bulgaria has the advantage of a strong fiscal position: the state has little foreign debt (12 per cent of GDP in 2008) and a budget surplus (3.2 per cent of GDP). This places Bulgaria in a good position to absorb the additional spending and loss of revenue that will inevitably come from the economic slowdown.

Romania

Contrary to the experience of most other EU countries, Romania's economic growth actually accelerated to 7.8 per cent in 2008 from 6.2 per cent in 2007. Growth continued to be driven by buoyant domestic demand, which in turn was boosted by high wage growth and easy domestic credit and investment. However, the global financial and economic crisis finally caught up with Romania by the end of the year.

Credit started to tighten and investment to slacken in the third quarter. By December, as a result of the sharp downturn in major export markets, industrial production was 18 per cent down on December 2007. Falling output was most marked in oil processing, metallurgy, road vehicles, electrical machinery and apparatus which declined between 28 and 61 per cent (National Bank of Romania, 2008). Business and industrial confidence indicators plummeted and consumer confidence was not far behind. Consequently, private consumption, growing rapidly since 2005, was slowing by the end of 2008 and is forecast, at best, to be only marginally positive in 2009.

Labour markets continued to tighten, albeit only slightly, for most of 2008 but by the end of the year short-term factory closures and a cessation of hiring heralded the first signs of a reversal. Wage increases in 2008 averaged 23 per cent and continued to outpace productivity gains, resulting in a marked increase in unit labour costs. Together with a depreciation of the local currency and supply-side pressures, high wage settlements contributed to accelerating inflation in early 2008 but, later in the year, aided by lower energy prices, a good harvest and the emerging economic slowdown, inflation started to moderate.

Two deficits continue to dog Romania – the current account and budget deficits. The current account deficit fell to 12.9 per cent of GDP in 2008 from 13.6 per cent in 2007. Import growth, although still strong, started to fall in 2008 but the biggest reduction will occur in 2009 when the downturn in domestic demand really starts to gather pace. Export growth in 2008 was faster than in 2007 but slowed towards the end of the year as euro area markets started to feel the impact of the global crisis. Depreciation of the local currency and FDI-driven improvements in manufacturing competitiveness will not prevent falling export growth but they will help offset its worst effects. However, the burgeoning budget deficits and reductions in FDI inflows, which have covered a major part of recent current account deficits, will continue the high dependency on external borrowing and expose the economy to external financial shocks.

Romania has been following an expansionary, pro-cyclical fiscal policy in recent years. Accordingly, the budget deficit steadily increased to 5.2 per cent in 2008. As a result of the downturn and continued fiscal loosening, the deficit looks set to continue its expansion. Given its external imbalance and the tightness of global credit, further unrestrained government spending could result in financing difficulties.

Conclusion

The impact of the international financial and banking crisis began to bite in the real economies of the non-euro area EU members by the end of 2008, marking a significant turning point in their economic performance – a turning point which threatened social and political tension in many countries. The size and timing of the impact varied but these countries were generally hit by a double whammy. First, domestic demand, which had been the main contributor to growth across the region in recent years, was badly hit by declining credit conditions, loss of consumer and business confidence and the drying up of credit. Secondly, given the international nature of the crisis, export markets contracted and the external sector was, for the most part, unable to take up the slack in demand.

One noticeable feature of late 2008 was the reassessment of strategies for membership of the euro area. Latterly, several countries had seen their target date for euro area membership slide further into the future. However, the crisis has highlighted the vulnerabilities of relatively small, open economies to large-scale currency movements in times of economic crisis and tension. The currency board arrangements in the Baltic states, for example, restricted the possible responses of governments to the crisis. Consequently, several countries started to reconsider the benefits of membership of the euro area as a source of stability in a time of economic upheaval. However, unless the eligibility criteria for euro area membership are relaxed, which is unlikely, the deterioration in public finances brought about by the recession will restrict euro area expansion until recovery is well under way.

References

Commission of the European Communities (2008) 'Economic Forecasts: Autumn 2008'. *European Economy*, No. 6/2008.

Commission of the European Communities (2009) 'Interim Forecast: January 2009'.

IMF (2009) 'IMF Executive Board concludes 2008 Article IV Consultation with Bulgaria'. Public Information Notice (PIN) No. 09/34. Available at: «http://www.img.org/external/np/sec/pn/2009/pn0934.htm».

National Bank of Romania (2008) 'Monthly Bulletin', 12/2008.

WTO (2009) 'World Trade 2008, Prospects for 2009'. Press/554. Available at: «http://www.wto.org/english/news_e/pres09_e/pr554_e.htm».

JCMS 2009 Volume 47 Annual Review pp. 277–283

Chronology: The European Union in 2008

NICOLA CORKIN
University of Birmingham

At a Glance

Presidencies of the EU Council: Slovenia (1 January–30 June) and France (1 July–31 December).

January

1	Slovenia as the first of the 2004/07 enlargement Member States takes over the Presidency of the European Union.
1	Malta and Cyprus adopt the euro.
23	EU commission publishes its Environmental Aid Programme – a mixture of old measures such as CO_2 emission trading to ensure competition but also new measures under the polluter pays principle with increased concentration on investment in renewable energy sources.
24–26	Informal council meeting of justice and home affairs ministers. Consideration was given to the strengthening of family law matters and access to the courts. Further attention was paid to higher co-operation in criminal matters.
29	Slovenian and Maltese parliaments ratify the Lisbon Treaty.
29	The ECJ rules that Member States are not obligated to ensure that personal data is disclosed in civil procedures relating to copyright law.

29   Business roundtable with the Commission agrees on the
            necessity to design an early warning system for financial crises
            and high risk credits.
30   Council approves new aviation security rules and extends the
            duties of the European Aviation Safety Agency.

February

3   Boris Tadić is re-elected president of Serbia.
4   Romanian parliament ratifies the Lisbon Treaty.
7   French parliament (upper and lower house) ratifies the Lisbon
            Treaty.
15   Informal meeting of the education, youth and culture ministers
            resulting in the conclusion that multilingualism is an inevitable
            necessity for economic strengthening.
15   Václav Klaus re-elected Czech president.
17   Kosovo declares itself independent of Serbia.
18   Czech parliament (lower house) ratifies the Lisbon Treaty.
21–22   Informal meeting of the ministers of defence. The meeting
            focused on military capabilities and their development. The
            relationship between Nato and the UN was under discussion as
            well.
22   Northern Rock bank is taken into state ownership.
24   Cyprus elects Dimitris Christofias as president.
25   Council adopted a key paper on competitiveness and
            innovation and reached an agreement on the main elements for
            the launch of the fuel cell and hydrogen joint technology
            initiative.
28   Liechtenstein signs Schengen-related association with the
            EU.

March

1   EU–China maritime transport agreement enters into force.
2   Dmitry Medvedev elected president of Russia.
6   Belgian parliament (upper house) ratifies the Lisbon Treaty.
8   Maltese parliamentary elections won by Nationalist Party
            (Christian Democrats) with 49 per cent of the vote.
9   Informal meeting of trade ministers.

9	Spanish general elections – a coalition of the Spanish Socialist Workers Party and the People's Party gains most votes. Spain becomes the first European country with a female-dominated cabinet.
11	United Kingdom parliament (lower house) ratifies the Lisbon Treaty.
11–12	EU External Border Conference.
13–14	European Council met and focused on the renewed Lisbon Strategy, energy policy and climate change and the security of financial markets.
16–17	Informal meeting of ministers of sport. The meeting was designed to further progress with the white paper on sport and the 'Pierre de Coubertin' plan.
21	Bulgarian parliament ratifies the Lisbon Treaty.
28–29	Informal meeting of EU ministers of foreign affairs. The EU encourages China to re-establish a dialogue with Tibet.

April

1	Polish parliament (lower house) ratifies the Lisbon Treaty.
2	Polish parliament (upper house) ratifies the Lisbon Treaty. The president does not sign the Treaty and ratification halts.
4–5	Informal meeting of ECOFIN aimed at improving the infrastructure for clearing and settlement for securities transactions.
9	Austrian parliament (lower house) ratifies the Lisbon Treaty.
10	Belgian parliament (lower house) and Slovak parliament ratify the Lisbon Treaty.
11–12	Informal meeting of environment ministers. The meeting focused on the need to achieve a greater synergy between climate change protection and conservation of biodiversity.
13–14	Berlusconi elected Italian prime minister.
14–16	Informal meeting of ministers for competitiveness concerned with the further development and co-ordination of the European Research Area.
23	Portuguese parliament ratifies the Lisbon Treaty.
24	Danish parliament and German parliament (lower house) ratify the Lisbon Treaty.

May

5–6   Informal meeting of the ministers of transport and
          telecommunication. There was an agreement for environmental
          sustainability and energy efficiency as the basis for providing a
          sustainable environment for future generations.

7   Brian Cowen becomes Irish Taoiseach.

8   Latvian and Lithuanian parliaments ratify the Lisbon Treaty.

11   Serbia National Assembly elections. Democratic Party (Social
          Democratic) achieves 38 per cent as strongest party.

14   Meeting of ECOFIN agrees more transparency and control of
          the financial markets. They also decided on taxing exorbitant
          bonuses for managers.

16–17   EU–Latin America summit.

23   German parliament (upper house) ratifies the Lisbon Treaty.
          However two pending cases at the German constitutional court
          lead to a halt in the ratification process.

25–27   Informal meeting of agriculture ministers laying down a
          framework for the future development of CAP 2009–13.

29   Luxembourg parliament ratifies the Lisbon Treaty.

June

1   Macedonian National Assembly Elections. Democracy for
          Macedonian Unity (Christian Democrats) emerge as strongest
          party with 49 per cent of the vote.

5   Dutch parliament (lower house) ratifies the Lisbon Treaty.

5   Treaty infringement case brought against Germany relating to
          the legislation giving VW national advantages.

10   EU–US summit on strengthening the strategic partnership and
          fostering a competitive economy.

12   Irish referendum on the Lisbon Treaty: rejected by 53.4 per
          cent to 46.6 per cent.

11   Estonian, Finnish and Greek parliaments ratify the Lisbon
          Treaty.

18   United Kingdom parliament (upper house) ratifies the Lisbon
          Treaty.

18   The European Parliament passes a draft law on the treatment
          of illegal immigrants. This directive forms the first European
          Union legislation on immigration in which parliament has full
          co-operation.

| 19–20 | European Council debates ratification of the Lisbon Treaty, high food prices and the Eastern Partnership of the European Neighbourhood Policy. Also the declaration that Slovakia fulfils the Maastricht Criteria for joining the euro. |
| 26 | Spanish parliament (lower house) ratifies the Lisbon Treaty. |

July

1	France takes over EU Council Presidency.
2	Commission presents legislation in the areas of labour and social law for discussion.
3	Cypriot parliament ratifies the Lisbon Treaty.
7–9	G8 Summit.
13	French Presidency proposes Union for the Mediterranean at the EU Mediterranean Summit.
15	Spanish parliament (upper house) ratifies the Lisbon Treaty.
23	Italian parliament (upper house) ratifies the Lisbon Treaty.
31	Italian parliament (lower house) ratifies the Lisbon Treaty.

August

7–8	Georgia launches military attack on South Ossetia.
9	Russian troops enter South Ossetia.
12	Georgia and Russia agree to preliminary ceasefire.
13	Council adopts a declaration that the solution to Caucasus crisis must be based on the principle of sovereignty and territorial integrity of Georgia.
26	Russia recognizes the independence of South Ossetia and Abkhazia.

September

1	Extraordinary European Council on the Caucasus crisis.
15	Lehman Brothers files for bankruptcy.
21	Slovenian parliamentary elections. Social Democrats emerge as strongest party with 30 per cent of the vote.

October

| 4 | Crisis meeting of the Heads of State and Government of France, UK, Germany, Italy, Luxembourg with the head of the European Central Bank, the Eurogroup and the Commission. |

6	EU-27 leaders publish a declaration on the stability of the financial system.
7	Meeting of ECOFIN in Luxembourg. Discussion concentrates on the safeguards for private assets and the breaking down of tax heavens.
8	Russia completes withdrawal of troops from Georgia.
15–16	European Council decides on prioritization of stabilizing international financial markets.
24–25	EU–Asia (ASEM) summit.
26	Lithuanian parliamentary elections won by coalition of Homeland Union, National Resurrection Party and Liberals' Movement of the Republic of Lithuania.

November

3	EU foreign ministers hold informal meeting to discuss the situation in eastern Congo.
7	Informal meeting of the Heads of State and Government of the European Union to prepare the international summit on the economic crisis later that month.
14	EU–Russia Summit.
15	International summit on the financial crisis in Washington, DC.
20	Swedish parliament ratifies the Lisbon Treaty.
20	EU agriculture council reaches agreement on the CAP health check.
26	Czech Constitutional Court rules the Lisbon Treaty not to be in violation of the national constitution.
26	China cancels summit with the EU over the visit of the Dalai Lama.
26	Commission presents an aid package to stimulate the economy.
30	Romanian parliamentary elections won by Social Democratic Party with 33 per cent of the vote.

December

11–12	European Council. Plan to reduce CO_2 emissions as well as plans for encouraging economic growth and combating the economic crisis with a programme of €200 billion economic stimulus package.
17	Commission adopts temporary framework for Member States to tackle effects of credit squeeze on real economy through state aids.

18	The 2009 Budget is presented in the EP with increased financial means for the innovation programmes to combat economic downturn.
19	Accession meetings with Croatia and Turkey.
22	Second Brazil–EU Summit.
23	European Commission allocates €12.4 million in humanitarian aid to vulnerable Palestinians and Iraqis. This is a reaction to the urgent calls for help by UN institutions.
23	Commission approves Italian recapitalization of financial institutions and the modification the UK proposed for its banking system as well as a wide range of other measures regulating the financial services in Germany, Latvia and Spain.
30	Commission approves real economy crises measures (two German aid packages are approved).

Index

Note: Italicized page references indicate information contained in tables.